Ius Gentium: Comparative Perspectives on Law and Justice

Volume 88

Ius Gentium is a book series which discusses the central questions of law and justice from a comparative perspective. The books in this series collect the contrasting and overlapping perspectives of lawyers, judges, philosophers and scholars of law from the world's many different jurisdictions for the purposes of comparison, harmonisation, and the progressive development of law and legal institutions. Each volume makes a new comparative study of an important area of law. This book series continues the work of the well-known journal of the same name and provides the basis for a better understanding of all areas of legal science.

The *Ius Gentium* series provides a valuable resource for lawyers, judges, legislators, scholars, and both graduate students and researchers in globalisation, comparative law, legal theory and legal practice. The series has a special focus on the development of international legal standards and transnational legal cooperation.

More information about this series at https://link.springer.com/bookseries/7888

Hanna H. Wei

Sociocultural Otherness and Minority Justice: A Study on China

Springer

Hanna H. Wei
Qingdao Institute of Humanities and Social Sciences
Shandong University
Qingdao, China

ISSN 1534-6781 ISSN 2214-9902 (electronic)
Ius Gentium: Comparative Perspectives on Law and Justice
ISBN 978-981-16-9754-8 ISBN 978-981-16-9752-4 (eBook)
https://doi.org/10.1007/978-981-16-9752-4

This Springer imprint is published by the registered company Springer Nature Singapore Pte Ltd.
The registered company address is: 152 Beach Road, #21-01/04 Gateway East, Singapore 189721, Singapore

Introducing Sociocultural Otherness and Minority Justice

Contextual Background

This book is not a collection of China's problems, let alone failures, but a reminder of the complexity of the country's realities and that everything has more than one meaning and each cause has more than one effect. Contemporary China is a strange, fascinating and seemingly impossible combination of fossilised ideologies and, in many respects, an incredibly wide range of choices and opportunities. The fixity of public discourse contrasts dramatically with the plurality of possibilities for many in sociocultural and private domains, giving rise to confusions, misunderstandings, and contrasting interpretations as to why this is the case. One interpretation is that, despite being known for its autocratic characteristics rather than democratic tendencies, the all-powerful ruling Party does allow more freedom and room for diversity, if not divergence, than many in the West thought, so long as the exercise of freedom does not have detrimental effects on the rule of the Party, which explains why while public discourse is tightly controlled, those aspects of life which are not considered to have the potential to negatively impact on the official discourse are allowed some colorfulness. Contrasting with this view that all is under control and intentional is another interpretation that simply says that, in a country as vast and complex as China, it is just not possible to control everything.

The author's view is somewhere in the middle. Large-scale economic reforms and limited political liberalization in the past few decades have not only resulted in tremendous economic growth but also the state's diminished control of the private sphere. Coupled with increased opportunities for ordinary Chinese to experience anything Western either directly or indirectly, past decades have witnessed a rise in individualism and a growing sense of personal identity, especially among the younger generation. However, despite social and cultural relaxations in many respects, the development of liberal spaces is highly restricted. Leaving detailed analysis to later chapters, it is necessary to mention in passing here some noteworthy characteristics of the Chinese context to enable proper understanding of the larger context.

In *Discipline and Punish* (1977), Foucault traces a shift in the eighteenth and nineteenth centuries in the technologies of control brought about by the rise of surveillance techniques, which sees the delineation of 'normal' and 'abnormal' replacing direct violence as a technique of power and control, which is maintained through a normalizing process in which 'the whole indefinite domain of the nonconforming is punishable' (Foucault 1977, 178). Certain groups, behaviors and life choices are deemed abnormal through labeling and systematic stigmatization. In contrast to oppression in the form of direct violence and forceful punishment, the dominator is abstracted, disembodied, invisible yet everywhere. Most importantly, control is exercised through the controlled, domination is exercised through the dominated, during which process and through the technique of the self, individuals alter themselves using an internalized disciplinary gaze to bring their conduct into compliance with a given rule, in order to escape the peril of being viewed as abnormal—of being labeled 'the other'.

While this phenomenon of what Foucault calls 'the arts of existence' does not apply to all categorizations of otherness covered in this book, the techniques of self-molding, self-discrimination, self-stigmatization and even self-censorship are key characteristics of the lived realities of many who constitute 'the other'. This of course is not solely a Chinese phenomenon but rather confronts and challenges all that do not belong to the mainstream in all cultures to varying extents. State control is a vastly complex and sophisticated mechanism that drives and maintains the processes of 'othering' through creating pressure for conformity and driving everyone toward the ideal state of being—and in the case of sociocultural minorities, often with the backing of the majority and widely held sociocultural norms. In other words, it is not just the state that exercises domination and control; it is a sophisticated collective effort involving everyone—the state, the people, the majority and the minorities themselves. The proper understanding of this phenomenon requires knowledge not only of Chinese history, culture and politics but also of psychological and sociological theories, on which later chapters will draw.

Another noteworthy characteristic of the Chinese reality is that, for many years, political symbols, slogans and rituals no longer saturated everyday life of the Chinese to the extent they did during the Maoist era. Recent years, however, have witnessed a revival, resulting in continuous hegemony of representation in which only certain symbols, ideas and narratives may be referenced in the public sphere, although diverse beliefs, nonmainstream norms and practices permeate all institutions and social levels. Similar questions regarding whether this is intentionally designed or constitutes loopholes may be asked but hard to answer with any degree of certainty. However, what does appear certain is that this disconnection, or perhaps mismatch, between static official representations and the reality which does manifest some degrees and forms of diversity, is taken for granted by the people who willingly conform to the custom that, some ideas may be expressed in public, while others only in private among trusted friends and family. Which is which, one just knows.

The nature and degree of this learned habit and collective willingness to cooperate cannot be overemphasized, and the reasons why the Chinese are so 'easy-going' are psychologically, socially, culturally, historically and politically complex but at the same time also very simple—the comprehension of which is key to understanding the nature of and reasons for the processes of 'othering' related to many sociocultural issues, some conscious and other unconscious. As will be shown throughout this book, the processes of othering are often more of a result of the masses' wilful acceptance of the norm of cultural conformity, often out of a cultural as well as psychological need for stability and harmony, rather than of direct immediate oppression of the state. To emphasize the people's 'willingness' is not to pretend there is no deliberate pressure. However, to oversimplify such pressure as purely political and top-down is to grossly misinterpret the reality which has given rise to unique challenges, challenges that are symptomatic of very complex and continuous interactions between collective memories filled with historical pains, sociopolitical habits learned from past conflicts and oppressions, insecurities generated by contemporary challenges and social problems, as well as hope for a safe and prosperous future—many of which it is psychological theories, not political or legal theories, that can best explain. It is within such a uniquely challenging context, characterised by incredible powerfulness and unbelievable weaknesses, that this book presents a situational analysis of what it means to be a sociocultural 'other' in China.

Presumptions as Starting Points

It seems sensible to begin a book with presumptions, as they are the most stubborn obstacles to accurately interpreting reality, and recognizing them at the outset of any work constitutes the first step in the right direction. Among many, the author wishes to highlight three of these obstacles. First, it is erroneous to presume that the reality of Chinese minority rights is all bad news. Different categories of minorities have different lived realities, and within the same category, there is also significant internal diversity that calls for observational and analytical attention to detail. On this point, it is necessary to point out that this book has a selective focus and not all minority issues are covered. Attention is focused only on those that most vividly reflect the difficulties and challenges in the unique Chinese context. To serve this purpose and considering that 'minority' has a specific meaning under international minority rights law, the terms 'the other' and 'otherness' are employed instead to reflect the width and complexity of the issues in concern as well as these groups' positioning in society.

Rightly or wrongly, not much time or effort has been spent on the construction of the notion of 'otherness'. Rather, it has been taken to be a matter of fact as consisting of social, cultural, political, ethnic and ideological categorizations, according to which someone who constitutes 'the other' is by definition different from the vast majority, different in terms of gender, class, age, race, cultural background, religious beliefs, political affiliations or simply life-style. 'The other' may be different in physical appearance, of different sociocultural background, of different behavioral or sexual orientation; 'the other' may also represent competing values and interests to those of the majority and thereby causes conflicts and clashes, or may even be considered to pose a threat to the interests of the society, the people, the state. In other words, while some categorizations of 'the other' are positive, i.e., being different in a positive way, some are neutral, others are negative to varying degrees and in their respective ways and consequently considered threatening.

It is not beyond the realm of imagination that such a topic is unlikely to present an overly bright picture, which leads to the second presumption that the author wishes to highlight, namely, that injustice and oppression are always due to the evilness of an authoritarian government. This is a key presumption that this book wishes to challenge, although it is not always apparent, which renders an express statement necessary. As already mentioned and will be explored in detail later in the chapters, the lived reality of 'the other' in China is highly complex because it is symptomatic of the interplay of a wide range of intertwined reasons, including historical pains from the colonial era, political instabilities in modern history, the size and population of the country, the serious social problems that the country has to deal with—all of which become the heavy baggage that the country carries in its dealings with divergence and otherness, many of which are constant reminders of the histories that the people do not wish to remember, and of a present that the country is not good at confronting. Rather than goodness or badness, it is the mere facts of the country's past and present that render old habits die hard and many problems unresolvable. In addition, when bad things are done by good people is when justice is most difficult to realize.

This must not be taken to be a valid excuse for violations for rights, which leads to the third presumption that this book wishes to challenge. Western fascinations with Chinese human and minority rights issues are constant, although such fascinations are to a certain extent based on a fixed impression and static understanding of many issues, which has led to preliminary conclusions that may or may no longer be valid. One such preliminary conclusion is that as long as China's dialog with the West does not stop, those aspects of the country's minority situation that are currently problematic will improve. The author, critical of such optimism, argues that closer observation of emerging political facts in conjunction with analysis of the country's changing diplomatic stance on many issues in recent years will reveal otherwise. What could this mean in terms of the future prospects of recognition of sociocultural otherness remains to be seen, although in the age of COVID-19 when hardliners begin to take center stage and well-meaning transnational dialog becomes increasingly difficult, for a breakthrough of any sort to take place would require first and foremost minute attention to the details of actual reality.

Objectives of the Book

The primary objectives of *Sociocultural Otherness and Minority Justice* are threefold. The first is to present a tentative analysis of the living reality of being 'the other' in China, with the specific aim of not only presenting a critical picture of the complex Chinese situations, identifying main concerns and key challenges but also and especially drawing attention to the fact that while some issues have remained unchanged and persistent, others have only recently emerged or have evolved to be of a different, considerably more complex, nature than before, owing not only to a rapidly changing political climate but also to a new global environment in which the balance of power has shifted and continues to shift.

The second objective is to focus attention on the interaction between factors that affect if not determine the effectiveness of recognition and rights protection, be they historical, political, social or cultural, especially on whether these factors are mutually reinforcing or in conflict with each other. An examination of how these factors interact opens up a rich domain of inquiry for those interested in how recognition or the lack of recognition can affect the behavior of individuals, society and societal norms, institutions and institutional norms, formal and informal laws, politics and political norms—and vice versa. By showing that understanding the intersection between these myriad systems is especially important for accurately interpreting the Chinese reality, the author argues against understanding the rights ideals or pushing for a particular form or direction of protection in a vacuum.

Related to this is the third objective, which is to bring attention to new trends and developments in the field of minority rights and sociocultural diversity in China, some of which are easily identifiable whereas others are much less detectable, some impact each other while others are relatively isolated incidents, and while some are straightforward others remain easily misinterpreted. The background is a newly emerged and seemingly surprising phenomenon in China that has not received much critical attention or scholarly engagement, namely, the rapid enlargement of the scope of human rights. This is different from the gradual enlargement of the scope of human rights in the West taking place in recent decades, which despite having attracted debate and criticism, has mainly served the purpose of moving human rights beyond claims solely against the state to contest rights violations by nonstate actors. The Chinese phenomenon has a much less clear nature with obvious political and strategic purposes, which renders the country's seemingly new intense interest and involvement in human rights a sign of caution.

Outline of the Book

Following this *Introductory Chapter,* which sets the tone and outlines the book's overall thesis, structure and purpose, provides an overview of the background, contents and key arguments of each chapter, the project commences in Chap. 1 with gender and sexual identity and thoroughly examines the interplay between the realms of law and policy, history and tradition, foreign influences and modernisation in both the constitution of gender topics and the construction of the identities of gender minorities in Chinese society. Through identifying presumptions and misconceptions, the author focuses on two interrelated topics that the Chinese find most difficult to openly discuss—homosexuality and male sexual abuse—creating two groups of minorities that are most vulnerable and least protected. Despite a significant increase in the degree of sexual tolerance in Chinese society, this part nevertheless highlights how each of the realms of history, tradition, culture, politics, law and policy individually and combined constitutes a stubborn obstacle to the knowledge-building of these two topics and in turn hinders legal and social recognition of these two groups, which would only come about with tentative learning and genuine appreciation of their needs. Opening with gender and sexuality helps set the tone for the entire book by highlighting what each and every category of 'the other' has in common that renders their recognition and fair treatment difficult to come about in a conventional and totalitarian country—taboo, shame and blame.

Following these observations, Chap. 2 presents an analysis of the interaction between social norms and health issues through an exploration of cultural tradition and beliefs, psychological and psychiatric practices as well as the role of the state in the treatment and protection of the rights of people living with serious health issues, with two sections focusing respectively on mental illnesses and HIV/AIDS. These two topics are chosen for their status as the leading stigmatised health conditions in China today and their unique ability to demonstrate what it means to be 'the other' purely due to one's state of health, to reveal how health-related stigmatisation works through complex and delicate associations with morality and fear, and how it interacts with a web of structural determinants. While acknowledging the *individual* risk factors and responsibilities associated with these illnesses, *contextual* factors that have rendered certain groups of people forever more vulnerable than others are the focus of attention to show how the state, society as a whole, healthy people along with those living with these illnesses together make these conditions truly sufferable.

Chapter 3 examines the impact of state reforms on the lives of individuals, identifying major transformations and challenges that have occurred in the lives of those who have been most affected, emphasizing both the unique political and economic background against which these changes have taken place as well as their exceptional pace and scale. The positive impacts of China's transformative reforms in the past few decades on the country as a whole have been plain for all to see, which Chap. 3 fully acknowledges; it nevertheless draws attention to the much less talked about aspects of how these transformations have changed the lives of individuals, particularly those changes that have been foreseeable, long-lasting and challenging. Recent academic works on Chinese internal migrant workers and so-called shidu parents (aging parents who have lost their only child) are critically analyzed in detail. These two groups are chosen for their stronger ability compared to others to reveal the power of the state over the individual, the interactions between state-imposed reforms, which have been designed for the greater public good and a bright future for the entire country, and the life choices and realities of those who have made enormous contributions, even sacrifices, to make all this possible.

Chapter 4 casts a critical gaze over Chinese minority rights laws and policies related to two classic minorities under international law—ethnic and religious groups—to identify areas of success and problems of design and implementation. While ethnic and religious minorities are the most systematically protected 'otherness' on paper, conflicting evidence of the degree of tolerance of diversity and effectiveness of protection demands closer examination of state interactions with these groups. Showing considerable respect to the complexities and particularities of the

Chinese context but nonetheless trying to avoid an overly contextual approach, the twofold aim of the chapter is, first, to provide an overview of the development of the regime, especially the relevant laws, policies and programmes protecting ethnic diversity and religious freedom, focusing not only on legal reforms but also on the changing attitudes of both the government and the general public; second, to identify key challenges and obstacles to better recognition and to evaluate the plausibility of possible remedies. It is firmly within the wider context of Chinese culture, society and politics that the exploration of the possibility of a more just, functional and realistic regime for the protection of ethnic and religious diversity is carried out.

Chapter 5 examines changing societal and personal perceptions of intimacy and their interaction with traditional values and state-imposed behavioral norms. Part I looks at commercial sex at a time when the party-state has once again turned conservative, with public discourse on sexuality increasingly conducted according to considerations that are historically and traditionally Chinese. The chapter does not take a side between the abolitionists and those who want prostitution legalized, but rather focuses on the contextual reasons behind changing perceptions, draws attention to the great diversity of personal motivations and individual circumstances, compares and contrasts the variety of ways of looking at the subject while emphasizing that it concerns a wide range of questions such as sexuality, the institution of marriage, internal migration, social inequality, even the construction and perception of modernity. Along similar lines, by examining the social origins, determinants and functions of cohabitation, extramarital relations and singlehood in a pro-marriage conservative country, how cultural tradition and morality interfere with and shape people's private life is examined in Part II, in so doing the commonly presumed power relations and social expectations are re-examined. A connection between identity politics and the search for intimacy is also made, emphasizing the interplay between unsatisfied basic human needs on the one hand, and social, economic, cultural and other factors on the other.

Chapter 6 looks at the old topic of *freedom of expression* from two minority angles—the seldom talked about artistic freedom, and the so-called 'Human Flesh Search Engine' (HFSE) as a form of online collective action that strongly resembles democratic participation. Drawing on political, legal and artistic theories in combination with analysis of historical and recent incidents in the Chinese contemporary art field, Part I provides an interdisciplinary analysis of the possibility of accommodating controversial art forms in China and explores the complexity and value of 'otherness' to art and to Chinese culture generally. Part II examines HFSE in the context of *offline* social, cultural and political conditions that have not only shaped people's *online* behavior but also determine how they communicate generally in real life. HFSE is seen as a telling phenomenon that depicts how the state and its people interact and how participation and expression nonetheless take place in a controlled social space. Hence, despite its irrational and in some situations violent nature, tentative attention ought to be paid to the individual and collective emotions behind, the realities that have generated such emotions, and why people choose to express emotions in this particular way.

In *Conclusion: Beyond Otherness*, the author concludes the project and makes a definitive statement on the reality and future of the protection of sociocultural otherness in China. Three broad and interrelated categories of uncertainties within the Chinese context will be explored: conceptual, methodological and institutional. While recognizing that we all deploy assumptions, protocols and stipulations when identifying, organizing and framing issues of debate, and it follows that all discussions of minority rights, including but not limited to those covered in this book, imply a like simplification and framing of inquiry, the author calls for a more tentative, more critical and continuous scholarly engagement with Chinese minority issues both within China and internationally. By identifying persistent concerns and evolving challenges, this concluding chapter carefully considers the manners in which old debates might be transformed to deal with new, unsettling situations.

Reference

Foucault, Michel ([1977] 2020), *Discipline and Punish: The Birth of the Prison,* Penguin Classics

Contents

Chapter 1
Gender Roles and Social Justice

1.1 Introduction: When Nature Clashes with Culture

Gender and sexuality in the Chinese context are vast issues that deserve the dedication of several volumes. This chapter has picked two closely related topics out of a large pool of possibilities that concern sexual identity and minority justice in China—homosexuality and male victims of sexual abuse—which are examined together due to their close connectedness, similarities as well as differences. They are similar in that, first, publicly expressing views on both topics in China today still causes varying degrees of rejection, although people, especially urban people, have grown much more tolerant than before. Second, public discourse on both topics is fraught with contradictions, as while recognition, acceptance and improved rights protection of both categories of people are increasingly advocated, they continue to be labeled and stigmatised as sexual perverts (in the case of homosexuality) and people not worthy of protection (in the case of male victims of sexual abuse).

They are different in that, first, while homosexuality officially entered public discourse in China in the 1980s, male sexual abuse as a topic only began to emerge very recently in the past few years. Second, while it is still very difficult for Chinese homosexual men and women to be open about their sexual orientation for fear of social condemnation, with the increase in cultural tolerance, which has enabled the expansion of homosexual identities and communities, an increasing number of them are able to come out, with or without having to suffer any consequences. Comparatively speaking, male sexual victims are under greater pressure to remain silent, fearing shame and social isolation. Third, China still lacks laws and policies that recognize sexual and gender minorities or protect them from discrimination and unfair treatment on the basis of their gender identities, although there are a number of institutional policies on education, health care and workplace rules that serve protection purposes, whereas some male sexual victims are partially protected by Chinese criminal law due to the 9th amendment, the impact and limitations of which will be examined in detail in Part II.

H. H. Wei, *Sociocultural Otherness and Minority Justice: A Study on China*,
Ius Gentium: Comparative Perspectives on Law and Justice 88,
https://doi.org/10.1007/978-981-16-9752-4_1

By examining these two topics together, this chapter aims not only to identify the difficulties and challenges they each face, explore the historical, cultural, social and political roots of hostility and stigma but also to establish connections between the two groups in terms of common causes of rejection and discrimination.

1.2 Part I: Homosexuality, Ideology and Rights

Research into homosexuality in China seems to show a tendency to separate theory (i.e., gender theory, queer theory, sexuality theories) from historical, social and other empirical perspectives on same-sex relations in the Chinese context and that existing, especially the newer, Chinese literature on homosexuality seems mostly to take the form of collection of individual stories and experiences. This gives a twofold impression. First, gender and sexuality theories and models are Western inventions that cannot readily apply to the Chinese reality without running the risk of perpetuating a colonialist epistemology (Liu 2015, 21). Second, it makes one wonder whether Chinese scholars are under invisible (or visible) pressure not to dig too deep into this controversial subject, even though the sociocultural atmosphere is increasingly tolerant toward same-sex relations. Both impressions are not unfounded.

Despite its decriminalization in 1997 and removal from the nation's official list of mental illnesses in 2001, homosexuality remains a taboo subject, which means that reliable information in the Chinese language, both primary and secondary, least of all official, is not easy to come by. Since the appearance in 1992 of the very first book published in Mainland China on homosexuality—*Their World: A Study of Homosexuality in China* by Li Yinhe and Wang XiaoBo—there has not been that much Chinese scholarly attention given to the fast-growing and the world's largest homosexual population, which has been estimated at approximately 70 million. Once in a while a book will be published in English written by Western or Chinese scholars based abroad who seek to explain the living realities of homosexual men and women in China, which shows that scholarly attention has not left this issue, but that it tends to come from abroad due to local sociocultural and political constraints on thought and expression.

This is a key reason for the lack of publication of theoretical, structural, scholarly work on homosexuality in China—the sociocultural and political atmosphere prevents one from exploring topics that are considered controversial let alone presenting them critically in great detail. The pressure may not always be deliberate, constant or even carry any consequences but is certainly felt. This renders telling the lived stories of homosexual people a safer way of exposing the issues and inviting public attention and debate. However, presenting the reality of Chinese homosexuality simply as collections of individual experiences and stories has serious misleading effects on the course of advancement of homosexual welfare and rights in China, in that it gives the erroneous impression that homosexuality, or queerness, is nothing more than being grounded only in the subjective encounters and perceptions of affect, emotion, desire, shame, conflict, harm, and loss.

As is the case with any individual experience in the field of human and minority rights, each individual story always reflects something structural and fundamental. Homosexuality concerns the constitutive sociality of the self, which requires not only focusing on the queer discourse itself but also important questions of cultural diversity, cross-cultural dialog, tolerance of otherness, socioeconomic welfare and equality, respect for the full enjoyment of private choices, as well as constructive participation in the public domain. All of these require systemic studies and understanding of the production and reproduction of power in society, which a nation that claims to thrive on Marxism is supposed to be in a rather informed position to begin with. None can deny the validity and unique contribution of an individual's stories, but stories alone do not tell the full story.

Part I of this chapter has a threefold purpose. The first is to present a critical picture of the historical evolution of homosexuality and its stigmatisation in China, debunking the common Chinese belief that it is a recent Western import. The second is to analyze in detail the types and intensities of discrimination homosexual men and women face, emphasizing that discrimination comes from both outside and within the group. Socioeconomic inequality is the key focus of attention when discussing internal discrimination. The third is to compare and contrast what works abroad and what works in China in the advancement of queer welfare and rights, hoping to show that while queer communities around the world have not evolved along the same path, to varying extents and in different ways, liberal values of individual freedom, privacy, tolerance and diversity have guided them all.

1.2.1 Same-Sex Attraction in Chinese History

It is not widely known that the history of homosexual relations in China is perhaps as ancient as the history of Chinese culture. According to Chinese natural philosophy, a healthy human body would display the right balance between *yin* and *yang*, which tend to shift throughout the life cycle of both males and females, and that a physical body could conjugate many forms, be they male or female, young or old, robust or delicate (Mann 2011, 138). Along similar lines, classical Chinese medicine also defines health or illness in terms of the relative balance of *yin* and *yang*, and represents gender as to some extent fluid (Mann 2011, 87). As a result, until the twentieth century, neither intellectuals nor medical specialists were trained to view the human body in static binary terms as they do now.

During much of China's long ancient and imperial period, same-sex attractions were not only accepted as natural but also celebrated through tales, folk songs and classical poetry, but studies of the history of Chinese homosexuality focus predominantly on homosexual men with very rare reference to lesbianism, which is noteworthy but not surprising. The earliest recorded homosexual relations between Chinese men seemed to be those between emperors and their male favorites in the Zhou Dynasty (1122–256 B.C.), during which period men were said to be free to show affections to and engage in intimate relations with other men. During the

Western Han era (187–180 B.C.), ten of the eleven emperors were noted in historical records to have been openly bisexual either with male favorites or had homoerotic relationships (Hinsch 1992, 35–36). Renowned ancient scholar Sima Qian claimed in his monumental *Records of the Grand Historian* that unlike imperial wives and concubines, male companions were kept not only for their sexual attractiveness but also for their talents and administrative capabilities (Hinsch 1992).

During the liberal and prosperous late Ming era (1368–1644), homosexual relations were said to have become a kind of fashion and existed among men of every social class but were most visible among a small circle of elite males—the literati, who pursued homoerotic relations for cultural refinement as well as adventure. Long-term relationships with young male entertainers, servants and male prostitutes were often formed, symbolising powerful social status and cultural taste; young men and boys were also indispensable at their parties and gatherings, again emblematic of the host's wealth, status and refined aesthetic taste (Zheng 2015, 35). Scholars would write about their homoerotic relations in their writings, indicating that homosexuality at the time was not only normal and popular but also a recognized source of excitement, envy and public admiration.

Despite a change of general atmosphere from the Ming Dynasty, celebration of homoerotic sentiments, both socially and artistically, continued into the Qing Dynasty (1368–1911), during which period such sentiments would develop even further into a symbol of aesthetic taste and a form of romantic idealism. Historical records around this time also recounted tales of homosexual relations between the emperors and their male subordinates; homoerotic themes continued to be elaborated in well-known classic novels such as *Dream of the Red Chamber* and *The Golden Lotus* (Hinsch 1992, 147; Zheng 2015, 36). It was during this period that it became particularly apparent that the sexual ideal was embodied by young, delicate, feminine, *male* bodies, which has been attributed to the fact that the Qing Dynasty was intensely patriarchal (Zheng 2015, 36).

Continuing the late Ming pattern, the predominant type of same-sex relation during the Qing period was also that between elite men (literati, officials, wealthy merchants) and young actors who often played young female roles in traditional theatre such as the Beijing Opera. There existed 'guidebooks'—*hua pu* ('flower book')—that gave patrons detailed instructions on how to locate famous young male actors at the entertainment quarters (Zheng 2015, 37). Competing views exist, however, as to whether these same-sex 'relationships' were 'friendships' or more, with some inferring that they were of a sexual nature (Hinsch 1992, 131–132), while others insisting that they were friendships that did not extend to sexual relations (McDermott 1992).

It should be noted that historically, it was rare for a same-sex relationship to occur between men of similar age or similar social status, as a power hierarchy was widely considered to be necessary at the core of any relationship, heterosexual or homosexual, in order to keep it stable, and that as long as same-sex relationships observed the order of social hierarchy, they were in alignment with Confucian moral requirements (Zheng 2015, 38). Another social precondition seemed to be that family responsibilities had to be fulfilled, thus the vast majority if not all of the elite men in homosexual relations would already have been in a heterosexual marriage, having fathered children (Zheng 2015, 39). Interestingly, as will be shown later, such practice of living a double life is also commonly practised among homosexual men and women in China today. The difference is perhaps that during the imperial period double lives were lived openly, to the knowledge of the 'weaker party', whereas nowadays, as will be shown below, except for those increasingly common fake marriages formed upon mutual contractual agreement, formal or informal, many heterosexual people married to homosexual men or women in modern day China do not actually know their other half's real sexual orientation (Wang et al. 2019; Zhu 2018).

It was not until the 1860s when institutional reforms were initiated following a series of military defeats and concessions to foreign invading powers that the status of homosexual practice began to change, and stigmatisation of which gradually became official and intensified during the Republic period (1912–1949), with the word 'homosexuality' first emerging in the Chinese language in the 1930s. National crisis caused patriotic Chinese intellectuals to voice severe critique of the Chinese tradition. They would translate and introduce Western knowledge into China hoping to bring about modernisation—part of such knowledge, among Western sciences, philosophies and religions, was homophobia. These intellectuals started to attack male homoeroticism as the epitome of the many fatal flaws of Chinese culture and society, labeled homosexual men as not only weak but sick, and asserted heterosexual masculinity to be a means to empower the nation. Homosexual practices were rapidly transformed from once a symbol of social status into a reprehensible and distasteful behavior symbolising 'sickness of the nation' (Jeffreys and Yu 2015, 72). The intellectuals did not stop at attacking homosexuality but also called for all people to discipline their sexual desires, denounced prostitution, masturbation, and premarital and extramarital sexual relations.

This call for all sexual activities to be strictly regulated was enforced with an iron fist in the Maoist era (1949–1977), which forcefully maintained a heterosexual, marital and reproductive sex model wherein sex was legitimate only for the purpose of reproduction within marriage. Sexual desires continued to be demonised as decadent and incompatible with neither the interests of the state nor the ideals of socialism, as they would debilitate people's energy that should be devoted entirely to building the socialist nation. Sex for reasons other than reproduction (for instance premarital sex, extramarital sex, prostitution, same-sex relations) was deemed deviant and corrupt, in need of policing and punishment. In the absence of laws directly prohibiting consensual same-sex activities, such relations were subject to a wide range of administrative and disciplinary sanctions under the charge of 'hooliganism'.

During the Cultural Revolution (1966–1976), homosexual people were classified as 'bad elements' under the 'five black categories' along with landlords, rich peasants, counterrevolutionaries, and rightists. Upon discovery of same-sex activities, individuals would receive administrative punishments such as detention, persecution, reform through education or labor, disciplinary sanctions such as withholding wages and suspending Communist Party membership (Zheng 2015, 42). While the Cultural Revolution has been described as the darkest age for homosexual people in China, and it has also been said that this was the only period in Chinese history in which people had been sentenced to death for homosexual activities, there is also the contrasting view that the complete breakdown of society in fact provided opportunities and the necessary freedom for people not only to discover their homosexuality in secret but also to form long-lasting homosexual relationships (Worth et al. 2017).

While the Cultural Revolution is long gone, and with the rapid changes taking place in Chinese society in recent decades, private life has undergone a slow but sure transition, in which the importance of sexual pleasures for their own sake rather than for reproductive purposes has at last gained recognition as proper, which has been attributed to be an unintended consequence of the one-child policy (implemented in the 1980s and now officially abolished) (Pan 2006). However, one should not be too quick to label such an environment as 'accommodating' for homosexual people, as the sexual pleasures recognized are those experienced *within marriage*—an institution into which same-sex attracted people are not legally allowed to enter in China. Despite claims that China has been undergoing a high-speed sexual revolution since the 1990s, producing a sexually open-minded new generation and affecting societal perceptions of homosexual activities, it would be wrong to underestimate the conservativeness of modern Chinese society, especially in regard to sex life. This, in conjunction with a general political atmosphere that requires obedience and comprehensive conformity, has sustained widespread expectations and apprehensions that have continued to cause and sustain discrimination against sexual otherness.

This lengthy presentation of the history of homosexuality in China serves three purposes. First, it shows that homophobia was an import but homosexuality was not. Second, it provides historical evidence that many of the modern elements of discrimination of same-sex attracted people have their roots in history. Third and related, it provides the background for arguing *against* the optimistic assertion that the fact that both theistic religions and fundamentalist movements lack strength in China renders the country less homophobic or that it has the potential to be less homophobic than those countries in which such religions or movements have a powerful existence. History shows that such an assertion has ignored the country's living past of the nineteenth and twentieth centuries and has underestimated their long-lasting impact on social attitudes today.

1.2.2 Discrimination: External and Internal

1.2.2.1 Structural and Societal Discrimination

Same-sex attracted people in contemporary China have entered from a period of systematic denial and hostility into a phase of greater visibility and empowerment, while stubborn obstacles, challenges and a wide range of forms of discrimination remain both outside and inside the homosexual community. While widespread prejudice exists in society, the degree varies in different regions and different social environments, and the various forms interrelate and impact each other. There are four main sources of external discrimination and two of internal discrimination that deserve close attention, and it makes sense to start with those with roots in the history presented above.

In *Being LGBTI in China: A National Survey on Social Attitudes toward Sexual Orientation, Gender Identity and Gender Expression*, the United Nation's Development Programme (2016) presents the telling findings that, compared to university campuses, schools, workplaces and religious communities, it is families of sexual minorities that have the lowest degree of acceptance of sexual minorities in China (UNDP 2016, 16). This points to the first and perhaps most deep-rooted source of external discrimination of homosexuality in the country, namely, that despite modernisation and rapid changes, old Confucian family ethics remain very influential in China, creating great pressure for people of a certain age to get married, have children and fulfil family responsibilities in ways that society approves (Shi et al. 2020). Undoubtedly, the long-running (and now abandoned) one-child policy has also been a key reason why Chinese parents place enormous pressure on their children to raise families.

The individual is in tight relation with the social environment and its expectations, from the power and moral influence of which one cannot easily break free. While this is not automatically 'discrimination' per se, it does produce enough pressure under which a person's behavior will always to some extent reflect their social relations and interactions with the outside world—a phenomenon that has been studied by psychoanalysts (Flugel 1945[1955], Chap. 5). Evidence of which is that many same-sex attracted people in China would in fact define a 'normal life' as one of being in a heterosexual marriage with children, and rather surprisingly, many oppose the idea of gay marriage for fear of 'standing out from the crowd' (Zheng 2015, Chap. 6).

Various studies show that the majority of same-sex attracted people in China are in a heterosexual marriage (Wang et al. 2019; Pan 2017a; Zheng 2015, 152; UNDP 2016, 24), and that an increasing number have chosen to avail themselves on websites or other social flatforms to match with other same-sex attracted people who are willing to enter into a fake marriage ('*xingshi hunyin*') with them, which both parties would use as a cover for their homosexual identity in front of others, especially their families. As of 2 December 2021, the number of registered users on *ChinaGayLes.com*, a not-for-profit dating website for the sole purpose of arranging fake marriages for homosexual people, was 459,960, and since the website began operation in 2005, 55,195 couples have successfully entered into fake marriages through arrangements made on the website. The fact that such a website is allowed to operate in the tightly controlled Chinese webspace, especially considering that such arrangements openly contradict the generally accepted societal and familial codes of conduct, is a sign that widespread discrimination against homosexuality is officially recognized as a problem, to which fake marriage as a solution for the lack of any other is officially tolerated.

In contrast to such overt arrangements, some people (mostly homosexual men) would simply trick another heterosexual person into marriage, have children, generating in themselves the erroneous belief that they have fulfilled gendered and familial expectations and are therefore entitled to carry on with homosexual relations behind their legal partner's back or even with their knowledge, paying little attention to their feelings of hurt. There is no information or studies on the children born into such families, which would be very telling of the living realities of these arrangements and their impact on those within, which would be both hard and irresponsible for outsiders to imagine. Gay rights activist groups have in recent years started to take such behavior very seriously. While recognizing same-sex attracted people's emotional and physical needs and that tricking people into marriage is largely due to the immense social pressure to conform and fear of discrimination and social isolation, these organizations have put great efforts into drawing attention to the heterosexual party's rights and the immorality of tricking someone into marriage for personal gain or whatever reason. The largest gay activist organization in China—PFLAG China (short for 'Parents, Families and Friends of Lesbians and Gays of China')—even provides talks to teach heterosexual people, especially women, how to recognize the signs of danger of being tricked into a union so that they can effectively protect and defend themselves.

A second source of discrimination, especially for homosexual men, is evident in a public debate that went viral on Chinese social media on maleness just over a year ago. In recent years, China's popular media and commercials have been filled with young male stars with feminine and alluring appearances, who the public nickname 'fake women' (*weiniang*). This phenomenon has been attributed to the popularity of Japanese animation and comic games, in which male figures all display feminine beauty and apply extensive make-up, who are believed to appeal to a large population of audiences ranging from school girls to women of old age. It is unclear how the attack on 'fake women' started, but very soon it evolved into a debate on the loss of Chinese manhood and its threat to the nation-state—just like in the late Qing Dynasty and the Republic era during which the feminisation of males was seen as a sign of national weakness and a key reason for colonial domination of China.

Given that media images of homosexual men are also always overly feminine, similar to the 'fake women', understandably, this anti-feminised-men discourse has an overwhelming anti-gay flavor. In attacking 'sissy men', public discourse one-sidedly denounces feminised and homosexual men for violating the natural order of things, and claims that it is only through men fulfilling gender-appropriate code of conduct by being heroic, fearless and militaristic that society may be harmonious and the nation may be strong. This linkage between masculinity and strength, gender and nationhood, is clearly painful collective memory speaking out loud in modern context. Once again, 'a man behaving not like a man' has become seen as a threat to the state, although not carrying the same sense of urgency as historically.

Leaving aside the unlikelihood of homosexual men weakening the state and causing another round of colonization of China in today's world, this public discourse on maleness has brought to attention a third source of discrimination of same-sex attracted people, particularly same-sex attracted men—media representation. Images of homosexual men are almost always couched in effeminate representations, which simplistically distorts reality. And since ordinary heterosexual people lack the opportunity to truly get to know homosexual men, not least because the latter are seldom open about their sexual orientation for fear of discrimination, they tend to take media representation as *the* representation and internalise the idea that all homosexual men appear feminine and all feminine-looking men are likely to be homosexual, while at the same time having the historical memory playing in the background that feminine men was a symbol of the weakness, sickness and danger to the state.

A related fourth source of discrimination is the linkage between homosexuality and danger, more precisely, the danger of deviance, criminal behavior, and illnesses, which are all connected. All social groups and societies have rules of behavior that intend to be obeyed and passed on. These rules define social situations and the kind of behavior appropriate to these situations, specifying some actions as right and others as wrong, some as wrong but tolerable, and others simply deviant. There are many ways of defining deviance. For instance, statistically speaking, if a behavior varies widely from the average, it may be considered deviant; medically speaking, if a behavior reveals the presence of a disease, be it mental or physical, it may be considered deviant; sociologically speaking, if a behavior or social process is dysfunctional and tends to disrupt the stability of the society (presuming the society knows what constitutes functional and what its ultimate goals are), it may be considered deviant; or, if a behavior or way of life is considered to have failed to obey collective rules, it is often considered deviant (Becker 1963, 4–8).

Surveys of public opinions on homosexuality in the past few decades reveal that, despite showing signs of greater tolerance, especially among young people and in large cities, in the Chinese public's eye, homosexuality is deviant in all of the above ways (Zheng 2015, 52–54). This is evident in that despite homosexuality being neither a crime nor an officially regarded mental illness, some public hospitals and private clinics in China continue to offer so-called 'conversion therapy', which is clearly based on the assumption that homosexuality is a choice that may be reversed, an illness that needs to be treated, a problem that ought to be corrected.

This association with deviance has caused many to believe that homosexuality is brought about by some sort of problem or disorder at some stage of a person's life, for instance unhealthy upbringing, violent family environment, gender confusion, which would all serve to inject into the minds of homosexual people hatred toward society and cause them to use extreme measures to gain revenge, such as child molestation, rape, abetting others to become homosexuals, blackmail, and deliberate transmission of sexually transmitted diseases—all rendering it necessary for a healthy and orderly society to be heavily guarded against the homosexual threat (Zheng 2015, 57).

The sense of being under threat, in danger, is particularly strong in regard to associating homosexuality with serious diseases, especially HIV/AIDS, the history and details of which will be the focus of the next chapter. Public discourse about HIV/AIDS began to take place in the early 1990s, which was around the same time that homosexuality became publicly visible, which means that from the very beginning, China's HIV/AIDS epidemic has been a platform on which a particular image of homosexuality is portrayed—a corrupt Western import. Growing public attention to HIV/AIDS underscored the intrinsic tie between homosexual activities and the spread of the disease, and homosexual men became identified as a high-risk group of the disease.

While homosexual transmission has indeed been a main cause of HIV/AIDS in China, which cannot be denied, it is noteworthy that in fighting the epidemic, China often employs the strategy of scaring people away from contracting the disease, which further strengthens stigma related to the illness and those identified as high-risk groups (Kleinman et al. 2011, 242). Over the years, media coverage has also reflected a shift from an utter denial of the existence of HIV/AIDS, of homosexuality, to a campaign to link and demonise both, with the former being interpreted as rooted in promiscuous and perilous lifestyles, and the latter thereby becoming linked with everything that is considered promiscuous—prostitution, incest, sexual abuse, rape—all factors portrayed as leading to the widespread transmission of HIV/AIDS and other sexually transmitted diseases (Zheng 2015, 51). The danger of homosexuality is thereby considered proven—by immorality and fatal diseases.

1.2.2.2 Discrimination Within the Homosexual Community

Discrimination hardly ever only comes from outside of a social community, in that as long as there is external discrimination in the wider society, there will be some form of internal discrimination within the group itself, reflecting, reacting to, or even imitating external injustices. A review of the literature suggests that within the Chinese homosexual community, largely due to and through interaction with the societal reality and external discrimination, there are two noteworthy phenomena that may constitute sources of internal discrimination, both reinforcing *heterosexual* gendered norms and sociocultural expectations as a result of homosexual people's interactions and negotiations with the gender discourse in China, which defines the 'normal life' as not only heterosexual but also with some social status and relatively wealthy.

In her studies on Chinese homosexual men, Zheng (2015) reveals that within the Chinese homosexual community, men are either a '1' or a '0', with the former symbolising the penis and identified as the male role, and the latter symbolising the vagina and identified as the female role. Some choose their own role, often based on their sexual position in their first sexual experience with someone who has already self-identified as a 1 or a 0; others focus more on which gender roles they tend to play in the relationship and let the cultural categorization of personal traits and characteristics help them decide their self-identification as a 1 or a 0. For instance, even if a homosexual man has experienced the inserted position of 0 with another man, he may still self-identify as a 1 because of personal traits, and even if a man enjoys the inserting position of a 1, he may well self-identify as a 0 due to his personal traits (Zheng 2015, 78). Zheng's studies show that most 1 s choose the inserter's role to satisfy their physical needs, whereas most 0 s are believed to have endured the pain caused by receiving in order to satisfy their psychological needs. In other words, gender roles lead to sexual positions, and gender roles lead to sex roles, not the other way around (Zheng 2015, 79).

The 'personal traits' that these homosexual men rely on for self-identification are clearly associated with idealised and stereotypical masculine and feminine qualities leading to different expectations and obligations. For instance, while a 1 is supposed to take the role of the husband who is meant to be aggressive, rational, protective, financially supportive, and sexually free, a 0 is meant to take on the wife's role who is supposed to be passive, emotional, delicate, financially dependent, needy, and faithful (Zheng 2015, 82). Clearly, the gender division of 1 and 0 imitates the hegemonic gender expectations in heterosexual relationships in Chinese culture. Furthermore, Zheng (2015, 78) also shows that within the homosexual community, men even refer to each other as 'husbands' and 'wives' in alignment with their allocated gender roles and that it is commonly believed among them that a relationship is most stable when it is made up of a 1 and a 0 rather than two 1 s or two 0 s.

While it is wrong to assume that all 1 s and 0 s conform to gender roles and expectations, this 'natural', almost exact, imitation of heterosexual gender roles suggests that there is prestige and respect associated with the male role, and social stigma and inferiority attached to the female role, causing some 0 s to present themselves as 1 s and attempt to erase feminine characteristics in their outer behavior. This is interesting considering and as mentioned before, the mainstream media tends to always present homosexual men as overly feminine—or perhaps this is a reason why overly feminine homosexual men are discriminated against within their own community—a case of external discrimination causing internal discrimination causing self-denial, self-criticism and assimilation. It would be worthwhile to conduct detailed studies and surveys from the perspective of psychology on the subjective personal reasons why social stigma is attached to the female role within the homosexual community, other than assuming simply that it reflects the patriarchal norms of the wider Chinese society.

Another internal source of discrimination within the homosexual community that also imitates that of the wider society is social hierarchy, which brings out the issue of 'minorities within minorities', which causes us to pause and think that, when we talk about gay rights in China, what exactly and whose rights are we talking about? Chapter 3 will examine the living reality of some of the underclasses in contemporary China based on the observation that the Chinese system functions on a clear division of classes despite claiming to be a classless socialist society. While the elites have unlimited powers and resources, the underclasses live in a very different state. Studies show that a similar class structure exists within the Chinese homosexual community, consisting of, in Zheng's (2015) terms, gold-collar, red-collar, white-collar, blue-collar and gray-collar homosexual men and women. 'Gold collar' refers to people who hold high-level managerial positions in large state or foreign companies; 'red collar' refers to party officials and employees of government institutions, party agencies or administrative authorities; 'white collar' refers to well-educated mental labor workers; 'blue collar' refers to manual labor workers; and 'gray collar' commonly refers to university students who occupy that gray area between white and blue collars, being capable of both mental and physical labor work (Zheng 2015, Chap. 4).

Nothing has yet to be written either in Chinese or a foreign language about the homosexual practices of gold and red collars in China because information on them is most difficult to gather, as out of all classes, they fear the most that the revelation about their sexual orientation will cost them everything, especially social status. Very limited and competing information exists regarding their sexual behavior, with some suggesting that these high-class homosexual people treasure emotional attachments and have romantic homosexual relationships, while lower-class people tend to be after physical pleasures and have mainly casual sexual encounters; others disagree and show that the former are in fact much more likely than other classes to purchase sexual services or rent money boys to satisfy physical sexual desires free of emotional entanglements, which they take great care to ensure for fear of disclosure and blackmail (Zheng 2015, 101–103). While the other classes of homosexual people are far from free of fear of disclosure of their sexual identity, they are at much greater liberty to visit public cruising areas such as parks, online chatrooms, bars and bathhouses. Those who are unable to attract potential sexual partners in these usual ways, especially if due to lack of physical appeal, tend to either purchase sex or visit bathhouses where dark rooms would mask their appearances (Zheng 2015, 105). All of these places are targets of regular police surveillance, which effectively prevents higher classes from visiting.

As will be noted in Chap. 3, increasing inequalities, especially along the rural–urban divide, have produced a Chinese population keen on drawing class distinctions to their advantage, either based on wealth, social status, educational level or one's roots. This is also the case for the homosexual community, in which class differences are epitomised by values, habits and experiences associated with rural versus urban origins. Studies on Chinese homosexual men show that the homosexual community as a whole expresses moral repugnance and social discrimination toward those who are considered to be the lowest class of all homosexual men—those of rural origin, have a migrant status, engage in sex work, or are overly feminine (Zheng 2015, 110). The worst sufferers of insults and internal discrimination are rural migrants who engage in sex work in cities, the so-called 'money boys', the vast majority of whom are said to be heterosexual. Due to their background and work nature, they are considered uncivilised, immoral, disgraced and polluted within the homosexual community (Zheng 2015, 110). There is further internal hierarchy within this class of rural migrant money boys, ranging from low-tier, freelance, medium-tier to high-tier, determined by their place of work and the fees they charge (Zheng 2015, 111–112).

This presentation of the external and internal sources of discrimination leads to three conclusions that shed important light on the protection of the rights and welfare of same-sex attracted people in China. First, as is the case with any group, the homosexual community in China is not unified—variations in personal traits and social status prohibit them from uniting and speaking with one voice, which is often required when demanding better rights protection. Second, the homosexual community itself firmly embraces many of the ideologies and expectations of the *heterosexual* world, which further reinforce and internalize discrimination in the forms of prejudices and divisions, rendering challenging existing prejudices coming from outside of the homosexual community difficult if not impossible. Third and related, any attempt to understand let alone tackle the difficulties facing the homosexual community must be interdisciplinary and dive into a broad range of social and cultural issues in order to determine what might work and what might not work.

1.2.3 International Inspirations and Local Activism

One way of working out what might work and what might not work is by conducting a situational analysis within the Chinese context of Western strategies that are currently in place in the advancement of the rights of homosexual people. Legal protection aside, Western strategies to debunk common misunderstandings and prejudices against homosexuality typically have two key ingredients—advancement of scientific knowledge, and grassroots/NGO activism—both exist in China and function with great difficulty but have nevertheless generated progress.

The relevance of scientific knowledge with regard to homosexuality in the Chinese context is twofold: one concerns the nature of homosexuality, and the other concerns its association with HIV/AIDS. Since the Chinese culture and society are so convinced by the linkage between homosexuality and morality, surely the natural thing to do is to enquire whether or not a same-sex attracted individual has made a conscious moral choice to be homosexual or is genetically predisposed to homosexuality—which is, after all, central to the moral issues that homosexuality is said to have raised, as in order to make a person morally accountable for their actions, we need to be able to assume that they are making a conscious, free, moral choice.

Similarly, if homosexuality is labeled a disease of sexual perversion in need of correction and cure, one needs to first inquire about the evidence supporting such a conclusion and in what context, what the usual characteristics of sexual perversion are in comparison to those of homosexuality, in order to determine whether it is indeed a disease so labeled. In other words, much should be a matter of fact which may easily be explained by scientific, medical evidence and theories, which may well be conflicting with each other in some aspects, which is precisely the point of publicly presenting and debating them so that people may themselves reach informed conclusions, which will of course vary.

Not surprisingly, there exists no scientific data on theories and evidence that openly normalize homosexuality in the Chinese public domain, and once in a while if a person with status makes a statement to that effect, it still causes surprise, such as in December 2014 when a Beijing court ruled in favor of a gay man who had sued a clinic for giving him electric shocks to 'cure' him of homosexuality, where the judge stated expressly that homosexuality was not an illness and required no treatment (Kaiman 2014b). In China, even though doctors and psychologists are trained as scientists, when it comes to the subject of homosexuality, they seem to do nothing more than make simple conjectures about the causation and harmful effects of homosexuality, especially in terms of its linkage to HIV/AIDS, which would fit the cultural pattern in China without any empirical follow-up to test their validity. As will be shown in the next chapter, some counsellors and psychiatrists operate clinics that claim to be able to 'correct' homosexuality even after it was removed from the country's official list of mental illnesses in 2001. It seems that the cultural inclination for harmony has prevented psychologists, doctors and scientists from fully engaging with the topic or publicly expressing views that are contrary to those of the mainstream population. To be able to do so requires the existence of a free, rational and tolerant public space that is not easily angered by alternative points of view.

This is not to be interpreted as saying that the Chinese are not interested in science in regard to homosexuality. Quite the contrary. The Chinese are obsessed with the word '*kexue*', while the direct English translation being 'science' or 'scientific', the actual meaning is much broader and more nuanced. A quick look at China's mainstream media will show that the word '*kexue*' is everywhere—*kexue* policies, *kexue* development, *kexue* ideologies, *kexue* management—it is particularly frequently invoked in official political statements and speeches on modernisation, development and progress. While the word means 'science' or 'scientific' when used in scientific fields, within wider political and sociocultural contexts, it implies that ideas, practices and behaviors are well founded, rational, modern, and future oriented; the opposite '*bu kexue*' (not scientific) means backward, irrational, improper, and anti-modernization (Hood 2011, Chap. 6).

'Homosexual activities are *bu kexue/not scientific*' is a particularly common line of attack on homosexuality, especially among older generations, which clearly refers to sexual acts and their association with STDs and HIV/AIDS. Applying the notion of '*kexue*' to homosexuality signifies that there are things and behaviors that are inherently modern and proper, and there are things and behaviors that are by nature uncivilised and barbaric, as evident by serious diseases. By emphasizing the connection between homosexuality and illnesses, the intention is to cultivate a self-disciplined society whose sexual habits and behaviors remain on the safe and healthy side and regulate those that are not. It is by so doing, '*kexue*' stands in contrast to 'lax morality', and despite normally having the connotations of progress and modernisation, begins to have paradoxical meanings and now serves the oppositional purpose of keeping with tradition—the tradition that has had homosexuality demonised.

In other words, while the spread of scientific knowledge on the nature and social impact of homosexuality may ease fear and enable understanding in the West, it does not exactly serve the same purpose in China, as what the Chinese call 'scientific' in this context is not what the Western world calls scientific, and instead of sharing new data, enabling free flow of information in the generation of renewed knowledge as a truly scientific environment will do, its emphasis on the 'scientific ways' in fact serves the opposite purpose of presupposing right and wrong, sorting ideas, practices and behaviors into fixed categories of proper and improper, those that should be applauded and those that ought to be condemned. The scientific knowledge about homosexuality that has thus far received predominant emphasis is its connection to STDs, especially HIV/AIDS.

Thus, while the solution seems straightforward, which is to let science speak, let scientific knowledge on homosexuality circulate in the public space so that the society can begin to gain insight into what it truly is, may it actually be normal, which is the best way to ease fear and enable recognition; in reality, the *kexue* environment would not let this happen easily. However, official channels are neither the only nor the most effective means to spread such knowledge, which leads us to look to another important driving force in the advancement of rights protection of same-sex attracted people in the West and in China—grassroots activism and NGOs.

While grassroots queer movements around the world share the broad common goal of fighting prejudice and achieving social justice for sexual minorities, local realities differ substantially and present diverse challenges, rendering it necessary that very different strategies and priorities be put in place in different national contexts. This has raised questions regarding the usefulness of comparative studies and the workability of imported ideologies and strategies, especially whether there exists one single correct articulation of homosexual identity and life. Having said that, an examination of the five main forms of grassroots queer activism in China below will show that there are undoubtedly transnational hegemonic ideals and ways of articulation that are based on Western-style individualism and coming-out narratives, bringing attention to the fact that despite substantial situational and cultural differences, same-sex attracted people anywhere in the world share many similar difficulties and face common challenges, giving rise to similar if not identical activist strategies, with variations in degree of exposure, width of participation, and intensity.

The following paragraphs will show that the Chinese queer activist strategies are 'locally specific' not in the sense that they are completely new or unseen in the West, but that the very Western-style strategies have been appropriated, fine-tuned, or toned down, in order to circumvent censorship. The Chinese politics of homosexuality does have transcultural and transnational dimensions.

1.2.3.1 Online and Social Media Queer Communities

Queer online media in China has come a long way since it first emerged in the late 1990s, and due to the lack of positive representations of homosexuality in mainstream traditional media,[1] it has become an important platform for queer community-building, and the positive impacts are threefold. First, in terms of presence, with hundreds of LGBT websites in existence providing information on homosexuality-related issues, offering space for online support and interaction, documenting and broadcasting local and international queer events, the internet has become the main communication platform, cultural base and action arena for the Chinese queer community.[2] It is also an important source from which the nonqueer community, should they be interested, may gain insight into a world about which they know little, a world with a distinct collective identity and yet manifests great internal diversity.

Second, in terms of transnational information flow, the internet has enabled the global flow of queer-themed information and rights movements to reach and inspire Chinese queer communities, which have not only built up their confidence over the years and promoted them to rethink their sexual identities, but have also lent

[1] The only mainstream traditional media that has covered China's LGBT-themed issues seems to be the English-language news channel CGNT—China Global Television Network (previously known as CCTV-9), which is the international arm of the government-run China Central Television (CCTV) based in Beijing, well known for its censorship on sensitive domestic issues. For all the LGBT issues that it has covered, see https://www.cgtn.com/search?keyword=LGBT.

[2] Well known examples of such websites are: 'Ai Bai': https://www.aibai.cn; 'Queer Comrades': www.queercomrades.com; 'Dan Lan': http://www.danlan.org/.

them resources and inspirations to carry out activism in a difficult context. Despite having these important transcultural and transnational dimensions, the internet has enabled the Chinese queer community to form indigenous discourse by providing a participatory and reflexive environment for queer as well as non-queer people to share and communicate through blogs, chatrooms, storytelling, video sharing and other online resources and interactions (Jeffreys and Yu 2015, 82). Online activities often lead to or come hand in hand with offline strategies; for instance, watching online educational videos has led to offline discussions, lectures and panel sessions (Engebretsen and Schroeder 2015, 29).

Third and most importantly, in the age of the internet, the fact that information travels wide and fast means that exposure of injustice is much easier, despite that the Chinese cyberspace is subject to many constraints. On 13th April 2018, China's Sina Weibo, a Twitter-like Chinese-language social media platform, announced that all LGBT issues would be banned in its latest campaign to create 'a clean and harmonious' environment on its platform. Comics, games and short videos containing pornography, violence and homosexuality were classified as violating the platform's regulations. While this was not the first time LGBT issues were censored, it was the first time that normally taken-for-granted censorship generated a powerful wave of online protests within just hours after the announcement. Queer as well as non-queer people expressed their anger and opposition by posting pictures of rainbows on various social media platforms; same-sex couples posted personal photos of themselves to express solidarity and in support of LGBT rights; many quoted China's Constitution and legal provisions that were meant to protect all minorities and respect the dignity of all Chinese citizens, indicating that Sina Weibo's move was neither legal nor moral.

What was even more striking was that on 15th April 2018, *People's Daily*—the flagship Chinese Communist Party newspaper, published an editorial via its social media account criticizing Sina Weibo's announcement, stating that 'there is more than one sexual orientation, and both homosexuality and heterosexuality are normal', 'everyone is unique with different looks, skin color, height, weight, personality, ethnicity, nationality, and sexual orientation is just one of these differences', 'protection of sexual minorities' rights is what fairness and justice require', 'understanding difference and elimination of discrimination ought to be society's shared belief'. The piece went on to say that 'considering homosexuality as similar to pornography and violence is bound to cause public concern'.

This highly unexpected move by the Communist Party's flagship newspaper soon generated a great deal of public support, causing many to repost the editorial on their personal social media accounts. Some interpreted this editorial as a clear signal that the Chinese government had not only softened its attitude toward LGBT rights but also considered it fit to publicly admit it—not its usual style on controversial domestic issues. On 16th April 2018, just 66 hours after its announcement to crackdown on homosexual contents, Sina Weibo reversed the ban, announcing on its social media account that it would now only censor contents that were pornographic or violent. At the end of the announcement, it thanked the public for 'discussions and suggestions'—followed by three microphone emojis.

However, it was what happened *after* the reversal of the ban that was more telling if one was to accurately understand the situation. Until the appearance of this *People's Daily* editorial, many saw the propaganda of LGBT rights in China as being led by foreign media. Undoubtedly motivated by the unexpected government support of the queer community, some sought to take it further and extend it into a larger movement to mark the International Day Against Homophobia 2018. This was banned, and many online postings and discussions on the topic were deleted. This was a clear indication, and as this book will show throughout that, changes are taking place, but they are only allowed to take place if led by the government and within the firm boundaries drawn by the government. The government is particularly suspicious of any incident that may have the potential to develop into a larger movement. It is therefore also arguable that the *People's Daily* editorial in fact reveals not the government's softening attitudes toward LGBT issues but rather a hardening stance on Sina Weibo jumping the gun and appearing to be 'leading', although it was in fact merely 'following' the lead of the state to 'clean up' the public environment.

This reveals the major obstacle facing online queer activism in China—cyberspace is not free, in a complex way. Studies show that many gay and lesbian-oriented websites tend to be short-lived due to internet regulations and controls, and many lack financial resources and technical expertise to keep their websites safe from online pornography or hacking from other similar websites, possibly as a result of competition or conflicts (Ho 2007; Jeffreys and Yu 2015, 82–83). Furthermore, many queer websites practice self-censorship to avoid the risk of being shut down by government authorities, while others have become commercialised or sexualised to attract traffic—all will lead to misrepresentation of the queer identity (Ho 2007; Jeffreys and Yu 2015, 83). Consequently, the impact of online activism led by queer groups has been limited.

1.2.3.2 Gay Pride

While Gay Pride events are far from the main or most widespread form of queer activism in China, it stands out from the crowd not least because it is rather surprising that such 'flashy' events, in great contrast to the other grassroots queer activist initiatives which are all very low-key, really have been taking place in a country as culturally conservative and socially controlling like China. 2019 marks the 11th year of the Shanghai Pride Festival, the very first and by far the largest and most visible Pride festival in the Chinese Mainland.[3] Since 2008, the organizers' intention has been to present a multiday, multidimensional apolitical public event every summer, by staging a wide range of cultural activities in arts, music, drama, sports, educational exhibitions and forums, to 'show off' the Chinese queer community as a whole and as a culture to the rest of China with the intention of increasing awareness and

[3] For key information, past events and schedules of future events, see their bilingual official website: https://www.shpride.com/?lang=en. The fact that such a website exists and is continuously updated is also a good sign.

understanding. Since 2015, an important part of Shanghai Pride's programme has been its queer film festival, intended to be an important tool for public education on LGBT issues. With tireless efforts and enthusiasm of the organizers, volunteers, overseas connections[4] and considerable local support, Shanghai Pride has managed to become an annual event—despite consistently suffering setbacks and interruptions of the local police, which tend to take the forms of interviews with the organizers requesting detailed information before the events, sudden shutdowns or requests to slim down the programme, censorship of films and art exhibitions, and last-minute cancellations of prebooked venues accompanied by refusal to give explanations.[5]

A closer look at Shanghai Pride's official website reveals that, contrary to common misimpressions and what sometimes foreign media reports tend to suggest, the Chinese queer community has clearly been for many years deeply immersed in queer culture and queer rights politics in a way very similar to their counterparts in the developed Western world. An important difference is that their range of activities and topics, forms of presentation and especially volume of their voice have been tailored to meet the Chinese standard—evident, for instance, from the fact that Shanghai Pride is a Pride festival without a parade, as mass parades of any kind in China are nearly impossible to carry out and will cause grave concern not just to the government but also the general public. While it is sensible to assume that the cosmopolitan city of Shanghai is an exception, as while similar events are said to have taken place in other cities, there is no publicly available information on them whatsoever, it is nevertheless necessary to elaborate on three intertwined concerns to which Shanghai Pride has given rise, as they shed important light both on the relationship between Gay Pride events and the broader queer grassroots initiatives, as well as on some of the factors that have caused the formation of grassroots activists' coping mechanisms in China. These three common concerns are: location (and visibility), image by association, and identity politics.

First, the public and urban spatiality necessary for Pride events has the effect of equating Pride with urban citizenship and cosmopolitan atmosphere, which in turn has the unintentional consequence of excluding those without urban citizenship or living outside of cosmopolitan environments (Engebretsen and Schroeder 2015, 101). Such a divide can be regional as well as socioeconomic, in that people in less developed environments, with less social and economic means, not only have much less access to international and national queer information but also have less money and less free time to participate in such events, which could also carry greater risk and cause greater consequences of exposure for them than for those in large cities. This explains why in large cosmopolitan cities, due to greater exposure to homosexuality and closer proximity to the queer community, the general public is more receptive and acceptive of homosexuality and the associated events, whereas in less modern places, it remains a taboo.

[4] They list on their official website seven foreign consulates and one foreign state agency as partners in 2019 (Australia, UK, Denmark, Finland, France, Germany, Norway, and the Agency of Culture and Palaces of Denmark): https://www.shpride.com/sponsors2019/?lang=en.

[5] http://www.sohu.com/a/235999625_139533.

Second, Gay Pride is by definition public, colorful, with a strong, collective, coming-out and reaching-out emphasis, and it tends to give the (mis)impression that the LGBT community is not only loud but also homogenous, without national borders or internal diversity, which, in the political environment of China which is dismissive of both loud expressions of alien ideas and tight groups representing entirely different cultures especially if with well-established foreign connections, will naturally cause suspicion. This explains not only the police interventions at Pride events but also why, as will be shown below, most queer grassroots activism takes place in China either secretively or openly but with a cover, self-(mis)representing as something else.

This leads to the third point, which concerns expressions of the queer identity. The existence of Shanghai Pride and similar events is a sign that Western-style language and expressions of queer identity are workable in China, or at least in some regions or some cities, which must not conceal the fact that they are workable only to some extent, in that a variety of identity expressions exist and there are multiple versions of Pride. This calls into question the way we see the West–East divide both generally and in the particular context of homosexuality. It seems that rather than seeing this as different queer communities interpreting and expressing queer identity differently, which is inherently West-centric, it is better to recognize global queer activism as consisting of an expansive range of forms and degrees of expression, which is internally diverse and multicultural, interacting with and reacting to a wide range of local circumstances (Engebretsen and Schroeder 2015, 102).

1.2.3.3 Independent Queer Films

Films and documentaries have played a vital role in LGBT community-building and public education on homosexuality in the West. In China, LGBT-themed films do not meet the state's official requirements for public showing in cinemas or on television, but they may be shown discreetly in cafes, bars, galleries, restaurants or independent film salons, arguably due to loopholes in the law (Engebretsen and Schroeder 2015, 82). Some have also taken place in foreign consulates. This allows film makers, activists and viewers to form small gatherings to show, view and talk about the films and LGBT issues. Despite being small in size and therefore limited in impact, since they nevertheless have the sole purpose of showing censored images to the public, such events are viewed as a symbolic challenge to the status quo and protest against the government's tight control over information. Consequently, if brought to the attention of the authorities, especially when the events are of a certain size or have a certain name—for instance, 'queer film festivals', which distribute and consume a significant portion of Chinese queer films—such gatherings will normally be subject to police intervention and government censorship, as evidenced by, among others, the forced closure of the first Beijing Queer Film Festival in 2001, the first Beijing Gay and Lesbian Culture Festival in 2005, and the Beijing Independent Film Festival in August 2014—the very first complete shutdown in the prominent film festival's 11-year history (Kaiman 2014a).

Confronted with pressures and risks, the organizers of the Beijing Queer Film Festival had to rethink their strategies by initially incorporating the festival into other officially allowed film festivals and labeling queer films as 'avant-garde' and 'nonpolitical'. Gradually, it gained its footing and is now an independent annual event (with a new name), featuring predominantly queer films, documentaries and short films produced in the Chinese mainland as well as from other parts of the world. In recent years, similar to other independent film festivals in China, the Beijing Queer Festival has developed a coping mechanism in the form of a guerrilla-style organizing strategy comprising various tactics to circumvent official censorship. For instance, multiple screening venues will be selected, and contingent screening plans are designed, so that if one venue is shut down by the police, the festival may still continue at another (Tan 2019; Bao 2016); it has also experimented with online streaming and onboard screening on trains and buses (Bao 2018, 92). However, despite having survived, due to reasonable fears of the organizers and audiences, the impact of the festival has been limited, although such guerrilla-style festival-organizing tactics have opened up the question as to what constitutes a film festival (Bao 2017, 95), which in the Chinese context has significant practical consequences.

Furthermore, as part of a social movement, it is important that such events may benefit as many as possible, which is difficult to achieve considering the Chinese reality. However, in recent years, efforts have been made and attention has been given to those who do not have easy access to such resources for financial, geographical or other reasons. For instance, as part of its outreach programme, the Beijing Queer Film Festival has in recent years sponsored those from small cities or remote regions to attend the festival (Bao 2018, 93); Beijing-based queer film makers have also organized the China Queer Film Festival Tour to let people outside of Beijing and across China gain access to international, Asian and Chinese queer films in a relatively safe and inclusive environment. Relying heavily on collaboration with local hosts and different gay and lesbian groups, upon reaching an agreement with local collaborators, the organizers in Beijing would send them the selected films and accompanying publicity materials. All viewing events are documented, and feedback is collected and reviewed.

While official censorship remains the greatest challenge, such touring events have also encountered significant regional discrepancies in economic, social and cultural development, as well as vast differences in the audiences' personal taste and preferences, causing the need to constantly rethink details of film selection, tailor-make viewing programmes and adjust expectations according to local circumstances (Engebretsen and Schroeder 2015, 84). However, over time, the tours have contributed to LGBT community-building in China by enabling film makers to interact with fellow filmmakers and audiences, promoting experience-sharing, discussions and debates about LGBT rights issues, recording and archiving the stories that the participants share, attracting journalists to the events to enable understanding and therefore less biased media representation, consciously encouraging gay and lesbian groups to break barriers, collaborate and build good relations with each other for a common cause (Engebretsen and Schroeder 2015, 84–85). More importantly, such tours (and film festivals) tend to lead to further discussions and events, which will prolong interest and debate by generating more insights and understanding. Thus, overall, despite their limited impact, the fact that such events have survived and grown at all demonstrates strong potential for Chinese queer activism.

1.2.3.4 Organizing Against HIV/AIDS

However, while both are open to the general public, the impact of Gay Pride and queer film festivals is probably felt mostly inwards by the queer community itself, as it is mainly the same-sex attracted people themselves who tend to participate in these events, and that social stigma and censorship mean that their impact, despite growing, is severely restricted in the wider nonqueer society. What does connect the queer community more closely with the wider society is another important and better-known form of queer activism—the fight against HIV/AIDS. It is also an area of Chinese queer activism that may be compared and contrasted more directly with its Western counterparts, in that while the existence of active queer communities preceded the AIDS epidemic in the West, and governments prioritized research and policies on HIV/AIDS *as a result of* or *in response to* the political activism of the queer communities, in China it has been the opposite—the queer community became visible only *because of* the AIDS epidemic (Jeffreys and Su 2018, 100), which explains many of the deep-seated presuppositions and widespread discrimination against the community.

However, at the same time, it is also this connection to HIV/AIDS that has provided opportunities in recent decades for queer activism to grow in China. Since the early 2000s, when the Chinese government finally decided to confront the HIV/AIDS epidemic after years of denial, men who have sex with men have been identified as high-risk, and as the next chapter will show, both international organizations and the Center for Disease Control and Prevention of China have since closely engaged the queer community in the fight against HIV/AIDS. One of the main reasons for such engagement is that while the government has shown willingness and real efforts in behavioral intervention in high-risk groups (for instance, intravenous drug users, illegal blood donors, commercial sex workers, gay men), the social stigma associated with homosexuality has caused serious problems in identifying infected individuals, as they usually hide their sexual orientation and the vast majority are in a heterosexual marriage, rendering it necessary to have insiders working from within the vulnerable group to help tackle the disease.

It seems that in the fight against HIV/AIDS, a community base and a large amount of resources (internal as well as external) are a necessary combination, as while the former provides legitimacy of existence of the queer community in a society that is known for severely constraining the activities of such organizations, the latter helps sustain the community's development and enables it to fight the disease (Sutherland and Hsu 2012, 134; Engebretsen and Schroeder 2015, 197–199). It is also important to note that while the Chinese government is normally very suspicious of foreign 'interventions', this is one area in which it welcomes international assistance and has been consistently receiving funds from foreign organizations and donors. In fact, until the early 2000s, China's HIV/AIDS programmes were mainly supported by Western countries such as the United Kingdom and the United States, various United Nations agencies and multilateral agencies, as well as private donors such as the William J Clinton Foundation and the Gates Foundation (Wu et al. 2011).

However, foreign assistance is subject to heavy constraints even in this field. For instance, community-based queer organizations are not allowed to apply directly for global or foreign funds but may only rely on the government financially (Zheng 2015, 138). While the government now funds the vast majority of its HIV/AIDS-related programmes and projects, where it does receive international funds, they are always directed first to the government, which will then pass them on to community-based organizations. This 'filter model' was initiated by the China-UK HIV/AIDS Prevention and Care Project launched in 2001 by the UK's Department of International Development and largely followed by other international donors in the field (Engebretsen and Schroeder 2015, 196).

Furthermore, while online activism, independent queer film-making and Gay Pride all in their own ways go against the mainstream and challenge the government, HIV/AIDS-related activism sees the queer community in partnership with the state. From the queer community's point of view, this collaboration signifies a certain degree of official acceptance and recognition, generating a sense of purpose and usefulness in being able to tackle a serious problem that has disproportionately affected the group. This sense of purpose is evident, first, in the fact that there are said to be over four hundred grassroots NGOs, 'government-organized NGOs' and online HIV/AIDS networks working together or individually to combat the epidemic in China, and second, in the observation that some of the queer groups have dedicated so much attention and effort to HIV/AIDS work that they have neglected broader community-building activities (Engebretsen and Schroeder 2015, 86).

Given the limited influence that NGOs are allowed to have in China, it would be unrealistic to expect their presence to be able to cause any fundamental change on their own. The existence of so-called 'government-organized NGOs' is a sign that, first, the government recognizes the value and therefore necessity of the work of NGOs; second, it also worries about their existence—perhaps precisely due to their value and necessity—and expects them to exercise their power only in accordance with principles and values of the state and not to be too nongovernmental. This explains why these organizations are much more influential and visible in China in areas such as HIV/AIDS in which they work closely with the government than in those areas in which their agenda or methods do not accord exactly with those of the state.

Community-based queer organizations spread all over the country. Notably, the leaders, volunteers and participants of these groups and networks are almost exclusively same-sex attracted people (Zheng 2015, 125). Additionally, many of these organizations, NGOs or support networks do not have the words 'gay', 'homosexual' or 'same-sex' in their names; neither do they ever publicise themselves as such, giving the impression that they are not queer organizations but groups advocating for public health. This once again draws attention to the constrained space within which they are allowed to operate, namely, within state-drawn fixed boundaries and move in specific ways—in this particular context, as a kind of outsourced social service provider, a collaborator, not a leader (Hasmath and Hsu 2016). An important but not the only reason for such positioning is their lack of permission to apply independently for international funds, and thus have to depend on government agencies or government-backed NGOs in order to participate in this worthy cause, which requires them to shape their tactics accordingly. This again debunks the wishful thought that as the NGO sector grows in China, some fundamental change will take place to challenge the status quo and social norms. It will not, as nongovernmental organizations in China are not nongovernmental.

However, their contributions in the fight against HIV/AIDS as part of queer activism should not be overlooked. Studies on the structure and function of such organizations show that although their internal workings, style and focus vary, on the whole their style is nonconfrontational and typically includes staging events to raise public awareness of HIV/AIDS, organizing and conducting peer education, providing a safe space in which same-sex attracted people can seek emotional and psychological support and counseling, organizing trips and other group activities for community-building so that members may acquire a strengthened sense of belonging, as well as maintaining hotlines to provide practical advice such as on testing, safe sex practices and other related issues (Miller 2016; Sutherland and Hsu 2012, 117).

Nonconfrontational methods are also employed to negotiate with multiple sectors in society and the state with the purpose of influencing mainstream discourse on the relationship between homosexuality and HIV/AIDS, which typically include open letters and online postings that repeatedly emphasize homosexuality as neither illegal nor a mental illness, and that queer groups are indispensable in the government-led fight against HIV/AIDS (Zheng 2015, Chap. 5). Such efforts should all be recognized, but it does give the impression that such groups are only relevant when they do HIV/AIDS work led by the state, further enhancing society's presumption that homosexuality is responsible for the spread of HIV/AIDS—'why else would you be so invested in the fix if you did not break it in the first place?'.

1.2.3.5 Parental and Family Support for LGBT

Despite the tight political atmosphere, the biggest obstacle facing same-sex attracted people in China is not political but sociocultural, and rejection by the family could cause more harm and damage than societal discrimination. It is thus promising that a newly emerging form of grassroots queer activism has been dedicated to supporting parents and families of same-sex attracted people, helping them especially the older generations to learn how to approach the issues, understand diversity in sexual orientation and the needs and difficulties of those living as a sexual minority in China, with the aim of generating vital familial support for same-sex attracted people. While there are such organizations around the country, by far the most influential and the largest in size is the grassroots organization PFLAG China, short for 'Parents, Families and Friends of Lesbians and Gays of China'. Founded in 2008 and named after the American organization PFLAG, PFLAG China's work has thus far reached over 50 cities.

Having recruited thousands of volunteers (many of whom are family members and friends of LGBT people) and employing means such as public lectures, helplines and counseling as well as other activities and forms of dialog, its goal has been to facilitate communication and understanding between LGBT people and their families, make the LGBT community visible and understandable not only to the general public but first and foremost to those closest to them, to enable respect and self-respect, recognition and self-recognition.

As the name of the organization suggests, its work intentionally revolves around families and friends of LGBT people. All educational means and activities are used *on* the parents as well as *by* them. For instance, PFLAG China organizes lectures and seminars to educate parents of LGBT people on sexual diversity and how to come to terms with their children's homosexuality. Similar lectures and seminars are also available to the general public, some of which are given by the parents themselves who will present their own lived experience of being the families of LGBT people and how to cater to their emotional needs in a generally unsupportive societal environment. PFLAG China operates hotlines to receive phone calls from family members of LGBT people, listen to their concerns, and provide practical advice and emotional comfort. When the author last checked, from Monday to Friday every week, the hotlines were operated by parents and family members of LGBT people themselves. On Saturdays, the volunteers would take over, and on Sundays, the psychologists would be in charge.

A particularly noteworthy arrangement of PFLAG China is its annual National Conference, which has been taking place in different cities since 2009 as well as on cruises. Bonding, recreational and educational activities take place over the few days, bringing together LGBT people and their parents, family members and friends across the country, with the aim of providing a chance for them to communicate together as a community, and helping parents and family members understand and accept minority sexual orientation, thereby generating family support and internal recognition. PFLAG's WeChat account has documented some of the eleven national conferences thus far, presenting moving details of personal accounts of volunteers, participants and family members, reflecting also on the problems encountered while organizing the events, paying particular attention to the coming-out stories and the parents' reactions, especially how their feelings toward their children's homosexuality change as their understanding increases. Many young LGBT people invite their parents to the national conferences with the sole purpose of coming out to them, hoping that their acceptance will be easier to come by when surrounding by other LGBT people and their families who are ready to offer guidance and support, knowing that they are not alone.

In contrast to Gay Pride and queer film festivals, more nuanced strategies such as those of PFLAG China will be far more effective in China in terms of generating social acceptance and increasing understanding, simply because they are more likely to *be allowed to* be effective in the Chinese sociocultural reality. First, the very fact that they are low-key and gentle renders them more likely to be viewed in a positive light by a society and a government that value harmony above all, which means these strategies are more likely to survive than others. Second, while gentle they hit the nail on the head, in that families and friends provide the closest and most constant support to LGBT people, the lack of which causes the most immediate and heartfelt hurt. By aiming to generate understanding within the family through inclusive educational and community-building activities, intervention is direct yet very intimate. Third, people are always more likely to listen to those who are like them, with similar experiences, especially similar negative experiences, rendering that when LGBT parents speak to other parents who are yet to come to terms with their children's homosexuality, they are more likely to get through. This is the key reason why PFLAG China is keen to recruit parents and family members as volunteers to help spread the word.

Fourth, targeting parents and family members may effectively solve some of the serious social problems that nonacceptance of homosexuality has caused in Chinese society, for instance, fake marriages. Since people enter into fake marriages with the sole purpose of hiding their real sexual identity from the family and other loved ones, if families and friends understand and respect sexual diversity and accept their homosexuality, there will be no need to fake their sexual identity and hence no need for fake marriages. This relational understanding of the issue also leads to a fifth, important but often ignored point: when speaking of supporting the queer community, it is necessary to remember that the parents and families are very much part of that community, and that in order for them to be able to afford support to their children, they themselves need support in the first place for the challenges they themselves face. This is the most valuable contribution of organizations such as PFLAG China, namely, that parents and families, rather than being expected to automatically offer one-way support and respect to their homosexual children, are recognized as minorities in need of assistance and support, brought together into a safe and friendly arena to relate to each other, to realize self-help by helping others, thereby maintaining a community in which not only they can find similar others but also maintain an environment in which they are the powerful majority for once.

1.3 Concluding Part I

Upon examining the facts and trends, how optimistic should one be regarding the future of recognition and rights protection of same-sex attracted people in China? To answer this question, three preliminary conclusions of Part I may be presented. First, it would be expecting too much to think that, despite some evidence of growing tolerance, China will become friendly toward homosexuality any time soon. A key reason for this is, second, that in order for fear and stigma to go away, there needs to be a free and tolerant space in which issues about homosexuality may be openly talked about, competing and diverse information and opinions may be compared, contrasted and debated, so that people may reach meaningful conclusions themselves after constructive evaluation of all the information available. Despite improvements in some circumstances, such a space generally does not exist.

Third, in regard to minority issues in the Chinese context, the power of *existence* is always greater than the power of *resistance*. It is highly arguable that the improved living reality of Chinese homosexual people has been brought about not by *fighting* for their rights but by simply *exiting,* in the sense of consistent, gradually increased but not overly ambitious visibility, so that after a while the society begins to notice and becomes more accustomed to the idea that homosexuality is a fact, during which process more and more people, while not necessarily understand or accept homosexuality, have at least learnt to turn a blind eye and let others be. However, as Part II below will show, turning a blind eye is not always a strategy.

1.4 Part II: Male Victims of Sexual Abuse

On 29th August 2015, the Standing Committee of China's People's National Congress adopted the 9th amendment to the Criminal Law of China, which came into force on 1st November 2015. Among other changes, article 237, which originally read 'whoever, by violence, coercion or other means, forces, molests or humiliates a *woman* (emphasis added) shall be sentenced to imprisonment of not more than five years or criminal detention', was amended to read 'whoever, by violence, coercion or other means, forces or molests *any other person* (emphasis added) or humiliates a *woman* (emphasis added) shall be sentenced to imprisonment of not more than five years or criminal detention.'[6] For the very first time in Chinese history, men became legally recognized as possible victims of sexual molestation.

The aim of Part II is fourfold. First, six years have passed since the amendment, during which lawsuits have emerged, to which attention should be given when conducting theoretical and sociocultural analysis. Second, there has been a serious lack of Chinese legal academic attention to male sexual abuse, and the issue continues to be presented in the legal field mainly as 'stories' rather than matters of academic concern, for reasons that this part of the chapter will examine. All published academic works in China are made available on the National Knowledge Infrastructure website, on which a search for key words such as 'male sexual abuse' or 'male sexual rights' showed merely 17 results on 17 June 2020, indicating either a lack of academic attention or unwillingness of journals and newspapers to publish. A few studies conducted by Chinese academics have been published in foreign journals in the English language in the past decade, e.g., those of Professor Chen Jingqi of Peking University, Professor Catherine Tang of the Chinese University of Hong Kong, Professor Edward Chan, and the meta-analyses conducted by Kai Ji and Professor Xiangming Fang. However, all of them concern '*child* sexual abuse', which of course covers '*male child* sexual abuse'; none, however, examines 'male sexual abuse' as a general category or pays attention to male adults, as this chapter does.

Third, limited attention coming from the legal field has been paid to the technical details of the law, e.g., appropriateness of penalties in given circumstances, while this part places the legal technicalities within the wider context of Chinese culture

[6] Official website of the National People's Congress:
http://www.npc.gov.cn/npc/c12488/201508/9bded7f9cb6449c5a84e410ec6da0d5a.shtml.

and tradition that have given rise to particular societal views of gender and sexuality as well as corresponding conceptions of sexual health and sexual justice. Fourth, the author marries existing sociological literature, surveys and reports published in the Chinese language with theoretical legal analysis inspired by Western sociolegal theories, hoping to bring attention to this seriously underresearched topic.

1.4.1 Contextualizing Male Sexual Abuse in China

While all countries prohibit sexual abuse in general, as a definition both legal and moral, 'sexual abuse' is largely dictated by local norms and therefore varies from culture to culture, society to society, and legal system to legal system. Consequently, the key elements, precise wording, structure and scope of the offence vary considerably in different countries. However, in its simplest form, countries that have laws governing sexual abuse tend to agree that it can cover any unwanted sexual activity by one person on another, which is improper or harmful, by the use of threat, coercion, violence or manipulation, and may cover a wide spectrum of forms and degrees of force. Male sexual abuse has long been a taboo subject in China. It is visibly present yet carefully concealed by the victims who are too ashamed to speak out and by a society that is too ready to ignore. It has been six years since the 9th amendment came into force, although both its legal impact in terms of disclosures and lawsuits, and its social impact in terms of bringing public attention to the matter as well as inspiring debate and understanding, have been limited. But as cases continue to reach the courts, sexual violence against men and boys has gradually become visible in the public arena if not yet acknowledged as a problem worthy of attention.

Publicly available data on male sexual abuse in China are very limited; hence, the exact extent and seriousness of the problem are unknown. There are signs that the change of law has had some albeit limited impact. First, there has been a quiet yet noticeable increase in the number of cases reported by mainstream media and decided in courts. China Judgments Online shows that since the amendment came into force, there have thus far been 62 court cases of male molestation, out of which 58 judgments have been made public, although this number is significantly lower than that of female molestation, which is approximately 4000 in the same period.[7]

Second, cases with very similar facts have produced different results before and after the change of law. In a 2012 preamendment case, a deputy headmaster of a secondary school attached to the East China Normal University sexually molested boys attending the school over a period of several years, for which he was merely sacked from the position without having to go through further investigation or bear criminal charges, as Chinese criminal law at the time did not recognize males over the age of fourteen as victims of sexual crimes.[8] In contrast, in a 2016 postamendment

[7] See http://wenshu.court.gov.cn/website/wenshu/181217BMTKHNT2W0/index.html?pageId=e362190fef0e94b0c1c609e5dd91d931&s21=强制猥亵.

[8] See http://news.ifeng.com/society/2/detail_2012_06/29/15649027_0.shtml.

case with comparable facts, a male teacher took home three male students, coerced them into drinking until drunk and then sexually molested them in their sleep, for which he was taken to court by the boys' parents, found guilty of forced molestation and sentenced to three years in jail.[9]

Third and related, media reports on male sexual abuse before the 9th amendment were all restricted to describing basic facts and often lacked follow-up information on the outcome of the case, whereas in the postamendment reports, all suspects were reported to have been subjected to coercive measures. It should be noted that not all judgments of these reported cases have been found on China Judgments Online, which could either mean that the information in the reports was incorrect, or that the courts considered them unsuitable for disclosure, or that the suspect only received administrative detention. Furthermore, despite an increase in the number of lawsuits and media disclosures, male sexual abuse remains seriously undercontemplated and underresearched, and the lack of Chinese data and ready availability of Western data also give the misimpression that this is very much a Western problem, behind which misunderstanding there is a network of reasons why the idea that males may be victims of sexual crimes is difficult for the Chinese to digest.

1.4.1.1 Masculinity and Social Expectations

Social expectations are particularly powerful in China. Expectations about the male gender role and male (hetero)sexuality significantly impact not only society's and women's understanding of gender and sexuality but also men's reception of their own sexual victimisation (Lowe and Rogers 2017), enhancing fixed conceptions of masculinity and gender-specific 'must-have' qualities. The sources of such expectations are various.

The first and most obvious are the biological differences between males and females, causing the misimpression that men are always assertive in sexual acts while women passively receive; thus, if a man is unwilling, even if the perpetrator forces the man against his will, the act cannot be completed. Therefore, if the act has been completed, the man must have been willing in the first place. This argument is based on the misconception that, first, to constitute 'sexual abuse', the act in question has to be completed sexual intercourse, which is ignorant of the fact that various means of sexual abuse do not involve penetration; second, patriarchal societal norms of men's masculinity and physical invulnerability rule out the possibility that the perpetrator could be a woman and give rise to the constant need to explain why the male victim did not fight back (Cohen 2014; Cook and Hodo 2013).

The second is the anthropological argument that gender inequality appeared only when agriculture emerged. This explains the long-lived patriarchy of historically agriculture-dominated China, which is said to be the most complete and one of the most sexist among all world cultures due to Confucian emphasis on hierarchy and order (Li 2005), under which cultural customs and social norms are created by

[9] See http://courtapp.chinacourt.org/zixun-xiangqing-46352.html.

men, followed by women. Much has changed with the transformation of China's old economy characterised by gender-based labor division and limited work options for women, sustaining a static construction of manhood and maleness. But thousands of years of history have left their mark on the nation, which continues to function under the influence of traditional beliefs in both public and private domains, where men in general remain the key providers, bearing duties of generating wealth and advancing prosperity for the family. With such duties come the voice to speak and the power to decide, for the family and for the women.

Third, men having control over ideological mechanisms means that they are also responsible for the construction of social ideals and gender roles. Despite continuous and rapid social changes in recent decades, gender-specific 'must-have' qualities have not changed entirely. Women's honor and morality, although not as much as before, remain tightly connected to chastity, whereas those of men are much more variable and relaxed. These expectations learned, sustained and passed on are believed to have maintained the stability of the Chinese family and society and continuously reinforced the dominant self-awareness of men, sustaining a very narrow and specific definition of masculinity (Louie 2002), which causes confusion when expectations are not met, for instance, when men are sexually abused. This constitutes a key reason why men in patriarchal societies are highly unlikely to speak out about abusive experiences, especially if committed by a woman.

1.4.1.2 Public Opinion and Associated Stigma

A related second reason is that due to the presupposed strengths of men and presumed weaknesses of women, the latter tend to be considered more deserving of protection, and society is much more ready to offer sympathy and protection to female than male victims and much more willing to condemn male perpetrators than their female counterparts. Social psychology has proposed a number of theories to explain public attitudes toward victims of crime, three of which are particularly relevant to Chinese perceptions of male victims of sexual abuse.

First, due to a natural need for predictability and control, the public tends to unintentionally or intentionally look for aspects of victim behavior that could have contributed to their victim status, hence holding the victim responsible for their own victimisation (Wood and Gannon 2009). Consistent with this theory, male victims are often treated suspiciously by the public, as according to the Chinese 'male code', the male involved in a sexual act would be expected to have enjoyed the experience no matter how it happened in the first place and in what form it continued. This is comparable to a provocatively dressed female being blamed for having been raped—you asked for it so do not complain. While studies reveal that victims commonly report erections and even ejaculations while being raped, these are uncontrollable and physiological responses that do not necessarily mean the act itself is being 'enjoyed' (Cook and Hodo 2013). Cases show that after sexual assault, many men typically experience physical and psychological problems, including but not limited to self-doubt, anxiety, sexual dysfunction and suicidal tendencies (Stemple and Meyer 2014). There exist Chinese cases in support of these findings, but they are hardly known or talked about.[10]

Second and related, the victim's gender influences blame attribution, especially in cases of domestic violence. Studies find that police officers are more reluctant to become involved in cases of domestic violence if the victim is male and are much more willing to attribute more blame to male victims (Steward and Maddren 1997). It has been reported that over 30% of families in China have experienced some form of domestic violence, and more than 15% of the victims are male[11]; and according to the latest data published by the Supreme People's Court, out of all the divorces filed between 2016 and 2017, 14.86% were due to domestic violence and 8.57% were committed by women on men,[12] although it is unclear what percentage was of a sexual nature. Furthermore, the Chinese public as well as male victims tend to readily assume that family law and public security regulations protect only women; it is seldom known that in several provinces, local branches of the All-China Women's Federation, the key women's rights organization in China, have set up offices or hotlines to receive and settle complaints brought forward by male victims.

Third, when making judgments, the public is often guided by emotions and attitudes toward a certain minority status, rendering public responses to victims of certain crimes predictable (Wei 2016a, b; Lyons 2006). In other words, it is attitudes towards particular *groups' collective characteristics* rather than the *victim's individual* characteristics alone that determine attribution of fault (Lyons 2006). Of particular relevance to male victims is the finding that homosexual victims tend to be held more accountable and judged more harshly than heterosexual victims (Wood and Gannon 2009), and fear of others' presumptions of one's homosexuality is a major factor that prevents heterosexual male victims from speaking out. A heterosexual male victim in Hong Kong reports that having been molested by another man and experiencing erections during the incident caused him to fear that he might be gay.[13] Such 'internalised homophobia' reflects social stigma attached to same-sex attracted people, placing male victims under double pressure for being a sexual minority (perceived or real) and for having been violated.[14] Some gay men consider sexual abuse punishment for their homosexuality, which enhances self-stigmatisation and causes some previously comfortable with their sexuality to become uncertain following victimisation (Lowe 2018).

It is important to note that despite the media often giving the impression that it has a good understanding of societal opinion on sexuality and sexual offences, reliable data regarding public attitudes in China are lacking. While attitudes toward offenders of the most serious crimes are often loud and clear, we in fact know little about societal opinion regarding sexual offences of a less violent nature, which many forms of male

---

[10] See, for instance, http://www.sohu.com/a/260250725_100286752.

[11] See http://www.sohu.com/a/51256593_128238.

[12] See http://courtapp.chinacourt.org/fabu-xiangqing-87622.html.

[13] For more information, see https://www.thestandnews.com/society/看見性侵-5-3-背後-看不見-的男性受害人/.

[14] See http://cusp.hk/?p=8050.

sexual abuse tend to be. Recent Chinese court decisions reveal a range of degrees of violence in male sexual abuse cases: out of the 58 cases of male molestation that have been made public, 33 were committed when the victim was asleep or drunk, 13 involved the use of violence, and the rest were nonviolent. This is in great contrast to molestation cases with female victims, the vast majority of which have involved the use of violence as court decisions reveal.[15] This gives the impression that male molestation is less violent and therefore less serious than female molestation. Less serious crimes often mean less public attention and less recognition.

1.4.1.3 Sexuality: Research and Education

Due to thousands of years of feudal and Confucian influences, the Chinese have always been shy to speak about sex. While modern Chinese society has long moved on from the Cultural Revolution when the social atmosphere was one of absolute moral purity that inhibited any talk, study or education of sex or sexuality (Li 2014), as a subject most closely relevant to anyone's life and a reliable indicator of social change, except a marginal number of specialists, sex and sexuality have very much been absent in serious academic studies (Huang and Zhang 2018). In great contrast to Chinese scholars' apparent indifference is Western scholars' persistent interest, as evident in a large number of high quality academic output covering a wide range of topics concerning Chinese sexuality, causing the irony that when researching topics related to sex and sexuality in China, Chinese scholars often need to refer to Western literature.

The lack of academic research correlates to the absence of comprehensive sex education, which is an essential means to build up knowledge of and right attitudes toward sexuality-related issues. Although various forms of sex education are supposed to exist in secondary schools and universities, their effectiveness is in serious doubt.[16] On the one hand, the country lacks decent textbooks on sex education; on the other hand, teachers' and parents' conservatism causes widespread unwillingness to educate about sex and sexuality properly with the provision of critical details and knowledge (Liang 2016). Sticking with the basics would mean that, among others, sexual abuse is excluded from the syllabus for being too controversial.

1.4.1.4 Lack of Human and Minority Rights Culture

Inadequate education is reinforced by a weak human and minority rights culture. Wei (2016b) has argued in a different context that asking the 'minority question'

---

[15] See http://wenshu.court.gov.cn/website/wenshu/181217BMTKHNT2W0/index.html?pageId=1094e3df91d4a581b22693481faf8450&s21=强制猥亵.

[16] For example, see 'Survey of HIV/AIDS Infections Among University Students: The Unreturnable Classroom': http://china.cnr.cn/yaowen/20150907/t20150907_519786597.shtml;

'Hit Hard by HIV/AIDS: 80% of Infected University Students Had Same-Sex Partners': http://www.shuoshuokong.org/zixun/2018/47991.html.

in China is not easy, as the nation does not speak the rights language comfortably, values harmony and civil obedience above all, rendering minorities, be they people, points of view or ways of life, 'out of place' for association with the unknown, disobedience and dissent, in which category male sexual abuse belongs. In such a collectivist culture, people tend to develop the habit of readily dismissing an issue as unimportant or unworthy of attention, especially if the number of those affected is small and their degree of societal recognition is low.

It is thus particularly important to point out that the number of Chinese male victims is not as small as presumed. According to a survey conducted by renowned sexologist Professor Pan Suiming, in 2010 alone among the total Chinese population between the ages of 18 and 61, as many as 1/10 of the men had been *raped*, although given the lack of legal recognition none had been reported or investigated as such (Pan and Huang 2013). Pan also revealed in another report that the number of men in the same age range who had experienced unwanted sex had grown between 2000 and 2015 from 10% to 16% (Pan 2017a, b), and that while the rate of female rape dropped from 6.3% to 3.0%, that of male rape rose slightly, from 4.0% in 2000 to 4.1% in 2015 (Pan 2017a, b).

These figures are so shockingly high that the author had to repeatedly scrutinise them and found that, in the first report Pan had controversially equated 'unwanted sex' with 'rape' (Pan and Huang 2013),[17] in other words the rate of 1/10 was in fact that of 'unwanted sex' rather than 'rape' legally speaking. And in the second report, while the rates of 10% and 16% did refer to 'unwanted sex' as he wrote, the rates of 4.0% and 4.1%, respectively, seemed to be those of what he described as 'violent sex', which almost matched the Chinese legal description of the crime of rape, but not exactly (Pan 2017a, b). It is necessary to remember that the 9th amendment does not recognize men as possible *rape* victims.

There also exists a 2013 report of Guangdong Provincial Center for Disease Control and Prevention, which shows that out of all male students in senior high schools, provisional colleges and universities in Guangdong Province, male students are 2.2–2.3 times more likely than their female counterparts to experience unwanted sex.[18]

1.4.1.5 Blurred Boundaries Between Law and Morality

Male sexual abuse is very telling of the nation's sense of justice, which in many ways remains habitual, bound up with moral standards, social norms and emotions, rather than inspired and sustained by universal ideals or independent critical thinking. While it is common to blame it on the judicial system's lack of independence, the role of tradition must not be understated.

First, Confucianism gradually became the mainstream thought in the middle of the Western Han Dynasty and began to penetrate China's legal system with Confucian

[17] He states expressly in the text that 'all unwanted sex should be considered rape'.

[18] See http://cdcp.gd.gov.cn/mtbdlist/content/post_1108083.html.

ideals. The law began to restrict and prohibit behavior that failed to conform to Confucian moral standards, giving legal standards a strong moral flavor, thereby blurring the boundary between law and morality (Ma 2008). Confucianism required legal rules to be founded upon moral norms, causing a long line of feudal emperors to rule by virtue, not law (He 2017). It was not until the mid-nineteenth century that law gradually developed into an independent social science, although traditional cultural and moral influences lingered on. In fact, one of the key principles of the current Chinese government's 'rule of law with Chinese characteristics' approach is precisely 'the integration of the rule of law with the rule of virtue' (Xi 2017).

Second, the influence of morality over law was traditionally most evident in relation to familial relations, and sexuality, which were products of natural ethics as well as manifestations of social morality, were legal as well as ethical relations that required the regulation of both law and morality (Chen 2010). A good example was the Tang Code, penal code of the Tang Dynasty and one of the greatest achievements of traditional Chinese law. By synthesising legalist and Confucian interpretations of law, crime or noncrime, light crime or serious crime, were all determined according to propriety, guided by the 'three principles and five virtues', one of which being 'the husband guides the wife', reflecting women's subordinate status in traditional sexual and familial relations. These Confucian ethical and patriarchal ideals remained the core of the Chinese moral code for a long time—arguably they still are but to a much lesser extent.

This has meant that, third, Chinese sexual culture and sexual crimes were/are also under the all-encompassing influence of traditional morality. Under such a system, sexual conception and behavior were/are magnified to measure a person's general character, rendering anything to do with sex a moral matter. Consequently, people would restrict their sexual behavior with moral principles and standards; some were/are self-imposed and voluntary, while others were/are mandatory due to societal pressure (Yu 2014). It is noteworthy that traditional Chinese ethics considered sex morally shameful and that sexual abuse historically only covered activities that were considered detrimental to the integrity of matrimony and stability of the family and community. Unlike in much of the West where debates about sex and sexuality are constant and open, revolve around right or wrong, normal or abnormal, crime or sin; in China, the topic of sex is much neglected, considered inappropriate to be openly discussed or paid too much attention to (Li 2014). When it comes to sex and sexuality, the Chinese have a sense of *shame*, not a sense of *crime*.

1.4.2 Forces of Change

It is thus easy to understand why gender- and sexuality-related issues in China are often seen as falling within the domain of morality and social decency rather than law and justice, causing standards and criteria of judgment of the two fields to merge, creating gray areas in which 'illegal' becomes 'immoral' and vice versa. Additionally, although not all sexual crimes take place in private, many do. The element of privacy differentiates sexual violence from other types of crime, which often means that in the absence of witnesses, laws and regulations are difficult to implement, neither is the negative impact of the offences on those involved easy to determine. Furthermore, China has always been more concerned about the impact of sexual violence on the family and society at large rather than the welfare and interests of the individual. But things have started to change recently, which has both enabled and hindered research development on male sexual abuse.

1.4.2.1 Gender Relations and Changing Power Balance

In a patriarchal society, what is more difficult to comprehend than men being sexually abused is that the perpetrator may be a woman. It is only in a society in which women have visible social status that this becomes imaginable. Chinese women today enjoy much greater financial independence and gender equality than when Confucianism ruled supreme, although it is arguable that China is more patriarchal now than it was during the Maoist era when gender equality was politically prioritized, resulting in a large number of women being appointed to leadership positions. When the transition toward a market economy commenced in the late 1980s, state support for gender equality began to take a backseat to the promotion of rapid growth. Continuous emphasis on efficiency resulted in widespread layoffs, as fewer workers were needed despite greater economic output, especially affecting married women with dependents. While such gender discrimination in the workforce is perhaps less a result of government policy than of employers' greater freedom over labor, there is no doubt that intense competition has caused traditional patriarchal traditions to reassert themselves, now coated with economic efficiency.

Yet, none can deny that Chinese women's material comfort and financial security have increased incredibly since the reforms commenced, lifting their general position in society and expanding their activity fields from within the family to the public sphere. The latest data published by the National Bureau of Statistics (2018) reveal that the proportion of female employees in the whole of China was 43.1% in 2016, 43.5% in 2017 and 43.7% in 2018; the number of female professional and technical personnel in state-owned enterprises and institutions has also been rising, accounting for 47.2% in 2015, 47.8% in 2016, and 48.6% in 2017; and the number of women sitting on the supervisory boards has also been increasing, accounting for 40.1% in 2016, 41.6% in 2017 and 41.9% in 2018. With an increasing number of women benefiting from career opportunities, increasingly fewer are dependent on their husbands or family, giving rise to a new sense of self, renewed constructions of manhood by women, and of womanhood by men.

Furthermore and related, while traditional conceptions and images are far from undermined, as women become increasingly prominent in the workforce by occupying greater positions of authority with supervisory and managerial powers, an increase in sexual harassment in the workplace directed against male coworkers is foreseeable (Cook and Hodo 2013). This is backed by a rising number of Chinese media reports on female superiors molesting male subordinates or female teachers molesting male students,[19] which psychologists have explained on the rise of feminism as a result of enhanced female social status (Mei 2017). However, none of these reported cases has led to legal actions.

Changing power balance in the public domain is also reflected in private family life and sexual relations in which the historically subordinate and passive role of women is no longer. This is not to deny that many traditional familial ideals and practices have endured; rather, men, as a social class, have lost the inherent power to dominate over family matters, and relations between family members are increasingly based on affection, mutual understanding and equality. Not that these elements were entirely absent in traditional families, but that the traditional family would place greater emphasis on the honor of the family as a whole and the sustainment of order and structure according to the wishes of male elders, whereas the modern family pays more attention to individual interests and wishes, demonstrates greater tolerance for divergence from traditional teachings and well-established social norms. Marriage and family are no longer for the purpose of reproduction and inheritance; people are now more willing and able to acknowledge that affection, love and sex can bring not only physical pleasure but also spiritual fulfilment, the pursuit of which no longer causes an overwhelming sense of shame.

The controversial documentary *China's Sexual Revolution* claims that the nation has been undergoing a high-speed sexual revolution since the 1990s, producing not only a sexually open-minded new generation but also a booming albeit illegal sex industry. The dramatic effects on the family and marriage are evident in the fast-rising rates of cohabitation and divorce, which have been increasing since 2000, with the latest data showing that as of 2018, the divorce rate in China climbed to that of 3.2 divorces per 1,000 inhabitants.[20] Although sex without or outside marriage is still not entirely socially accepted, it is widely practiced by both men and women and attracts much less condemnation than before, which the sexologist Professor Li Yinhe (2008a, b) calls 'revolution in the bedroom'. None of these would seem 'revolutionary' had one not known that in ancient China Confucianism espoused the virtues of silent and obedient women who stayed home and served their husbands and sons; foot-binding was promoted in the Song Dynasty as a way to foster sexual segregation and enhance chastity by making it difficult for women to move around; widows in the Qing Dynasty who committed suicide to avoid remarriage were enshrined and honored with the establishment of *zhenjie paifang* (chastity arches); and during the Cultural Revolution (1966–1976) when sexuality was the greatest taboo, women were required to wear unisexual clothing and forbidden from getting stylish haircuts or wearing make-up.

Yet, 'sexual revolution' is nevertheless an exaggeration perhaps in that while it is happening, it is very quiet and that Chinese society on the surface at least retains its clear moral boundaries and remains characteristically conservative. Attention has been given to the impact of this 'revolution' on the lives of ordinary people—more

[19] See http://news.sina.com.cn/s/2005-11-03/00037340055s.shtml.

[20] Statista Research Department (2020), *'Divorce rate in China from 2008 to 2018'*, Feb 27, 2020:https://www.statista.com/statistics/279449/divorce-rate-in-china/.

precisely, ordinary *women*. This is understandable since it is widely held that only women need sexual liberation, as men already enjoy greater freedom. However, the impact on men should perhaps not be examined in terms of *their* 'liberation' per se but in relation to how the sexual liberation of women impacts men. In particular, as women become sexually more open-minded and much less easily surprised by previously unheard forms of sexual activities and indeed abuse, what could this mean for men? Thus far research from this angle is limited.[21]

1.4.2.2 Changing Attitudes Toward Homosexuality

As stated earlier, a key reason why male sexual abuse is hard for the Chinese to accept is its presumed association with homosexuality. While the presumption is erroneous, it is not entirely without reason. It is vital to note that *all* of the 58 male sexual abuse lawsuits since the 9th amendment have been crimes committed *by men, on men*. While this does not automatically render those involved gay, the possibility cannot be ruled out either.[22] If sexual relations between men are not recognized socially as 'proper', the status of men as victims of sexual abuse, especially if committed by men, will also not easily be recognized, and male sexual abuse committed by men risks being branded as sodomy rather than violation of one man's rights by another.

The long history of homosexuality in China has already been presented in detail in Part I and shall not be repeated here, although a brief reminder is necessary that largely due to the lack of a monotheistic religion, homosexuality has historically been treated with much less animosity in China than in the West, and that it was not until the 1860s when institutional reforms were initiated following military defeats and concessions to foreign invading powers that the long homosexual tradition was censured, and stigmatisation intensified during the Republic period when homosexuality was condemned as 'sickness of the nation' (Jeffreys and Yu 2015). This connection between sexuality and state was further enhanced in the People's Republic, in which homosexuality was criminally punished as hooliganism and sodomy until 1997 and remained on the government's Classification of Mental Disorders list until 2001.

Pan (2017a, b) has shown in four nationwide sexuality surveys conducted between 2000 and 2015 that public attitudes have grown much more nuanced if not exactly friendly toward homosexuality in the past few years. The increase in the number of gays and lesbians publicly coming out has contributed to society's toleration if not understanding of them. Two widely publicised cases are worth noting. A Beijing court in December 2014 ruled in favor of a gay man who had sued a clinic for giving

[21] Examples of Chinese works in which women's increased sexual freedom has been named as the cause of rising criminal sexual behavior are: Kang, S. H., & Zhang, X. H. (2016) *Criminology*. Beijing: Peking University Press, 252, and Mei, C.Q. (2017). *Criminal psychology*. Beijing: Law Press, 182.

[22] Out of all 58 published judgments of male sexual abuse cases thus far, only 4 have stated expressly that both the perpetrator and the victim were gay. The sexual orientation of those involved in the other cases were unknown.

him electric shocks to 'cure' him of homosexuality, where the judge stated expressly that homosexuality was not an illness and therefore required no treatment (Kaiman 2014a, b). This was a landmark moment and the very first gay rights victory in a Chinese court.

Similarly worth noting was the well-known gay activist Fan Popo suing the then State Administration of Press, Publication, Radio, Film and Television (SAPPRFT) for ordering video sites to take down his gay-themed documentary 'Mama Rainbow' (2012) featuring the real-life stories of six mothers with homosexual children, which the agency denied having done so. The Beijing No.1 Intermediate People's Court ruled in December 2015 that the SAPPRFT was truthful in stating that it had not requested the film to be taken down while leaving it unclear who did.[23] This was nevertheless widely celebrated by the Chinese gay community as an unprecedented victory over state censorship. And the film was back online.

Furthermore, as Pan (2017a, b) observes, the Chinese public tends to focus more on gay men than lesbians; hence, the fact that men may be victims of sexual abuse committed by other men has become at least imaginable if only due to the erroneous presumption of homosexuality. However, public attitudes may be changing, it will take a long time for discrimination to ease. In August 2015, China's National Health and Family Planning Commission (2015) and the Ministry of Education (2015) issued a joint notice promising to increase efforts on HIV/AIDS prevention and education in universities, where according to their data, sexual relations between men were the main cause of the rapid increase in HIV infections in recent years. While it should be applauded that the Chinese government has finally taken steps to confront the long-existing problem of HIV infections among young people, its identification of male homosexual relations as the main cause of the spread of the disease has caused a new wave of fear and attacks on homosexuality. This will likely rearouse stereotypes surrounding what constitutes a 'victim', which could lead to criminal incidents not being recognized as sexual abuse if the victim is a *homosexual male* rather than a *heterosexual woman.*

1.4.2.3 Renewed Political Atmosphere

Families and social relations typically adjust their patterns of behavior in response to changing political circumstances (Jankowiak and Moore 2017). None of the above changes would have occurred without a *renewed*, not *free*, political atmosphere, the impact of which on gender and sexuality is unique. Unlike in the West, where struggle in the sexual sphere was historically between religious abstinence and secularism, in China, it has been characterised by the interaction between politics and the private life of the individual, or more accurately, the dominance and control of the former over the latter. After the founding of the People's Republic in 1949, sex became regarded as the political enemy of the revolution, ultimately leading to the 'asexual culture'

---

[23] Judgment of Fan Popo *v.* SAPPRFT http://wenshu.court.gov.cn/content/content?DocID=8f605b66-4d40-49b3-90f8-fd7dc75d01ad&KeyWord=%E8%8C%83%E5%9D%A1%E5%9D%A1.

during the Cultural Revolution, recognizing sex for productive purposes only. Since entering the period of recovery in 1976 and especially since the economic reforms commenced, state control over sexual matters has been increasingly relaxed in that absolute repression has gradually been replaced with social guidance (Pan and Huang 2013).

In '*How Censorship in China Allows Government Criticism but Silences Collective Expression*', King, Pan and Roberts (2013) describe the Chinese people as 'individually free but collectively in chains'. They argue that, contrary to common belief, the overall purpose of the vast and sophisticated Chinese censorship effort is *not* to suppress criticism of the government; it is to eliminate information and discussions associated with events that have '*collective action potential*', which may threaten the Party's hold on power (King et al. 2013). This explains China's apparent loosening of the constraints on public expression by allowing social media to flourish, producing a large quantity of negative expressions and critical comments about the government. This is a conscious effort to carefully balance freedom of expression and media openness on the one hand and state censorship on the other, in order to learn about the public's concerns, with the ultimate aim of legitimising the state and maintaining regime stability. It is in such a tightly controlled yet increasingly albeit selectively relaxed atmosphere that historically sensitive issues of gender and sexuality, which are not categorically considered by the government as having *collective action potential*, have been *allowed* to become topics of public discussion, making wider dissemination of educational messages on male sexual abuse a realistic possibility in the near future.

Having said that, whether an issue is of collective action potential is not necessarily determined by what it says but how it is said. A good example was the month-long detention of the 'Feminist Five' by Chinese authorities in March 2015, which was widely reported in the West but never mentioned in China. At the time the activists were planning an anti-sexual harassment rally on 7th March, for which they had recruited volunteers through social media flatforms. There were several explanations why they were detained. First, they had over the years become influential sexuality advocates who had been using creative methods to express concerns and spread their views, turning their personal expressions into public demands. Second, the planned event was to take place around the same time as China's annual legislative session, during which period the government would always take stricter measures for stability maintenance. Third, this type of activism in China would always be linked to foreign meddling—a common tactic to discredit domestic movements. In other words, the timing of the event and its clear collective feminist action potential eventually led to government crackdowns. This appears to contrast greatly with the relaxation of attitudes mentioned on the previous pages, but in fact only confirms that in China it is not always about what you say, but how you say it, and indeed when you say it—don't make it overly political then you might well just be fine.

1.4.3 The Way Forward: Challenges and Possibilities

Evidently, the obstacles to appreciation of male sexual abuse are multifaceted and demand multifaceted solutions.

1.4.3.1 Starting with Legal Flaws

It ought to be recognized that the relationship between legal changes and public perception of gender and sexuality issues is complex, but the former helps reshape conceptions if not generate immediate acceptance. Hence, to move Chinese discussions about male sexual abuse forward, it is important that the public may be guided to know and debate the contributions and limitations of the 9th amendment to article 237. The two obvious contributions are, first, the suffering of *some* male victims of *some* sexual crimes is at last addressed by law; second, although Chinese gender and sexuality issues have received some scholarly attention within the country, the focus has been on women, and the amendment serves as a reminder that gender issues also include men's issues. However, more important than recognizing contributions is to identify limitations and be realistic about the law's likely impact, which will be limited due to three major flaws.

Men Cannot Be Humiliated?

First, the postamendment Chinese law still recognizes only women as possible victims of 'humiliation', a crime similar to molestation in some respects but differentiates significantly from it for the former's public element—humiliation tends to take place in front of others, thereby causing shame and damage to the victim's honor and reputation. Examples include a wide range of behaviors, such as making sexual remarks, indecent exposure, ripping off another's clothes in public with an intent to humiliate, forcing one to perform masturbation on oneself, and so on, all of which may be done by men to women, men to men, women to women, women to men. There is no reason why the law should protect female victims only.

Men Cannot Be Raped?

The second flaw of the 9th amendment is that it makes no change to article 236, which specifies the crime of *rape*—only women may be victims. Not that in China a person who commits an act on a man which would have been categorized as 'rape' had it been committed on a woman would not be held accountable at all; in theory, such a person would be held responsible for 'intentionally injuring' another and sentenced under article 234 of the criminal law, or if the victim is a member of the family, for 'mistreating family members' under article 260. But in reality, for reasons already explained, most male rape victims would prefer to settle the matter privately due to confusion, shame and fear of damage to reputation and consequent social isolation.

The fact that article 236 remains unrevised is hardly surprising, as for the cultural and ideological reasons that this chapter has presented, China is not ready to recognize male rape despite the increase in the number of male rape incidents noted by the media. Given that the Chinese press is under tight state control, the increased exposure of male rape on mainstream print media such as *Legal Daily* and *Xinhua News* indicates that the topic is not considered morally so dangerous that it ought to be censored, which might not have been the case a decade ago. There is thus reason to be hopeful that male rape, like homosexuality, will attract growing attention from the public and the state, generating more information and open debate, hopefully leading to reasoned conclusions and timely revision of the law.

Insufficient Protection for Male Minors

If failure to recognize *adult* male rape victims is for the time being forgivable, the neglect of *minor* male rape victims is much more alarming, which constitutes the 9th amendment's third crucial flaw.[24] In this respect, China's criminal law as it stands affords female minors better protection than male minors, as while article 236 clearly excludes *all* males including *male minors* as possible victims of rape, it does provide that sexual relations with girls under fourteen is considered rape with or without consent. And according to the revised article 237, like adult men, boys are now recognized as possible victims only of the crime of molestation, not of humiliation. The situation is made worse by the fact that while article 49 of the Chinese Constitution forbids physical abuse of children, 'child abuse' is not clearly defined in Chinese law, and neither the Criminal Law nor the Law of the People's Republic of China on Protection of Minors has a provision specifically on 'child abuse'. Those who have committed offences on children would usually be prosecuted under article 234 for 'intentionally injuring another', and if the child is a family member, under article 260 for 'maltreating family members'. It is important to note that unless the intentional act has caused severe injuries, disabilities by especially cruel means, or death, punishments under both articles are light—not more than three years under article 234 and not more than two years under article 260.

1.4.3.2 Raising Awareness and Societal Recognition

The best protection never comes from law but society. Sexual violence is known to disproportionally affect women, but the true prevalence of male sexual assault is

[24] Various cases of rape of boys have been reported by the Chinese media over the past few years, an example being in 2011 a boy of ten from Shanxi Province was raped by an older male living in the same village and was left to die in the fields: http://news.ifeng.com/society/1/detail_2011_01/27/4470550_0.shtml.

underestimated due to underreporting (Zilkens et al. 2018). Of critical importance is the simple acknowledgment that males can indeed be victims of sexual abuse—they must first be known to exist before they may possibly be understood, recognized and helped. A few years have passed since the enactment of the 9th amendment, but the country is largely unaware of the change of law. Indeed, unawareness of the revised law has been raised in court as defense for the accused who claimed to not know that his behavior was a criminal offence, which the court rejected.[25]

Media and the Internet

The mass media is, on one level, simply a medium of communication and mediator of information. But this is not all it is. It has authority, credence and credibility; it legitimates social knowledge while simplifying or even inventing it; and it is a prime source of learning, socialization, and normalization (Cohen 2014). For Chinese society to be in a position to protect male victims, it needs to possess the necessary knowledge and right attitude toward male sexual abuse, which would require, among others, issues of male sexual abuse gaining access to traditional mainstream media to enable representation and exposure in the public arena. As discussed earlier, since the topic of male sexual abuse is not considered to be either morally dangerous or having collective action potential by the government, and since it has already begun to be acknowledged as an existing problem, it is foreseeable that it might gradually find its way into mainstream media and become more visible publicly, however slowly. It is vital that this visibility does not primarily involve 'professionals' or 'experts' talking about the relevant matters but should rather aim at enabling self-presentation of the victims themselves in whatever way they feel comfortable and protected.

A comparison could perhaps be made with how homosexuality first gained public visibility in China, and by looking at the difficulties that gays and lesbians have encountered, it is also possible to foresee the sorts of issues that raising public awareness of male sexual abuse might have to confront. Until very recently, lack of access to traditional mainstream media was the main factor that prevented positive representations of homosexuality in China (Jeffreys and Yu 2015). With the fast spread of HIV/AIDS since the early twenty-first century, the necessity of prevention programmes has risen, which has increased the visibility of gays and lesbians as well as discussions about homosexuality in public, which for a long time mainly involved medical experts talking on television about homosexuality being a disorder responsible for the spread of a life-threatening disease, granting no space to gays and lesbians themselves to tell their own stories. This drove them in the 1990s to start building discourses on the internet, which, despite also being under tight state control, was a much more participatory and reflexive place than traditional media for them to share information and form relationships and join communities, producing

[25] Judgment of the Liu Chenggang Case: http://wenshu.court.gov.cn/content/content?DocID=45ab5183-8b87-49b9-a3ff-a72100c61544&KeyWord=%E5%88%98%E6%88%90%E5%88%9A%7C%E7%8C%A5%E4%BA%B5.

a large number of active websites, chat rooms and personal blogs (Ho 2007; Jeffreys and Yu 2015). It is foreseeable that those male victims who are willing to speak about their experiences will also find the internet more approachable, inclusive and supportive. The fact that online information travels fast and far would also mean that their stories could reach more.

Having said that, homosexuality-oriented websites tend to be short-lived due to internet regulations and checks, lack of funds and technical knowledge, hacking from other gay websites due to competition or personal conflicts; many also practice self-censorship to avoid being shut down by the authorities, while others have become commercialised or sexualised in order to attract attention (Ho 2007). While male victims do not have the exact problems, they are also not as large in number or as organized, it is nevertheless also possible for them to encounter similar issues such as posts being deleted from websites or chatrooms should they be considered morally dangerous or sexually explicit. It would be worthwhile to consider the possibility of setting up a special-purpose website dedicated to male sexual abuse, not only providing theories, facts and information on where and how to get help, but also granting the victims a safe and open space to speak about their own experiences while feeling protected and respected.

As to who should be responsible for such a website, first, for all the reasons this chapter has presented, it might be unrealistic to expect male victims spontaneously to set up and maintain such a website; second, if left to the NGOs, funding and staff might be an issue, not to mention that China does not allow NGOs to operate in quite the same independent way as they do in the West; thus and third, it might be more realistic at the moment for a government body to set up such a website in the fashion of China Women's Network, Chinese Women's Research Network and Women's Voice, all maintained by the All-China Women's Federation to provide information on news topics, research projects, books and conferences related to women's studies in China, covering issues such as gender inequality, domestic violence, and sexual abuse. Just as the hotlines of the Women's Federation also handle men's complaints, the Federation may well consider maintaining a website similar to those for women, collecting and presenting similar information but in relation to men, with the specific purpose of letting the public know that domestic violence and sexual abuse also happen to men.

Furthermore, once again in comparison to queer groups, it has also been noted that although the internet is crucial to queer groups in their efforts to share information and combat discrimination, gay-initiated online activism has very limited influence on the general heterosexual public, in that even if gays and lesbians could talk freely about anything they like on the internet, few heterosexuals are interested in listening (Jeffreys and Yu 2015; Chase 2012). This will also be a problem for male victims speaking out. However, it is possible that, should their stories be allowed to travel online, male victims might receive more sympathetic listeners than gays and lesbians, but their influence will remain limited unless access to the traditional media is also granted.

Hotlines and Help Services

First, China can take inspiration from the well-established hotlines of the All-China Women's Federation and set up male sexual abuse hotlines to provide victims with consolation and practical help. Women's hotlines have played an important role, especially since the implementation of the Anti-Domestic Violence Law. Hangzhou city published in February 2019 the country's very first anti-domestic violence whitepaper, in which the city's Women's Federation revealed that in the three years since the coming into force of the Anti-Domestic Violence Law, while the total number of reported incidents of domestic violence first showed a decline in 2018, those involving male victims continued to increase in the city, although the number was 22 in 2018 which was small, and it was not said how many were of a sexual nature.[26] While at the moment the women's hotlines also handle men's complaints, should male sexual victims' hotlines be set up, it would be better if they were for men only, for all the cultural and ideological reasons already examined would prevent men from seeking help using a general hotline let alone a women's. Furthermore, with the broad internet coverage in China, online reporting of sexual abuse could also be a realistic option, especially considering that many might find direct verbal presentation of sexually abusive experience psychologically and emotionally challenging and would therefore prefer writing from a safe distance away.

Second, the last decade has seen an increase in the number and range of support services available for survivors of sexual crimes in many Western countries, and the collective voice of male victims has started to be heard, albeit slowly, although the quantity and quality of service provision remain inconsistent (Lowe 2018). China needs to start paying attention to the advantages and limitations of these Western policies and institutional designs. In particular, it is vital to think carefully before initiation of any policy of, first, that the psychological needs of male victims differ from those of female victims and that the stigma attached to them are also different; second, even within the same gender group, individual diversity cannot be overemphasized, giving rise to the necessity of multiple means of treatment and comfort (Lowe 2018; Zilkens et al. 2018). Greater education and training will also be needed for primary service providers because they are a crucial first point of contact for male victims in crisis, as negative experience during this first contact with service can severely set back or even stop further engagement (Lowe 2018). More practical work will be needed to enable the spread of best practice across all relevant bodies, although in the absence of actual policies and support programmes, it is too early to speak of cooperation.

1.4.3.3 Recognition Through Education

While media exposure and public discussion can enable clarification and critical reflection on standards, values and problems, they do not necessarily cultivate agency

[26] See http://www.hangzhou.gov.cn/art/2019/2/28/art_812270_30574024.html.

or increase capacities to truly understand male victimhood or to influence or change the environment in which prejudices occur. Corrigan and Penn (1999) have identified in a different context three types of strategies for challenging and changing public stigma: *protest, education* and *contact*. While *protest* appeals to a moral authority to challenge disrespectful attitudes and stigma with the aim of stopping them, *contact* facilitates interaction between stigmatised groups and the public—and those who stigmatise; *education* compares and contrasts myths and facts in order to disseminate the correct knowledge and diminish prejudice and discrimination (Corrigan and Penn 1999; Wood and Gannon 2009).

China's political atmosphere is not one that listens well to *protests*; and in order to be willing and able to facilitate *contact*, society needs to have not only the right knowledge of and attitude toward male sexual abuse but also enough male victims willing to speak up—at the moment and in the near future this is unlikely. At the root of the problem is lack of understanding and recognition due to lack of knowledge and apprehension, which may best be solved with *education*, which is the most systematic and thoughtful way to undermine stigma through provision of knowledge, although its effects could take time to show with no guarantee of positive results.

School-Based Sex Education

To be able to talk openly about male sexual abuse, it is necessary to first be able to talk openly about sexual abuse, and to educate about male sexual abuse properly requires educating first about sexual abuse properly, which would require, among others, school-based sex education to be allowed to play its role. While the content and methods of delivery of sex education should be tailored to meet the specific needs of targeted audiences who vary in age, socioeconomic status and cultural background, in order to be effective in the Chinese context, school-based sex education should have the following characteristics.

First, sex education needs to be properly integrated into school curricula with designated times for administration rather than being left to the wishes of specific schools or teachers. It is also essential that the programmes be long rather than short, with repeated reruns and follow-up 'booster shots' to reinforce earlier knowledge. At the moment, sex education in Chinese schools tends to be very short, something that needs to be 'mentioned' and quickly got out of the way. The cumulative effect of sex education is not recognized, and it is impossible for knowledge to improve without further continuous exposure to similar educational programmes (Davis and Gidycz 2000).

Second, while passive methods of teaching are necessary for passing on basic information, it is important that active participation is enabled in the form of frank and honest discussion and debate, which are particularly difficult to achieve in the Chinese classroom. Third, targeted explicit training, such as behavioral rehearsal, is necessary for teaching specific skills to and encouraging behavioral change in younger audiences. Research suggests that without behavioral rehearsal, any subsequent transfer from knowledge to behavior in potentially abusive situations is unlikely

(Melton 1992). Considering that it is difficult for people, especially children, to speak about sexual abuse, behavioral rehearsal in this respect should also include practising disclosure and reporting. This is backed by research that shows that trained children are more likely than untrained children to disclose abusive incidents (Wurtele 2002).

Fourth, school-based sex education should cover 'controversial' topics such as same-sex relations and male sexual abuse and have the teaching materials standardized and taught by trained professionals who would allow space for honest exchange of information. Designers of such programmes should be alerted to the fact that, fifth, the contents of such programmes tend to be designed primarily to meet the protection needs of women and girls and may not provide adequate knowledge and training for men and boys. For reasons previously examined, men and boys are less likely to realize that they can be sexually abused and thus are more likely to be engaged in risk-taking behavior and treat abusive experiences as experimentation rather than victimisation (Briggs and Hawkins 1997), which makes it more not less urgent for them to be properly educated on such matters.

It is worth noting that despite a large number of studies and programmes, there currently exist no *conclusive* experimental evaluations of whether school-based educational programmes actually help prevent sexual abuse, male or female. Indeed, some have suggested that child-focused sex education places too much responsibility on children than they could and should possibility bear (Melton 1992). Similarly, there exists no conclusive evidence as to whether school-based sex education casually enables better recognition of male sexual victims. However, Western empirical findings may not be conclusive; they are more reassuring than discomforting, which means that similar programmes may well be workable in the Chinese context. Although considering China's political and sociocultural particularities, cultural sensitivity must firmly be borne in mind to avoid unintended consequences.

One such unintended consequence could be increased anxiety among children in the wake of programme exposure. This would require the development of a multisystemic educational network targeting not only children but also parents, teachers and the general public, so that society can work on these issues together, so that children do not bear unnecessary burden.

Notes on Sex Education Outside School

Chinese studies have shown that baseline knowledge of concepts and behaviors related to sexual abuse is very low among preschoolers (Zhang et al. 2013), and current preschool programmes all thus far aim at increasing very young children's skills-based knowledge on what to do in potentially abusive situations—and the results are positive (Kenny et al. 2012). Studies employing follow-up reports suggest that in general, knowledge gained at the preschool stage can be maintained over time (Wurtele et al. 1992), which suggests that should children be exposed to the idea of male sexual abuse, they are able to retain the key albeit most basic information—if only the simple idea that boys may also be victims of sexual abuse.

Apart from distributing facts, an important secondary goal of teaching young children about sexual abuse is to mitigate the negative consequences of abuse, i.e., to help them not feel guilty or at fault, which rests on the 'burden of responsibility' argument drawing attention to the role of family support. There is little research on parents' involvement in formal or informal educational programmes that aim at preventing sexual abuse within the family or in other contexts. Since large numbers of male sexual abuse take place within the family, it is important that parents are educated to be sensitive to their children's vulnerability to sexual abuse and to promote positive communication within the family. One obvious yet often unacknowledged problem in terms of parental involvement is that sometimes the parent is the abuser. There is also no easy way to teach children about possible dangers coming from those to whom they are close and who are supposed to protect them.

In addition to preschool, school-based and familial education, all of us receive life-long education through the 'societal curriculum' of the socializing forces of society, which in the modern Chinese context and regarding male sexual abuse specifically may be divided into three types according to the provider, medium and means of operation: digital education on digital media or the internet, thematic education provided by organizations or agencies with special functions, and exhibitions held at public venues (Wang 2019). Audios, podcasts and short films posted online may be straightforward and widely accessible ways to raise male sexual abuse awareness. Exhibitions and educational events may also be held at cultural venues and public libraries to spread the word.

Additionally, many of the measures taken by the Women's Federation in advancing women's and children's rights, such as public lectures on domestic violence, women's rights campaigns, and children's welfare awareness week, are also applicable to educating the community on male sexual abuse. The Women's Federation, relevant government departments or the courts are also in a good position to invite legal professionals, sociologists or sexologists to give thematic public lectures, as well as organize educational events such as knowledge contests, small-scale seminars and consultations to popularise basic legal knowledge in the local community. All of these methods have long been running in China as part of state governance to promote a 'correct' understanding of written laws at the local level, none of which has yet to touch upon male sexual abuse.

1.5 Concluding Part II

Male sexual abuse is not only a unique perspective from which to study gender and culture in China, but also a classic illustration of how social norms and formal laws impact each other and the lived experiences of social minorities. Part II of the chapter has aimed to show that the slight and largely unnoticed 9th amendment is a small but important step for China to take, but its conservatism speaks for itself, hence its limited impact. The reality is that the law may have changed a little, society may have changed a great deal, the underlying traditional Chinese conception of masculinity and social perceptions of gender and sexuality remain largely intact, and these norms are so ingrained and self-reinforcing that people do not realize the extent to which they shape individual and collective perception and behavior. The revised law is many steps ahead of sociocultural norms, which would usually mean that the law is unlikely to be consistently enforced. Therefore, of vital importance to bringing about recognition and protection is to change existing sociocultural perceptions of male sexual abuse, which has already happened since the amendment. But in order for this to continue, it is essential that more male victims can speak up and that free flow of information on theories and facts of male sexual abuse is enabled to generate informed debate and critical understanding, which would be a daunting task. All things considered, it is safe to predict that despite the first step in the right direction, justice on a large scale for Chinese male victims of sexual abuse will take a long time.

References

Bao H (2017) Queer as catachresis: the Beijing queer film festival in cultural translation. In: Beery C, Robinson L (eds) Chinese film festivals: sites of translation. Palgrave Macmillan, London, pp 79–100

Bao H (2016) Queer filmmaking in the People's Republic of China' at http://theasiadialogue.com/2016/08/22/queer-filmmaking-in-the-peoples-republic-of-china/

Bao H (2018) From "Celluloid Comrades" to "Digital Video Activism": queer filmmaking in postsocialist China. JOMEC J 12:82–100. https://doi.org/10.18573/jomec.171

Becker HS (1963) Outsiders: studies in the sociology of deviance. The Free Press, New York

Briggs F, Hawkins RMF (1997) Child protection: a guide for teachers and child care professionals. Allen & Unwin, Sydney

Chase T (2012) Problems of publicity: online activism and discussion of same-sex sexuality in South Korea and China. Asian Stud Rev 36(2):151–170

Chen W (2010) Research on legislation of marriage and family law in China. Mass Press, Beijing (in Chinese)

Cohen C (2014) Male rape is a feminist issue: feminism, governmentality and male rape. Palgrave Macmillan, Basingstoke

Cook PW, Hodo TL (2013) When women sexually abuse men: the hidden side of rape, stalking, harassment, and sexual assault. Praeger, California

Corrigan P, Penn D (1999) Lessons from social psychology on discrediting psychiatric stigma. Am Psychol 51(9):765–776

Davis MK, Gidycz CA (2000) Child sexual abuse prevention programs: a meta-analysis. J Clin Child Psychol 29:257–265

Engebretsen EL, Schroeder WF (eds) (2015) Queer/Tongzhi China: new perspectives on research, activism and media cultures. NIAS Press, Copenhagen

Flugel JC (1945) Man, morals and society. Penguin Books, Harmondsworth

Hasmath R, Hsu JYJ (2016) NGO governance and management in China. Routledge, Abingdon

He BS (2017) Traditional legal culture and value of China. Law Press, Beijing (in Chinese)

Hinsch B (1992) Passions of the cut sleeve: the male homosexual tradition in China. University of California Press, Berkeley

Ho WW (2007) The gay space in Chinese cyberspace: self-censorship, commercialisation and misrepresentation. China Aktuell J Curr Chin Affairs 36/4:45–73

Hood J (2011) HIV/AIDS, health and the media in China: imagined immunity through racialised disease. Routledge, Abingdon
Huang YY, Zhang YY (2018) Sexual debates among feminisms. Sociol Rev China 6(06):71–83 (in Chinese)
Jankowiak WR, Moore RL (2017) Family life in China. Polity Press, Malden
Jeffreys E, Gang S (2018) Governing HIV in China: commercial sex, homosexuality and rural-to-urban migration. Routledge, Abingdon
Jeffreys E, Yu H (2015) Sex in China. Polity, Cambridge
Kaiman J (2014a) Beijing independent film festival shut down by Chinese authorities. The Guardian, 24 Aug 2014. https://www.theguardian.com/world/2014/aug/24/beijing-independent-film-festival-shut-down-china-freedom
Kaiman J (2014b) Chinese court rules 'gay cure' treatments illegal. The Guardian, 19 Dec 2014. https://www.theguardian.com/world/2014/dec/19/chinese-court-gay-straight-conversion-clinic
Kenny MC, Wurtele SK, Alonso L (2012) Evaluation of a personal safety program with Latino Pre-schoolers. J Child Sexual Abuse 21:368
King G, Pan J, Roberts ME (2013) How censorship in China allows government criticism but silences collective expression. Am Polit Sci Rev 107(2):326–343
Kleinman A et al (2011) Deep China: the moral life of the person. University of California Press, Berkeley
Li YH (2005) Gender relationship. East China Normal University Press, Shanghai (in Chinese)
Li YH (2008) Learning from sexuality. Epoch Literature and Art Press, Changchun (in Chinese)
Li YH (2008) Public attitudes toward homosexuality. Community 15:48–49 (in Chinese)
Li YH (2014) The observation in sociology. China Federation of Industry Press, Beijing (in Chinese)
Liang JH (2016) Studies on the marriage, family and gender (V). Social Sciences Academic Press, Beijing (in Chinese)
Liu P (2015) Queer Marxism in two Chinas. Duke University Press, Durham
Louie K (2002) Theorising Chinese masculinity: society and gender in China. Cambridge University Press, Cambridge
Lowe M (2018) Male sexual assault survivors: lessons for UK services. J Aggress Conflict Peace Res 10(3):181–198
Lowe M, Rogers P (2017) The scope of male rape: a selective review of research, policy and practice. Aggress Violent Beh 35:38–43
Lyons CJ (2006) Stigma or Sympathy? Attributions of fault to hate crime victims and offenders. Soc Psychol Quart 69:39–59
Ma HB (2008) Legal thoughts and social changes. Tsinghua University Press, Beijing (in Chinese)
Mann SL (2011) Gender and sexuality in modern Chinese history. Cambridge University Press, New York, p 138
McDermott J (1992) Friendship and its friends in the late Ming. In: Institute of Modern History (eds) Family process and political process in modern Chinese history, Part I. Academia Sinica, Taipei, pp 67–96
Mei CQ (2017) Criminal psychology. Law Press, Beijing (in Chinese)
Melton GB (1992) The improbability of prevention of sexual abuse. In: Willis DJ, Holden EW, Rosenberg M (eds) Prevention of child maltreatment: developmental and ecological perspectives. Wiley, New York, pp 168–189
Miller CJ (2016) We can only be healthy if we love ourselves: Queer AIDS NGOs, kinship, and alternative families of care in China. AIDS Care 28(sup4):51–60. https://doi.org/10.1080/09540121.2016.1195481
National Bureau of Statistics (2018) Monitoring report of the program of China's women development (2011–2020) of 2018. See http://www.stats.gov.cn/tjsj/zxfb/201912/t20191206_1715998.html
National Health Commission and the Ministry of Education (2015). 'Notice on setting up HIV/AIDS reporting system and further strengthening HIV/AIDS prevention and detection in schools and universities.' nhc.gov.cn. 10 August 2015. (in Chinese). http://www.nhc.gov.cn/xxgk/pages/viewdocument.jsp?dispatchDate=&staticUrl=/jkj/s3585/201508/e4c8a1e6809c4a8e9c49f7f8708873d1.shtml&wenhao=

Pan SM, Huang YY (2013) Change of sex: the sexual life of Chinese in the 21st century. China Renmin University Press, Beijing (in Chinese)
Pan SM (2017a) Gay or Nay: China's changing attitude towards homosexuality. Sixth Tone. 9 Dec 2017. http://www.sixthtone.com/news/1001348/gay-or-nay-chinas-changing-attitudes-toward-homosexuality
Pan SM (2017b) The "Sexuality" of Chinese from 2000 to 2015: the main data analysis of the four national total population sample surveys. 1908 Ltd., Hong Kong (in Chinese)
Shi X et al. (2020) Heterosexual marital intention: effects of internalized homophobia, homosexual identity, perceived family support, and disclosure among Chinese gay and bisexual men. J Homosexual 67(4). https://doi.org/10.1080/00918369.2018.1547558
Stemple L, Meyer I (2014) The sexual victimization of men in America: New data challenge old assumptions. Am J Public Health 104(6):e19–e26
Steward A, Maddren K (1997) Police Officers' Judgments of blame in family violence: the impact of gender and alcohol. Sex Roles 37:921–933
Suiming P (2006) Transformation in the primary life cycle: the origins and nature of China's sexual revolution. In: Jeffreys E (ed) Sex and sexuality in China. Routledge, London, pp 21–42
Sutherland D, Hsu JYJ (2012) HIV/AIDS in China—the economic and social determinants. Routledge, Abingdon
Tan J (2019) Networking Asia Pacific: queer film festivals and the spatiotemporal politics of inter-referencing. Inter-Asia Cult Stud 20(2):204–219
UNDP (2016) Being LGBTI in China: a national survey on social attitudes towards sexual orientation, gender identity and gender expression
Wang L (2019) A study on the boundary consciousness of social education. Nanjing J Soc Sci 5:150–156 (in Chinese)
Wang Y et al (2019) Behind the rainbow, "Tongqi" wives of men who have sex with men in China: a systematic review. Front Psychol 10:2929. https://doi.org/10.3389/fpsyg.2019.02929
Wei HH (2016a) A dialogical concept of minority rights. Brill Nijhoff, Leiden & Boston
Wei HH (2016b) Asking the minority question in China. J Comparative Law 11(2):214–234
Wood J, Gannon T (2009) Public opinion and criminal justice. Willan Publishing, Cullompton
Worth H, Jing J, McMillan K (2017) 'Under the same quilt': the paradoxes of sex between men in the cultural revolution. J Homosex 64(1):61–74
Wu Z et al (2011) The integration of multiple HIV/AIDS projects into a coordinated national programme in China. Bull World Health Organ. At https://www.who.int/bulletin/volumes/89/3/10-082552/en/
Wurtele SK, Kast LC, Melzer AM (1992) Sexual abuse prevention education for young children: a comparison of teachers and parents as instructors. Child Abuse Negl 16:865–876
Wurtele SK (2002) School-based child sexual abuse prevention. In: Schewe PA (2002) (ed) Preventing violence in relationships: interventions across the lifespan. American Psychological Association, Washing DC, pp 9–25
Xi J (2017) The governance of China (II). Foreign Languages Press, Beijing (in Chinese)
Yu HX (2014) Traditional sexual customs and cultural essence in China. Commercial Press, Beijing (in Chinese)
Zhang W, Chen J, Feng Y, Li J, Zhao X, Luo X (2013) Young children's knowledge and skills related to sexual abuse prevention: a pilot study in Beijing, China. Child Abuse Neglect 37:623
Zheng T (2015) Tongzhi living. University of Minnesota Press, Minneapolis
Zhu J (2018) 'Unqueer' kinship? Critical reflections on 'Marriage Fraud' in Mainland China. Sexualities 21(7):1075–1091
Zilkens RR, Smith DA, Mukhtar SA, Semmens JB, Phillips MA, Kelly MC (2018) Male sexual assault: physical injury and vulnerability in 103 presentations. J Forensic Leg Med 58:145–151

Chapter 2
Social Norms and the Right to Health

International attention on contemporary Chinese issues tends to focus on those that are politics-related, for instance, free speech, corruption, and authoritarianism. While they are important and worthy of continuous close examination, they are also vast topics that are far away from the everyday living of ordinary people in a nondemocratic state, in which constructive participation in politics is irrelevant to the vast majority. In such an environment, rightly or wrongly, nothing political can compete with the importance of everyday living—in good health.

Chinese society is a complex society with numerous health issues worthy of attention. There are the more conventional ones such as physical disability, medical care for the poor, elderly care; there are also the newer ones emerging or intensifying in recent years, for instance health issues related to pollution, food safety, both of which have been in the spotlight during the past decade. And needless to say, the enormous medical and social challenges presented in the past two years by COVID-19 will be the focus of much attention in the years to come. But being unhealthy does not automatically render one 'the other', as not every health issue involves 'othering', which is a complicated social process involving multiple actors and factors.

It is for this reason that this chapter examines only two health issues—mental illnesses, and HIV/AIDS—for their status as the two leading stigmatised health conditions in China today and their unique ability to demonstrate what it means to be 'the other' purely due to one's state of health, to reveal how health-related stigmatisation works through association with morality and fear, and how it interacts with a complex web of structural determinants. While acknowledging the *individual* risk factors associated with these illnesses, those *contextual* factors that have rendered certain groups of people forever more vulnerable than others are the focus of attention, in order to show how the majority, the whole society, the state and those living with the illnesses together make these conditions truly sufferable. Both topics have some connections with the issues and concerns raised in Chap. 1, which has in various ways laid the foundation for the analysis here. Thoughts on the relation and interaction between some binary concepts, such as the private and the public, weakness and

H. H. Wei, *Sociocultural Otherness and Minority Justice: A Study on China*,
Ius Gentium: Comparative Perspectives on Law and Justice 88,
https://doi.org/10.1007/978-981-16-9752-4_2

power, physical and moral, safety and danger, rights and duty, are present throughout the chapter.

2.1 Part I: Mental Health: Personal Right or Public Duty

2.1.1 China's Mental Health Reality: Context and Background

A mental illness or psychiatric disorder is generally considered to be a mental or behavioral pattern that causes varying degrees of distress or impairment of personal functioning, which may be persistent, relapsing and remitting, or occurs in a one-off episode (Bolton 2018, 6). For a mental state to be classified as an illness, there needs to be some form of professionally diagnosed dysfunction that varies from illness to illness. Mental illness is now firmly on the list of China's top national health concerns, causing researchers, medical professionals, drug companies and service providers to rapidly develop new initiatives, products and services to meet growing demands. However, whether or not China is experiencing a mental health 'crisis' is debatable. The point of divergence is not whether mental illness is a serious problem in the country—this is beyond doubt, as various sources independently confirm both the scope and seriousness of the phenomenon in terms of the number of sufferers and variety of illnesses.

For instance, the China Mental Health Survey, set up in 2012 and funded by the National Health Commission and the Ministry of Science and Technology, was the country's first nationally representative survey on mental disorders. The Lancet Psychiatry in March 2019 published its findings of interviews and screenings of 32,552 people in 31 provinces for mood disorders, anxiety disorders, alcohol-use and drug-use disorders, schizophrenia, eating disorders, impulse-control disorders, and dementia. The findings estimated that 16.6% of Chinese adults had experienced some form of mental disorder at some point in their lives, with anxiety disorders being the most common and depression on the rise (Huang et al. 2019a, b).

Additionally, in 2019, China published its very first Blue Book on mental health, reviewing the general psychological condition of its entire population of 1.4 billion. Among its findings, it is revealed that an estimated 154 to 210 million Chinese have mild to moderate mental health issues, 28 to 42 million have moderate to severe mental health problems; urban population generally has better mental health than rural population—in that 13.8% of the former have mild to moderate mental health issues and 2% have moderate to severe problems, 18.3% of the latter have mild to moderate issues and 2.6% have moderate to severe problems; by the end of 2017, China had 33,400 psychiatrists, 6,000 psychotherapists, fewer than 30,000 practising psychological consultants, leaving a shortage of almost 1.3 million according to WHO recommended level of one psychological consultant per 1,000 people (NHC

2019). The WHO also estimated that in 2020, mental illnesses were likely to have accounted for one quarter of the overall burden of disease in China (Yang 2018, 2).

There is no doubt that mental health services in China are inadequate and resources are extremely limited, as evident in, among others, the country's mental health worker-to-patient ratio being much lower than the world average (WHO 2017). While the Chinese government has made consistent efforts over the years to improve both the quality and quantity of the relevant services, official efforts have not been focused on structural causes of the country's mental health problem. For reasons related to stability and governance, the state does not wish to be seen as publicly admitting that its mental health problem is at least partly caused by rapid structural transformations in society over the past few decades. The point of divergence concerns the cause of this widespread problem, whether existing and emerging care and treatment efforts constitute genuine care or control in disguise, and to what extent mental health should be analyzed in conjunction with and using the tools of politics.

In *Mental Illness and Psychology*, Foucault famously claims that both the form and ethology of madness ought to be sought not in the body or psyche but in the history of their discursive construction (Foucault 1976). As is the case with any social issue, comprehensively understanding China's mental health reality requires situating it within the country's larger historical, cultural, social, economic and political context, paying close attention to the influence of Confucian ideology, lived experiences of ordinary people during the Maoist era, and new emerging features of the country's present. In great contrast to Western thought, which treats individual rights as divine, Confucian ideology emphasizes personal duties and collective goals; the Chinese 'self' builds on its value for and contribution to society at large rather than expression and development of individuality and particularity. Under such influence, mental health is considered to be concerning oneself but validated through ties with the family, community and the nation, realized by doing the right thing and living up to responsibilities and expectations.

Heavily embedding the self in familial and social networks shapes how the Chinese people suffer, what they consider to be stressful, and how they think about, cope with and respond to stress. This explains why mental health issues in China are frequently associated with stress arising from the family environment or intergenerational relationships (Yang 2018, 29). It is also for this reason and in sharp contrast to the West that mental health in China has a strong moral element—the lack of mental health is not only viewed as having psychological and psychiatric problems but more so as a sign of moral weakness and irresponsibility.

This explains not only the association of mental health with shame but also why Western-style counseling and psychotherapy, which emphasize expression of the self and exercise of personal autonomy, may not work and may even be detrimental in the Chinese context—they do not fit the Chinese relational and moralistic sense of either self or health (Yang 2018, 27). This of course depends on the precise type and nature of the mental illness in concern as well as the individual characteristics of the person in question. Another explanation of the tie with shame and guilt is the fact that during Mao's era and especially the Cultural Revolution, mental illness was viewed as a sociopolitical evil and ideological pathology caused both by personal weaknesses and foreign influence, causing 'antipatriotic' and 'counterrevolutionary' behavior that ought to be corrected and punished in labor camps (Yang 2018, 27). While such overly dramatic labels are no longer attached to mental illnesses, as this chapter will demonstrate, for various mental illnesses, China continues to place the burden of mental health on the individual, sees them as attention-seeking and needy, seeks to 'correct' them rather than nurture them back to health, expects them to get back in control, reform and adapt to the requirements and expectations of the society by adjusting their attitudes, values and emotions.

It is important to remind ourselves that there are many different types of mental illnesses; some are traditionally recognized, while others are newly emerging, born out of the modern context, relations and interactions. As will be demonstrated in later sections, the wide range of mental illnesses corresponds to a wide spectrum of attitudes toward them, depending very much on how strongly the said illness is viewed as a *moral* problem. This moral orientation is based on the presumption that mental problems are self-induced, and since the self is the cause of the issue, it should also be the cure (Yang 2018, 35–36). By individualising mental health issues, individual responsibilities take center stage, and attention is distracted away from structural, political, social, cultural and economic factors, which are not within the individual's control.

In *Where the Anxiety of the Chinese Came From,* a book published in Chinese, Mao (2013) identifies sources of distress among the Chinese population, which include widening income gaps, rising housing prices, social injustice, unemployment, high pressure examination-centered education, food safety, and pollution. While the government has taken steps to tackle these issues in some aspects, the link between these structural impetuses for stress on the one hand and mental illnesses on the other has not been made specific; consequently, the former has not been addressed as such.

As the rest of the chapter will show, while it is important to focus on the individual, and while the author does not entirely agree with the claim that the state has made a deliberate effort in the field of mental health to distract attention from serious societal problems (Yang 2018, Chap. 1), it is vital not to overshadow the role of the state and contextual factors in the generation and expansion of negative emotions leading up to or causing mental illnesses. As the examples in Sect. 2.1.2 will show, it is detrimental not to be able to distinguish between negative emotions and illnesses at a largely psychological level on the one hand, and those triggered, intensified, sustained, and then ignored by outside forces. Making such a distinction is of course often a very difficult task.

2.1.2 Who's Ill and Who's not?

2.1.2.1 Treatment Gap

Traditional theories of Chinese medicine did not treat mental disorder separately from physical illness, and considered its cause to be an imbalance of the internal organs, giving rise to a treatment approach that focused on the restoration of physiological function and internal balance, so mental health did not become an independent field until the 1800s when Western missionaries began to build mental institutions in China, although war and social disruption during the first half of the twentieth century halted its developments. It was not until after the founding of the People's Republic in 1949 and especially after the end of the Cultural Revolution in 1976 that the field of mental health began to revitalise, and it has only been in recent years that attention starts to turn to the enormous gap between the need for and actual provision of treatment. Research reveals that approximately 190 million Chinese individuals are in need of professional counseling or psychiatric treatment (Yang 2018), and this number is likely to continue to increase. However, an estimated over 90% of those in need of care and treatment are said to have failed to reach professional help (Phillips et al. 2009), and according to the government's Blue Book on mental health, 74% of those questioned in the survey said they had no idea where to obtain psychological counseling (NHC 2019).

There are six possible obstacles in the Chinese context that may prevent someone with mental health problems from seeking appropriate help. First, mental health resources in China are extremely limited as well as unequally distributed, and the country's psychiatric hospitals treat only severe mental disorders and pay little attention to the more common types. The lack of a qualified workforce, as already noted previously, may be partly due to a general lack of recognition of mental health and partly due to severe underdiagnosis, resulting in a serious mismatch between demand and provision. The geographic maldistribution of resources, especially the urban–rural divide, means that the majority, especially those in rural areas, have no access to professional help when in need.

Second and related, out-of-pocket costs of mental healthcare are high due to insufficient public funding. While in 2012 the government expanded healthcare insurance coverage to include the treatment of severe mental disorders (the key word being 'severe'), there were/are enormous variations in actual reimbursement rates depending on a variety of factors, such as region, age, sector of work, and whether the person was/is retired or not. Generally speaking, high-income areas and major cities have significantly better coverage and higher reimbursement rates than less developed places. For instance, Shenzhen covers six major mental illnesses such as schizophrenia and paranoia in its health insurance plan and has a reimbursement rate of up to 90%; Beijing covers six major illnesses and has a reimbursement rate of 70% with no maximum limits. Needless to say, for the vast majority of mental illnesses that are not covered by insurance, people need to pay full expenses. It is also necessary to bear in mind that health insurance in China is not portable, so that if one is to seek medical care outside of one's city of residence, they need to pay full expenses.

In comparison to situations in the cities, Xu et al. (2018, 385) note that mental patients in rural areas, both insured and uninsured, use significantly less inpatient mental health services than urban patients, and he offers several explanations. One is lack of professional services, two is greater travel time and distance involved in seeking care, three is that they simply cannot afford the high costs of inpatient services due to low insurance reimbursement rates for rural patients, which are on average more than 20% lower than those in urban areas (Xu et al. 2018, 387). Taking into account the enormous income disparities along the urban–rural divide, professional mental healthcare is simply too expensive for rural patients.

Third, apart from monetary costs, nonmonetary costs are also high, especially due to stigma, the functioning of which will be examined in detail in Sect. 2.1.4, but some foundational points should be highlighted here. Stigma in a collectivist culture such as China has much to do with basic moral common sense and fundamental social values upon which the country is based and managed. People stigmatise against others or themselves not always because they lack sympathy or are ignorant, but because others' or their own behavior or mental state are inconsistent with shared social norms. Being mentally ill, especially being depressed, is viewed very differently from being physically ill; it is considered more an attention-seeking weakness that renders one a burden on one's family and society. There is also an association with risk, which explains why certain mental disorders cause more stigmatisation than others, simply because the patients are considered more dangerous. These will be explored further in detail in Sect. 2.1.4 of this chapter.

Fourth, it seems that mental healthcare in China increasingly relies on psychopharmacological treatment, and since healthcare providers, especially public hospitals, rely heavily on profits obtained from prescription drugs as their main source of revenue, there is the common belief that such drugs may be prescribed based not on necessity or safety but on profit margins. Many people in both cities and rural areas simply cannot afford long-term psychiatric drugs or hospital care, and prefer to interpret their mental illnesses in nonbiomedical terms and therefore seek alternative relief, for instance, from traditional Chinese medicine or even superstitious healers (Yang 2018, 131). There is also widespread mistrust and stigma against psychopharmaceutical drugs, especially for illnesses such as depression. It is widely believed that once starting to take medication, one will get addicted, which will lead to serious long-term consequences. As a result, many would prefer self-help over professional treatment by adjusting oneself, keeping positive and socially engaged, and exercising more.

Fifth, a closely related issue that may also have contributed to both keeping people away from professional help and to the shortage of mental health workforce is the intense relation between the medical profession and patients in China. This is a widely reported phenomenon in recent decades that has given rise to terms such as 'medical disturbance' and 'medical violence', describing situations in which due to the patients' or their family members' distrust on the accuracy of the diagnosis or the suspicion that the medical institution is after profit, they or the people they hire verbally or physically attack the medical staff in question either to gain compensation, or simply to make a scene, or to take revenge with the aim of causing injury or even death. Violence against the medical profession has increased dramatically over the past decade, and it is easy to understand why people with mental health problems may be considered to be more prone than others to demonstrating such unreasonable or violent behavior in the face of unsatisfactory treatment. While distrust may keep patients away from professional help, fear may render the mental health workforce inadequately staffed.

Sixth, a very important obstacle to people seeking help is that they simply have not recognized their mental health problems. Various studies have concluded that mental health recognition in China is poor and that individuals with better recognition have a greater endorsement of seeking help (Huang et al. 2019b; Gong and Furnham 2014; Wu et al. 2017). The causes of poor recognition are easy to identify: lack of public education and awareness of mental health, severe stigma, tendency to consider mental health symptoms as signs of personal deficit, or attribution of socially and culturally appropriate labels to mental illness symptoms (Huang et al. 2019b).

2.1.2.2 Classification

While it may be difficult for the general public to recognize mental illnesses, professionally, the third version of the Chinese Classification of Mental Disorders (hereafter CCMD-3) is the clinical guide for diagnosis. The CCMD-3 is very similar in both structure and categorization to the International Statistical Classification of Diseases and Related Health Problems (ICD) of the World Health Organization and the Diagnostic and Statistical Manual of Mental Disorders (DSM) of the American Psychiatric Association, although with some notable variations in terms of wording and culture-specific diagnoses. While the diagnoses of depression and schizophrenia contain similar criteria to the ICD and DSM, which are readily applied in the Chinese psychiatric field, the precise wordings of some diagnoses are different; for instance, 'impulsive personality disorder' in the CCMD-3 is called 'emotionally unstable personality disorder' in the ICD and 'borderline personality disorder' in the DSM.

A good example of a Chinese culture-bound diagnosis is the so-called 'qigong deviation', which is traditionally used to indicate that something has gone wrong during or as a result of qigong practice, which could refer to a wide range of traditional Chinese self-cultivation exercises, causing an 'imbalance of qi (energy)' and undesirable somatic and psychological effects. Symptoms may include sensations and pain in the head or body, self-consciousness, panic, uncontrolled spontaneous movements, neurasthenia, mood disorder, visual or auditory hallucinations, and paranoia (Yang 2018). The CCMD-3 makes a diagnosis based on the subject being demonstrably normal before qigong exercises; psychological and physiological reactions appearing during or after the practices; complaints of abnormal sensations during or after qigong exercises; diagnostic criteria do not meet other mental disorders such as schizophrenia, mood disorder or neurosis. 'Qigong deviation' has also been recognized as a culture-bound syndrome outside China, for instance, in the 4th edition of the DSM (DSM-IV) of the American Psychiatric Association, in which it is described as 'an acute, time-limited episode characterised by dissociative, paranoid, or other psychotic or nonpsychotic symptoms that may occur after participation in the Chinese folk health-enhancing practice of qigong.'

Even more culture-specific and telling of the Chinese reality are the new forms of mental disorders, while some have recently been officially recognized, others, despite being commonly talked about as 'illnesses', are in fact unaccepted social behavior.

While it is beyond the author's expertise to know whether all mental illnesses have, to varying degrees, a sociocultural cause, drawing on Foucault's view that mental illnesses are socially and culturally constructed and Kleinman's view that culture shapes experiences of suffering (Foucault 1976; Kleinman 1988), it seems reasonable to say at least that the line between 'mental illness' and 'social deviance' is not always clear. Among others, two controversial Chinese examples may help us further explore the sociocultural causes and construction of seemingly psychological and mental problems.

2.1.2.3 'Internet Addiction': Medicalization of a Social Problem?

With an estimate of 802 million active internet users, China has by far the largest internet population in the world, and in 2008, it became the first country to classify 'internet addiction' as a clinical disorder (Yang 2018, 68). Internet addiction, or pathological internet use, refers to an excessive compulsive need for the use of the internet to the extent that it interferes with daily life. While various studies conducted in different countries have confirmed the serious health consequences caused by excessive internet use, it as a mental illness remains contested internationally. While problematic internet use may include many subtypes of behavior, such as cyber-relationship addiction, cyber-sex addiction, online gambling, excessive online shopping, compulsive web surfing (Young 1999), 'internet addiction' in the Chinese context seems to refer specifically to excessive online gaming, which, while the 5th edition of the DSM (DSM-V) does not list as a proper illness, it does list it as a condition warranting more clinical research before it could be so labeled.

It was, however, officially recognized by the World Health Organization in June 2018 as a full disorder and defined in the 11th edition of the ICD (ICD-11) as a pattern of gaming behavior characterised by impaired control to the extent that gaming activities take precedence over other interests and daily activities, and that this pattern of problematic behavior continues and escalates despite negative consequences. For such a disorder to be diagnosed, the pattern of behavior must be sufficiently severe and has directly resulted in significant impairment in personal, familial, social, educational, occupational or other areas of an individual's functioning life and would normally have lasted at least 12 months.

The WHO's decision caused much controversy, as it was believed to have been reached under pressure from Asian countries, especially China (which claimed in 2017 that up to 27.5% of its young internet users were addicted). Internet addiction has long caused serious concerns in Chinese society, especially among parents and educators, giving rise to a variety of forms of controversial 'treatment' ranging from corporal punishment and involuntary confinement to electroconvulsive therapy, causing severe physical and psychological damage to those being treated and in some situations causing death. It is important to note that the government has not turned a blind eye to widespread maltreatments: electroconvulsive therapy for internet addiction was formally banned in 2009 by the Ministry of Health; the country's first ever Mental Health Law came into effect on 1st May 2013, aiming to safeguard the dignity and medical privacy of those being treated and to prohibit involuntary treatment of any form unless certain strict criteria were met; in its 13th Five-Year Plan (2016–2020), the government promised to increase investment in national support for mental healthcare; and in 2017, 22 ministries and departments jointly issued the first guidelines on improving mental health in the country, focusing especially on promoting awareness and education and increasing access to mental health services across the country (Yang 2018, 7).

In other words, as is often the case in China, it is not in the absence of laws or regulations that dubious forms of treatment have continued to function all over China, but in spite of them, causing one to wonder whether, as it is often heard, that the country is simply too big for the government to manage effectively, or whether there is something much deeper and structural that provides a sanctuary in which maltreatment is not just secretly condoned but genuinely considered to be right and necessary in many situations by many people. Possible answers to these questions may shed light on many other controversies covered in this book, and the well-documented maltreatments considered below are telling of what Chinese society considers to be good or bad, well or unwell, and more importantly how it judges the worthiness of people who are unwell in particular ways.

The most commonly used treatments for internet-addicted adolescents in China are military-style boot camps, correctional clinics or rehab centers. It has been widely reported that in the vast majority if not all cases, adolescents are sent to be 'corrected' against their will by their parents, relatives or teachers. Some are forcefully seized and sent to the camps, some are tricked into going, some are drugged by their parents or the clinics. Many such institutions impose severe corporal punishment, including but not limited to intense physical exercises, extremely long hikes, standing for hours without breaks, starving, whipping, and long confinement in tiny cells. Even more controversial is that some clinics conduct electroconvulsive therapy (ECT) on patients without anesthesia, causing great physical and psychological suffering in many cases, which, upon police intervention and extensive media exposure in some cases, has caused grave public concern and intense debate as to what constitutes appropriate treatment for internet addiction, especially considering that ECT may be legally administered in China for some disorders such as schizophrenia and is believed to be effective.

The most controversial figure in the field of internet addiction treatment in China has been Dr Yang Yongxin, a self-labeled 'national expert on internet addiction' who in 2006 established his notorious center for internet addiction treatment attached to the Linyi Psychiatric Hospital in Shandong Province. This center was famous for a special therapy invented by Yang—'Xingnao' (brain-awakening)—which would require electroconvulsive therapy to be implemented to treat internet addiction. Before admission, parents or guardians were asked to sign away their guardianship of the patients to the hospital in full knowledge that electric shock therapy and psychiatric medication would be used.[1] Once admitted, the patients would be confined and subject to brain-awakening therapy along with military-style training and other forms of 'treatment' at the will of the staff.

Undercover reporters and former patients at Yang's center reveal that ECT was frequently employed not only as a treatment for internet addiction but also as a form of punishment for having broken some rules, such as eating chocolate, locking the bathroom doors, sitting on Yang's chair without permission and so on. It was revealed in August 2009 by *News Probe,* a China Central Television investigative programme, that the center had been using a DX-IIA electroconvulsive therapy machine banned in 2000 for harmful effects on the recipients, such as severe muscle spasms, extreme physical pain and psychological damage.[2] While under pressure, the center switched to a different machine, the same investigative programme showed that discomfort and harm were intentionally sought after by Yang during ECT in order to achieve what he deemed to be desirable results. In other words, he was not only aware of the pain caused, he was intentionally causing it and considered it the very reason why the treatment 'worked'.

As to what constitutes 'worked', there have been a number of media reports as well as Yang's and the patients' own accounts which note that immediately after receiving the ECT treatment, the recipients would break down in tears, humbly kneel in front of their parents, beg for forgiveness and promise they would never do it again. However, it is highly arguable that such behavior is more survival instincts and a tactical move to avoid further pain than signs of genuine remorse and guilt. This is backed by the statements of several former patients who claim that they would pretend to surrender, to have been transformed, just so that the treatment would stop and they could go home. Yang would also demand that the patients must apologise to their parents and relatives for their addiction immediately after receiving electric shocks, threatening to do more if they failed to do so, causing many parents to believe that the treatment really worked as their children appeared so humbled and reformed. Other than the fact that such inhumane treatment is torture, it is easily imaginable and indeed backed by statements of Yang's former patients that such treatment would generate hatred rather than remorse.

Having said that, there have been reports that many really have been 'cured' of internet addiction after 'treatment' at the center, evident from the fact that after checking out, they have returned to normal life and have either stayed away from the internet or have started to use it sensibly. However, since neither the safety nor the effectiveness of the center's methods was beyond doubt, in July 2009, the Ministry of Health banned the use of ECT in treating internet addiction. But it never did stop. In fact, there have been reasoned speculations and leaked recordings of screaming coming out of the center's ECT treatment room (known as Cell 13)

[1] It is essential to note that in the vast majority (and probably all) of the known internet addiction cases in which ECT is involved as part of the treatment, it has been conducted with the parents' or the guardians' full consent. This point will be further explored later.

[2] Available at http://tv.cntv.cn/video/C10435/5300e9841e654ed85d4c4887d0220369. According to state media reports, such treatments have also been used on the elderly who are mentally ill, same-sex attracted people, rebellious children, and even pregnant women.

that seem to suggest that the center, despite having been closed down officially and confirmed by the hospital upon inquiry, is still operating in secret, and it is certain that Yang is still a doctor at the hospital—never investigated, never disciplined, let alone punished. This is very strange considering that the abovementioned investigative programme of *News Probe* was aired in 2009, meaning that it was more than ten years ago that people began to realize something was seriously wrong; besides, it is usually assumed that exposure by the state controlled China Central Television would constitute the clearest possible indication that the government had taken a stance against you.

In addition to Yang's center and ECT, in the past two decades, there has been a dramatic increase in the number of reported cases of physical abuse occurring at such clinics and camps, causing physical injuries and several deaths, although it is hard to say whether such an increase has been due to relaxed media censorship on this particular topic or simply an increase in the number of cases. In 2007, after having been severely beaten at a correctional center in Chongqing, a teenager attempted suicide three times by jumping off a building. In 2008, a youth ended up with kidney failure after being beaten and forbidden from drinking water at a correctional center. In 2009, 15-year-old Deng Senshan was found dead 8 hours after being sent to a correctional center in Nanning; it was reported that the teenager was beaten by his trainers at the center. Additionally, in 2009, 14-year-old Liang Pu was taken to the hospital with water in the lungs and kidney failure after 'treatment' at an internet addiction center in Sichuan. In 2011, Xiao Jun of Guangzhou ended up with broken bones for entering the recreational area of a correctional center without permission. In 2014, 19-year-old Guo Lingling of Zhengzhou died at an internet addiction center with multiple injuries to the head and neck. Also in 2014, 14-year-old Xiao Tao was tied and hung by the hands on a horizontal bar for having eaten a biscuit at the correctional center, resulting in ischemic necrosis of eight fingers.

In 2016, 16-year-old Chen Xinran tied and starved her mother to death in revenge of being sent to a correctional center in Heilongjiang Province from which she had escaped. In 2017, 18-year-old Li Ao was found dead with multiple external and internal injuries two days after his parents sent him to a military-style boot camp in Fuyang, Anhui Province. In April 2018, a 13-year-old boy was suffocated and died after getting into a fight with his trainers at a correctional school in Jinan, where young people demonstrating internet addiction, antisocial behavior as well as those experiencing depression, anxiety, and even romantic feelings for someone were sent to be 'corrected'; before the incident took place, the local government had already realized the school had been providing illegal 'treatments' and had ordered it to close down, the process of which was ongoing at the time and now completed.

These are just a few examples of cases reported in the mainstream media or social media. While each and every single exposure led to closure of the center in concern, it still begs the question of why these incidents were allowed to take place in the first place. It is also impossible to know the exact number of injuries and deaths, not least because the majority of such cases are likely not to have been brought to public attention. One should resist the urge to blame it all on those who run the correctional centers, for they would not be able to function without popular support, and that their continual operation is enabled by sociocultural attitudes and especially the patients' (very often minors) own parents and guardians, driven by fear, powerlessness, and misapprehension of the causes and nature of their loved ones' addiction. It is necessary to examine some of these factors in detail.

The first sociocultural factor that sustains tolerance and even praise of this kind of treatment is the collectivist culture of shame and guilt, the feeling of which often emerges when one believes they have violated a moral order, a societal norm. The ultimate purpose of Yang Yongxin's inhumane treatment is through the imposition of pain and fear to force people into admitting they are wrong, feel shameful and guilty, and remember the pain physically as well as mentally so that they will reframe from doing the act for which they are punished ever again. The sense of shame is also likely to be a main reason why these parents would send their children to such correctional centers to be 'treated' so inhumanely, which is related to the concept of 'face', 'losing face'—feeling shameful and distressed when one or a loved one fails to present a good image of oneself or cannot live up to societal or familial expectations, thereby causing shame to the family (Yang 2018, 30). In many of the cases, without the parents' consent and support, physical punishment would not have escalated into violence.

A related second sociocultural factor is paternalism, that of the parents, the society and the state. When it comes to social rights and wrongs, China tends to employ a very narrow conception of normality. There is often only one right answer, only one type of behavior or personal image that is acceptable, any divergence or deviation would be considered wrong, abnormal, in need of correction and treatment. This not only emphasizes the individual as the source of their own problems, thereby deflecting attention away from underlying causes and broader factors, but also imbeds into people's minds that facilitation of the 'harmonious society' is facilitation of conformity and sameness, which requires controlling, being controlled, and being in control. As many parts of this book show, paternalism, a key characteristic of authoritarian China, is manifested in many of the country's policies, laws and styles of governing. It is also embedded in the private domain and especially parent–child relations, in that despite visible democratization of Chinese family life in recent decades, parents still tend to discipline children with a broader stroke than their Western counterparts.

In *Internet Addicted Adolescents*, another *News Probe* episode on internet addiction aired in November 2004, Tao Hongkai, yet another controversial expert on internet addiction though with a rather positive image, makes the point that such addiction among adolescents is always symptomatic of problems in the family home, especially poor parental techniques and lack of meaningful emotional connection. In other words, it is a social, relational, problem comparable to alcohol addiction and drug addiction that requires not only working on the individual but also and especially on their social relations. Furthermore, it is also unlikely to have been caused by just one factor, but rather by a network of intertwined factors—familial, educational, societal—with the first, Tao claims, being determinant. Thus, instead of treating only the symptoms, it is necessary to search for and deal with the underlying causes, which may often be located in everyday details.

While each case is unique, many internet addicts seem to share a common feature—loneliness—due to lack of affection within the living environment, be they single-parent environment, lack of discipline, overdiscipline, trouble at school, poor communication with loved ones and so on. They also vary in age, while some are young children and others are adults. It thus seems that contrary to common belief, the internet is not the cause of addiction but rather a sanctuary where troubled people of any age may seek comfort and emotional escape for a great variety of reasons. For instance, young people 'hide' on the internet to escape the intense pressure and competition at all levels of Chinese education, which is well documented. Escaping from reality in this way is unfortunate and unhealthy, but in many respects, a natural response to problems that they are not capable of tackling; thus, rather than being pathological, 'ill', they are simply living in a psycho-social-structural dilemma from which they are unable to break free (Yang 2018, 69). This is not to diminish the seriousness of internet addiction or to turn a blind eye to the great many online games and related products that target young people and encourage addiction; but rather to emphasize its complexity and shine the spotlight on a common miscomprehension of the issue—that it is the addicts' 'fault' that they are behaving this way. As many interviews have shown, constantly being told that they are at fault and need to reform often worsen the problem.

This opens up two further areas of concern that are too vast and complex to be properly addressed in this chapter but ought to be highlighted nevertheless. The first is whether ignorance of the social causes of internet addiction is wilful or truly due to ignorance; the second and related is just how dangerous medicalization of social problems is. The answer to the second question largely depends on that to the first. Studies seem to show that people are not normally entirely ignorant of the underlying social causes, but somehow are insensitive, impatient, and even cruel in the way they choose to deal with the problems, and that it is often their genuine belief that methods of torture are the key to curing addiction. This begs the question—what has made the parents and the claimed experts so cruel? What are the driving forces that are pushing them to do such things in the name of good?

First, the personal characteristics of the parents certainly play a part, as not all addicted youths' parents would resort to this kind of method. Second, 'doing things the hard way' seems to be a common way of dealing with social deviance in authoritarian China, coupled with the fact that many Chinese parents often find it hard to talk about feelings with their children and especially about negative emotions, rendering it difficult for the children to be emotionally honest with difficulties in life. This is made worse by the fact that, third, intense competition at all levels and aspects of Chinese education as well as parents' high expectations tend to cause those who are not on top of things a sense of powerlessness and shame, which they would find hard to express and admit. Fourth, blindly and unconditionally depending on the so-called professionals—a habit no doubt at least partly nurtured by a system that discourages independent critical thinking—is what turns the parents into collaborators.

In other words, when we speak of medicalization of a social problem, we are not speaking of it in a vacuum; we are referring specifically to medicalization of social ills in an authoritarian state, in which environment social problems are much more likely to be medicalized as diseases than in a free democratic society. Placed in this context, it becomes apparent that medicalization of a social ill like internet addiction is dangerous not least because the term 'mental illness' stops one from examining the many subtypes of internet addiction and the many reasons for addiction, but also that without paying sufficient attention to individual circumstances and underlying causes, it becomes a tool of oppression, the effect of which will be worsened by the lack of treatment for broader contextual ills, allowing them to continuously function and produce even greater number and diversity of social ills.

What then might be the right way to treat internet addiction in the Chinese context? First, it is necessary to introduce restrictive measures to govern underaged people's access to online gaming sites, for instance, by requesting them to register with real identification when accessing certain sites so that their age may be noticed from the beginning, and by limiting the total amount of time they are allowed to spend on certain sites each day. Second, considering that the absence of parents is a common factor in almost all cases of internet addiction, parents need to realize that spending more quality time with their children may be a way out of their problem, as they are more likely to be able to notice their children's emotions and especially changes in those emotions, which would require, among others, employers to make it easier for parents to spend more time at home, for instance, by allowing flexible working hours (which is difficult to achieve in China). Third, instead of military-style 'correctional' training, interesting and worthy activities are likely to be able to distract people's attention away from the internet and give them a sense of purpose and strength.

2.1.2.4 The Complex Reality of Repetitive Petitioning

Even more controversial is another phenomenon that has increasingly been discussed as a psychological disorder, such as 'bigotry'—repetitive petitioning. Petitioning is a traditional means of seeking justice that is firmly rooted in Chinese history. The modern petitioning system, *xinfang* (literally means 'letters and visits'), is an official administrative channel for hearing complaints and grievances that cannot otherwise be resolved through normal procedures or formal channels. *Xinfang* bureaus and practices exist uneasily alongside and sometimes within formal legal institutions, and that the National Public Complaints and Proposals Administration, government departments and agencies, courts as well as local petitioning bureaus receive letters, calls, personal visits, and in recent years through emails, text messages or via apps, to hear from individuals or groups their complaints and grievances, which could relate to a wide range of issues covering both individual appeals for justice and organized challenges to local official decisions; some are legally cognisable, others are not.

The usual procedure is that the petitioners begin their attempts to redress at the local level, and after initial screening and selection by *xinfang* officials, the issue will be channelled to respective departments. The progress of settlement will be monitored and communicated to the filing party. Only if the issue is unresolved or they are unsatisfied with the results may petitioners move up the hierarchy level by level and eventually to Beijing. However, in reality, especially if attempts at the local level have repeatedly failed or if corruption during the process of screening is suspected, many petitioners would take their cases directly to Beijing, which is considered by many to be least corrupt, least biased, and indeed most powerful. This would cause lower-level governments a great deal of annoyance and stress, leading many to do whatever they can to stop petitioners from going directly to Beijing, or if they have already reached Beijing, to bring them back through persuasion or by force. But the reason for the annoyance caused by petitioners skipping the lower-level bodies to reach higher-level institutions is precisely what renders *xinfang* a necessary compliment and alternative to formal institutions and channels.

First, the static structure of the Chinese bureaucratic system gives *xinfang* its logic. Each level of government is subordinate and responsible to the next level up. With a few exceptions, the central government directly manages only down to the provincial level, which in turn manages down to the prefecture and the city level, which manages the county level, which manages the township level. Such a structure has created difficulties in terms of information transmission, among others, in that the higher the government is, the less directly it faces the people and their everyday concerns, causing it to lack a direct and independent source of information. Instead, it receives reports from the lower-level government, creating possibilities of intentional or unintentional misinformation. Thus, by enabling the people directly to come in contact with higher up governments and institutions through x*infang*, the inherent deficiency of the bureaucratic system is supplemented (Chen 2014, 92; Yang 2018). This is particularly necessary considering, second, corruption and local protectionism are widespread at local levels, causing people to lack faith in lower-level governments and justice systems.

A related point is that the Chinese justice system is subject to the heavy influence of administrative powers, so when people are unsatisfied with the justice system at the lower levels, ironically but also sensibly, they would habitually consider taking the case to administrative powers higher up rather than appealing within the legal system to be the most effective way forward. In so doing, the centralization of political power is strengthened, not weakened. It should also be noted that since the second-instance decision is final in China, those who are not happy with the decision will either have to apply for a retrial or petition. Considering the fast increase in conflicts demanding resolution in recent years, the existence of *xinfang*, in spite of all its flaws and controversies, seems necessary, as it is a mechanism that fills the loopholes in the official channels, loopholes that are unlikely to disappear without changes of the bureaucratic structure and China's style of governing—which are both unlikely to change any time soon. In other words, while *xinfang* is often defended from the point of view and needs of the petitioners, it may also be defended based on the needs of governing and functioning of the official channels.

It is against this background that we examine how petitioners are treated. Treatments vary depending on many factors, such as the local receptiveness of *xinfang*, the nature of the issue petitioned, and the methods used and so on. There have been many reported cases in which force was used to prevent the petitioners from taking the claims forward; there have also been cases in which the petition reached the very top and a wide range of mechanisms were speedily mobilized to resolve the issue in concern; there have been cases in which the petitioners were forcefully sent to mental hospitals; there have also been cases in which those forcefully hospitalized later sued the local authorities, the police or other institutions, won and received compensation.[3] While it is beyond the scope of this chapter to examine every single aspect of the complex functioning of the *xinfang* system, it is necessary to consider some factors that may render a petitioner a 'bigot'.

An important factor is the means employed. A range of troublemaking tactics are reported to have been used by petitioners, and some are violent. It is such tactics and the disturbance so caused that have in recent years turned *xinfang* into a negative word, although at the same time the trouble-making tactics are believed to signify the petitioner's significance and importance, helping draw attention from Party and government leaders and especially from those who normally lack the incentive to take them seriously, thereby distinguishing themselves from the moderate petitioners who often fail to gain sufficient attention to have their issues resolved, encouraging more to turn themselves into trouble-makers especially in the absence of high costs (Chen 2014, 99). A good example of such 'troublemaking' tactics is collective action, in which events petitioners in effect become protesters who have no intention of following the normal procedure of taking the petition level by level up the hierarchy and instead tend to demand direct dialog with the local leaders, who, in such circumstances, do often speak with them directly, and even if the petitioners fail to arrange a meeting with the leaders, an action of such nature is likely to cause the *xinfang* officials to report it to those in charge as cases demanding special attention (Chen 2014, 109).

Another important element is repetitiveness. Ever since its founding, the *xinfang* system has been differentiating repetitive petitioners from first-timers (Chen 2014, 113). Both *xinfang* officers and society at large tend to consider the former wicked, addictive, suffering from bigotry demonstrating symptoms such as imaginary or exaggerated grievances, delusional expectations and irrational vindictiveness and aggression toward imagined persecutors (Yang 2018, 59), and the reasons for disapproval are probably more sociocultural than political. Once so labeled, attention becomes focused on their disgruntled nature and disturbing behavior, causing the willingness to listen and consider their claims to diminish. There are experienced 'career petitioners' who either for themselves or on someone else's behalf consciously cause disturbance or blackmail the government for personal gain, but there are also those with genuine grievances who are emotionally and/or mentally out of control due to years of failed petitioning.

In any case, repetitive petitioning is a sign of bureaucratic ineffectiveness and therefore a problem for the receiving end to solve, but the regime is probably more concerned with the impact of such behavior on the wider society—that more people may imitate such behavior and become repetitive petitioners themselves. This collective potential renders repetitive petitioners more dangerous than others, also underlining the political as well as sociocultural reasons why such people are considered unacceptable.

---

[3] See the case of WU Chunxia of Zhoukou, Henan Province: http://www.chinanews.com/sh/2014/05-21/6197557.shtml.

However, the fact that they are being talked about as sufferers of mental illnesses (without being actually on the official list of recognized illnesses) is telling of the behavioral expectations on individual members of an authoritarian state, which determine the standards according to which people are positioned in society. It is clear that both internet addiction and the so-called 'petitioning bigotry' are symptomatic of confusion, stress, fear and sometimes greed in a society packed with conflicts and unmet needs. The way that these social problems are medicalized or pathologized reminds one of the pathologizations of unaccepted social behaviors in the Maoist era, when blame was always sought within the individual rather than in the wider society in which injustice, confusing contradictions and unbreakable barriers were the source of many people's difficulties. There were consequences then, there are consequences now.

2.1.3 *Impacts: Health, Social, Economic and Human Rights*

Issues concerning the consequences or impacts of mental illnesses, especially mistreated or untreated mental illnesses, do not receive much public attention in China unless something of a violent nature has taken place; for instance, if a schizophrenic person has stabbed someone to death, then it makes the news. While it is beyond the scope of this chapter to comprehensively examine how mental illnesses impact the individual and society, and it is wrong to speak of all mental illnesses as a whole, it is necessary to note that generally speaking, their impact has four interrelated aspects: health impact, social impact, economic impact, and human rights impact.

The extent to which mental health disorders have become an increasingly important cause of disease burden in China has already been examined in the first section of this chapter, quoting findings from the China Mental Health Survey, China's Blue Book on Mental Health, and the World Health Organization. In addition, research has found that mental health disorders, along with musculoskeletal disorders and sense organ diseases, are the three leading causes of YLD (years lived with disability) in China (Zhou et al. 2019, 1149). But the full impact of mental disorders extends well beyond such calculations, as they contribute to the development and outcome of many chronic diseases, such as diabetes, cardiovascular diseases, cancer, and HIV/AIDS, through their impact on unhealthy and risky behavior, nonadherence to prescribed medical regimens, and diminished immune functioning (Prince et al. 2007). People with schizophrenia, bipolar disorder and major depression also have an overall increased risk of mortality than the general population as a consequence of untreated mental or physical health conditions, and lack of access to high quality mental health services is a major cause of the problem (WHO 2009).

A recent phenomenon in this respect is the fast-rising suicide rate among Chinese officials. While complete data are not available, Chinese media reports suggest that at least 243 officials, from the central government to local authorities, committed suicide between 2009 and 2016, with the bulk of the deaths occurring after 2013 (Wang 2018), and between 2016 and now there have been periodic news reports on officials committing suicide. These deaths have identical features in that the causes of these suicides are always rapidly identified by employers and investigators as mental illnesses—depression, anxiety, excessive pressure and exceptional stress, and so on. Official reports often provide statements from colleagues and family members, who would play the role as eyewitnesses revealing personal details about the deceased such as 'having been in a bad mood for a long time', 'very stressed lately', 'suffering from insomnia', and 'having been taking psychotropic drugs for a long time', all aiming to highlight their suicides as the result of personal psychological and mental issues. It is unknown whether medical experts are ever involved. Some reports have also linked the deaths to the anti-corruption campaign, suggesting that the suicides have taken place due to fear of punishment and possibly to protect others.

Chinese suicide is a highly complicated phenomenon into which this book does not attempt to dig, and suicide of officials is undoubtedly the most complicated of all, not least because evidence is impossible to obtain; hence, the truth is impossible to prove. For ordinary people, reports of officials committing suicide supposedly due to mental health issues are the most vivid revelation of the health impact of mental illnesses, but whether so being reminded helps people think about mental health in the right way is unknown. How many people would actually look beyond those eye-catching news stories to examine the unexamined is unknown.

Even more diverse, far-reaching and hard to measure than the health impact of mental illnesses is their social impact. So far Chinese studies seem to have gone along the same lines as those conducted in other parts of the world, namely, that attention is focused on the mental health of particular groups, such as low-income families, rural women, homeless people, students, and prisoners. In other words, socioeconomic and gender inequalities have been identified as major factors contributing to the higher incidence of certain groups' mental stress and difficulties, and the connection between mental health and educational inequality and unemployment is also highlighted.

In addition, the mental well-being of so-called 'left-behind children' (children who remain in rural areas while their parents leave to work in cities) has become an increasing concern for academics and the government. Due to the absence or limited parental support and guidance, these children face a wide range of serious developmental and emotional challenges, and are more prone to mental health problems, especially mood swings, depression, anxiety and trauma. They are yet another good example of how structural and social changes impact individual lives, and how individual lives and state of health (physical, emotional and mental) impact the functioning and health of society.

Social impact always goes hand in hand with economic impact, understandably particularly in China. At the individual level, due to widespread discrimination as well as intense competition at finding a job in the grim Chinese job market, in order not to be denied job opportunities and to be treated fairly at work, many would hide their mental illnesses, rendering themselves uncared for and the conditions unattended to. People with mental disorders are at greater risk of becoming unemployed than their healthy peers, as the illnesses affect their abilities to accumulate human capital and cause reduced productivity. Once unemployed, they will lose all employment-related pension and health coverage and possibly descend into poverty as a result, which is likely to expose them to more risk factors for the development or worsening of mental illnesses, for instance adverse living environment, inability to afford treatment, no educational or career opportunities, substance abuse, and violence—which will affect not only themselves but also their families and social relations.

They also impose a huge economic burden on the entire society. While the latest official data are lacking, studies over the years have revealed that in 2013, the total annual costs of mental disorders in China were 88.8 billion US dollars, accounting for over 15% of China's entire health expenditure and 1.1% of its gross domestic product—this was when the vast majority of people with professional mental health-care needs had not received help (Xu et al. 2016); in 2017, the total economic burden of mental disorders in children and adolescents was 1·191 billion US dollars (Xu et al. 2019); the estimated total annual costs of dementia in China were predicted to reach 69 billion US dollars in 2020 and 114.2 billion US dollars in 2030 (Xu et al. 2017); the total direct economic burden for patients with severe mental disorders for the period of 2014 to 2017 was 734.5 million US dollars, and the indirect burden within these four years was 8.9 billion US dollars in total (Xie et al. 2019).

2.1.4 The Human Rights Impact Through Stigma

The human rights impact of mental illnesses is best examined through the process of stigma, which has an individualistic focus and involves a set of social processes. When human differences are highlighted, certain persons are discredited for possessing some undesirable characteristics, causing the separation of 'us' and 'them', resulting in emotional and psychological reactions on both sides, and status loss and reduced opportunities for the stigmatized (Yang 2007, 979). Theorists from multiple disciplines have proposed models of how mental health stigma affects the individual's emotions and behavior, emphasizing the internalization of stereotypes as a key, very damaging, coping mechanism to avoid threat to self-esteem and social rejection and to minimize devaluation of worthiness. This often leads the individual to conceal symptoms and treatment from others and withdraw from social contacts, generating harmful effects such as feelings of shame and guilt, which will further worsen one's psychological condition and negatively affect one's social and vocational opportunities (Yang 2007, 979). There are also models and more recent research that focus on structural mental health stigma and discrimination, which originate from historical, social, political and economic sources, both intentional and unintentional, and claim that it is the societal-level conditions, sociocultural norms and discriminatory institutional policies rather than interpersonal encounters that really constrain the opportunities and affect the well-being of people with mental illnesses (Hatzenbuehler 2016; Corrigan et al. 2004). Three core elements of the stigmatizing mechanism have thus been identified: public stigma, i.e., discrimination from the general population, self-discrimination as a result of internalization of stereotypes, and structural discrimination.

2.1.4.1 Varying Degrees and Expressions of Stigma

The Chinese media plays a key role in how people view and react to mental illnesses. What the public believes is very much conditioned by what they read and hear on the news. Regarding the most serious disorders, such as schizophrenia, media reports on schizophrenic patients' threatening disruption of order in society give the impression that they are the ultimate sick and violent people suffering from the most serious disorder of the brain, which is much more complicated, more unpredictable, harder to treat and therefore much more dangerous than psychological illnesses, which explains why schizophrenia is the most stigmatised mental health condition in China (Lee et al. 2016; Yang 2018), although different people experience stigma differently.

The various ways how schizophrenia-related stigma works in China have been recorded, be they public, self-induced or structural (Yang 2018, 2007; Li et al. 2017): it is challenging for people with schizophrenia to communicate with others as they are widely perceived as dangerous, which would cause them to feel misunderstood, embarrassed, ashamed, angry or afraid; such negative emotions generate feelings of inferiority and significantly enhance the internalization of stereotypes; people especially those in the less developed areas or are less educated like to make fun of the schizophrenics; families with schizophrenic patients often have to move frequently as the neighbors have an issue with having them nearby; it is difficult for people with a schizophrenic history to find someone to date or marry; it is also very hard for them to find a job unless their health status is concealed; interestingly and in contrast, stigma may also be of strategic value to the patients and their families, in that it is possible to take advantage of people's fear for personal gain, for instance to make a scene in public in order to have one's demands satisfied (Yang 2018, 106). Similarly, people afflicted with milder mental illnesses such as stress and depression could also manipulate the diagnosis for personal advantage, for instance, to gain attention or to cover for their academic failures.

There are two main reasons that the degree of stigma associated with depression is much lower than that associated with people with schizophrenia. First, at an estimate of 95 million people suffering from various types of depressive disorders, depression has in recent years become the most widespread form of mental illness in China, and for that reason, it has received much, if not enough, publicity and attention. With increased exposure comes public knowledge and enhanced understanding, which tend to ease stigma—sometimes knowing that something is a common occurrence is enough to ease fear, which causes stigma. Second, unlike schizophrenia, which is considered a disease of the brain, people tend to attribute depression to anxiety, stress, weak personality or weak will, which means it is easier to cure and therefore less threatening. This is important as how the illness is perceived influences if not determines how it is treated.

While the diagnosis of depression is included in the Chinese Classification of Mental Disorders, given the diverse interpretations as to its cause, there is a wide range of perspectives as to how it may be resolved, including physical exercises, emotional self-adjustment without professional intervention, moving into a new environment, and professional medical treatment and psychological intervention. Other than the fact that high-quality professional help is not readily available outside of large cities, given the stigma attached to mental illnesses in general in China, some people hide their depressive symptoms by acting normal or appearing particularly positive, it is also a cultural belief that if they continue to act normal and appear happy, the seriousness of their depression will decrease, which will eventually lead to a complete cure. The social side of appearing normal is to avoid causing trouble and worry to those around and to sustain social harmony. Once again, the burden is on the individual.

Of all those who feel the need to hide their depressive symptoms, owing to fear of discrimination hindering their political future, Chinese officials are probably under the most intense pressure to appear normal. The phenomenon of depression of officials is good demonstration of the relationship and interaction of public stigma and self-stigma, with the former encompassing the reactions of the general public to people exhibiting depression, and the latter the prejudice that depressed people feel toward themselves as a reaction to public stigma, causing concealment of symptoms which requires a great deal of self-control and acting out, creating distorted self-image and self-imposed isolation, which will in turn lead to inconsistent diagnosis and treatment (Yang 2018, 116). The purpose and limited space of this book do not permit an in-depth examination of mental disorders of Chinese officials, which is a very unique angle to examine Chinese culture and politics and demands tentative analysis and attention.

2.1.4.2 Face and Social Dignity

While theory tends to define stigma psychologically and emphasizes its negative impact on the individual, stigma, particularly in the Chinese context, also has a sociomoral aspect that serves the purpose of maintaining a particular collective identity and thereby sustaining a sense of belonging. This sociomoral aspect functions through the concept of 'face', which is central to Chinese social identity and ties the individual with their family. Having roots in Confucianism that upholds harmony and hierarchy, the process of 'maintaining face' or 'saving face' functions as a form of social capital that drives people to act according to established norms and appear good and respectful; otherwise, one is to 'lose face' socially and morally. This explains both self-stigma and stigma expressed by the family members of mental health patients, in that the perceived incompetence associated with mental health problems causes embarrassment to the family and lowers its social and moral status. In a way, mental health patients have become nonpersons who are seen as having lost their abilities to fulfil social obligations and maintain social standards that ought to be fulfilled and maintained by full persons. Therefore, they are not treated as full persons accordingly.

'Face' also explains the parents' harsh reactions to their internet-addicted children—to behave disruptively and socially unhealthily is considered to signify moral and ethical failure on the part of the addicts, the parents and guardians, the family as a whole, which is to lose face both individually and collectively as a family in front of others. This is an important point to note—the moral blame is applied, real or perceived, not just to the individuals but also to their entire family. Parents fear that society's judgmental attitudes toward addicts will be extended to their parents and the family, which will cause social exclusion by weakening or breaking social networks that link them to other people, opportunities and resources (Yang 2018, 105). Similarly, repeated petitioning is considered by many to be face-losing, as it contradicts the widely accepted social norm of fitting in and never making a scene—it is too persistent and confrontational. Thus, by treating internet addicts or repetitive petitioners with discrimination, disrespect, and even humiliation, people are consciously or unconsciously protecting and advancing social and moral norms and status both of their own and of the entire society. It is in this way that stigma not only causes individual pain but more importantly also functions as a form of governing—self-governing as well as societal governing.

2.1.4.3 Stigma as Control

This requires attention to go deeper into the fact that stigma seems to be stronger and more damaging in contexts in which practices and programmes that effectively enshrine human rights and humanitarian values are weak or absent, for instance, in a society that functions on social control, of which stigma can be a vehicle. In order to avoid stigma and fit in, people with mental health problems and their families would conceal symptoms and deny illness. By acting in conformity with the 'normal' healthy majority, they are upholding the societal norm of being good and strong in front of others, thereby maintaining social harmony and stability on the surface. By shouldering the burden of illness entirely on their own and having to seek help in secret if at all, the pressure they bear can be tremendous, but self-governing at least in the short term is achieved.

The spirit of societal governing is revealed in various local policies, regulations and the Mental Health Law of China. For instance, it was reported in the summer of 2016 that the Public Health and Family Planning Bureau of Shuangliu District of the city of Chengdu, Sichuan Province, offered monetary rewards to anyone who would identify and report suspected sufferers of psychiatric and mental illnesses. This caused debate on social media despite the official explanation that it was for the sole purpose of providing better care to those in need (who ought to be identified first), which might not have been entirely persuasive, as this type of reward-driven mass mobilization is often employed in reporting criminal activities and corruption in China. Understandably, therefore, to avoid being identified and reported to the government, mental health sufferers would have to hide their symptoms. This would be particularly relevant to those sufferers of serious mental illnesses, as the Mental Health Law provides that psychiatric patients who are considered to potentially pose a threat to others could be forcefully detained and hospitalized (Yang 2018, 122).

2.2 Concluding Part I

It is important to recognize though that element of 'care' is not entirely missing, but just not as visible as it should be. There have also been positive signs in the development of community solutions, as evident in the widely reported Shanghai café, which helps young people with autism develop their communication skills by offering them jobs and diminishing public stigma by fostering direct contact in a friendly environment. While the mental health reality of China is very complex, what is clear beyond doubt is that mental illnesses are far more than individuals' suffering but bear social meanings and reflect complex cultural realities, which are dominant factors in how the sufferers are treated as 'the other'. While in a nondemocratic society, it is beyond the control of ordinary people to truly contribute to and make a real difference in bettering the mental health care system, the least one can do is to recognize that since each individual suffers differently, knowing of and understanding people's subjective experiences of living with mental health difficulties and with stigma can inform us of what is really at stake in 'the other's lived reality.

2.3 Part II: HIV/AIDS: Private Sufferings Versus Public Safety

Another seriously stigmatised condition—HIV/AIDS—is perhaps an even more vivid demonstration of the lived realities of health minorities. The country's changing perspectives and evolving governing techniques are telling not only of the difficulties and hopes facing health minorities in general and those living with HIV/AIDS in particular, but also of the functions of stigma, both socially and self-induced. While HIV/AIDS is not the only serious infectious disease that has been troubling China, being the greatest epidemic of our time, and noting that China reported a 14% surge in new cases at the end of September 2018 with 40,000 in the second quarter alone, to say that how this disease is dealt with in a country so populous can significantly affect the health of the world is not an overstatement, which is why in recent decades the United Nations especially the World Health Organization has paid tentative attention to the control and education of HIV/AIDS in China, which have gone through several stages of attitude evolution and strategy development before reaching the current state.

2.3.1 *From Disease of Foreigners to Disease of 'the Other'*

For the past decades, HIV/AIDS has been widely considered to be a foreigners' disease, consequential of contact with Westerners and their free lifestyle; thus, upon the recording of the first AIDS death of a foreign tourist in China in June 1985, the initial strategy was to stop the disease from entering the country. But the fact that the death happened in Beijing made China realize that this once upon a time distant disease was now rather close to home. Thus, despite firmly labeling the disease as foreign, there were also attempts to stop transmission within the country from the very beginning through laws and regulations against drug use and prostitution. Authorities were also given the power to isolate HIV/AIDS individuals. However, as was the case in many parts of the world, the traditional public health methods of containment and isolation of infected individuals proved somewhat ineffective, a key reason being that China was going through rapid economic and social changes at the time, which had led to, among other things, nationwide movement of population, increased drug use and changing sexual behavior. The situation was worsened by the fact that while imported blood products were banned since September 1985, illegal collection and commercialisation of blood and plasma within the country had been out of control until an outbreak of HIV/AIDS in blood donors in the early 1990s, which forced the government to introduce fierce countermeasures—following initial attempts to cover up.

In December 1989, China recorded its first HIV outbreak among drug users who injected drugs using nonsterile equipment in the country's western and southwestern border regions, including Xinjiang, Yunnan and Guangxi, linking the spread of the disease to drug-using cultural practices among some ethnic minority groups and thereby establishing a domestic dimension of the epidemic in contrast to the earlier interpretation of it being entirely foreign and imported (Jeffreys and Gang 2018, 9). In 1990, the Ministry of Health set up the National AIDS Committee. In 1992, the National Health Education Institute set up the country's first HIV/AIDS counseling hotline, as the country announced a medium-term plan on the prevention and control of the disease. In late 1994, the first HIV outbreak in commercial plasma donors and recipients of blood transfusions in poor provinces such as Henan was recorded. Around the same time, China signed the Paris Declaration at the International AIDS Summit, which called on national governments to formulate effective prevention programmes and treatment policies. In January 1995, the national HIV/AIDS sentinel surveillance system was set up, and in May, all blood and plasma collection stations were shut down. In September 1996, the first condom trials were launched. In November 1997, the first workshop on effective intervention strategies commenced.

By July 1998, HIV/AIDS had been reported in all 31 Chinese provinces, autonomous regions and municipalities, with over 70% of the cases being in the countryside. In October, the Law on Blood Donation took effect, which required health authorities to standardize blood collection and banned collection for commercial purposes. In November, the Medium-Long Term Plan on Prevention and Control of HIV/AIDS 1998–2010 was issued, setting a target of keeping the HIV-positive population below 1.5 million. In 1999, the Ministry of Health issued administrative guidelines emphasizing the recognition and protection of the rights of people living with HIV/AIDS. In October 1999, the first needle-exchange programme trials began. In June 2001, the first five-year Action Plan on HIV/AIDS Prevention and Containment (2001–2005) was issued. In August 2002, the government announced that infections rose by 67.4% in the first half of 2001 compared with the first half of 2000 and that the country was facing an epidemic. In December, the first antiretroviral therapy and prevention of mother-to-child transmission trials commenced.

In the early 2000s, China's commitment to evidence-based HIV/AIDS policies began to accelerate and started to show positive effects, with significant developments taking place in 2003 and 2004, when the country's health authorities began actively working with the United Nations and other international agencies. In September 2003, China pledged a set of anti-HIV/AIDS measures at the 58th UN Assembly's special session on AIDS, promising a wider range of responsibilities on prevention and control, including international cooperation, laws and regulations, establishment of control centers, and free treatment for the poor. In December, Premier Wen Jiabao visited a Beijing hospital and publicly shook hands with AIDS patients in a deliberate bid to eliminate social discrimination. Additionally, in December, the 'Four Frees and One Care' policy was initiated, introducing free antiretroviral treatment for rural and urban residents without medical insurance or with financial difficulties, free testing services to newborn babies and to prevent mother-to-child transmission, free voluntary counseling and testing, free schooling for children orphaned by AIDS, and care and economic assistance to households of people living with the disease. At approximately the same time, the Ministry of Health and the United Nations Theme Group on HIV/AIDS jointly issued an assessment report, estimating that China had 840,000 HIV-positive people, of whom 80,000 had developed AIDS.

In February 2004, the State Council's AIDS Working Committee responsible for developing a comprehensive policy framework was established. In March, methadone maintenance treatment trials commenced. In April, Vice-Premier Wu Yi made an unprecedented step by openly advocating behavior intervention for high-risk groups at a national working meeting on HIV/AIDS. In November, President Hu Jintao visited AIDS patients in Beijing in yet another bid to eliminate discrimination. In January 2006, the Chinese Ministry of Health, UNAIDS and the World Health Organization jointly issued an assessment that lowered the estimated number of HIV/AIDS cases in China to 650,000, showing a significant reduction of almost 200,000 compared with 2003. Three important steps were taken in the same year: the first was the AIDS Prevention and Control Regulations, and the second was the coming into force of the State Council's second Five-Year Action Plan to Control HIV/AIDS (2006–2010). While both pieces were bold, they were passed 20 years after the first case was identified in the country, indicating that the development of a national structure had been the result of a very long and at times chaotic process. The third was the launch of a national, web-based HIV/AIDS information system by the National Centre for AIDS/STD Control and Prevention at the Chinese Center for Disease Control and Prevention, greatly improving data collection and analysis and has since been an important source for epidemiological research and a key tool for the implementation of national programmes (Wu et al. 2019, 459).

In February 2009, an official report announced for the first time that HIV/AIDS had become China's leading cause of death among infectious diseases (Information Office, Ministry of Health 2009; Wu et al. 2019, 464), and that while before 2009 the majority of new cases were related to contaminated blood transfusions, sharing of drug-injecting equipment and mother-to-child transmission, sexual transmission has become the main cause of new infections since 2009 and now accounts for over 94% of all new cases in the country, causing what some describe as 'sexualisation' of AIDS response in recent years with certain vulnerable groups being targeted, as will be shown below (Jeffreys and Gang 2018, 10, 144).

Since then, China's HIV/AIDS policies have become more confident and more rights-based in many respects. In 2010, the State Council lifted its travel ban on people living with HIV/AIDS entering the country. In the same year, the 'Five Expands Six Strengths' policy was introduced with the aim of enhancing HIV/AIDS education, testing and relevant care services. The third Five-Year Action Plan (2011–2015) was launched in 2011, which emphasized the importance of the involvement of civil society in the fight against the disease. The fourth Five-Year Action Plan (2016–2020) was introduced in 2016 and contained three important changes in state policy. The first was that the UNAIDS 90-90-90 Targets were adopted as a national narrative—by 2020, 90% of all people living with HIV would know their status, 90% of those diagnosed would receive sustained antiretroviral therapy, and 90% receiving antiretroviral therapy would have viral suppression; the second was that the CD4 count-based ART eligibility criterion was eliminated; the third was the introduction of the new 'One4All' strategy—a streamlined and accelerated protocol for people to obtain a diagnosis, complete clinical staging and initiation of treatment (Lu et al. 2020, 365).

In many respects, China appears more westernised on HIV/AIDS than on mental health, as evident in its prevention work which closely mirrors dominant paradigms in international and Western social research with regard to the prevention of HIV/AIDS and intervention programmes, which stress the identification of high-risk populations, risk-taking behaviors, and the provision of national surveillance and education so that people can acquire facts of the disease and learn how to self-protect (Jeffreys and Yu 2015, 125–126). High-risk groups include intravenous drug users, commercial blood donors, male long-distance drivers, male migrant workers, female sex workers, people who engage in casual, premarital, extramarital or nonmonogamous sex, men who engage in sexual behaviors with other men whether they openly self-identify as gay or not. High-risk behaviors mainly include needle-sharing and unprotected sexual intercourse, both homosexual and heterosexual.

As the sections below will show, while the targeting of high-risk groups is correct and necessary, it also worsens discriminated groups' already marginal position in society by officially associating them with disease and danger, sustaining a misbelief that HIV/AIDS affects only the disadvantaged, 'the losers', 'the other', preventing deep and structural re-examination of the dominant moralistic approach that considers the infection and spread of HIV/AIDS solely to be the result of irresponsible and risky behavior of individuals. It is important to identify factors over which the individual has control. It is also essential to shed the spotlight on the factors and forces outside their control, pushing them into risky situations and rendering them more vulnerable than others in respective ways. Paying more attention to the structural determinants does not deny that risky individual actions play an essential part, but rather reminds us of the larger reasons behind and places individual behavior on the contextual and historical terrains that have largely been missing in China's public understanding of HIV/AIDS. By surfacing the wider economic, social, cultural and political determinants of HIV/AIDS, understanding of the functions of health-related stigma will become clearer by focusing more on how stigma relates to and interacts with inequality.

2.3.2 *Beyond the Individual: Economic, Cultural and Social Determinants*

2.3.2.1 Economic Inequalities

It might be too simplistic to announce that HIV/AIDS is a disease of poverty, as UNAIDS data suggest that some of the wealthiest African states have the most serious HIV/AIDS problem (Sutherland and Hsu 2012, 27), rendering it necessary to issue a mental note that a wealthier state (i.e., one with high per capita wealth) may also have higher levels of inequality, and that it might be inequality rather than overall poverty of the country that has a more direct connection with the country's reality of HIV/AIDS. Furthermore, while looking at HIV/AIDS contextually as a social phenomenon through inequality, it is important not to consider inequality generally but rather to examine the specific contributions of specific types of inequality. This is the trickiest issue in conducting such a project, in that it might be unclear which type of inequality is relevant and should be analysed, and also that since different inequalities inevitably interact with each other, the precise relationship between any specific type with the HIV/AIDS reality might be difficult to identify, along with that the complex relationship between different types of inequality might be inadequately addressed, leading to unreliable and overly simplistic conclusions.

Having said that, it is nevertheless possible to identify various inequalities that are particularly relevant to driving the HIV/AIDS epidemic in the Chinese context. The first is income inequality. Its association with overall health standards has already been established internationally, especially in the developed world, and the connection between income inequality and HIV/AIDS in China is evident in that the regions with lower levels of human development (particularly Henan, Yunnan and Guangxi provinces) generally have more infections than regions with higher levels of human development (for instance Guangdong, Beijing and Shanghai), and regions with greater income inequality and lower literacy have higher rates of infection than those with smaller income inequality and higher literacy. Second, there are wide disparities within provinces between rural and urban areas, with infection rates in the former being significantly higher (Sutherland and Hsu 2012, 58). It is, however, important not to readily presume that we fully understand the relationship between income inequality and HIV/AIDS. In the Chinese context in particular, income inequality contains important information about the country's development stage and process, is associated and interacts with many other factors, such as migration, urbanization, education, and social cohesion, which all, individually and working together, have an impact on the dynamics of HIV/AIDS, rendering the precise portion of each's contribution hard to determine.

2.3.2.2 Public Health and the Healthcare System

Since how well HIV/AIDS is managed in a country largely depends on its overall standards of health, it is reasonable to claim that if a country's overall healthcare system is inadequate, its capacity to manage HIV/AIDS is unlikely to be high. Despite the common impression that the wealthier the state is, the better and more resourceful its healthcare system will be, it has been argued that China's successful economic reforms in the past few decades have not strengthened but weakened the country's healthcare system (Sutherland and Hsu 2012, 100). While this view is overly simplistic in the sense that the pre-economic reforms Chinese society was much less complex than it is now, hence the two societies may not actually be comparable, the observation deserves close attention as it reveals how China's healthcare system has characteristically changed over the past few decades and how these changes have impacted people living with HIV/AIDS.

Before the economic reforms commenced in 1978, while urban healthcare was streamlined, China's national healthcare system since 1949 served the country's rural population, which constituted the vast majority, through communes under the Rural Cooperative Medical Scheme. Care was provided by barefoot doctors with little training, based in villages and towns with minimal medical facilities. Yet they seemed to have been able to meet the needs of the population and that the health system as a whole appeared to be rather successful and was held to be the model to emulate (Sutherland and Hsu 2012, 100). This was possibly because people's medical needs at the time were simple and basic, expectations were low, the diseases were nowhere near as diverse as today, and HIV/AIDS not yet existed.

It was during the period of the economic reforms symbolised by fiscal decentralization and introduction of market forces that the healthcare system came under review and began reconstruction in the 1980s, which saw much of the state's responsibility for health provision shifting toward local governments, the share of the central government's health spending dramatically decreased, and much of the health system was privatized. In cities, as an increasing number of people were no longer employees of state-owned enterprises, they lost their social security and health benefits, leading many, starting in the 1990s, to have to pay their health costs out-of-pocket, which caused access to healthcare services to fall dramatically during this period. The situation was more serious in rural areas as great rural–urban divergence began to show in terms of health standards and access to services as a result of the sharp decline in state financing. While this was partly offset by local government subsidies, it severely affected the country's ability to address a variety of health problems, especially in rural areas, where rising health costs were a significant factor in pushing families below the poverty line.

It seems that as the country became rich, the healthcare system became pro-rich, as evident in the pro-urban distribution of national resources and the growing popularity of expensive private health services in large cities. Increased costs of healthcare would force many in need to forgo treatment, which would be of particular concern to HIV/AIDS patients, many of whom lived in poorer rural regions of the country or belonged to poorer households in the cities. Noting these problems, China launched the New Rural Cooperative Medical Care System in 2005 as part of comprehensive health reforms with the specific aim of making healthcare more affordable for the rural poor, under which 800 million rural residents gained basic, tiered medical coverage, with 30–80% of the medical expenses paid by the central or provincial governments. Urban residents now obtain their healthcare either through purchasing health insurance or paying for treatments. While the overall standards have improved, expenses and quality of care vary greatly from hospital to hospital and city to city, and services in large cities are significantly better than those in smaller towns and rural regions. Care provided by private hospitals is of much higher quality than that provided by public hospitals and also vastly more expensive.

In such a reality and knowing both the extent and potential of the country's HIV/AIDS epidemic, Chinese leadership has pledged strongly to strengthen the prevention and treatment of HIV/AIDS, especially for the poor. Since the implementation of the Four Frees and One Care policy in 2003, China has been committed to providing universal access to HIV medication. However, while patients may have access to discounted medication subsidised by the government, the cost of long-term healthcare may still be too high to be affordable for many households. Apart from direct medial costs, indirect costs such as transportation, loss of time and income also affect the patients' decision as to whether to seek professional assistance (Sutherland and Hsu 2012, 103). Besides, similar indirect costs incurred by the family member who acts as the carer also contribute to the overall financial burden of those living with HIV/AIDS, which can be further and more precisely examined by dividing these people into so-called high-risk groups.

2.3.2.3 Same-Sex Relations and HIV/AIDS

Despite consistent government advances in HIV/AIDS education, testing and treatment, the number of infections has been increasing every year, with the most visible increase occurring among men who have sex with men, which, despite worrying, is also in part a reflection of the expansion of surveillance, behavior interventions and testing in the country. It was already highlighted in Chap. 1 that homosexuality became a visible public phenomenon in China at the exact same time as men who had sex with men became identified as a target group in the country's HIV/AIDS response (Jeffreys and Gang 2018, 100), rendering that since the very beginning, same-sex relations between men have been linked to this serious disease, which explains the long-lived and widespread discrimination and vividly demonstrates how infection routes determine why, how, when and where people living with HIV/AIDS experience discrimination.

China's health authorities first began issuing plans and guidelines for conducting HIV/AIDS prevention programmes that targeted men who had sex with men in the late 2000s. For instance, in late 2007, the Chinese Center for Disease Control and Prevention (CDC) and the National Center for AIDS/STD Control and Prevention (NCAIDS) issued the Guidelines for Interventions into AIDS-Related High-Risk Behaviors Among Men Who Have Sex with Men; in 2008, the Ministry of Health released a document entitled AIDS Prevention Pilot Programme for Men Who Have Sex With Men, indicating that health authorities would carry out pilot projects in 61 cities across the country between 2008 and early 2009 to promote safe sex through condom use, and to conduct HIV/AIDS testing for 21,000 men in order to establish a clear statistical baseline for infection rates, and to develop diagnosis and medical care facilities across the country. This project was described by UNAIDS as 'the first of its kind in Asia' and the 'largest such study undertaken anywhere in the world' (Jeffreys and Gang 2018, 96–97). In 2016, the CDC and NCAIDS issued the Guidelines for Interventions to Prevent AIDS Among Men Who Have Sex with Men, demonstrating the ongoing but also altered nature of the interventional measures targeting this group, in that the Guidelines outlined behavioral surveys and interview questions for health authorities and NGOs to 'map' the social and sexual practices of this group, identifying not only the physical places for homosexual sociality in a given city but also the virtual spaces for men to meet men, as well as asking these men to comment on the prevalence of HIV/AIDS among their circle and on how the provision of information on prevention, testing and treatment may be improved.

Apart from state-level guidelines and implementation plans, since the late 2000s, local-level branches of the CDC have organized large-scale public health interventions aiming to provide men who have sex with men with information about HIV/AIDS prevention, testing and treatment. It is interesting to note that in a society in which all actions are state-led and government-monitored, in regard to HIV/AIDS interventions targeting men who have sex with men, it has become common practice for the CDC to contract social organizations to carry out the programmes and to provide rapid testing and treatment services. In other words, while the initiative was taken by government health authorities in the first place along with the introduction of guidelines and implementation plans, it is often the social organizations that do the actual work on the ground, conducting surveys, distributing CDC-produced information booklets, visiting places frequented by men who have sex with men, conducting educational programmes in various contexts, and providing rapid testing and forwarding the results back to the CDC. This reliance on social organizations is because while such organizations are limited in number and power, their staff and volunteers have easier access to men who have sex with men, many of whom distrust government authorities and worry that involvement with them will lead to their sexual orientation and health status being revealed to their families and employers, with detrimental consequences.

Such worries are well founded. First, due to widespread fear of the disease and the government's consistent tendency to treat public health issues as a matter of national and societal security, it is likely that certain personal information will be revealed in some way to the families and employers of those in concern. Second, while homosexual practices are widespread in both urban and rural China, it is often the case that a homosexual man is legally married to a woman or has female partners to avoid social discrimination, and that many of them have never been tested for HIV/AIDS and do not use condoms during sexual activities with men or women (Wang et al. 2015). Maintaining a heterosexual front is important to them, rendering fear of exposure understandable. Third, as noted in the previous chapter, while Chinese law prohibits discriminating against HIV-positive people in employment, there have been several reported cases in which people are rejected during recruitment processes or sacked for the sole reason of being HIV-positive.

Details of the lived reality of this group may be revealed by examining, first, how successful the tailor-made prevention programmes are and, second, the shortcomings of these strategies and the general characteristics as well as the particularistic nature of the discrimination and stigmatisation that they face. First, it is difficult to say how the success or failure of the prevention programmes are to be measured, which, as is the case with all such programmes, depends on their purposes and side-effects. In terms of fulfilment of purposes, the latest data show that men who have sex with men present an increasing national health challenge and that various factors determine the seriousness of the disease within this group: HIV is more prevalent among those aged over 50, less educated, those who seek sex in saunas, massage parlours and bathhouses, and those who live in the southwest (Dong et al. 2019). Interestingly, it has also been found that although knowledge of HIV/AIDS is high among men who have sex with men, the rate of consistent condom use is low, reflecting the complexity if not presenting a challenge to the hypothesis that knowledge build-up and consequent behavioral change are key to HIV prevention (Dong et al. 2019). As later sections will show, similar results have been found in studies on other high-risk groups, in which good knowledge does not necessarily lead to sensible behavior.

Second, the success of any initiative also depends on its side-effects. The most noteworthy contribution of identifying men who have sex with men as a target group is that it has made a previously invisible group visible, thereby saving their lives, also rendering it possible for society to gain knowledge and to deal with the HIV/AIDS problem more openly. However, this important contribution also constitutes the most serious and inevitable side-effect, in that these men's image as major contributors to the spread of HIV/AIDS in China is further enhanced, causing more discrimination and stigmatisation, which would render their lives even more difficult and prevent some from coming forward and seeking help. As will be noted below, similar to the situation of commercial sex workers, men who have sex with men as an HIV/AIDS high-risk group are particularly stigmatised because the construction of the type and degree of stigmatisation that they face is tightly connected to the presentation of homosexuality in China, which, as Chap. 1 has shown, has never been positive. Also as Chap. 1 notes, consistent public efforts to ease discrimination do not make discrimination disappear, and old cultural and social beliefs remain strong, especially among older generations. While anti-discriminatory measures are now recognized as necessary in the fight against HIV/AIDS by the government, as demonstrated not only by its engagement with gay NGOs, discrimination continues to create obstacles for prevention, education and treatment, and self-identified homosexual men continue to marry women to avoid social stigma (Jeffreys and Gang 2018, 114).

Third, experience around the world shows that gay communities and organizations should be allowed to play a bigger role in the fight against HIV/AIDS in order for the interventions to be precise and effective, as men who have sex with men naturally trust their own communities more. While the illegality of prostitution has made it difficult for NGOs to work with sex workers, the increased tolerance of homosexuality has seen the number of nonprofit organizations working on HIV/AIDS awareness programmes for men who have sex with men gradually increasing (Jeffreys and Gang 2018, 103–104). While government actions have demonstrated recognition of the necessary contributions of NGOs, they have also made it clear that the freedom of such organizations is subject to heavy limitations and often restricted to carrying out the government's work. Many NGOs have developed links with local governments or agencies and regularly conduct HIV outreach programmes, historically often with international funding. Since much of such funding is no longer available, such as that from the Global Fund to China, which ended in 2013, NGOs now have to apply for funding from government authorities, which further compromises the sustainability of their independence, and the focus of their work will be increasingly determined by the government's preferences, which often means being loud about the technical aspects of HIV/AIDS and silent about other issues. This severely limits their impact.

Fourth, some subgroups within the category of men having sex with men also create additional difficulties, for instance, the so-called 'money boys'—usually young men from poor rural areas who work in the cities as male prostitutes and provide sexual services to both men and women. They belong in another high-risk group: sex workers.

2.3.2.4 Commercial Sex Work and HIV/AIDS

The general laws and policies on prostitution and their implications will be examined in Chap. 4. This part considers only the implementations of HIV/AIDS interventions targeting people who sell sex for a living, commonly via entertainment and leisure venues, illegally. The very first significant regulatory instrument that explicitly linked prostitution with sexually transmitted diseases in contemporary China was the Notice of the State Council on Resolutely Banning Prostitution and Curbing the Spread of Sexually Transmitted Disease (1986), in which the Ministry of Health was required to establish sentinel surveillance sites to monitor the extent and spread of STDs. Local governments were called on to investigate hotels, motels and entertainment venues, severely punish those who organize or engage in prostitution by sending them to re-education through hard labor, introduce compulsory self-funded health checks for STDs, transfer the results to public security organs, and inform the workplaces and families of those tested. At this time, while STDs in general had begun to be recognized as a homegrown problem, HIV/AIDS was still viewed as an imported foreign disease that could be managed through border controls, policing and banning prostitution through coercive strategies, which remained the primary means of controlling the spread of prostitution-related HIV/AIDS until the late 1990s (Jeffreys and Gang 2018, 61–62).

The utility of condoms in preventing HIV/AIDS was not completely unrecognized at this early stage, although discussions were very limited in the context of prostitution, not least because prior to the 1990s direct and indirect censorship ensured that state-controlled media did not discuss the topic of prostitution in any detail unless within the parameters of Party-directed discourse on the matter such as moral condemnation and nationwide crackdown—the use of condoms in prostitution was outside such parameters not least because it would give the impression that those engaged in prostitution were worthy of protection, or that by encouraging the use of condoms the government was in effect tolerating or even encouraging sexual promiscuity, which would not have been a socially acceptable thing to do at the time, or now, in the Chinese mainland, where such work and workers are underground and seriously stigmatised.

However, two quiet but significant moves in the early 2000s constituted evidence that while China was unlikely to change its moral positioning regarding sex work or sex workers, it was willing to care for the health of those involved, if only for the protection of public health rather than out of concern for the wellbeing of the sex workers, thereby, in a sense and as a side-effect, acknowledging that stigmatization was problematic at least, again, in the sense of disease prevention rather than out of concern for the sex workers. The first move was renaming condoms 'safety sheath' from 'pregnancy avoidance sheath', probably in order to shift attention away from them being a contraceptive device and toward the understanding of them as a personal hygiene device for disease prevention; the second was renaming prostitutes 'sex workers', a largely morally neutral term with Western feminist origin. Understandably, the first term did not generate as much debate as the second, as while the first change signified a mere technical shift in the understanding of the functions of condoms, without having added anything new to existing knowledge or having challenged dominant perceptions in any fundamental way, the second did—simply by calling prostitution 'work'.

This was not the intention of the Chinese government. Rather than aiming to ease stigmatization, the change of terminology was more likely to have been entirely pragmatic, namely, to adhere to international standards, considering that it took place at the same time as the country launched its 100% Condom Use Programme in the early 2000s. The transnational health intervention in collaboration with the World Health Organization aimed to prevent sexual transmission of HIV/AIDS by transforming the behavior of those engaged in the sex industry. Four pilot projects were initially launched in rural county-level cities that were not associated with particularly high HIV infection rates rather than in major cities or places with high infection rates (Jeffreys and Gang 2018, 26). Unlike other state-led projects that would always be accompanied by intense publicity, media exposure of these projects was deliberately avoided for the fear that their sensitive nature might be construed as offering protection and granting legitimacy to the banned sex industry, which would likely cause public outcry and create difficulties for further projects (Jeffreys and Gang 2018, 38). It was also feared that these projects would be viewed as signs of the presence of an epidemic, causing panic and endangering the local economy and tourism (Jeffreys and Gang 2018, 41). These four projects (and a later fifth in cooperation with the UN Population Fund) were either covered in short reports that either did not mention the sex industry or received detailed media coverage only after their conclusion, which caused a great deal of public interest and generated intense debate (Jeffreys and Gang 2018, 40–53).

The fact that the government felt the need to hush it up and just do without talking about something that was protective of the health and interest of the general public reveals a great deal of the difficulties facing sex workers then and now in regard to HIV/AIDS. First, the implementation of any protective measures within the sex industry would run the risk of giving the impression that the government is validating immoral conduct. People would have difficulty understanding that while at face value it protects a particular group, ultimately it is to protect the general public and the entire society. Once a matter of health becomes an issue of morality, parents in particular would become worried as to how such policies would affect their children's worldviews and behavior; married couples or those in a stable long-term relationship would also be concerned whether such projects and the rationale behind them would have the unintended effect of promoting and increasing promiscuous sexual behavior outside marriage and stable relationships, thereby causing fear and anger, enhancing existing stigmatization of sex workers.

Second, prostitution's illegal status regularly attracts police-led crackdowns, and the implementation of the 100% Condom Use Projects or any such protective measures would seem to contravene state laws and regulations. Article 358 of the Criminal Law of China stipulates sentences of between 5 and 10 years of imprisonment for anyone who organizes or forces others into prostitution, rendering the running of businesses that facilitate sexual services a criminal offence. This, along with the fact that the possession of condoms was/is widely considered evidence of sex work during police raids, explains why it is so difficult for those who own or operate entertainment venues to cooperate with the state in the implementation of such projects (Jeffreys and Gang 2018).

Third and related, such measures could also be interpreted as a sign of inability or unwillingness of the state and the police to crack down on an illegal industry, either giving the misimpression that prostitution is no longer illegal, or causing doubts in the capability of the authorities as well as chaos to law enforcement in general. It is also possible that the government's involvement in such projects could be considered embarrassing by the general public, as now it appears to be 'managing' rather than 'policing' commercial sex-selling (Jeffreys and Gang 2018, 50). All of these factors would give the government and the police reasons to keep things quiet, which could hinder knowledge-building of sexual transmission of HIV/AIDS.

The misimpressions may be explained away by recognizing that these projects and relevant protective measures are pragmatic and responsible governmental approaches to public health protection, considering that prostitution is the oldest trade in the world that is unlikely to disappear any time soon, legal or illegal, and that the official stance has never changed, namely, that prostitution is illegal. However, the social reality and socially induced difficulties would mean that, fourth, sex workers often have to adopt various other measures to attempt to ward off potential STDs, including HIV/AIDS, such as external-use cleansing products, preintercourse antibiotic injections, or simply use their own judgment as to which client might be safe. These measures are not only ineffective in protecting against HIV/AIDS but have also resulted in serious health problems and frequent abortions (Dewey et al. 2016, 34). It has also been reported that during crackdowns, the police would require hospitals to hand over personal information of patients with STDs so that they could be located, causing many sex workers to seek healthcare from unlicensed, low-priced and low-quality clinics (Dewey et al. 2016, 35).

Fifth, given that in order to increase earnings, it is important for sex workers to enhance their image, it has also been noted that sex workers spend less money on healthcare than on body-altering drugs and cosmetic surgeries, which would drain their financial resources fast, rendering them unable to afford proper, long-term regular treatments for HIV/AIDS should they ever be in need. The difference money makes is also revealed from another angle in a study that finds that high- and middle-tier female sex workers have a significantly lower risk of infection than lower-tier sex workers, suggesting that interventions in this group should be diverted to high-risk subgroups such as drug-using and low-tier sex workers (Zhang et al. 2015).

2.3.2.5 Mobile Populations and Migrant Labor

Rural-to-urban internal migrant workers have also been characterised as among the most vulnerable to HIV infection by the Chinese government and the international community as a result of a wide range of structural inequalities, which will be explored in greater detail in Chap. 3. This group was first listed as a priority for intervention in China's second Action Plan for the Containment and Prevention of HIV/AIDS (2006–2010),[4] which urged local authorities to promote education, testing and care for this group with a goal of reaching 80% of the migrant population by the end of 2010; the third (2011–2015) and fourth (2016–2020) Action Plans also listed internal migrant workers as a main focus group. For reasons that, first, issues concerning internal migrants are not usually politically sensitive and therefore not often subject to censorship (unless protests demanding better pay and better treatment are involved, which have happened but never been openly reported), and second, that rural-to-urban migration, although not unique to China, has been a telling phenomenon and key to understanding China's economic rise in recent decades, there has been a decent amount of academic and societal interest in the living and working experiences of migrant workers in the cities. The various intertwined factors that render them particularly vulnerable to HIV infection are also those that render them vulnerable in general both as a class and as individuals.

The most obvious is the relative poverty in which they live and work, both at home and in their host cities. Huge economic inequalities between rural areas and cities in

---

[4] While the first Action Plan (2001–2005) mentioned only migrant workers returning from work from abroad. Internal migrants were not mentioned.

China have pushed many rural-born people to leave their native home and move into large cities in search of work opportunities. Once settled in the cities, they tend to engage in low-paid and labor-intensive work and often have to live in poor or heavily constrained conditions such as in *chengzhongcun* (literally 'village in the city') or factory dormitories, which means that the vast majority are only able to provide for and look after themselves in the host cities and have therefore to leave their wives, husbands or partners behind in their native villages for extended periods of time and only return home very infrequently. Such disruption to stable sexual relations and proximate familial support would generate a great deal of loneliness as well as physical urges, causing many to seek alternative sexual relations in the host cities, be they long-term and stable, or short-term and casual such as in the form of visitation to prostitutes based at cheap hair and massage salons, potentially heightening their vulnerability to HIV infection (Dai et al. 2015, 1–9).

Furthermore, research has shown that not only do male migrants tend to engage in unprotected sex with multiple partners, including sex workers, low rates of condom use have also been reported among female migrant workers, both married and unmarried, who seem to be more worried about getting pregnant than getting sexually transmitted diseases (Jeffreys and Gang 2018, 124–125). The reasons are financial, ignorance of the danger involved, and sexual habits in the form of irresponsible attitudes and risky practices over extended periods of time. Younger female migrants face higher risks of infection due to lack of knowledge of the disease and safe sex practice as a result of inadequate or absence of sex education in their conservative rural hometowns, leaving them ill-prepared for the increased opportunities to engage in sexual activities in their host cities (Lu et al. 2012; He et al. 2012; Huang et al. 2014).

While it is unclear which reason is dominant and most common among this group, and indeed it is simplistic to speak of them as 'a group' due to the wide range of professions and personal circumstances, considering the lived experiences and shared characteristics of this group, money is a very serious issue, not only that some are unable to afford consistent use of protection, but also that they do not tend to seek testing or treatment services because of financial concerns and fear of being stigmatized or losing their jobs should they test positive (Wang et al. 2010). This is unfortunate, as it has been state policy to distribute free condoms to which both urban residents and migrant workers are entitled. Though it seems that many people are neither aware of this policy nor know where to collect. Testing should also be free according to the 'Four Frees and One Care' policy.

Once in a while the media will report on migrant workers being fired for testing positive for HIV/AIDS despite the fact that the law prohibits discrimination on this ground, although it is safe to say that the vast majority of cases have not attracted media attention. Nor is firing on this ground restricted to this group, as the next section will show, in recent years cases begin to appear in court challenging employers' decisions, although it would be wrong to say that plaintiffs receive much sympathy from society or that employers would refrain from doing so in the future—not only that the law hardly ever comes to mind at the stage of firing and that it is easy to find a way to appear nondiscriminatory and bypass the law, but also that due to fear of social stigmatization, few—least of all the migrant workers who are among the most powerless in society—are willing to openly challenge such decisions as it would mean revealing one's health status, and that even if such challenges are presented, even successfully, due to the moral positioning of this disease the society is not on their side.

Despite a number of policy changes in recent years designed to improve social services for migrant workers, it remains the case that they are not entitled to subsidised medical welfare in places other than their place of household registration (Li et al. 2004, 551), and that although free access to antiretroviral drugs was mandated by the 'Four Frees and One Care' policy for those in need, research shows that rural-born migrants living with HIV/AIDS are often unable to access free antiretroviral drugs in cities. For instance, in 2010, Beijing, one of the major destinations for internal migrants, made free antiretroviral drugs available only to migrant workers with a temporary residential certificate, which clearly aimed to spread the burden of cost for disease prevention and treatment across local governments (Jeffreys and Gang 2018, 126). But many migrants do not possess a residential certificate, as it costs money and requires original documentation that must be obtained in person from the local government at their place of birth.

In addition to financial difficulties and limited access to healthcare, lack of awareness and knowledge of the disease has played a key role in this group's vulnerability to infection (Yang et al. 2015). This was officially recognized in the second, third and fourth Action Plans for the Containment and Prevention of HIV and AIDS, which recommended providing HIV/AIDS education as part of occupational work trainings for rural-to-urban migrant workers, and urged government departments and businesses to provide educational materials and condoms in educational institutions, workplaces, as well as during health and safety and vocational trainings. The National Rural-to-Urban Migrant Workers' AIDS Prevention Education Project was launched in late 2005 along with an implementation plan jointly issued by the State Council AIDS Working Committee, the Publicity Department of the Chinese Communist Party Central Committee, the Ministries of Agriculture, Construction, Health, and Labor and Social Security, the National Population and Family Planning Commission, the State Administration for Industry and Commerce, the All-China Federation of Trade Unions, the Central Committee of the Communist Youth League, the All-China Women's Federation, and the All-China Federation of Industry and Commerce. This across-the-board institutional cooperation reflects official recognition of the vast complexity of implementing an educational project of this nature for China's internal migrant population.

The plan also outlined the respective responsibilities of all involved. For instance, during major holidays and planting/harvest seasons state-controlled media was to broadcast at least 10 hours of HIV/AIDS education programmes, state publications were to publish at least 10 pieces of HIV/AIDS material; the Ministry of Health was tasked with producing education materials and organizing peer training sessions for relevant government departments and agencies; departments and agencies associated with the Ministry of Agriculture were required to provide migrant workers with HIV/AIDS education as part of their vocational training programmes; those associated with the then Ministry of Construction (now Ministry of Housing and Urban–Rural Development) had to distribute HIV/AIDS awareness and prevention booklets to migrant workers on construction sites and conduct relevant on-site trainings and education; those affiliated with the Ministry of Labor and Social Security were obligated to provide migrant workers with at least 2 hours of HIV/AIDS education as part of their prejob training; the National Population and Family Planning Commission was required to widely distribute information on HIV/AIDS prevention as well as to provide an HIV/AIDS information booklet and free condoms to migrant workers retuning home during the Chinese New Year and for seasonal agricultural work; departments associated with the State Administration for Industry and Commerce were tasked to conduct HIV/AIDS awareness programmes for migrant workers in private enterprises at least twice a year and to make sure that each worker was provided with information booklets; while the All-China Women's Federation made migrant female workers their target, the All-China Federation of Industry and Commerce focused on mobilizing real-estate developers and managers of service industries, and the Communist Youth League was to coordinate HIV/AIDS education through existing training programmes for young workers and spread the knowledge among young migrants through a variety of means including booklet distribution and peer education.

2.3.2.6 Have Interventions Worked?

Since then, numerous initiatives operating on the same basis of organizational cooperation have been ongoing, aiming to continuously enhance HIV/AIDS education for internal migrant workers. The overall impact may be assessed from three angles, although evaluation should take into account the fact that local implementation of national policies and the availability of services vary a great deal due to differences in political will and resources (Hood 2015, 357).

First, there has been evidence, based on large-scale studies, that awareness of HIV/AIDS especially regarding the means of infection has increased among rural-to-urban migrant workers postintervention (Zhang et al. 2018, 36–37); education has also caused positive attitude and behavioral change (Li et al. 2014), as evident in an increase in the use of condoms during sexual activities due to enhanced knowledge of HIV/AIDS among migrant workers (Zeng et al. 2019); but there has also been contrasting evidence that despite the increase of knowledge of the high risk of infection without condoms, many migrant workers still fail to use condoms consistently (Jeffreys and Gang 2018, 124); systemic long-term cross-site intervention in both urban and rural areas has been found to be highly effective in improving migrant workers' HIV/AIDS knowledge, attitude and behavior—the key words are 'cross-site' and 'long-term' (Li et al. 2014); it has been reported that interventions must focus on migrant-sending rather than migrant-receiving locations to ensure that education reaches the family members and spouses (Dai et al. 2015); a decrease in the use of commercial sexual services in this group has also been reported although the drop has not been dramatic (Zhang et al. 2018, 36–37); notably, male migrants who have had sex with commercial sex workers have been found to have significantly more knowledge of HIV/AIDS and better perception of vulnerability than those who have not (Yang et al. 2015, 329); those who participate in a social organization, be they political parties, alumni associations, peer groups, cultural and sports clubs or NGOs, have better awareness of HIV/AIDS, revealing that social capital and sense of connectedness are important for the floating population in the fight against the disease. But due to low income and limited resources, only a small proportion belong to a social organization.

Analyses of risk groups should draw attention to how different workplace settings impact knowledge-building. When one speaks of migrant workers, it is easy to presume we are referring only to male migrants and forget about the females who make up over 30% of the migrant workforce. The majority of rural-to-urban female migrants work in the service industries such as hotels, restaurants, factories, and entertainment establishments, which confer different levels of risk. There has been research that comparatively examines the HIV-related sexual behavior of migrant women in these three work settings and finds that those working in entertainment venues have significantly better knowledge of HIV/STD but are also more likely to report unprotected sex and multiple abortions than those who work in restaurants and factories (Huang et al. 2016). This shows that knowledge increase does not necessarily lead to responsible sexual behavior, the nature of work is determinant, and knowledge makes little difference if the work setting does not encourage consistent sensible sexual behavior. This indicates that prevention strategies must be tailor-made to be workplace-sensitive. For instance, while for migrant women working in entertainment venues, attention should focus on reducing unprotected sex and unintended pregnancy and increasing testing, for women working in factories and restaurants, attention should focus on enhancing knowledge-building regarding the disease and self-protection (Huang et al. 2016, 603).

The second angle from which to evaluate the interventions is to see if there are changes in the infection rate. Data show that infections have been increasing rapidly in the past few years. According to the joint estimate of the CDC, UNAIDS and the WHO, by the end of 2018, there were an estimated 1.25 million people living with HIV in China, with 80,000 new infections reported in 2018, an increase from 57,194 in 2017, while an estimated 30% of infections had not been identified. The continuous increase in infections should not, however, simplistically be interpreted as an indication of failure of interventions, as the increase may be associated with a number of factors.

First, internal migration continues to push large numbers of migrant workers from the more conservative countryside or poorer regions into large cities where there are more opportunities for sexual encounters and for jobs that carry a significant risk of infection, such as those in entertainment venues and salons, in which many migrant women work. It should be noted, however, that prevalence among female sex workers has overall declined in recent years, suggesting that interventions, especially condom use promotion and increased access to counseling and testing, have worked, and that the disproportionately high HIV burden among female sex workers in the southwest of the country has been said to be drug-related (Zhang et al. 2015, 81).

Second, although homosexuality is still not widely accepted in China, attitudes have changed and tolerance has increased, having led to homosexual activities being more visible, possibly explaining the rising infections among men who have sex with men. The fact that many are married to women while continuing to have same-sex partners acts as a bridge for the disease to transmit from this high-risk group to the general population. Third, rising infections may also be due to the increase in the testing rates in high-risk groups as well as among the general population. Fourth and related, developments in both testing and treatments also mean that those infected are now living longer lives, which will translate into a higher total number of infections in the country.

The third angle from which to evaluate the interventions is to look at whether professional and societal attitudes toward HIV/AIDS have changed. The government's initial response to the epidemic as well as targeting high-risk groups, albeit necessary, have to a large extent strengthened stigma related to the illness, but in recent years, increasing attention has been given to the role of stigma in causing social injustice and imposing additional suffering upon those infected, for instance educational materials now tend to contain anti-discriminatory information. A particularly noteworthy move in the past two decades has been the use of public figures and celebrities as image ambassadors for the government or for UN HIV/AIDS initiatives, indicating a shift toward engaging citizens in self-initiated and self-sustained behavioral change through 'advertising' and public education led by well-known public figures, in addition to large-scale government-backed workplace and community-based interventions (Jeffreys and Gang 2018, 134). As is the case in the West, a unique advantage of celebrity-endorsed HIV/AIDS communication is its particularly intense focus on the anti-discriminatory message, which is often conveyed powerfully and convincingly.

While tackling the disease and the risen insecurities from the critical site of stigma is a move in the right direction, in today's China, HIV/AIDS stigmatization remains widely tolerated, accepted, legitimized, and even praised as a necessary price to pay in return for good public health, for the larger portion of society to be safe and healthy. This should be looked at from two perspectives. First, HIV/AIDS-related stigma has much to do with society's sense of morality, in that the disease and getting infected are judged by local meanings and criteria of good or bad, moral or immoral, which immediately lead to another moral judgment about the goodness or badness of the patient as a person—getting a disease that is commonly transmitted through sex or drug use is bad, and the possibility of passing it on to others renders those infected a danger to society (Kleinman et al. 2011). In other words, HIV/AIDS-related stigma is very much a natural moral response that shows what truly matters to Chinese society, and that is security, both physical in terms of good health and psychological in terms of absence of fear. This is why stigma is unlikely to easily go away.

Second and more to the point, once the affected population is divided into high-risk groups, revealing invisible structural determinants to HIV/AIDS thereby rendering it a social disease, it becomes necessary to lean closer and reask: when we speak of HIV/AIDS-related stigma in China, what are we really speaking of? An answer may be attempted by examining the role of the media in the stigmatization of those living with the disease, especially through how the mainstream media as well as social media portray the illness and those infected, and how such presentation has evolved over the years and whether patterns and forms of stigmatization have changed accordingly.

2.3.3 Stigma and the Role of the Media

Looking at media representation since the commence of the epidemic, it is clear that the ways the Chinese population, especially the urban population, is informed about HIV/AIDS have shifted over time, both in terms of means and platforms of communication, and how the virus and those infected are portrayed—from complete initial silence and denial, to emphasizing on the danger and immorality of the disease and those infected, and then to adopting a more caring voice and incorporating messages of anti-discrimination into educational programmes and campaigns.

The public now receives information about HIV/AIDS from increasingly diversified media platforms, including traditional state media, the internet, social media and networking sites. While information is more readily available than before, there is seldom any critical or self-reflective analysis on stigmatization due to tight restraints placed upon expression. Technical information is of course essential in terms of facts provision and promotion of safe sex practices, for instance, but without combining it with the more in-depth materials that guide people in reasoning and critically thinking about deeper issues such as discrimination, the impact of technical information is likely to be compromised, and functioning alone, it may even stir up more fear, discrimination, and even hatred.

Media presentation of high-risk groups has evolved in recent years, producing positive results in the context of HIV/AIDS. Regarding men who have sex with men, positive or at least neutral presentations of homosexuality were absent from state-controlled media until recent years, with even the Communist Party's mouthpiece *People's Daily* speaking openly in support of anti-discrimination on the ground of sexual orientation, although such incidents have been very rare. In contrast, while the irreplaceability and contributions of migrant workers to China's economy have been widely recognized, in the context of HIV/AIDS, media presentations continue to send out the message that they are vulnerable to infection for their class-associated poor qualities, such as lower levels of education and income. While these factors are indeed closely related to HIV vulnerability, how they are presented requires tentative thinking, and more attention needs to shift toward structural determinants, as already examined. Compared to other high-risk groups, discrimination of this group should be the easiest to tackle, so long as their contribution to society and value are publicly recognized.

Much less fortunate are sex workers, as while the media may help ease discrimination against particular groups by normalizing their unique characteristics (e.g., homosexual men) or praising their contributions (e.g., migrant workers), it is impossible for the media to normalize let alone praise prostitution in the Chinese culture in which it is illegal and immoral. However, social media has made an important contribution in recent years, in that articles have appeared to tell the personal stories of those engaged in the sex industry, some written by sociologists and others by journalists, giving the hated profession a human face, all seeking to show that many have been driven into the industry by financial hardship and rely on emotional support from the sisterly bonds established at work with other sex workers in order to survive socially. The message is that everyone has a story, do not judge so readily unless you have listened first. How exactly these social media reports may ease or have eased discrimination in the context of HIV/AIDS needs closer examination.

2.3.4 New Trends and Forgotten Issues

Thus far, this chapter has shown that the way that China handles both mental illness and HIV/AIDS has gone through different stages with varying aims and strategies at each, producing very different results and impacts. This gives rise to the necessity to pay close attention to new trends both in terms of emerging issues as well as changes in attitudes. It is also important to dig up neglected issues—be they neglected purposefully, due to negligence or ignorance, or as a result of having been labeled unworthy of attention.

2.3.4.1 New Trends

Three emerging issues of concern should be highlighted here. The first is that, contrary to the enduring misconception that HIV/AIDS is a disease of the young, the number of older people (mainly men) who are infected has increased sharply in recent years. The latest data show that in 2018, 24,465 men over 60 were living with HIV/AIDS, compared to 8,391 in 2012 and 19,815 in 2017, accounting for 16.46% of the entire HIV/AIDS-infected population. It is unclear whether this is a new phenomenon or an older issue previously hidden from public sight.

There are several explanations for this sharp rise. First, it is surprising to many that sexual transmission has been the main means of infection for 90% of the infected elderly, leading to the culturally shocking and socially very uncomfortable realization that older people have sexual needs. Second and related, since elderly sex is associated with shame and never talked about, and older people's options for sexual fulfilment are severely limited, they either have to supress their sexual desires or consider the illegal way out—a news report revealed at the end of 2018 that 80% of the infected elderly had admitted to having had sex with commercial sex workers. Third, older people tend to have very poor knowledge of HIV/AIDS and consider using protection unnecessary even for sex with prostitutes. This is due to the fact that, fourth, until recently following greater media exposure, older people's sexual needs were presumed not to exist; hence, no proper sex education was previously considered necessary. It was as late as 2017 that they became listed as a target group for intervention in the country's Thirteenth Five-Year Action Plan for HIV/AIDS Prevention and Treatment. Fifth, stereotypes and stigma also prevent older people from getting tested and treated.

The second emerging issue of concern is that the infection rate among young students is rising fast. Apart from youth curiosity and an increasingly open sexual culture, the key reason for this is the absence of comprehensive sex education, which is an essential means to build up knowledge of and right attitude toward sex-related issues. Although various forms of sex education are supposed to exist in secondary schools and universities, the sharply rising HIV infection rate casts doubt over their effectiveness. Teachers' and parents' conservatism causes widespread unwillingness to educate about sex and sexuality properly in the classroom. This is unfortunately coupled up with overly simplistic education on HIV/AIDS—on many university campuses, HIV/AIDS education means handing out free condoms once a year on the World AIDS Day, giving the impression that sex is encouraged rather than that HIV/AIDS must be taken seriously.

The third, rather promising, trend is that the number of court cases challenging HIV/AIDS-related discrimination is rising, signifying growing rights awareness. There have been some notable cases in the field of labor discrimination. In June 2017, a 28-year-old HIV-positive man won a lawsuit against his former employer, a quasi-governmental food inspection company, for firing him for being HIV positive. Having previously lost twice, first during labor arbitration and then in a lower court, he became the very first person in the country to receive a judgment in which discrimination based on HIV status was ruled illegal. He also filed a lawsuit against the local government to review the legitimacy of its physical examination standards for government employees, as according to Chinese law, HIV testing should be voluntary, not compulsory. A hearing date is yet to be set. In April 2018, a municipal district court in Sichuan Province issued a mediation settlement under which the plaintiff, an employee who was sacked after having been diagnosed as HIV-positive, was reinstated and awarded compensation for loss of earnings. In October 2019, a man in Guizhou Province filed a lawsuit against Maotai, China's largest liquor company, for rejecting his application for a full-time position after discovering that he was HIV-positive. He had been working with a third party associated with Maotai for two years and had passed both the written examination and the interview for a full-time position. A decision has yet to be reached, although it is widely speculated that the plaintiff will win.

2.3.4.2 Issues Demanding Attention

Consistent with this book's call for tentative contextual analysis of health issues and the belief that the cure for any disease tends to have a social aspect, and especially bearing in mind the stigma attached to these illnesses, it would be worthwhile to start paying systemic attention to two important issues. The first is the impact of HIV/AIDS on close personal relationships and social relations in general. There has been increasing critique in the field of HIV/AIDS studies in the West on the distinction between biomedical and social dimensions of HIV/AIDS, calling for any disease response to meaningfully engage with the patient's everyday life and be integrated into their social relations and practices to generate stable support on the ground (Kippax and Stephenson 2012; Auerbach et al. 2011). Over the years, a very limited number of articles have been published in Chinese on how social relations and the environment impact patients' experience of living with HIV/AIDS, all reaching the unsurprising conclusion that the quality of social relations and the supportiveness of the social environment have direct and enormous impacts on how patients cope, especially in terms of medical compliance and progression of the disease, hence calling for greater social and familial support.

Furthermore, hardly any study has sought to look in detail at the problem from the other direction, namely, how being infected changes one's personal relations with those around. It is an easily imaginable fact but needs empirical examination and tentative analysis. First, it seems impossible to fully understand how social relations affect a patient's healing experience unless how the patient's infection has affected their social relations is examined first—things can get better only if we know how they got worse in the first place. Second and related, despite increasingly visible efforts from the government and NGOs to bring about social acceptance of HIV/AIDS patients, Chinese society as a whole continues to see them as a threat due to deep-seated beliefs and prejudice. Clearly, theories and good intentions are not yet taking root, which calls for more tentative intervention targeting those who are the closest to the patients—intimate partners, families, friends, coworkers, healthcare professionals—before one can expect anything from society as a whole. Since a patient's nature of relation with each of these groups varies greatly, it is important that studies be conducted on each separately, hopefully leading to purposefully designed intervention policies with the aim of generating understanding in each group and, very importantly, teaching technical skills of support for those living with this very challenging disease.

In addition to studying social relations according to the varying closeness of these groups with the patient, it is also necessary to, third, examine the urban–rural divide in this context. It seems reasonable to assume that the impact of HIV/AIDS on social relations in large cities should be smaller than that in rural areas, not least because there is greater privacy in the cities and hence easier for the patient to continue living a normal life without or with little judgment from others. For the same reason, it is also easier to keep 'the secret' within the family; hence, the family as a whole is able to live a normal life without or with little judgment from others, and when the family is not under external pressure or feeling shame, it is in a better position to play the supportive role. Also, due to the more cosmopolitan urban atmosphere in which HIV/AIDS information is more available than in rural areas, urban people as a whole are probably more willing and able to talk about their experiences so long as anonymity is ensured; hence, there is a greater chance of generating comprehensive understanding, humane treatment and skilful support.

In contrast, in poor rural areas where privacy is an alien concept and individual lives center around social relations, the situation may be more complex. One study found that the lower a rural person's socioeconomic status (e.g., living standards, income) was, the more likely they were to report that HIV/AIDS had a serious impact on their social relations (Zhang et al. 2011, 71). This is easy to understand, as a poorer person would need to rely more on the extended family, friends and the local community for caregiving and financial support. Any additional demand due to the illness is likely to put undue strain on close social relations, especially as the disease progresses. Age and education level should also be relevant factors. Currently, the number of studies on this topic is not large enough to compare and contrast, and different sampling strategies and ways of measuring stigma may produce different and even conflicting findings.

The second issue deserving more academic and public attention concerns the so-called minorities within minorities, namely, the most vulnerable among the population living with HIV/AIDS, for instance, the elderly, rural women, and children (including healthy children with HIV-positive parents and children who are themselves infected). A quick search tellingly reveals that almost all the academic works on HIV-positive minorities within minorities in China are papers written in English by Chinese scholars published in foreign journals, and while there are some media reports on the living realities of these people, serious academic works are lacking in the Chinese language. This perhaps explains why thus far intervention in the form of HIV education is flat and simplistic and no way near reflecting the complexity and seriousness of the issues involved—because critical reasoning and presentation of complex facts tend to be in a language that is not easily accessible to the general public, which hinders knowledge-building, especially self-education and self-reflection. This, however, will not change any time soon due to constrained freedom of expression and publication.

2.4 Chapter Conclusion: Health is a Right, not a Duty

In order truly to understand an illness it is essential to know what needs to be analyzed from the social science perspective, as while bringing a disease to public attention and revealing its technicalities relies on scientists and medical professionals, finding its cure and allowing those infected, affected, to live with dignity and a sense of safety, extend beyond medicine and into the larger sociocultural arena. While this chapter as well as the rest of the book have adopted a contextual approach, it is important to recognize its limitations—that a direct causal link is often hard to establish.

Apart from the societal structural determinants that this chapter has covered, there is another even wider, deeper, and even more powerful contextual factor that can explain the nation's emotions and hypersensitivity in the field of health—its colonial suffering. The ways that concepts of health and standards of healthy behavior are expressed in China reflect how strongly the preservation of individual and collective health is entrenched as a sociocultural norm. The vital importance of staying healthy, normal and free of any form of sickness is tied to suffering and humiliation during the nation's encounters with foreign invading powers in the past two centuries, during which period China was labeled 'the sick man of Asia', of which mental illnesses and HIV/AIDS today are reminders, causing the society to view the ill as dangerous and shameful, as if they have let the nation down. While many positive changes in the right direction have taken place, this part of history, so vividly remains alive in collective memory, means that it will take time for more people to accept that health is a right protected by the state, not a duty owed by the individual.

References

Auerbach JD, Parkhurst JO, Caceres CF (2011) Addressing social drivers of HIV/AIDS for the long-term response: conceptual and methodological considerations. Glob Public Health 6(Suppl. 3):S293–S309

Bolton D (2008) What is mental disorder?: an essay in philosophy, science and values. Oxford University Press, Oxford

Chen X (2014) Social protest and contentious authoritarianism in China. Cambridge University Press, New York

Corrigan PW, Markvwitz FE, Watson AC (2004) Structural levels of mental illness stigma and discrimination. Schizophr Bull 30(3):2004

Dai et al (2015) Sexual behavior of migrant workers in Shanghai, China. BMC Public Health 15(1067):1–9

Dewey S, Zheng T, Orchard T (2016) Sex workers and criminalization in North America and China: ethical and legal issues in exclusionary regimes. Springer, New York

Dong M-J et al (2019) The prevalence of HIV among MSM in China: a large-scale systematic analysis. BMC Infect Dis 19:1000

Foucault M (1976) Mental illness and psychology. Harper & Row, New York

Gong AT, Furnham A (2014) Mental health literacy: public knowledge and beliefs about mental disorders in mainland China. Psych J 3:144–158

Hatzenbuehler ML (2016) Structural stigma: research evidence and implications for psychological science. Am Psychol 71(8):742–751

He D, Zhou Y, Ji N, Wu S, Wang Z, Decat P et al (2012) Study on sexual and reproductive health behaviors of unmarried female migrants in China. J Obstet Gynecol Res 38:632–638

Hood J (2015) Untangling HIV in China: social, political, economic, and global-local factors. In: McLelland M, Mackie V (eds) The Routledge handbook of sexuality studies in East Asia. Routledge, Abingdon, pp 356–371

Huang W, Operario D, Dong Y, Zaller N, Song D, He H et al (2014) HIV-related risk among female migrants working in entertainment venues in China. Prev Sci 15:329–339

Huang W et al (2016) HIV risk and sexual health among female migrants in China. Health Promot Int 2016(31):595–605

Huang Y, Wang Y, Wang H (2019a) Prevalence of mental disorders in China: a cross-sectional epidemiological study. Lancet Psych 6(Issue 3):211–224

Huang D, Yang L, Pescosolido B (2019b) Understanding the public's profile of mental health literacy in China: a nationwide study. BMC Psych 19:20

Information Office, Ministry of Health (2009) Ministry of Health releases notifiable diseases in China in January 2009 and in 2008. Bulletin of Ministry of Health, pp 65–67

Jeffreys E, Su G (2018) Governing HIV in China: commercial sex, homosexuality and rural-to-urban migration. Routledge, Abingdon

Jeffreys and with Haiqing, Yu, , 2015.Jeffreys E, Haiqing Y (2015) Sex in China. Polity, Cambridge

Kippax S, Stephenson N (2012) Beyond the distinction between biomedical and social dimensions of HIV prevention through the lens of social public health. Am J Public Health 102:789–799

Kleinman A et al (2011) Deep China: the moral life of the person. University of California Press, Berkeley

Kleinman A (1988) The illness narratives: suffering, healing and the human condition. Basic Books, New York

Lee E-M et al (2016) Public stigma in China associated with schizophrenia, depression, attenuated psychosis syndrome, and psychosis-like experiences. Psychiatr Serv 2016(67):766–770

Li X et al (2004) HIV/STD risk behaviours and perceptions among rural-to-urban migrants in China. AIDS Educ Prev 16(6):538–556

Li N et al (2014) A cross-site intervention in Chinese rural migrants enhances HIV/AIDS knowledge, attitude and behavior. Int J Environ Res Public Health 2014(11):4528–4543

Li J et al (2017) Stigma and discrimination experienced by people with schizophrenia living in the community in Guangzhou, China. Psychiatry Res 255(2017):225–231

Lu C, Xu L, Wu J, Wang Z, Decat P, Zhang WH et al (2012) Sexual and reproductive health status and related knowledge among female migrant workers in Guangzhou, China: a cross-sectional survey. Eur J Obstet Gynecol Reprod Biol 160:60–65

Lu F et al (2020) Evolution of HIV/AIDS policy. In Wu et al (eds) HIV/AIDS in China: epidemiology, prevention and treatment, Chapter 18. Springer

Mao Y (2013) Where do Chinese anxieties come from? [中国人的焦虑从哪里来]. Qunyan Press, Beijing

National Health Commission of the People's Republic of China (2019) Blue book on Chinese mental health. http://en.nhc.gov.cn/2019-11/15/c_75812.htm

Phillips MR, Zhang J, Shi Q, Song Z, Ding Z, Pang S, Li X, Zhang Y, Wang Z (2009) Prevalence, treatment, and associated disability of mental disorders in four provinces in China during 2001–05: an epidemiological survey. Lancet 373(9680):2041–2053

Prince M et al (2007) No health without mental health. Lancet 2007(370):859–877

Sutherland D, Hsu JYJ (2012) HIV/AIDS in China—the economic and social determinants. Routledge, Abingdon

Wang et al (2010) Correlates of HIV/STD testing and willingness to test among rural-to-urban migrants in China. AIDS Behav 14(4):891–903

Wang S et al (2015) Heterosexual partnerships and the need for HIV prevention and testing for men who have sex with men and women in China: a qualitative study. AIDS Educ Prev 27(2):126–138

Wang X (2018) 'Why are so many Chinese officials killing themselves?', South China Morning Post. https://www.scmp.com/week-asia/opinion/article/2175401/why-are-so-many-chinese-officials-killing-themselves. Accessed 1 Dec 2018

World Health Organization (2009) Discussion paper 'Mental health, poverty and development'. https://www.who.int/nmh/publications/discussion_paper_en.pdf

World Health Organization (2017) Mental health atlas 2017 member state profile: China, Geneva: World Health Organization. https://www.who.int/mental_health/evidence/atlas/profiles-2017/CHN.pdf?ua=1

Wu Z et al (2019) History of the HIV epidemic in China. Curr HIV/AIDS Rep 2019(16):458–466

Wu Q, Luo X, Chen S, Qi C, Long J, Xiong Y, Liao Y, Liu T (2017) Mental health literacy survey of non-mental health professionals in six general hospitals in Hunan Province of China. PLoS One 12(7):e0180327

Xie M et al (2019) The socioeconomic burden of severe mental disorder in China, 2014–2017: a prevalence study. bioRxiv, December 2019. https://www.biorxiv.org/content/10.1101/867432v1

Xu J et al (2016) The economic burden of mental disorders in China, 2005–2013: implications for health policy. BMC Psychiatry 2016(16):137

Xu J et al (2018) Rural–urban disparities in the utilization of mental health inpatient services in China: the role of health insurance. Int J Health Econ Manag 2018(18):377–393

Xu J et al (2017) The economic burden of dementia in China, 1990–2030: implications for health policy. Bull World Health Organ 95(1):18–26

Xu L et al (2019) The economic burden of mental disorders in children and adolescents in China: a cross-sectional study. Lancet 394(S48)

Yang J (2018) Mental health in China. Polity, Cambridge

Yang LH (2007) Application of mental illness stigma theory to Chinese societies: synthesis and new directions. Singapore Med J 48(11):979

Yang B et al (2015) HIV knowledge among male labor migrants in China. BMC Public Health 15:323

Young K (1999) The research and controversy surrounding internet addiction. Cyber Psychol Behav 2(5):381–383

Zeng C et al (2019) The mechanism of theory-based HIV behavioral intervention on condom use among rural-to-urban migrants in China: the mediating roles of HIV knowledge and condom use self-efficacy. Health Behav Res 2(3)

Zhang Y et al (2011) Impact of HIV/AIDS on social relations in rural China. Open AIDS J 2011(5):67–73

Zhang L et al (2015) A systematic review and meta-analysis of the prevalence, trends, and geographical distribution of HIV among Chinese female sex workers (2000–2011): implications for preventing sexually transmitted HIV. Int J Infect Dis 39(2015):76–86

Zhang R et al (2018) Achievement of interventions on HIV infection prevention among migrants in China: a meta-analysis. SAHARA-J J Soc Asp HIV/AIDS 15(1):31–41

Zhou M et al (2019) Mortality, morbidity, and risk factors in China and its provinces, 1990–2017: a systematic analysis for the Global Burden of Disease Study 2017. Lancet 394:1145–1158

Chapter 3
Structural Reforms and the Individual

3.1 Introduction: The State and the Individual

One of the key elements of Western political philosophy is the nature of the relationship between the state and the individual, a subject of which it perhaps makes little sense to speak in the Chinese context, in which the notion of self-identity seems to lack a cultural basis and the individual is in many respects a disciplined member of a much larger collectivity. The easiest way of conducting such an analysis though is through class analysis, which always draws attention to difference and inequality—difference and inequality of wealth, social standing, lifestyle, opportunity and power. It also highlights the interaction and overlap between different kinds of inequality, examines their relation to sources of power and authority, and how they reinforce privilege and disadvantage. This is particularly the case in China.

To examine China's class make-up, to acquire where class differences and inequalities come from, is essentially to debate the extent and consequences of a landmark decision of the Third Plenum of the 11th Central Committee of the Chinese Communist Party in December 1978 to turn its back on the politics and style of governing of the Maoist era and officially began a period of comprehensive reform and modernisation. This historic meeting put in place a new comprehensive development strategy that would introduce market principles into the socialist system, decentralize administration, separate the functions of the ruling Party and those of the government, minimize the role of the government in economic management, and open the country's domestic economy to international opportunities and global interactions—all of which would eventually transform the country beyond anyone's imagination.

The positive impact of this brave step in economic terms has been plain for all to see. Since 2003, China has been the world's largest foreign direct investment destination country; in 2005, it became the world's third largest trading country, behind the US and Germany; in 2010, it surpassed Japan as the second largest economy in the world just after the US, seen as the engine of regional and world economic growth

H. H. Wei, *Sociocultural Otherness and Minority Justice: A Study on China*,
Ius Gentium: Comparative Perspectives on Law and Justice 88,
https://doi.org/10.1007/978-981-16-9752-4_3

(Goodman 2014, 5). In more precise terms, since the beginning of the reforms in 1978, GDP has risen tenfold; unprecedented and consistent economic growth at the rates of 9.5–11.5% occurred in the period of 1978–2013 (though GDP per capita has always been low due to the size of the population), creating countless opportunities and lifting tens of millions out of poverty; average wages rose while absolute poverty decreased from 41% of the population to 5%.

However, the negative aspect of the reform, especially in sociocultural terms, and the extent and form of its precise consequences both in the short-term and in the long-run, are less discussed. This is not because class or inequality is taboo in China—neither is—a state that is run by a political party drawn on the Marxist tradition is very familiar with such topics, and it readily admits that class division and grave inequalities are serious social problems in the country. What the state is not willing to admit directly or fully is that many contemporary inequalities have been the direct results of the very successful socioeconomic reforms, before the commence of which the country was in a state of remarkable equality—an equality of poverty, but equality.

The reforms have resulted in a class formation that has much in common with that in modern Western societies, but it is also differentiable from the latter due to its unique situational context and mixed characteristics—it is a class formation in a Communist party state with an economic system in which, while market principles have been in place, they constantly have to interact with, and are subordinated to, tight state control. In other words, as is the case with many things in China, it is not exactly this and not exactly that. Part I of this chapter looks at the relevant issues through examination of one subordinate group characterized by possession of physical labor, lack of educational qualifications, total or partial absence of protection of state laws and regulations, and much lower pay—rural-to-urban migrant workers.

It is important to note that class analysis is not the only angle to examine state-individual relations and how actions of the state impact the choices and everyday living of the individual. Each country has unique challenges that often generate incomparable, sometimes controversial, policies or programmes. One of such is the one-child policy. China has been experiencing extraordinary demographic changes with respect to the rising number of older persons in the population. Official data show that at the end of 2019, those over 60 constituted 18.1% of the population, and that by 2025, the total number of this age group is likely to reach 0.3 billion. In recent years, increasing public attention has been focused on the problems of an aging society, within which a unique group has begun to generate discussions and debate—*shidu parents*. 'Shidu' literally means 'losing the only one', and shidu parents, or shidu families, or shidu elderly people, are those whose only child has passed away and, for whatever reason but often due to old age, are unable to conceive or adopt another child, and the reason that they only had one child was due to China's long-running but now abolished one-child policy. Part II of this chapter presents an analysis of the unique difficulties facing this group.

There are three main reasons that internal migrant workers and shidu parents have been chosen to be the focus of attention in this chapter. First, in comparison to other groups, they possess a stronger ability to explain how, in a society characterized by rapid changes, socioeconomic constraints as well as unlimited possibilities and sometimes unpredictable movements, inequalities and the associated discrimination often come hand in hand with, even are caused by, continuous development that has benefited a great number of people. Second, they highlight what is at the very center of many forms of inequality and discrimination in China today—urban–rural divide, stigma attached to certain sociocultural backgrounds, occupations, and ways of family life. As these two examples will show, in a country that now has the largest number of millionaires and billionaires in the world and yet collective memories of being poor and hungry are still vivid, people know the importance of having money, which has driven many to take brave steps to seek opportunities for great socioeconomic gains sometimes at huge physical and psychological costs. Third, these two groups are the most representative and straightforward examples of how state policies and changes in state policies enormously impact the individual.

Furthermore, this chapter calls into question what really makes someone a disadvantaged member of society—is it occupation, qualification, income, social position, nature and outcome of interaction with the state, or all of the above? Analysis of these two groups sheds light on some of the determinant factors and draws attention to the socioeconomic, cultural and political reasons that have caused some people to become worse off in their respective ways compared to others in society, not necessarily in economic terms, and attention is drawn to the interplay of this wide range of intertwined reasons that has made these two groups 'the other', not just 'minorities'. However, it is worth remembering that these people, despite suffering hardship and discrimination in their respective ways, have also benefited under the new, however unequal and unjust, system in their respective ways, and may arguably have been much worse off should the reforms have never taken place, although the two scenarios are not exactly comparable.

3.2 Part I: Transformations and Rural Migrants in Urban China

On 18 November 2017, a fire broke out in an industrial neighborhood in south Beijing, killing 19 people, 17 of whom were migrant workers in the capital. City officials immediately declared a ruthless 40-day campaign against 'illegal structures', which had for years housed millions of migrant workers who had left their home in rural areas and came to Beijing to work on construction sites, in restaurants, delivery companies, factories, retail shops, casual work or as domestic laborers. Soon images and videos began to appear on social media showing notices issued by authorities threatening to cut off electricity and water in illegal buildings that housed migrants, streets clogged with clothes and belongings after migrant workers were given little time to pack up and leave, and official documents ordering evictions of 'low-end population'.

While the haphazard nature of the mass evictions made it impossible to determine exactly how many migrants had been displaced, how many decided to leave Beijing and went home, and what happened to those who decided to remain (or indeed if they were allowed to), these images and videos soon generated a violent wave of criticism on Chinese social media, which was unusual for a population that was entirely unfamiliar with any constructive form of democratic expression against the government on issues of injustice. A large number of posts and articles started to appear online attacking the mass evictions and were reposted frequently and widely; some people started wearing t-shirts with 'low-end population' printed on front in protest and in solidarity with those evicted; academics signed open letters criticizing the lack of due process and calling those involved uncivilized abusers of human rights.

The government soon responded and denied they were targeting migrant workers or ever having used the expression 'low-end population', insisting that safety was its only concern. It soon started to tone down even more by calling on relevant authorities to pay attention to the welfare, housing needs and future employment prospects of those evicted. While exactly how, whether, these were implemented was unknown, these mass evictions left a visible scar on the face of Beijing and gave rise to one of those rare occasions when Chinese voices of criticism drowned out those of international rights groups, although soon posts and articles started to disappear, and the whole thing was eventually forgotten. These evictions were also an important reason why the author decided to include in this book rural migrants as a group of 'the other'—not merely a 'minority'.

3.2.1 Rural Migrants: Some Introductory Basics

China's economic transformations and rise as the 'factory of the world' in the past few decades have been accredited to timely policy change and successful state-led reforms. It is seldom viewed as a victory of global capitalism—which it was. At the end of the 1970s and having reached the stage of rapid expansion, capitalism managed to destroy potential barriers erected by socialist nation-states for capital flow and technological transfer and successfully incorporated socialist regimes into the process of capital accumulation, which rapidly generated a huge wave of industrial relocation from advanced capitalist states to developing countries such as China (Ngai 2016, 4). It was against this global background that the Chinese state turned its reformative vision into workable pro-market initiatives and put great efforts into integrating itself into the global system by, for instance, joining international bodies such as the World Trade Organization. Until recently, when talking about this period of reform and opening-up, the focus has solely been on the country's rapid capital accumulation at an unprecedented pace, little attention has been given to a direct consequence of this incredible transformation—the emergence of a new working class comprising over 273.9 million individuals whose household registration is rural but engage in nonfarming work either in or outside of the village or town of their household registration (National Bureau of Statistics 2020).

It is important to be clear at the outset about the various definitions of 'rural migrant'. The figure of over 273.9 million above as revealed by the National Bureau of Statistics refers to '*nongmingong*'—a literal English translation being 'peasant worker', which covers both those individuals with rural registration but work *within* the area of their household registration but not in farming, and those with rural registration but work *outside* of their area of household registration. The latest government data reveal that in 2019, out of all peasant workers who work outside of their area of household registration, over 135 million were working in cities (National Bureau of Statistics 2020). Only them are covered in this chapter, as being away from home, rural-to-urban migrants are a telling angle to study inequalities and labor relations, especially what is lacking in available services in their host cities, particularly housing, education, medical care, and emotional support. For laborers who do not leave home, these are less of a problem.

There are three main reasons why the number of rural migrants in urban China is so large. First, during the reform era, China adopted from the very beginning an export-oriented economic model and turned China into the workshop of the world, which required a massive number of laborers. This ought to be considered in conjunction with the second factor that, despite some exceptions and regional differences, the Chinese countryside is in general rather poor, lacks opportunities and has comparatively speaking low demand for labor, which pushes hundreds of millions of mainly young rural workers to move from the countryside into big cities in search of employment opportunities and a future. Third, the process of reform took place under the strict guidance of the state, which not only determined China's direction and pace of socioeconomic development, but also had a forceful impact on the everyday life of individual members of society, especially rural migrants. As will be shown throughout this book, effectiveness-oriented top-down application of state power, despite many positive effects especially in terms of speedy development, has also been the cause of many ills in the lives of 'the other'.

Out of all the subordinate classes in contemporary China, the living realities of rural migrants are the easiest to generalize and the hardest to solve. They are easy to understand in that in terms of background, this group is internally least diverse in comparison to others—as mentioned above, they are all individuals who come from rural areas, have a rural registration ('hukou') and who work outside of their village or town. Despite socioeconomic reforms and rapid changes in many aspects, there has nevertheless been a bottom-line continuity of rural characteristics that defines rural life as opposed to urban life, rural people as opposed to urban people, and distinguish them from the living realities of other groups either within or outside of the same class category. Therefore, overall, migrant workers share a great deal of sociocultural characteristics due to their largely similar backgrounds.

On the other hand, the difficulties and challenges they face are the hardest to solve because they are multidimensional and multilayered, created and sustained by the hybrid marriage of state power and global capital, generating new needs, new demands and new forms of control at both social and personal levels. As this chapter will show, living and functioning under the influence of such enormously powerful forces would mean that the lives of internal migrant workers are not within their control, dignity is a luxury they cannot always afford, and that their labor and much of their lives are commodities for sale, to be purchased not just by the capitalist market but also the socialist state. But what truly renders their situation hard to solve is not just the many exploitative features of the system but also the fact that the exploitative system sustains their and their families' livelihood, further rendering them powerless to acquire a louder voice or demand better protection.

The significance of paying closer attention to their rights and welfare is fourfold. First, at a number as great as over 273.9 million, rural migrants now constitute the largest working class in China, to whom it is difficult and unwise not to pay close attention. Second, in a society that is experiencing vast and complex social problems largely though not solely caused by fast economic development, an unhappy and large working class is a potential source of political unrest and social resistance. While China's political atmosphere means that any grassroot political or labor movement is unlikely to succeed, as the literature has reviewed and will be demonstrated in this chapter, there has been growth in the number of incidents where migrant workers demand better welfare and equal rights. Third, since the emergence of migrant workers is the direct result of China's economic transformation, studying migrants is a gateway to understanding many other societal problems in contemporary China that have also been due to economic development at an unprecedented pace, such as rural poverty, growing class division, overall inequality, and left-behind children, spouses and elders.

Furthermore and fourth, the significance of studying migrant workers goes beyond policy relevance. While China has in recent years been talking a lot more than before about human and minority rights, much of the talk is instrumental, in that rights are often viewed as means to certain ends, to achieve certain goals such as stability and harmony in society, rather than ends in themselves. It is only when they come into conflict with state interests or mainstream ideals that their weaker and unstable position may be revealed. This is not to say that society is cold-hearted or entirely ignorant of issues concerning the rights and welfare of migrant workers—quite the contrary. Migrant workers' rights have received growing attention in recent years both from academia and the general public, although such examination has not been used to directly challenge the position of rights beliefs in China. In other words, migrant workers are studied more as a phenomenon, without going deeper to search for or confront the fundamental causes, which this chapter and book seek to do.

There are various ways to conduct situational analysis on internal migrants. Comparative studies are worthwhile for instance, and may be conducted from three angles. The first is to compare the living realities of permanent residents of cities and rural migrants; the second is to compare older-generation migrants and younger new-generation migrants; and the third, on which this chapter will not touch at all, is to compare Chinese rural migrants with those in other countries that are at similar stages of development and have similar circumstances or characteristics. This third angle may be difficult, as Chinese economic reforms and development are in many ways unprecedented and unique. In addition to comparative studies, a number of articles published in English or Chinese contain in-depth case studies or interviews that are particularly useful in letting migrant workers represent and speak for themselves.

While the challenges and difficulties facing rural migrants in urban China are vast and diverse, and each individual case is unique, they may nevertheless be divided into four related categories: work-related hardship, housing, social integration, and emotional needs.

3.2.2 Employment and Dignity

While many changes have taken place in the past decades in relation to all aspects of rural migrants' working, living and social life, one thing has remained the same, namely, that the vast majority of them continue to concentrate in low-paid and labor-intensive jobs. This is despite a slight rise in the educational level among them, which has probably been due to the fact that the younger migrants (under 40s), who now constitute 50.6% of the entire migrant worker population, are better educated than the older generation (National Bureau of Statistics 2020). Studies have been conducted on the differences and similarities between older and younger generations of rural migrants in cities. Among the findings are: while the older generation of migrants continues to farm by returning home for planting or harvesting, the younger generation is much less likely to do so; younger generation migrants are more selective about jobs than the older generation and are more aware of economic opportunities and rights-related issues such as equal pay, insurance and vacation time; younger generation migrants are also more likely than the older generation to organize to quit jobs together, causing a shortage of workers in some industries (Wu et al. 2014, 27).

However, despite positive changes in both their awareness of rights and welfare and the physical environment in which they work, a comparative study on the various industries in which rural migrants heavily concentrate reveals that, despite being physically present in the city and contributing vastly to urban people's life and the economy, they themselves as a class have not been socially, culturally or economically integrated into urban life in ways that are meaningful, just or necessary. According to the National Bureau of Statistics (2020, Fig. 4), rural migrants working in cities are heavily concentrated in jobs such as manufacturing, construction, wholesale, retail, transport, postal services, warehousing services, hotels, catering, and handyman services. Despite many practical constraints, most cities now have temporary registration for rural migrants and allow more leeway for their self-employment. Many migrants engage in various types of casual work; some, as will be looked at in Chap. 5, also engage in illegal work such as prostitution.

This section looks at three categories of rural migrants—construction workers, factory workers, and domestic labor—not only because it is impossible to cover all but also and more importantly because these three categories can best demonstrate that examination of the lived realities of rural migrants in cities ought to be conducted against the background of China's economic reforms, the social and relational changes that restructuring has brought to society, as well as the relationship between the country's economic system and global capitalism.

3.2.2.1 Construction Workers

The latest government data reveal that 54 million rural migrant workers are working in the construction industry, accounting for 18.7% of the total rural migrant workforce, which registers a rise of 0.1% compared to the preceding year and remains the second most popular job choice for migrant workers after manufacturing (National Bureau of Statistics 2020, Fig. 4). It has been noted that labor studies have largely neglected the lived experiences of construction workers (Ngai 2016, 41), which is surprising and irresponsible considering that the Chinese dreams of modernity and global power have very much been carried by the country's construction industry, which is the largest in the world and had a value in 2020 of 1,049 billion US dollars. As the government plans to focus on improving the infrastructure in small- and medium-sized cities, the construction industry is likely to maintain continuous growth and contribute significantly to the country's GDP. However, construction workers are among the most poorly protected workers in the country in terms of physical and financial risks, for both historical and pragmatic reasons.

Society's perception of construction work has changed over the years. Under the socialist system and since 1958, construction work was organized under state-owned or collective enterprises and was considered skilled and very respected. While those working in state-owned enterprises enjoyed fuller protection and greater benefits than those working in urban or rural collectives, all in the industry were looked after by the state in the sense that all had their food provided and enjoyed regular albeit modest payments and reasonable working hours (Ngai 2016, 45). This practice was abruptly brought to an end by the economic reforms under Deng Xiaoping, which not only restructured the construction industry's administrative system and allowed greater autonomy in state-owned enterprises, but also established a competitive bidding system and brought back subcontracting, which was first brought into the country in the mid-nineteenth century by Western construction companies.

The Chinese government made several significant moves in 1984 that would have lasting impacts on the construction workforce. Among others, it requested state-owned construction enterprises to reduce the number of permanent workers and not to, in principle, recruit any permanent workers in the future except those who were absolutely necessary to keep the enterprise operational; general contractors and contracting companies were asked not to directly employ blue-collar workforce but should do so through employing subcontractors who were to be responsible for labor recruitment (Ngai 2016, 46). In this way, management became delinked from labor and field operations by a multitier subcontracting system, part of which millions of rural migrant workers are today.

It is this subcontracting system that has caused many of the problems that rural migrant construction workers face. Typically, at the very top of the system is usually a well-known property developer in a large city who is responsible for land reclamation and the overall design of the project. Responsibility for construction is shifted down the chain through a competitive bidding process to a state-owned construction company that takes charge of the project's management and equipment arrangement for its contractors. This construction company relies upon various 'big contractors' who are responsible for providing raw materials and labor recruitment. These 'big contractors' in turn relies upon 'small subcontractors' to recruit workers and manage the daily division of labor on the project. These 'small subcontractors' are further dependent on labor-use facilitators (who are usually their relatives or covillagers) to search for suitable workers in their own or nearby rural areas (Ngai 2016, 47). Most contractors and subcontractors operate without much to spare and lack access to a credit facility, and since the developers at the top do not make the bulk of payments to the contractors until the project is completed, both the contractors and subcontractors often face serious arrears and shortage of funds right from the commence of the project. This means that the rural migrant workers at the bottom of the chain have no choice but to become accustomed to not getting paid until the project is completed. And if the subcontractors make low or no profits or even a loss, the migrant workers receive little or no payment.

Wage arrears as a chronic phenomenon, along with the lack of proper employment contracts which makes it hard for migrant workers to take their employers to court in case of dispute, the lack of pensions, medical insurance, accident and injury cover and other benefits, as well as inadequate physical safety on site—all despite the existence of relevant laws and regulations such as the Labor Contract Law—have made the life of a construction worker sometimes a risky struggle. While the subcontracting system has been the key reason for many of these issues, insufficient project funding and the absence of efficient state oversight are also key factors. It is important to note though that the Chinese government has not turned a blind eye to these problems. Different levels' and departments' continuous attempts to regulate the industry and tackle nonpayment of wages have taken various forms and accelerated in the past few years.

The first takes the form of state issued guidelines and measures. In December 2017, the State Council issued the 'Assessment Methods for Guaranteeing Wage Payment of Rural Migrant Workers' to carry out between 2017 and 2020 annual assessment of provincial governments' performance in ensuring wage payment for migrant workers within their respective provinces. While these measures do not apply solely to the construction industry, since nonpayment of wages affects the construction industry disproportionately, they are particularly relevant to construction workers. Performance quality will be divided into three levels (A, B, and C, with C being the poorest), and the relevant governments and departments will be requested to take appropriate measures according to the assessment. Assessment results are recorded and will be taken into account when relevant government officials are being assessed for general work performance or promotion. Should there be any evidence of issues needing further investigation, they will be referred to Party discipline-enforcement bodies or even subject to legal punishments.

In the same spirit of the State Council's Assessment Methods, the Ministry of Human Resources and Social Security issued detailed guidelines in September 2018 for various levels of the government to follow in order to guarantee prompt payment of migrant workers' wages. Then, in January 2020, Premier Li Keqiang signed a State Council decree to roll out a regulation guaranteeing payments of wages to rural migrant workers, which came into effect in May 2020, not only introducing penalties for firms that failed to comply, but also requesting the main contractor to simplify the payment process and pay migrant workers directly. Also, no project or work would be allowed to commence without sufficient funds, or the relevant parities would be investigated.

The second takes the form of 'naming and shaming' with potentially severe punishments attached, which is controversial but has proven to be effective. In April 2017 and for the very first time, the Ministry of Human Resources and Social Security exposed on its official website details of ten cases of nonpayment of wages for migrant workers.[1] It then issued in September 2017 the 'Interim Measures for the Administration of "Blacklist" on Wage Arrears for Rural Migrant Workers', the enlistment on which would lead to serious constraints and joint punishments by thirty ministries and departments including the Ministry of Human Resources and Social Security, the National Development and Reform Commission, the People's Bank of China and the Ministry of Housing and Urban–Rural Development, which would seriously affect many aspects of the relevant company's everyday functioning, such as procurement, tendering and bidding, production permit, government funding, application of loans, even transportation and travel for those held responsible.[2] In July 2018 the first 'blacklist' of 14 companies and 6 individuals was published, in October and December 2018 a second blacklist of 25 companies and 5 individuals and a third of 26 companies and 4 individuals were published; the first and second blacklists of 2019 were published in January and April, naming 30 and 50 companies respectively; the first and second blacklists of 2020 were published in May and July, naming 30 and 50 companies respectively; the first blacklist of 2021 was published in January, naming 30 companies. Apart from these Ministry blacklists, there are also local blacklists serving the same purposes.

Simultaneously, as employers are being dealt with, various cities have set up what people call 'rights protection hotlines' for the sole purpose of creating a channel for rural migrant workers themselves to report nonpayment of wages and other issues that have adverse effects on their welfare. As demonstrated in other chapters with other groups, the emergence and spread of hotlines is a good sign, as it is additional evidence that the government fully acknowledges that nonpayment of rural migrants' wages is a serious and widespread problem, and that people who are most affected

[1] See http://www.mohrss.gov.cn/gkml/ldgx/ldbzjc/201802/t20180207_288087.html.

[2] There exists only a Chinese version of the document. See the official website of the Ministry of Human Resources and Social Security: http://www.mohrss.gov.cn/SYrlzyhshbzb/laodongguanxi/zcwj/201709/t20170930_278573.html.

have been recognized to be in need of a channel to speak for themselves and seek help. Periodically, various levels of government will publish the latest data as to the amount of owed wages being paid to the migrants, demonstrating that they have kept their word and mean business. There are also periodic enforcement actions to further ensure that employers are kept on their toes and reminded of their legal duties toward migrant workers. This is perhaps a good example of one of those good things about an authoritarian country, that once it realizes a problem and wants to deal with it, it can put things in action extremely fast and effectively. But it is not always easy for it to feel that sense of urgency.

Apart from wages, there are other employment-related issues, such as medical care and workplace safety, which this chapter does not examine in detail. The change in the government's attitude toward this group has no doubt raised awareness of the lived realities of rural migrant workers in the construction industry, and despite a general lack of public attention given to them still, in the past few years both societal attention and academic interest have increased, not only that these workers' contributions to the country's economy and urban life have increasingly been talked about, but also that they have been talked about from a rights perspective, emphasizing also that it would be against both traditional Chinese virtue and the principles of a socialist system to mistreat its workers.

3.2.2.2 Factory Workers

As the factory of the world, in the past few decades, China has repeatedly been confronted with allegations of running, or at least turning a blind eye to, sweatshops, which are characterized by mass violations of international and national labor laws and industry codes of conduct, such as low wages, excessive overtime and poor working and living conditions. It is difficult not to begin an examination of Chinese factory workers with the widely reported Foxconn suicides, which are both unique to Foxconn and representative of the general working and living reality of China's factory workforce—not in that suicides are common among factory workers, but that the Foxconn incidents are a lens through which we may examine not only the lives and struggles of Chinese factory workers (who are predominantly rural migrants) but also China's relationship with the global economy.

In 2010, international and Chinese media zoomed in on Foxconn—the largest electronics manufacturer in the world and currently ranks 26th on the Fortune Global 500 list—not because it is said to have employed over 800,000 people all over mainland China, or that it makes large profits by producing Apple iPhones, iPods, iPads, Blackberry, Kindle, Sony Playstation, Xbox, Nokia devices and so on—but because in 2010 alone, as many as 18 young workers aged between 17 and 25 committed suicide at its production facilities, resulting in 14 deaths and 4 serious injuries (Ngai 2016, 105). Despite Foxconn drawing on its vast resources to minimize the impact of these incidents, various bodies have conducted investigations into these suicides.

Among others (some are completed reports and others ongoing research), three reports deserve close attention and have produced very similar conclusions: first, a report competed by teachers and students from 20 universities on the basis of their joint investigation during the summer of 2010 on the working conditions and management practices at Foxconn facilities in various Chinese cities, which surveyed over 1700 workers and interviewed 300 frontline workers, engineers and management staff[3]; second, a report entitled 'Workers as Machines: Military Management in Foxconn' released on 12th October 2010 by Students & Scholars against Corporate Misbehavior based on their investigations (employing interviews and undercover methods) from May to September 2010 at two Foxconn facilities in Guangdong and Zhejiang Provinces[4]; and third, the Fair Labor Association (FLA)'s independent investigative report released in March 2012, which not only revealed serious noncompliance with the FLA's Workplace Code of Conduct and Chinese law but also suggested a detailed set of remedial measures to better protect the welfare and safety of the workers.[5]

All three reports were promoted by the string of suicides and presented very similar concerns, findings and remedial suggestions. First, Foxconn's frontline workers were under enormous work pressure and had to endure high production intensity and yet were poorly paid. Taking Foxconn's Shenzhen facilities as an example, no doubt promoted by the string of suicides, in June 2010, frontline workers' monthly basic wage was raised from 900 to 1200 RMB, which was only 100 RMB higher than the local minimum wage of 1100 RMB set in July 2010; in 2012, the Foxconn starting wage in Shenzhen was 1800 RMB, and the local minimum wage was 1500 RMB (Fair Labor Association 2012, 9). Reports show that all Foxconn production facilities' basic wages were just slightly over the local minimum wage and far below the local living wage, which meant that frontline workers were not able to maintain decent living standards in the cities (Students & Scholars against Corporate Misbehavior 2010, 6–7). Workers also reported that after the wage increase in June 2010, production intensity also increased, rendering the wage increase a decrease in effect (Ngai 2016, 126). The current Foxconn basic wage seems to be within the range of 2200 to 2650 RMB depending on the geographical location, which is extremely low. This explains why all Foxconn workers 'agree' to do overtime in order to maximise income, which is the second issue of noncompliance with industry codes of practice and legal requirements that these reports have found.

Excessive overtime has been common practice. Investigations found that during peak production periods, the average working hours per week at the Foxconn facilities exceeded both the Fair Labor Association's code standard of 60 hours per week as well as the Chinese legal limits of 40 hours and a maximum of 36 hours of overtime

---

[3] The report was released on 9th October 2010 and is available in Chinese only at: https://tech.163.com/10/1009/15/6IIHU0KT000915BD_all.html.

[4] Available at: https://www.somo.nl/wp-content/uploads/2010/08/military-management-in-Foxconn.pdf.

[5] Available at: http://www.fairlabor.org/sites/default/files/documents/reports/foxconn_investigation_report.pdf.

per month (Fair Labor Association 2012, 2). However, it is important to note that according to the Fair Labor Association's 2012 report, 48% of the workers surveyed in Shenzhen considered their working hours to be reasonable, and another 33.8% claimed that they would like to work more hours to make more money (Fair Labor Association 2012, 8). But according to the report of Students and Scholars against Corporate Misbehavior (2010, 7), much of the overtime was involuntary.

All of these were made possible by harsh management, which was the third serious issue revealed in the reports. Various studies and investigations have looked into and considered Foxconn's military leadership style the culprit for continuous suicides. In order to maximize productivity to meet heavy demands, a corporate culture of absolute obedience has been imposed on the workers, who are organized by a hierarchical management principle. Since the division of labor is so detailed that each worker serves merely as a cog in the machine, their job is to strictly implement the instructions from their line leaders and managers by mechanically repeating the simple movements that their particular line of work requires without thought or 'skill' strictly speaking.

Many have written about Foxconn's militaristic drilling at the start of each day on the production line, when management will ask the workers 'how are you?', to which the workers will respond by shouting in unison 'Good! Very good! Very, very good!' (Ngai 2016, 122). Similarly, and for the same purpose of training workers to be disciplined and efficient, line leaders would punish harshly those who talk on the line or fail to catch up with the high speed of work or make mistakes, including requesting all workers to stay behind to listen to the one being punished to read out loud a statement of self-criticism. Floor managers also like to give speeches to the workers at the beginning and end of each workday, to which the workers will have to stand to listen after a long shift of a standard 12 hours of work (Ngai 2016, 123).

Among these workers are student interns, the exploitation of whom is the fourth major issue of concern raised by the reports and investigations on Foxconn and as a widespread practice in China. Foxconn's seasonal but enormous intern labor force is made up of vocational school students, who, under the Chinese Education Law, retain a student identity during the entire period of internship and do not qualify for protection under labor laws or regulations due to lack of labor status. Consequently, any conflicts that may arise between them and the organization will not be handled as labor disputes and, for the same reason, they will not qualify for social security benefits or trade union membership. It has been said that these legal loopholes have enabled Foxconn's student internship programme to function in a way that raises output and increases profits by paying subminimum wages and offering little protection during the busiest seasons (Ngai 2016, 118).

Furthermore, the Fair Labor Association (2012, 11) made it clear that it was necessary not only to examine whether policies and procedures existed but also, more importantly, to examine whether they were implemented. They found several issues related to inconsistent policies, procedures and practices in terms of health and safety, and industrial relations. This is the fifth main concern. For instance, a general observation concerning health, safety and environment was low worker integration, in that the majority of workers were not involved in the health and safety committees, which were management-dominated, and had low levels of confidence in the management of such issues, some were even unaware of the existence and role of these committees, which were said to be mostly reactive rather than proactive in monitoring conditions. It was suggested that the implementation problems could be avoided if the workers could become more involved and improve their perception of health and safety issues through greater engagement. Foxconn agreed to enhance workers' participation in these committees and other union structures, and that new workers would receive information about the union and its activities during their orientation process (Fair Labor Association 2012, 12–13).

There is no doubt that Foxconn's great achievements, which were rendered possible by the influx of orders from the largest global brands, have pushed its workers to their physical and psychological limits (Ngai 2016, 112). There is also no doubt that these great achievements were a key factor that turned China into the workshop of the world and the second largest economy in the world, which brought the corporation very favorable treatments from various levels of government. There is also no doubt that the reason that Foxconn functions this way and works its workers to such extent is to meet the continuous demands from global brands in the accumulation of capital. Thus, instead of blaming it all on Foxconn and the like for lacking respect for workers' dignity and welfare, it is important to consider the structural and contextual factors that make this all possible. These factors can also explain why some injustices are willingly ignored or simply not considered to be problematic.

First, the dismantling and transformation of the socialist economic system into one that relies mainly on foreign and private investments has led to heavy reliance on export and massive use of migrant laborers, which renders keeping labor costs low to appear attractive both necessary and possible. Second, unlike in the previous decades, when big names such as Foxconn tended to be based in the more developed coastal regions, many have now moved inland and are treated very well by the local governments because the state wants them to use their resources and networks to help develop the less developed inland. Such expectations would turn into favorable government policies as well as protectionism. Third, the problem is never just with Foxconn but also if not more with those who order from it, which is why after the series of suicides, there were voices calling for Apple to move production out of China. Indeed, all reports on and investigations into Foxconn have called upon global brands to take responsibility and pay closer attention to its supplier's treatments of its frontline production workers.

It would seem that since the problems have been clearly identified, the solutions should also be clear and straightforward: better labor rights training for both the workers and the employers, let the trade union function properly and representatively, provide the workers with a wider range of support services caring for their diverse needs, enable opportunities for the workers to engage in recreational and educational activities, and so on. Furthermore, it is important to know that while Chinese workers are known for their discipline, efficiency and obedience, and despite the great sense of alienation that they are likely to feel in their host cities where they do not belong, they are not entirely powerless. Ngai (2016, 138) notes that workers' resistance has developed in recent years from a single means to multiple means, from single-factory participation to cross-factory joint actions, from only taking legal actions to launching various forms of collective actions—no doubt inspired by public discourses on labor rights in the past few decades and enabled by growing knowledge of the country's labor regulations and laws that not only protect their rights but also dissolve conflicts.

However, the reality is that both resources and opportunities for rural migrants are scarce, particularly considering the rural–urban divide, which means they are likely to put up with a great deal before taking actions, if ever. Besides, gender is another factor that must not be ignored. The majority of rural-to-urban migrants who end up working in factories are women whose experiences, concerns and needs are diverse. But while generally speaking, women in the younger age groups are more concerned with learning new skills and personal development, as they grow older and take on additional responsibilities as partners or mothers, their motivations and ambitions decrease, and their priorities shift toward finding and retaining a stable job. This perhaps answers the following question, which has puzzled many over the past decade: if Foxconn workers are treated so badly, why don't they just leave? The straightforward answer is that they are not exactly in a position to bargain.

3.2.2.3 Domestic Labor

Gendered labor also sustains China's domestic services sector, the development of which manifests four main characteristics under the influence of the economic reforms. The first is the unprecedented demand of domestic workers, for which there are three main reasons. First, economic restructuring and policy changes have meant that expenditures on health care, childcare and early education are either reduced, or that services have been privatized, creating a huge care gap waiting to be filled by other means. Second and related, the increasingly competitive market means that women who were once the primary caretakers in the family now need to spend significantly more hours at work than during the prereform era, creating a problem for fulfilling domestic and caring duties. This is further exacerbated by, third, the 'one child policy' (which has now been officially abandoned), which caused a significant decline in the fertility rate and a steady increase in the ratio of the elderly in the population, causing a rising number of families to hire others to look after their young, old and sick (Tong 2018; Hu 2011).

When there is demand, there is supply, which is the second characteristic. The number of domestic workers in China is an estimated 35 million. There are several reasons why the reforms have caused a huge supply of domestic workers in cities. First, the rural–urban divide means that many would move from the generally poor Chinese countryside into large cities in search of employment opportunities. In rural areas, female poverty is more severe than male poverty, which explains why many women who engage in domestic work in cities are from remote and less developed rural areas (Hu 2011, 45). Second, economic restructuring has in many ways also been a gendered social transformation, causing mass unemployment among urban female citizens, who would either remain unemployed or seek alternative, previously unconsidered, employment options (Tong 2018). Third, economic reforms also caused the decline or privatization of several old forms of childcare, such as government-funded public childcare centers, childcare centers attached to state-owned enterprises, and community childcare centers (Hu 2011). While private for-profit childcare facilities have grown rapidly in recent years, practical constraints such as high fees and parents' working hours being incompatible with day-care hours often mean that they are not an option for every urban parent, rendering hiring someone into the family still more desirable and practical. Fourth, China is a rapidly aging nation that generates great demand for domestic helpers for the elderly.

Nothing will work in China without government backing, which is the third key characteristic of and reason for the flourishing of the domestic service industry in recent years—despite remaining subordinate in all but name, it is now not only an officially recognized employment type but also a government-backed and actively promoted career choice. This is very significant considering that while domestic work has a long history in China, for much if not all of its history, neither its status as 'work' nor its role and contribution to the economy was properly recognized. And ideally speaking, domestic work is not supposed to exist under a socialist system, as it has the characteristic of class exploitation, although it never ceased to exist even during the Cultural Revolution when class struggle was reasserted. It should be noted that Hu (2011, 32) claimed the opposite on this point and stated that domestic service was completely abolished during the Cultural Revolution. This is wrong, as the lived experience of the author's family during that time proved otherwise—domestic workers continued to exist in better-off families of the intellectual elite or high-ranking cadres who were not denounced.

The motivation behind the government's postreform change of mind regarding the status of domestic services was less to do with creating jobs for rural migrant women than for laid-off urban women as a result of the mass unemployment caused by economic restructuring. While mass unemployment affected both men and women in the state sector, women were laid off on a larger scale because they were considered economically inefficient under the fierce demands of market competition. To solve the serious unemployment problem and encourage urban women to work, the government realized that it would be necessary to first recognize certain work as 'employment'. In August 2000, the Ministry of Labor and Social Security set up the National Occupational Standards of Domestic Workers and divided domestic workers into three levels of beginner, intermediate and senior according to their working skills, while the Ministry's Employment Training Technical Instruction Center published training materials for each level (Hu 2011, 33–34). It is important to note that when only rural women were involved in urban domestic work, it was not officially recognized as 'employment', and when laid-off urban women started to get into the field, the government changed its policy to turn domestic work into a semiproper occupation, indicating changing circumstances but arguably also unequal status between urban citizens and rural workers (Hu 2011, 33–34).

This also speaks of the fourth characteristic of the impact of the economic reforms on the domestic field, namely, that it has been gendered, as while male workers have been laid off too, they have not been targeted as potential laborers in this newly promoted flexible employment. Traditional domestic service work complies with a gendered division of labor anyway; now, such social expectations and role assignment toward women have been further enhanced institutionally. This provides a good angle to study the interaction between patriarchy and social transformation in modern China, and also renders it necessary to highlight specific issues of concern regarding the rights and welfare of domestic workers who are mostly rural women and particularly open to all sorts of exploitation.

First, paid domestic work in China, like anywhere in the world, lacks sufficient legal protection due to its precarious status, so the various laws and instruments that protect workers in an employment arrangement do not seem to apply to domestic workers. For instance, the Labor Law of 1995 does not cover domestic workers employed by individuals and households; the Regulation on the Insurance of Workplace Injury only applies to workers who have a labor relationship with work unit employers; the Supreme Court's Interpretation of Certain Issues on the Applicable Laws about Hearing of Cases of Labor Disputes ruled that disputes between individuals or households and domestic workers are not covered as labor disputes; the Labor Contract Law of 2008 also excludes domestic workers, as private homes are not legally considered work units, although since the Law covers outsourcing, technically domestic workers who are employed and sent to people's homes by agencies are covered.

Second, the working and living conditions are not always favorable, not only because the precise responsibilities are not always clear, rendering that the workers might end up doing a lot more than what they are paid for, but also that rural migrant workers are not covered by government social benefit plans and often lack medical insurance coverage. Even for those with medical insurance coverage, rural residents are reimbursed for medical expenditures in their hometown hospitals only, but migrant workers who live and work in cities have few opportunities to return home and receive treatment at their hometown hospitals, where both facilities and doctors' skills fall behind those in cities. The occasional news of wealthy families willing to pay a great deal of money for a highly experienced nannie reveals how parents in a child-centered society nevertheless hope to balance the child's best interests with their own career and free time, and it should not be doubted that many employers treat their domestic workers well and as part of the family. However, despite a general salary increase in recent years and the fact that much depends on precise responsibilities, it seems that most domestic workers are still underpaid considering their working hours and contributions (Hu 2011, 86). This is partly due to low rates of signing service contracts, but even with contracts, their interests are not necessarily secure due to ambiguous wording in the documents, which tends to be unambiguously partial to the employer and the agency (if one is involved). The low-end nature of domestic services work also means low stability, as potential replacements are plenty.

Third, unlike working in construction or factories, the nature and environment of domestic work means that it often involves feelings and emotions, making those doing the work, especially live-in caregivers who are far away from their own home and family even more vulnerable to mistreatment and exploitation. While Chinese studies from this angle are lacking, Western scholars have examined how the emotional attachments of caregivers may lead them into situations of manipulation, causing them to do things that are beyond their original contractual agreement and rendering them less likely to resist or report abuse. For this reason, some have labeled domestic work as 'affective labor', 'emotional labor', and even 'care penalty' (Hardt and Negri 2004; England and Folbre 1999; Hochschild 1983; Hu 2011).

It would be reasonable to assume though that domestic workers' general situation may improve soon and fast, as this group, or more accurately this sunrise industry, has received a great deal of government attention and backing in recent years. First, support has been expressed with the Notice Regarding the Implementation of the Domestic Services Project issued in June 2009 by the Ministry of Commerce, the Ministry of Finance and the All-China Federation of Trade Unions, according to which the domestic services industry is now officially a nationwide 'project' of the state; in July 2010, the Ministry of Finance and the Ministry of Commerce issued the Notice Regarding Issues Related to Organizing and Declaring the Domestic Services Industry and the Systemic Construct Project, launching pilot projects of developing the domestic services system in some cities; the State Council's Guiding Opinions Regarding Developing the Domestic Services Industry in September 2010 further announced that the industry was the government's focal development project and encouraged more people to seek work within it; the Notice Regarding the Launch of Building the Domestic Services Industry as a Standardized Profession issued by the Ministry of Human Resources and Social Security along with seven other official units in 2015 required the industry to standardize its services and personnel training.

Second, the government has encouraged trade unions, women's federations and the Communist Youth League to establish schools and training courses for domestic workers to improve their skills and abilities. And third, some local governments have also directly purchased domestic services for people and families with disabled or elderly members. All these are clear indications that the industry has become government-led. However, thus far, attention has been focused on the needs of the receiving end of domestic services, whereas those at the providing end are still in need of more efforts and recognition in addition to those from their own organizations. It is worth mentioning that, contrary to common belief as well as traditional union theory that the informally employed are unorganized and cannot establish unions, there exist a growing number of support services, aid committees and unions within the domestic sector in China with the purpose of identifying the needs and defending the rights and interests of domestic workers (Tong 2018).

3.2.3 Social, Cultural and Emotional Needs

Compared to the more measurable difficulties and challenges, rural-to-urban migrant workers' social, cultural and emotional needs are often overlooked—not only by the state and society but also by themselves. There are several interrelated aspects. The first is housing arrangements and settlement patterns, which not only indicate the welfare of migrant workers but also determine their sociability, affecting not only their own level of social and personal satisfaction but also how permanent urban citizens view and interact with them. In other words, housing is never just housing but places migrants in particular relationships with others and in relation to the physical environment. Housing arrangements are not exactly an individual choice but rather determined by many outside factors, two of which are particularly important—institutional constraints that take the form of household registration (*hukou*), and the type of work that the migrants do.

China's household registration system has long been associated with inequality and discrimination, and it both restricts the geographical mobility of the population and reinforces urban superiority. Under the earliest form of this system, which assigned each citizen a particular place of residence, rural residents were not allowed to migrate into the cities, and urban residents were not allowed to move between cities. While these barriers have gradually been removed in recent decades, enabling rural people now to move into the cities to find work and reside, for most migrant workers, it remains unrealistic to expect to settle in their host cities especially the larger ones. Not only that a local urban *hukou* continues to be an important qualification for accessing several types of urban housing, especially the more affordable housing, and tight settlement criteria aside, high housing prices and rising living costs mean that urban residency is beyond the reach of most migrant workers (Choi and Peng 2016, 36). There are of course variations among migrants living in the cities, but in general, residential mobility and quality are reliable indications of socioeconomic status and mobility, and that the majority of migrants are drifting in the bottom layer, housed either in crowded factory dormitories provided by their employers, free of charge or at minimal cost, or in cheap private housing provided by permanent urban residents (such as the so-called *chengzhongcun*, which literally means 'village within the city' or 'urban village'), as low cost and proximity to work rather than space and quality are their highest priorities.

The dormitory labor regime is characterized by the reconfiguration of daily labor production and afterwork space within a factory compound in which work and residence are highly condensed in the same location (Ngai 2016, 86). The advantages of dormitories are obvious. Since housing would otherwise be a big problem for migrant workers, dormitories solve this problem not only for them but also for company management by ensuring that workers regain the necessary energy in the shortest possible time, at the lowest possible costs, but also for the state by keeping the labor force stable and disciplined. In other words, beneath the surface of these apparent conveniences is strengthened managerial control and domination, ensuring that the workers spend their off-hours doing not much more than preparing for another round of production, effectively extending the production line from workspace to after-workspace. Not having sufficient control over their personal and social lives along with the lack of recreational and cultural activities could well multiply migrant workers' sense of alienation. In addition, research has shown that dormitory housing tends to have worse overall conditions than other housing types (Wu et al. 2014, 55).

Chengzhongcun, or urban villages, are more telling of the relationship between rural migrants and the city in which they reside. These are neighborhoods created as cities expanded outwards, enveloping areas or villages that were formally on the outskirts of cities. Although now physically within the city, the residents in these urban villages tend to have rural *hukou* status. They often expand their homes or build additional structures on their land to rent out to rural migrant workers at affordable prices, turning such neighborhoods into migrant-concentrated areas. Unauthorized construction and leasing of unsafe dwellings mean that these places are under a constant risk of being demolished by the government. Yet, such places satisfy migrant workers' basic housing needs and give them a sense of belonging and community among people who have similar backgrounds or are in similar socioeconomic situations. More importantly, it is a useful transitional space that provides flowing information and linkages with the city and urban life, and it is due to such connectedness that for the migrants, these places are much more than just static slums. Although it would not be right to overestimate their ability to provide migrants with a social mobility path, unless these neighborhoods are reasonably situated and operated—for instance, with the presence of public spaces, shops and businesses, accessibility of social services, proximity to schools and other public venues, transport links to the city center, and so on—they may well be poverty traps (Wu et al. 2014, 90).

Furthermore, apart from economic considerations, since cities are very different from migrants' hometowns in terms of cultural values and social atmosphere, living in concentration means being close to people like themselves who constitute social networks, and close to familiar values and behavioral norms. In other words, being spatially confined in this way means that they may have moved far (from their hometowns to the cities), but not that far (socially). And given the long-standing and comprehensive urban–rural divide in China, one may say that while these migrant workers have been put in the city, they are still out of the city, unless they can find a way to mix with the urban people and their culture, benefit from the rich cultural resources of the city. Given their general situation, whether or not this is a realistic expectation requires further in-depth studies, which this chapter does not provide.

Another neglected aspect of migrant workers' welfare is that of their emotional and psychological needs, arising out of their often long-term separation from their family and children. Economic pressure is not only the justification used by migrant workers to defend such separation, but also the reason they use to persuade their left-behind loved ones to accept this painful reality. However, this breadwinning capacity and the assurance that their family members are provided for cannot prevent the emotional costs. In addition to strongly missing their family and children, many migrants express pain, anguish, guilt deriving from their physical absence in their children's daily lives, or arising from their inability to provide their children with even better economic support, especially in the absence of hands-on parental guidance. This is why Montes (2013) notes that it is migration, being far away from home, that has created the opportunity for migrants to really get in touch with those deeper emotions that would normally be overlooked under normal circumstances. But migration also exposes migrants to urban parenting and the things that urban parents can provide for their children that they themselves are not able to, which will exacerbate their emotional turmoil and guilt (Choi and Peng 2016, 116). All these factors point to the necessity of establishing prevention, counseling and treatment services that are not merely accessible but more importantly should be tailor-made and cater to their specific needs.

3.3 Concluding Part I: Class Subject or Social Problem?

The lives of rural migrant workers are seldom recorded or studied. It is easy to overlook or consider them as members of a collective group and not individuals, because their rural background has in many ways deprived them of urban choices in terms of well-paid work, decent housing, sociocultural integration and emotional support, and despite their enormous presence and contribution in cities, they have yet to constitute a meaningful part of society. This is not to claim that Chinese cities can function without them—quite the contrary—their contributions are enormous, diverse and go far beyond city borders. Being a migrant involves a process of transforming individuals into working subjects, and of a reconstruction or reconfiguration of one's relationship with the family as well as the outside world, and if the first is simple, the second is not. Having examined in detail the challenges facing rural migrants in China, it has become even less apparent whether they are best studied as a class or as a social phenomenon. Either way, it seems fair to say that some of the positive policy changes that concern them are products of pragmatism rather than a genuine transformation in sociocultural values and ideals, which means there is always a risk that positive changes may be short-lived. But it might equally be argued in a more optimistic light that, unlike some of the other categories of otherness that are not able to enter public discourse, the fact that migrant workers' welfare as a subject has received open and public attention should generate some enduring influence and positive consequences.

3.4 Part II: Shidu Parents in a Child-Centered Society

Another group that has similarly received increasing public attention in recent years are 'shidu parents'. As the beginning of this chapter notes, 'shidu' literally means 'losing the only one', and shidu parents are those whose only child has passed away and, for whatever reason but often due to old age, are unable to conceive or adopt another, and the reason that they had only one child was due to China's long-running but now abolished one-child policy. In other words, what makes the experience of this group unique and differentiated from normal bereavement of losing a child which could happen to anyone in any culture, is that the shidu experience has been the unintentional but inevitable and foreseeable result of deliberate government action and forcefully enforced state policy, which, albeit proven beneficial in many respects, has had long-lasting impact on many, giving rise to the necessity of paying attention and indeed duty to care for this uniquely disadvantaged group. This is also a good time to talk about shidu parents, as the one-child policy has already been abolished, rendering the topic much less sensitive.

3.4.1 Policy Background and the Realities of Shidu

3.4.1.1 One-Child Policy Past and Present

China's one-child policy was possibly the boldest, largest and most controversial experiment in population control in human history. It was enacted in the 1970s and early 1980s in response to the country's explosive population growth rate during the 1960s, which placed a heavy burden upon the country's extremely limited resources and weak economy at the time. The rationale was that limiting each family to having only one child (with the exception of ethnic minority groups, those whose firstborn was handicapped, and in some areas families whose firstborn was a girl were also allowed another) would free up resources so that they could be spent on societal and national development which would eventually benefit all. It is easy to criticize such a policy from the standpoint of free choice and the Chinese tradition of having large extended families, but at the time the country had little choice when it was only just recovering from the devastating effects of the Cultural Revolution which brought the country to its knees, and the experimental economic reform policies were just putting into place.

It is similarly difficult to judge whether the policy was successful. On the one hand, it effectively limited population growth and released pressure upon the country's resources, which was indeed its goal. In addition, despite being politically incorrect, the policy was an important factor that allowed the country's economic reform to be carried out so efficiently. It has been said that had there not been the enactment of the one-child policy, China would have 0.4 billion more people right now on top of its 1.4 billion—an enormous burden for the Chinese economy which is currently the second largest in the world, let alone during the 1980s when it was at the bottom of the pile. Having said that, while the policy solved immediate problems at the time, it has also caused devastating consequences beyond its original goal, which have become increasingly visible in recent years.

The first is that since patriarchal traditional Chinese culture always preferred male children over females, the pressure of having only one child led to widespread abortions of female fetuses and abandonment of girls, especially in less developed rural areas, resulting in a heavily imbalanced sex ratio of the population. The second is that while the one-child policy was supposed to apply universally to all families except those officially recognized exceptions, in reality it was enforced unevenly and that many especially in the rural areas had more children and hid them from the authorities, resulting in inadequate upbringing and lack of legal status of these children, rendering them unentitled to many of the social security benefits, services and resources that were available to children with status. The third unintended but inevitable consequence is a rapidly aging population that will soon become a serious problem. There are four main reasons why shidu parents deserve keen attention from everyone.

First, this group is now at a large number and growing fast. While precise data are lacking, various resources reveal that there are over 1 million shidu families in China, and the number is growing at approximately 76,000 annually. Second, as will be examined below, while existing and improving, government and societal support is inadequate, which has led to increasing incidents of these families protesting and demanding better recognition and protection, which constitutes the third reason. Protests always attract the government's attention, but sometimes it is more out of concern for protesters' 'collective capacity' to cause trouble and instability than genuine concern for their welfare and rights. The fourth reason is that shidu families are a good way to cut into the Chinese reality to consider the short-term and long-term impact of authoritarian laws, policies and style of governing on the lives of ordinary people. This good case study of the collective verses the individual may not be sufficient to denounce completely the short-term positive impact of the one-child policy, it should be enough to cause serious consideration over progressive comprehensive compensation for past policies. While the author hesitates to call the one-child policy 'past injustice', its communitarian and pragmatic nature makes shidu families a uniquely Chinese problem with multiple dimensions and diverse implications.

The welfare of shidu families has attracted increasing attention from academia, society and government, although this emotionally sensitive and socially self-isolated group is hard to approach, rendering research and support difficult. In general, attention and limited studies tend to focus on the following themes. First, needs-based studies present the financial, physical, psychological and everyday living needs of shidu families, especially shidu elderly parents, and emphasize the urgency to improve existing inadequate policies and programmes in order to meet these needs. Second, policy-based studies examine existing programmes and policies issued by the central or regional and local governments to reflect local experiences and variations. Third, new patterns of social intervention focusing on empowerment have also been explored. Fourth, recognizing that protection of shidu parents requires not only government support in the form of policy and provision of resources and services but also, and more importantly, efforts from a wide range of institutions, individuals and especially the local community within which they live, efforts have been made to explore the reconstruction of their social life, especially through various means, including enabling education programmes targeting those around shidu families.

3.4.1.2 Policy Response and Existing Protection

Since 2001, several levels and branches of government have introduced policies and programmes to provide shidu families with various forms of compensation and assistance, although many remain guidelines and suggestions. While support is not entirely adequate, the state has not turned a blind eye to this group, which is currently protected under the broad category of 'family-planning households with special difficulties', which also includes one-child families with a disabled or injured child, although shidu families are only entitled to government support if the wife is over 49 and the couple has not given birth again or adopted any children. The local authorities' responsibilities in supporting these families are briefly outlined in article 27 of the Population and Family Planning Law of the People's Republic of China of 2001, according to which local governments must provide shidu families with 'necessary assistance and support' only if they could not give birth to or adopt another child. However, regarding what would constitute 'necessary assistance and support', the instrument contains no specific instructions, a lack of standardization could lead to difficulties in enactment, and it would be left to the local governments to decide according to local circumstances that would vary greatly. Additionally, the National Health and Family Planning Commission and the Ministry of Finance launched a pilot scheme in 2007 to provide modest financial assistance to shidu families. The Law on Protection of the Rights and Interests of the Elderly of 2013 also prescribes local responsibility for supporting childless older people. Also in 2013, the National Health and Family Planning Commission and four ministries jointly issued guidelines calling for further improvements in elderly care, medical care and social support for vulnerable families.

More specifically, currently there are shidu support policies at the level of the state, within the family-planning system as well as at regional and local levels. At the state level, there are four main aspects of support. The first is financial assistance. In August 2007 and starting with 10 pilot provinces and cities, China introduced a financial support system for parents whose only child was either disabled or dead. The system was formally implemented across the country in November 2008, according to which a fixed-rate monthly payment would be made to each of the parents until their death if their only child was disabled or dead, provided that the mother had reached the age of 49 and they had not had or adopted another child, which would terminate the grant. Each parent would receive a monthly payment of no less than 100 RMB if the only child was dead. In December 2013, the Health and Family Planning Commission together with four other government departments issued the Notice on Further Assisting Families with Special Difficulties in Family Planning, raising the *urban* monthly rate per parent to 270 RMB if the only child was disabled and 340 RMB if the only child was dead and the *rural* monthly rate to 150 RMB for disability and 170 RMB for death, starting in 2014. Regional and local variations in terms of rates were allowed according to local circumstances, and shidu parents could also receive other subsidies should they participate in insurance or social security programmes.

However, research shows that, for instance, in Chongqing, Shanghai, Beijing, Fujian and Shaanxi, subsidies in all five regions are lower than or close to the local minimum living standard. Hence, unless shidu families have other sources of income or pension, this financial assistance can do little to improve their situation. Furthermore, the previously mentioned rural–urban divide is also an issue in that there is a rural–urban gap in the amount of subsidies. The official explanation is the difference in living costs between cities and rural regions. But this fails to account for the fact that shidu parents living in cities are more likely than their rural counterparts to have pensions or other sources of income and support (Song 2014, 120).

In addition to the specific-purpose financial compensation, government guidelines have requested that four other main forms of support should be in place, although how and whether these are implemented vary greatly among different provinces and cities. On principle, these four areas are medical care, elderly care, social support, and family planning and adoption services. In view of the risk of possible diseases, the above-mentioned Notice proposes to include eligible low-income families with special difficulties in family planning in the state support schemes of medical assistance in order to provide them with corresponding help. For families with medical insurance that are willing to have another child, the expenses of the relevant procedures shall be included in the scope of payment, and for those without insurance, subsidies should be provided along with sufficient provision of information and guidance. Hospitals and other medical institutions are encouraged to establish 'green channels' to facilitate easy access to medical care and relevant services for these families.

Closely related is elderly care, which has become an urgent issue for China as an increasing number of shidu parents are getting old. Realizing this, the government has also introduced some policies, though there is a long way to go, including the provision of subsidies for qualified families and priority admission into old people's homes. The rural–urban divide is yet again at play here, apart from the financial assistance mentioned above, rural shidu parents receive much less help in other respects too, in that they tend not to have pensions, have little access to support resources or services, and have received much less attention from the government and the society at large than their urban counterparts.

Social support is no less important than medical and elderly care and is another focus of state-level policies. Social organizations, employers, social services and volunteer groups are urged to come together to provide shidu families with the necessary assistance, focusing especially on the previously neglected provision of psychological, emotional and spiritual support, the creation of a friendly and respectful social atmosphere, and the development of new ways to effectively solve their difficulties, especially those of poor rural families. For those shidu parents who are willing to adopt another child, when all other circumstances are equal, they have priority over their non-shidu counterparts. And when shidu parents pass away, local governments are encouraged to contribute to funeral services. Perhaps more importantly, a contact system for shidu families has been called for, along with the inclusion of the incapacitated members of these families into the national adult guardianship system.

In line with the state's policies, within the family-planning system itself, there are five interrelated focuses of support: everyday living, elderly care, health, emotional and psychological support, family planning and adoption services. Of particular importance is emotional and psychological support. As will be examined in Sect. 3.4.3 below, a large proportion of shidu parents suffer from serious mental illnesses as a result of their traumatic loss, such as posttraumatic stress disorder, loneliness, depression, anxiety, and increased risk of suicide. In this respect, local authorities have shown more flexibility in developing comprehensive approaches of support. Apart from financial assistance, some local governments, such as those in Kunming, Hangzhou and Guizhou, have developed multidimensional support systems to respond to shidu parents' varied needs (Lu and Lu 2014). Community-based support models have also been explored in some regions to provide more personalized assistance. Local government bodies have been urged to engage more actively with other social forces and organizations to bring about more effective protection, especially to create a more enabling and welcoming environment in which shidu parents may be more willing to actively seek help to deal with aging and other challenges (Chen 2018; Fang 2020).

3.4.1.3 Online and Offline Activism

This group's emotional sensitivity and social self-isolation mean that a reliable way of determining shidu parents' pains and needs is by restoring their own voice, enabling an environment in which they are comfortable and willing to talk without feeling pressured. Partly due to limited state support and insufficient attention from society, shidu parents have been driven to speak for themselves and demand, as a group rather than individually, better protection and recognition. Two ways are particularly noteworthy.

The internet has become a major platform for shidu parents to form communities, seek comfort, express concerns and demands, or simply talk to others in the same unfortunate situation or anyone who wants to listen. This means of communication is particularly suitable for this socially isolated group who needs both comfort and distance. They set up online chat groups to meet each other, discuss and debate relevant issues, coordinate and organize activities and events to form friendships and fight for recognition. In other words, these chat groups function as sources of mutual support, information, and sense of belonging. Research shows that participation in such chat groups has helped many shidu parents to better understand their social relations and position in society. By redefining their situation and through meeting others in the same situation, they are able to make the transition from isolated outsiders to a community with a unique but common social identity (Shen et al. 2016, 3). The opportunity to meet other shidu parents is a vital source of strength, and helps enable self-empowerment and recognition of the necessity of mutual support in their fight for a more dignified future by turning an individual claim into a collective appeal, hence magnifying the issue and maximizing the impact.

Such enthusiasm and confidence help spread online activities into real life, as an increasing number of shidu parents are no longer satisfied with online communication and activism. This is the second means that they have employed to let themselves heard. Small-scale protests staged by shidu parents in recent years demanding better recognition and protection from the state are a noteworthy phenomenon. The tightly constrained media and unfree public arena explain the lack of debate on this topic, so it is impossible to tell whether shidu parents have only in recent years begun to place the blame on the government and publicly demand compensation and recognition, or that they have always done so but have only in recent years chosen to voice it publicly, or that they also protested in the old days but it never came to media attention either due to oppression or indifference or both. In the old days people's thinking was more collective and tended to focus on what they could do for the country; nowadays there is growing albeit still limited sense of individualism, causing more people to hold the view that sacrificing the individual for the collective good is questionable if not exactly wrong. It is highly probable that many wholeheartedly supported the one-child policy and believed it to be good for the individuals and for the country, and until one lost one's only child, this belief might well have been unshakable.

Whether or not protest as a method is new, it is still necessary to consider why shidu parents would choose to let themselves be heard in this way, knowing that protests and petitions are highly controversial and socially hard to accept in Chinese culture. The first is the spread of social media, as already mentioned, which allows them to form support groups and organize events easily with collective support rather than mere individual efforts. The second is the parents' enhanced rights attitude, which has given them a new sense of entitlement to make demands. The third and most important is the fact that the one-child policy has now officially been abandoned by the state. While this is due to changing circumstances and needs of the country, it could also have been interpreted by the parents as the state recognizing at least partially the damaging effects of the policy and thus willing to compensate, since turning back the clock is impossible. The abolishment would also mean that criticizing the policy is now less politically risky than before, especially considering that the government in recent years has been actively pushing people to have more children—and failing—which contrasts particularly painfully with the childless reality of shidu parents.

Information on petitions and protests in China is difficult to gather, as such politically sensitive events are never reported. But Han (2017, 238–248) has recorded six petitions of shidu parents between 2012 and 2015, demanding various forms of assistance, compensation and recognition. While collective actions of this nature are not usually received lightly, it seems that all six petitions/protests were met with patience and kindness from government officials in Beijing, who listened to the parents' concerns and demands, thoroughly discussed the relevant issues with them or their representatives, and expressed gratitude for their advice and criticism. Their demands included standardization of financial assistance, establishment of old people's homes, lowering the age limit for state support, should they be able to have another child the costs of reproduction being taken care by the state in their entirety, and administrative compensation and so on. They also pushed for legal amendments so that their rights and interests could be officially recognized and protected by state laws.

While many of their demands could not be satisfied in the end, for instance the administrative compensation request was ruled to be lacking legal basis, and the reproduction costs demand was also not met; their petitions, bringing first-hand experiences directly to the central government's attention, had brought about some changes in the right direction, including but not limited to the above-mentioned Notice on Further Assisting Families with Special Difficulties in Family Planning, jointly issued by five ministries in 2013. However, the very title of this document sparked criticism, as many shidu families refused to be considered as just 'having difficulties', and insisted that government and public attention should focus on the causal link between the state-imposed one-child policy and their unfortunate situation. They argued for a clear differentiation between disadvantaged groups in need of state assistance, especially financially on the one hand, and shidu families who had made sacrifices for the collective good on the other. In other words, not every shidu family is after financial compensation, but all need recognition.

3.4.2 Sociocultural Sources of Shidu Otherness

It is important to be specific about what one means by 'shidu otherness'. Given shidu parents' unique circumstances as manifested by the challenges and difficulties they face, which will be examined in Sect. 3.4.3, their 'otherness' could mean 'discrimination', 'imposed or self-imposed isolation', 'particularly vulnerable', and 'different from other bereavement'. Each shidu case is unique while sharing common characteristics with others. Shidu parents are particularly vulnerable for three main reasons that are interrelated. The first is losing a child, the second is losing a child in a culture that traditionally values big family and now has care patterns that are adult children centered for aging parents, and the third is losing an *only* child and as a result of state policy no less. In particular, their unique situation should be understood in relation to two elements of Chinese tradition and culture. The first concerns the child's position in the family and in relation to the parents, and the second is death taboo.

A key feature of the Chinese family has long been the mutual dependency of its individual members, while everyone is expected to be family-oriented, the parents are child-centered, and the child is supposed to seek parental advice on matters that concern themselves and care for the parents when they are of old age. The parent–child relationship is extremely close, or at least such closeness is the sociocultural norm to which all should aim to adhere. The combined effects of the economic reforms and the one-child policy have caused huge demographic shifts in the past few decades, significantly weakening the power of the family elders, reducing the degree of patriarchy, and transforming both childhood experiences and child-parent relations. While the changes have been far from uniform—there are significant urban–rural divides as well as regional differences among others—the one-child policy has undoubtedly contributed to the emergence of a new generation of children (especially urban children) who enjoy much greater parental attention and investment as well as significantly greater power within families of dramatically diminishing size (Naftali 2016, 70).

It is easy to understand that while the decline of fertility rate has caused a rise in value of a child, on the other side of the coin is rising anxieties and concerns over all aspects of the only child's life, safety and development, placing parents under enormous and constant pressure, and it is easy to anticipate that parents in one-child families demonstrate child-centeredness significantly more than parents with multiple children. This is why while grief caused by losing a child is natural in any culture, research finds that Chinese shidu parents' grief appears to be more intense than that of grievers in other cultures and situations (Zheng et al. 2017). Besides, it has long been a cultural principle that Chinese children should take care of their parents when the latter reach an advanced age, which gives rise to well-founded and widely held expectations on the part of the parents, and consequently a great sense of loss when those expectations are not met. Another reason that elderly parents often have to turn to their children is that social security and medical insurance have only covered a small portion of the population, and that the rural population enjoys neither the standard nor the availability of services that urban residents do. In a way, filial culture has shifted the responsibility of elderly care from the state to the younger generation both in principle and in practice. This could potentially cause enormous problems if the younger generation is absent.

It is important to note that the Law on the Protection of the Rights and Interests of the Elderly, amended in December 2012 and came into effect in July 2013, went further and made it a legal responsibility of the children to pay attention to the parents' emotional and spiritual needs, not to neglect the parents, to visit or greet the parents frequently if living apart. Employers are also required to guarantee employees' rights to take days off to visit their parents. While the state's position is clear and which is in line with long-held traditional beliefs and cultural practices, in reality the ambiguity of the provisions—such as 'visit frequently'—renders the law hard to enforce and remains mostly a reminder and guidance. How frequent is frequent enough? How should those who have failed to comply be punished? Is it possible, and indeed is it right, to try and catch every single one of those children failing to look after their parents properly? Should it really be a matter of the law? Should the fact that young people nowadays are under intense pressure to make a living be taken into account? And most importantly and sadly also ironically, this official position on filial responsibilities should make it particularly easy for both the state and society to understand shidu parents' pains.

While the firm Chinese belief in filiality and respect for the elderly is undeniable, tradition tends to be a mixed bag containing some controversial elements. For instance, traditional Confucian beliefs consider having no posterity extremely nonfilial. The death of the only child means the end of the bloodline, which is a sign of bad luck. For that reason, those without children may be culturally stigmatized for having failed to fulfil the responsibility of carrying on the family name and going extinct, although nowadays such pressure perhaps comes more from the past and within than the social contextual reality, especially in cities. However, the power and influence of tradition-induced stigma is difficult to measure. When the law says one thing and tradition says another, most people are probably not aware of the law, but everyone feels and lives tradition, whether or not they agree with it.

Furthermore, traditional beliefs also consider death a negative event, even a taboo, which hinders the search for and acceptance of grief counseling or other forms of professional or social intervention, rendering the already vulnerable even more so. Death taboo means that people would avoid speaking of mortality as if merely mentioning it would cause the inevitable event to happen sooner. Adults would refrain from talking about death in front of children to protect them; people would pay extra money for mobile numbers and registration plates to avoid the digit 4 as it sounds like the Mandarin word for death; few people would write their own will or register as organ doners for fear of bad luck and cursing themselves. The consequence of not speaking of the subject is not only a lack of courage but also a lack of knowledge and the necessary skills to deal with the tragedy when it happens.

Relatedly, the many different types of death of the only child may also determine how parents suffer. Han Shengxue, a family planning official responsible for implementing the one-child policy at the local level and to whom people affected by the policy could go and register grievances such as difficulties in applying for birth permits, contesting fines or requesting financial support, interviewed over 100 shidu families and depicted their sufferings in his book entitled 'A Report on Shidu Families in China', published in 2017 and constituted his own critical reflection on the impact of the policy and first-hand trueful depictions of the misery of this unique group who he was in a unique position to get to know. The fact that this book, which was written in Mandarin, was able to come out in a country where censorship operated was proof that the topic was not taboo, especially that now the one-child policy has officially been abolished. Chap. 2 of Han's book contains a number of cases detailing the different types of death of the only child, including fatal diseases, natural disaster, suicide, death from overwork, murder, car accident, fire and explosion due to negligence. While these could potentially happen to any child, shidu parents' loss is distinguishable from others, as their loss and vulnerability stem from the dutiful fulfilment of state-imposed duties in the name of the greater collective good and advancement of country and society, which should entitle them to special recognition from the state. Hence, in the face of insufficient support and inadequate understanding of their situation, it is not beyond the realm of imagination that their sense of being let down is understated.

It is important to dig deeper into this fact that their loss is an unintentional but entirely foreseeable consequence of state policy. This direct causal link could have very complex and dubious impacts on the parents themselves, whose very personal suffering, anger and other symptoms will be examined in the section below, and those around them, whose reactions or lack of reactions are telling of their appreciation of the policy as well as how the state and the individual interact. As will be shown in Sect. 3.4.3 below, social isolation is one of the many consequences that shidu parents have to live with, which in turn will cause many other physical and psychological difficulties. Although often self-imposed, fearing what others think of them is likely to be one of the driving forces. Looking at the matter from the other direction is also telling—how will the fact that the one-child policy has directly caused shidu parents' hardship affect the opinion and action of others?

There are many possibilities: for many, the fact that 'shidu' is a consequence of the one-child policy does not necessarily play that big a part in their reception of the situation—losing a child is losing a child which will generate actions of sympathy and kindness from any right-thinking person; there might also be those who deliberately not make the mental connection between state policy and shidu situation, due to the habit of not wanting to talk negatively about the state; there might also be those who find 'shidu' and its cause too painful a subject, do not want to know the details of the cases and keep a fair distance from shidu parents; there might also be those who choose to keep a distance from shidu parents simply because they do not want to appear to be intervening in private matters.

Having said that, without any intention to cause offence, it might also be worthwhile to consider another possibility by examining the relationship between social memory and individual memory. Social memory is a collective memory form with which individual memory is in a complex interactive relationship. In a communitarian society, any individual expression is likely to have some traces of the 'text' of the collective and is constrained by the social structure. Through communication and interaction with other members of society, individual memory containing both information and emotion expands into the public arena to become social memory, through which a sense of belonging, recognition and comfort are generated. This process of 'socialization' might cause alterations in individual memory.

For instance, first, scattered information and unique details of individual stories may become integrated and standardized into a uniform text; hence, although each and every single shidu story is different, when told publicly, they take on many common characteristics and adopt very similar tones, and among others, all tend to emphasize the causal link between the one-child policy and the shidu experience, which is likely to conceal the great variety of individual experiences, the complexity of individual intentions, the role of individual choices, and especially the lack of uniformity in the implementation of the one-child policy, leaving many loopholes and gaps, rendering the use of force not always present due to lack of necessity. Second, through social interactions, individual emotions may transform into rational expressions through which voices may be heard and demands may be made. Third, individual memory may become selective and magnify the negative aspects while ignore the positive elements, intentionally or unintentionally. This is not at all to deny the genuine suffering of shidu families and the undeniable causal link between state policy and their loss; rather, it is to remind ourselves that there are gaps to fill in every story and to emphasize the variety of individual experiences and the degree of diversity of shidu needs.

3.4.3 Diversity of Needs and Challenges

Considering the growing population of shidu parents and the lack of systematic investigation of the diverse health consequences arising in this group, it is important to pay more attention to the different facets of health problems in shidu families so as to contribute to the development of a comprehensive support system.

3.4.3.1 Financial Hardship

As already noted, the Chinese government has taken measures to mitigate the negative effects of the one-child policy but has focused mostly on financial and material support, such as raising the national standard subsidy. It has been suggested that increased subsidies and other material support have not improved the situation of shidu parents, as the difficulties that are socially and culturally induced have not been tentatively addressed (Zheng and Lawson 2014). It is also wrong to assume that all shidu families are experiencing financial hardship. Han (2017, 244) notes the words of a shidu petitioner during an interview, who criticizes the state for labelling shidu families 'family-planning households with special difficulties', and says that many shidu parents are after state and societal recognition for their sacrifices rather than monetary assistance, as many do not have financial difficulties. Research has also noted that some shidu parents refuse financial and material support from the state as it arouses their helplessness and self-pity (Yin et al. 2018a, b). This is not to deny that many shidu families are experiencing financial difficulties, especially as they age, due to conditional and modest state financial support and lack of other income (Yu 2020). It is also important to remember that shidu parents whose children have died from a disease are likely to be in debt because they have spent a lot of money on medical care for them.

3.4.3.2 Mental and Physical Consequences

Comparative research on shidu parents and parents with living children finds that the former are significantly more vulnerable in mental and physical well-being in terms of health self-assessment, satisfaction with life, anxiety and depression, self-guilt, loss of self-worth, and chronic diseases (Yin et al. 2018a, b; Cao et al. 2018; Yu et al. 2020), and that mental challenges are one of the most obvious difficulties confronting this population. Many studies have suggested that death, especially sudden death, of a loved one is an important risk factor for mental illnesses such as depression and posttraumatic stress disorder (PTSD) (Yin et al. 2018a, b). General studies on parental bereavement provide important insights as well as theoretical and analytical perspectives to understand shidu families, but most of these studies are on losing spouses, siblings and other family members, very few are specifically about losing an only child, which raises different concerns and, as explained previously, in the Chinese context there are intertwined reasons which render losing an only child in China a rather different experience from losing an only child in another country. Research shows that Chinese shidu parents suffer from a number of mental difficulties. Below is far from an exhausted list.

Prolonged Grief

Prolonged grief disorder (PGD) is a qualitatively unique grief-related disorder distinct from ordinary grief, bereavement-related depression, anxiety, posttraumatic stress disorder and other mood disorders; it is also a disorder considered to be requiring further study. Individuals who suffer from this disorder experience notable dysfunction for atypically long periods of time following a significant loss, demonstrating core symptoms including an intense longing for the deceased accompanied by intense emotional pain. It is also characterized by difficulties in engaging in enjoyable social activities, a reduced ability to experience a positive mood, and refusal to accept the death of the loved one. Such bereavement difficulties persist or grow rather than diminish with time (Jordan and Litz 2014). So far little attention has been focused on the potential risks of prolonged grief in the Chinese population, let alone among shidu parents, causing a lack of empirical evidence as well as the absence of an explicit description of the full spectrum of symptoms experienced by shidu parents (Zhang et al. 2020).

Zhang et al. (2020) showed that a significant proportion (22.2%) of the shidu parents interviewed met the criteria for the disorder, and that significant differences existed between the PGD-positive group and the PGD-negative group in terms of the parent's gender, economic status of the family, age of the parents at the time of child loss, and time since loss: the PGD-positive group comprised significantly more females than the PGD-negative group; the economic status of 90.9% of the PGD-positive group was poor or moderate; the age of the parents in the PGD-positive group was three years older than those in the PGD-negative group; and the 'time since loss' in the PGD-positive group was shorter than that in the PGD-negative group. It should be noted that while 22.2% of the subjects were classified as PGD-positive, 62.4% of all the parents experienced daily longing, 40.9% experienced daily emotional pain, sorrow or grief, 37.6% demonstrated cognitive, emotional and behavioral symptoms of avoidance behavior daily, 36.9% had trouble accepting the loss, and 36.9% felt stunned, shocked or dazed daily (Zhang et al. 2020). Evidently, shidu is an extremely painful experience.

Post-traumatic Stress Disorder

Wang et al. (2021) conducted a literature review and meta-analysis using eight articles covering 2,722 shidu parents, of whom 1,270 were identified as PTSD cases. They found that the prevalence of PTSD among shidu parents ranged from 23.78% to 72.29%, and the pooled prevalence was 46.8%, which was significantly higher than that among bereaved Chinese adults and thereby confirmed that the loss of an only child was a significant predictor of PTSD. Nine risk factors, including demographic characteristics and loss-related features, were examined. Among the demographic characteristics, gender, education, and income were associated with PTSD in this group. Particularly worth noting is that, first, shidu mothers were found to be at a higher risk of experiencing PTSD than shidu fathers, which was consistent with previous findings. Females are believed to be more sensitive to stress hormones and threats, which possibly reduce their ability to manage stressful situations and cause them to behave more negatively when confronted with trauma. Hence, interventions for PTSD should pay more attention to shidu mothers.

Second, parents with higher education levels were found to be more likely to develop PTSD than those with lower education levels. This finding was different from the results reported by other researchers who found that the lower the education level the more likely it was to develop PTSD (Cadichon et al. 2017). It seems that the relationship between the level of education and PTSD prevalence among shidu parents needs to be further examined. Third, lower income was found to be associated with a higher prevalence of PTSD among shidu parents, which was consistent with previous findings that income had a negative association with general well-being and suicidal ideation (Wei et al. 2016; Wang et al. 2019b). And the influence goes both ways—the loss of the only child may not only cause mental illnesses but also entail financial hardship, posing a threat especially to later-life quality, ultimately aggregating mental illnesses of shidu parents. Considering the relationship between gender and PTSD, it would be worthwhile to examine in future studies whether gender may moderate the relationship between income and PTSD among shidu parents (Wang et al. 2021).

Among loss-related features, gender of the child and time since loss were predictors of PTSD among shidu parents. Shidu parents who lost daughters had a higher prevalence of PTSD than those who lost sons—a noteworthy finding considering that many in China still have a preference for sons over daughters. Wang et al. (2019b) and Zhang and Jia (2018) also explored the relationship between the gender of the lost child and PTSD in shidu parents, and found that mothers who lost daughters were more likely to suffer from PTSD than mothers who lost sons, indicating a deeper emotional bond between mothers and daughters. These findings once again emphasize that the mental health of shidu mothers is worthy of urgent attention. Perhaps more studies should also aim to further clarify the relationship between the gender of the child and the development of PTSD in shidu fathers. Furthermore, the longer time since loss was found to be associated with a lower prevalence of PTSD, and having a grandchild was found in this study not to be associated with PTSD among Chinese shidu parents, which contradicts the results of previous research. Calhoun et al. (2010) found that shidu parents' having a grandchild was significantly negatively associated with posttraumatic growth, which makes more sense than the findings of Wang et al. (2021), as in Chinese culture which regards filial piety and the continuation of bloodlines as of vital importance, the death of the only child fatally challenges shidu parents' value of continuation of the family line. In such a situation, having a grandchild is a comfort as the bloodline continues, which could alleviate some pain (Calhoun et al. 2010).

Two findings are worthy of particular attention. First, the age of the child was not associated with PTSD among shidu parents, which was different from the results of previous studies. For instance, Johannesson et al. (2011) found that parents who had lost younger children seemed to have a higher risk of developing mental disorders than those who had lost adult children. Second and perhaps surprisingly, the cause of the child's death was also not associated with PTSD among shidu parents, which contradicted the results of other research that found that PTSD was more severe after sudden and violent deaths than natural deaths (Rogers et al. 2008). Sudden or violent deaths were also found to be crucial risk factors for other mental conditions, such as grief, depression and anxiety disorders of bereaved parents, as such completely unexpected or unusually distressing events rendered parents unprepared and difficult to adapt to the death (Harper et al. 2014; Cao et al. 2018).

It is also important to note that while studies have recognized the mental and psychological consequences of losing a loved only child, very few have addressed in detail the physical effects. Yin et al. (2018a, b) showed that there was a higher morbidity in coronary heart disease, tumors, mental illnesses and other unclassified diseases among the shidu population than among the non-shidu population. These diseases and the consequent death are closely related to the long-term psychological suffering caused by losing the only child. It is important to note that the shidu parents in Yin et al. (2018a, b) became shidu only one year ago, and for parents who have been shidu longer, the physical as well as mental consequences could be significantly more severe than the study's findings suggest.

Suicide Ideation

Suicide, which is often regarded as a direct consequence of long-term mental disorders, is not well studied among Chinese shidu parents. As a major problem worldwide, it has been found to be one of the primary health causes of mortality. China had one of the highest suicide rates in the world during the 1990s—at approximately 23 deaths per 100,000 people—and suicide was one of the top five causes of death at the time. But the overall suicide rate has been decreasing rapidly over the past decades, which is in line with global trends. Data from the WHO show that China's suicide rate in 2016 was 7.9 deaths per 100,000 people; Chinese data show that the suicide rate in 2019 was 5.29 deaths per 100,000. The reasons for this continuous decrease are, first, controlled sale and purchase of pesticides. The majority of suicides committed in China had been through taking pesticides or poisoning. Nowadays, some of the highly toxic pesticides have been phased out, and pesticides can only be purchased at specific locations and with proof of identification of the buyer. Also, the decline in rural population who work on the farm and therefore have easy access to pesticides should also be a contributing factor. Second, a significant decrease in suicide among women could be a consequence of their rising social position and growing opportunities. And third, the success rate of suicide has dropped, owing to better awareness, improved suicide prevention programmes and medical care.

Suicidal ideation is an important predictor and inevitable stage for suicidal behavior, and studies have reported a high prevalence of suicidal ideation among bereaved parents. A study reports that Chinese shidu parents demonstrate a high prevalence of suicidal ideation at approximately 11.24% out of 507 respondents, which is even higher than that of the Wenchuan earthquake survivors (9.06%) (Wang et al. 2019a). There were significant differences among sociodemographic variables of social status, marital status, chronic disease, gender and education. Respondents in the poor group had the highest prevalence of suicidal ideation. Those who were in an unhappy marriage had a higher prevalence of suicidal ideation. Those with post-traumatic stress disorder were more likely to endorse suicidal ideation than those without. And those who had experienced stigma had a significantly higher prevalence of suicidal ideation. Suicidal ideation was also more prevalent among women, which could be attributed to gender roles and the general social position of women compared to men, particularly because mothers would tend to spend more time raising the only child and have a greater emotional attachment to the family (Wang et al.

2019a). Additionally, Lee et al. (2014) indicated that mothers were also more likely to suffer substantial financial stress than fathers after the death of a child. These findings suggest that, as is the case with other mental difficulties, suicide prevention for shidu parents should also primarily focus on females, especially those with financial difficulties.

3.4.3.3 Everyday Care and Elderly Care

This section will not repeat what has already been mentioned previously. It is necessary to point out, however, that while the government foresaw the issue of shidu elderly care arising from the one-child policy, it was perhaps too optimistic about its solutions, seemingly believing that the problem could solve itself through continuous economic development. Shidu elderly care is now a serious social problem in China. First, not all elderly people have stable sources of income, or enough income, to support themselves. While they are still young and healthy, this may not be a serious issue, as they age, the impact will be felt more vividly, as the costs of medical care, elderly care and burial have been increasing rapidly over the years. Second, there is a severe shortage of elderly care facilities and personnel in China, and the quality of elderly care is far from satisfactory especially in less developed places. According to the Ministry of Civil Affairs, at the end of 2020, there were over two million old people staying in 40,000 senior care homes, with only 370,000 personnel and 200,000 carers—in other words, every carer needs to look after 10 on average. Third, as already mentioned previously, it is Chinese tradition for parents to rely on their children for elderly support, and senior care homes are only considered to be the last resort under normal circumstances. This widely held sociocultural perception is likely to have an emotional impact on shidu parents, causing discomfort, intensified suffering and self-imposed social isolation.

3.4.3.4 Rural–Urban Divide

As is the case with many issues covered in this book, the rural–urban divide is also an important feature here. The exact size of rural shidu population is difficult to say due to a lack of official data. Despite the fact that many rural households did not adhere to the one-child policy, given that the death rate of rural only children is believed to be twice as high as that of urban only children, one may confidently say that the number of rural shidu families is rising. Most of the difficulties and challenges confronting urban shidu parents examined above are equally applicable to rural shidu parents but to a higher degree. For instance, while rural living costs are likely to be significantly lower than those in cities, since the average income of the rural population is also significantly lower than that of the urban population, and pension and insurance coverage is extremely low, financial hardship is likely to be one of the shidu difficulties. The situation could only worsen as rural shidu parents age and begin to have health problems, since medical services in the countryside are of a significantly lower standard than those in cities, which will not only worsen their financial situation but also leave their conditions improperly treated, particularly mental and psychological conditions that have not yet received proper recognition in the countryside.

However, the most serious challenge confronting rural shidu parents is likely to be inadequate social support. While the loss of the only child should be able to generate a great deal of sympathy from the local community, as is often the case in cities, research has found that the loss of the only child has often caused originally good social relations to rapidly deteriorate in the countryside due to the still widely held superstitious beliefs that the loss of a child and therefore the end of the bloodline is bad luck and karma. This will cause rural shidu parents to feel the discrimination, isolation and powerlessness particularly vividly, and the lack of communication with those around, lack of meaningful and supportive social relations, will not help rural shidu parents relieve their psychological stress or seek support. Such a general atmosphere implies many dangers, including but not limited to unattended elderly parents with long-term illnesses falling ill while no one is around, leading to delay in rescue. Also, stigma and taboo surrounding the loss of a child, mental disorders and suicide are likely to prevent those with serious mental difficulties, those who are thinking of taking their own lives, or those who have previously attempted suicide, from seeking the help they urgently need.

3.4.4 Micro and Macro Support

It is wrong to say that shidu parents' pains and needs are continuously overlooked by society, but society has not yet found the way to delicately look after them. As already mentioned above, there has been an increase in the number of case studies in recent years, which would inspire debate on current policies affecting shidu families. Their findings reveal that shidu parents do have various sources of support, including the state/government, community/society, family, and other individuals especially those with similar shidu experiences, with the former two constituting formal support systems and the latter two informal (Shen et al. 2016, 49). It has also been found that out of all possible sources of support and in order of preference, shidu parents most value support from their other halves, the government, followed by those with similar shidu experience (Shen et al. 2016, 49). Two things are worth highlighting.

First, while it is only natural that anyone's primary source of support tends to be their close relatives, the fact that when experiencing loss one immediately turns to what Charles Cooley calls 'primary group' in *Social Organization: A Study of the Larger Mind* (1909) for support is a sign that the society in which they are situated is a traditional one with characteristics of an agricultural society such as limited sources of state and societal support and underdeveloped third sector organizations, rendering it necessary for citizens in need of comfort to turn to informal support especially that coming from family members. Second, the fact that an equally large number of shidu parents expect some form of government support is perhaps more noteworthy. While in a developed welfare society in which the support system is efficient and responsive, expecting state support at difficult times is natural and may be interpreted as trust in the state; in China, the driving force behind such expectations is more likely to be politically charged emotions than anything else, telling of the relation between the state and its people, between the collective and the individual.

In an authoritarian country such as China, in which the interaction between the state and its people is not only limited but fixated on certain issues only, any support from the state by whatever means will also be interpreted in a limited and fixed way. While in developed welfare societies state support is considered entitlement and realization of rights, in communitarian China it is first and foremost representation of authority and mainstream societal recognition, which represents the widest possible support be it real or perceived. While state support or compensation is valuable to shidu parents, what makes it invaluable is precisely the fact that it comes from the state. Politically, this reveals the relation between the state and its people as one of giving and receiving; emotionally and as case studies and the small-scale protests show, an increasing number of shidu parents now consider the state's one-child policy to be solely responsible for their shidu status, hence expecting the state to make up for the loss they alone have to suffer as a result of fulfilling a controversial duty. All this should be remembered when reforming the support system.

3.4.4.1 Quiet Support and Timely Response

As a result of continuous advocacy efforts from various parties over the years, Chinese society is now aware of the unique situation of shidu parents and is willing and able to pay more attention, except that what might be the best way forward is unclear despite both the state and society recognizing the necessity of better protection. The best policy can only arise from tentative observation of the shidu reality, which should have two key features: the first is 'quietness', and the second is 'timeliness' or 'responsiveness'. Unlike the other disadvantaged groups covered in this book, both advocacy and support services related to shidu parents need to be relatively low-key given the unique psychological and emotional reality of the group. Apart from stigma, which may prevent shidu parents from telling the truth about their loss and its impact, it is also natural that some disadvantaged people do not want to be viewed by others as disadvantaged and weak, as evident in the fact that some shidu parents will make up stories about the whereabouts of their children, others never pick up government subsidies, and many live in relative social isolation. It seems that the best possible way of supporting them is by designing multidimensional and multilayered policies that are easily accessible, low-key but highly sensitive so as to detect and respond to shidu needs in a timely manner.

Using psychological interventions as an example, a low-key, sensitive and highly responsive intervention programme would divide shidu parents into stages, for instance, the early traumatic stage (when the loss has either just taken place or time since loss has not been long), the convalescence stage (or the calming down period when shidu parents have to an extent adjusted to the loss and begun to improve), and the stable period. During the early period, the methods used should be those of crisis intervention, taking full account of newly shidu parents' severe shock and intense pain, which would require the relevant personnel to quickly gain their trust in order to effectively communicate and efficiently respond. The aim at this early stage should be short-term, to detect dangerous signals and respond to problems when they occur. At the convalescence stage, methods should be more forward-looking, focusing particularly on helping shidu parents adjust to the childless new life, to maintain or build new social relations, and to explore the family's potential in self-betterment and social development. All methods of intervention should be carried out on the basis of having acquired shidu parents' first-hand account of their needs and difficulties. Reaching the stable stage should not mean the end of social intervention, although intervention can become more reactive and focuses more on observing the changes in shidu parents' situation and needs, especially as they approach old age.

3.4.4.2 Resilience and Empowerment

Resilience refers to one's ability to adapt to difficult situations and the capacity to recover quickly from difficulties; for instance, some shidu parents are able to exercise rational choices and initiate the healing process and recover more quickly than others. This positive psychological basis is the foundation upon which empowerment is built and becomes a possibility. The aim of empowerment is to develop and strengthen shidu families' original power, which enables further self-help and realization of self-worth through a number of possible means.

The first is peer support or peer guidance, which means that individuals with the same or similar experiences share information, ideas or behavioral skills with each other as a form of social support. It is an effective and reliable means of comforting and empowering people in difficulty and plays an important role in socially and psychologically supporting shidu families in need. It is essential that shidu parents should not only be given the opportunity to receive peer support; more importantly, they should have the chance of receiving adequate training so that they are able to play the role of the helper. Through helping and comforting other shidu parents with similar experience, helpers can discover their own strength and realize their own self-worth, thereby further enhancing their own mental health.

The second is recreational or educational activities in a group. Sociological theories hold that humans are natural social animals, for whom contact with others is a natural human need. And humans form groups normally out of two kinds of needs, the first is instrumental, the second is expressive. Expressive needs are satisfied in a group that provides emotional support and opportunities for self-expression so that group members may let out their emotions and desires, which can minimize feelings of loneliness. Furthermore, according to activity theory, elderly people with higher levels of activity are more socially adaptable and more easily satisfied than those with lower levels of activity, which is supported by research that shows that shidu parents who frequently take part in group recreational or educational activities are more energetic, happier, and even look younger.

The third and closely related is voluntary work. Abraham Maslow's hierarchy of needs holds that the needs for self-actualization, personal esteem and feelings of accomplishment are the most important and complex human needs. Based on this theory and to help shidu parents more actively reintegrate into society, some NGOs have established mutual aid associations and invite physically and emotionally capable shidu parents to join as volunteers. It is found that doing voluntary work can greatly enhance shidu parents' sense of self-identity and pride, causing both their mood and sense of responsibility to improve significantly.

3.4.4.3 Further Development

It thus seems that the three key aims of further policy development in this field should be to further increase public attention to the welfare of this group, to continuously improve provision of resources and services, and to build up shidu parents' own capacity to self-help as well as to help others. At the macro level, policies should develop a more compassionate approach and be more sensitive and knowledgeable toward shidu realities and challenges, particularly the degree of diversity of these realities and challenges. It is also important to reshape some of the existing state strategies to enable more inclusive and more equal access to support, and to consider whether it would be possible and appropriate, and if so under what circumstances, to expand some of the policies and services to cover those parents whose only child is disabled. More importantly, society's potential in supporting shidu parents is far from fully realized. For shidu parents to make better sense of their loss and to grieve better, policy-making and implementation should aim to create a grief-literate society for both the shidu parents and everyone else (Fang 2020; Breen 2020). This requires directing and integrating more public and social resources, both material and educational, medicating and coordinating the services and actions of different individuals, organizations, communities, governments, NGOs, and bringing them together into a tight coalition to cater for the diverse needs of shidu parents.

Furthermore, among other things, urgent attention needs to be paid to the development of more holistic policies for those largely neglected end-of-life issues. With the aim of helping and soothing a shidu parent who is dying, such care should aim to prevent or relieve suffering as much as possible and to maintain the quality of life while respecting the dying person's wishes. Shidu parents should be granted easier access to a greater range of information, resources and guidance so as to understand how to prepare for what is to come. A dignified and peaceful death means different things to different people, although it is common that people would choose to be surrounded by family and friends at their very last moments. But shidu parents may not get to choose. It is important for the relevant policies and arrangements to be discursive enough to take into account their unique circumstances and to ensure their wishes are fully listened to. Should these dying shidu parents not have anyone who is in a position to take care of the relevant procedures and costs, local governments ought to step in.

3.5 Concluding Part II: Exclusion and Opportunity

Part II has attempted to present an exploration of the dynamics of shidu parents' experiences in facing and dealing with their vulnerability as they age childlessly, reaffirming the observations of existing studies regarding their challenges and risks, which are wide-ranging. Unlike some of the other groups examined in this project, the case of shidu parents is relatively straightforward as in who should carry the duty and what more needs to be done, and compared to the other groups, it is also relatively easy for them to gain sympathy, societal recognition and state support, as the uniqueness of their situation and difficulties are easy to understand. Given that the one-child policy, which was the cause of their situation, has now been officially abolished, it has become increasingly easy to openly discuss, even magnify, its negative impacts—some of which, for instance a rapidly aging society—have been apparent for all to see and acknowledged by the state. It seems that this is one of many areas in China that would need to wait for the state to make a move first at the top and then things will move downward and spread. In this case, the state has already made a move. It is hoped that with accelerated aging occurring in China, more attention will be given to this group, which will be affected by it most uniquely.

References

Breen L et al (2020) Grief literacy: a call to action for compassionate communities. Death Stud. https://doi.org/10.1080/07481187.2020.1739780

Cadichon JM, Lignier B, Cenat JM, Derivois D (2017) Symptoms of PTSD among adolescents and young adult survivors six year after the 2010 Haiti Earthquake. J Loss Trauma 22(8)

Calhoun LG, Tedeschi RG, Cann A, Hanks EA (2010) Positive outcomes following bereavement: paths to posttraumatic growth. Psychol Belgica 50:125–143

Cao X, Chongming Y, Dahua W (2018) the impact on mental health of losing an only child and the influence of social support and resilience. OMEGA J Death Dying 80(4):666–684

Chen Y (2018) From passivity to initiative: resilience construction for child-bereft elderly to cope with pension risk. Soc Work Manage 17(1):63–68

Choi SYP, Peng Y (2016) Masculine compromise. University of California Press, Oakland

England P, Folbre N (1999) 'The cost of caring', annals of the American Academy of political and social science by sage. J Online 561:39–51

Fair Labor Association (2012) Independent investigation of apple suppliers. Foxconn Report Highlights. http://www.fairlabor.org/sites/default/files/documents/reports/foxconn_investigation_report.pdf

Fang C (2020) Dynamics of Chinese shidu parents' vulnerability in old age—a qualitative study. J Popul Aging. https://doi.org/10.1007/s12062-020-09293-4

Goodman DSG (2014) Class in contemporary China. Polity, Cambridge

Han S (2017) A Report on the shidu families in China (《中国失独家庭调查》). Qunzhong Press, Beijing (in Chinese)

Hardt M, Negri A (2004) Multitude: war and democracy in the age of empire. The Penguin Press, New York

Harper M, O'Connor RC, O'Carroll RE (2014) Factors associated with grief and depression following the loss of a child: a multivariate analysis. Psychol Health Med 19(3):247–252

Hochschild AR (1983) The managed heart: commercialisation of human feeling. University of California Press, Berkeley

Hu X (2011) China's new underclass: paid domestic labor. Routledge, Abingdon

Lee C, Glei DA, Weinstein M, Goldman N (2014) Death of a child and parental wellbeing in old age: evidence from Taiwan. Soc Sci Med. 2014;101:166–173

Johannesson KB et al (2011) Prolonged grief among traumatically bereaved relatives exposed and not exposed to a tsunami. J Trauma Stress 24(4):456–464

Jordan AH, Litz BT (2014) Prolonged grief disorder: diagnostic, assessment, and treatment considerations. Prof Psychol Res Pract 45(3):180–187

Lu J, Lu Y (2014) Analysis on the current issues and reforms of support schemes for shidu families. J Chin Acad Govern 2014(6):33–38

Montes V (2013) The role of emotions in the construction of masculinity: Guatemalan migrant men, transnational migration, and family relations. Gender & Society 27(4):469–490

Naftali O (2016) Children in China. Polity, Cambridge

National Bureau of Statistics (2020) The 2019 Monitoring Report on Rural Migrants (《2019年农民工监测调查报告》) , 30th April 2020, Beijing, at http://www.stats.gov.cn/tjsj/zxfb/202004/t20200430_1742724.html (in Chinese)

Ngai P (2016) Migrant labor in China. Polity, Cambridge

Rogers CH et al (2008) Long-term effects of the death of a child on parents' adjustment in midlife. J Fam Psychol 22(2):203–211

Shen C, Long X, Bingying S, Li, Pingjv, Qi T (2016) Research on the assistance and social support network for Shidu families (《失独家庭救助与社会支持网络体系研究》). East China University of Science and Technology Press, Shanghai (in Chinese)

Song Y (2014) Losing an only child: the one-child policy and elderly care in China. Reprod Health Matters 22(43):113–124

Students & Scholars against Corporate Misbehavior (2010) Workers as machines: military management in Foxconn. https://www.somo.nl/wp-content/uploads/2010/08/military-management-in-Foxconn.pdf

Tong X (2018) Gendered labor regimes: on the organizing of domestic workers in urban China. Asian J Ger Eur Stud 3:14

Wang Q, Ren L, Wenhao W, Weihua X, Yang W (2019a) 'The relationship between posttraumatic stress disorder and suicidal ideation among Shidu parents: the role of stigma and social support'. BMC Psychiatry 19:352

Wang Q, Xu W, Ren L, Wang W, Wang Y (2019b) The relationship between hope and posttraumatic stress disorder in Chinese Shidu parents: the medicating role of perceived stress. J Affect Disord 251:23–30

Wang Q et al (2021) Prevalence and risk factors of posttraumatic stress disorder among Chinese shidu parents: a systemic review and meta-analysis. J Affect Disord 282(2021):1180–1186

Wei Y, Jiang Q, Gietel-Basten S (2016) The well-being of bereaved parents in an only-child society. Death Stud 40(1):22–31

Wu F, Zhang F, Webster C (eds) (2014) Rural migrants in urban China. Routledge, Abingdon

Yin Q et al (2018a) An investigation of physical and mental health consequences among Chinese parents who lost their only child. BMC Psychiatry 18:45. https://doi.org/10.1186/s12888-018-1621-2

Yin Q, Zhuoer S, Weizhi L (2018b) Mini review: the mental and physical consequences of Chinese Shidu parents. J Ment Health Clin Psychol 2(3):1–4

Yu G, Lenny C-H, Yu F, Zheng Y, Liu X (2020) Exploring the lived experience of old Chinese "Shidu" parents who lost their only child: a phenomenology study. Cult Psychol 26(4):837–849

Zhang Y, Jia X (2018). A qualitative study on the grief of people who lose their only child: from the perspective of familism culture. Front. Psychol. 9:869

Zhang H et al (2020) Prolonged grief disorder in Chinese Shidu parents who have lost their only child.' Eur J Psychotraumatol 11:1726071

Zheng Y, Lawson TR (2014) Identity reconstruction as shiduers: narratives from Chinese older adults who lost their only child. Int J Soc Welfare 24(4)

Zheng Y, Lawson TR, Head BA (2017) Our only child has died—a Study of bereaved older Chinese parents. Faculty Publications, School of Social Work, George Fox University. https://digitalcommons.georgefox.edu/sw_fac/13

Chapter 4
Ethno-Religious Diversity and Sinicization

Ethnic and religious groups are classic minorities under international human and minority rights law, but their lived realities in China are not easy to evaluate, as while they are the most systematically protected 'otherness' on paper, conflicting evidence of the degree of tolerance and accommodation has demanded closer examination. While in general the situation of religion is considered to be worse than that of ethnic minorities, since religion is alien to the vast majority, it has not attracted as much interest, whereas much attention has been given to ethnic groups in the past decades both internally and internationally. While never having turned a blind eye to internal cultural, ethnic and religious diversity, China portraying itself as a harmonious state with a well-documented turbulent past has caused the country to hold unity, stability and territorial integrity above all, which makes the minority question—symbolized by difference, dissent, special treatment—a difficult one to openly ask let alone answer. This also sets the tone for the treatment of religions in China.

Studying Chinese ethnic and religious minorities is difficult, not only materials remain hard to acquire, the reliability of those that are accessible remains open to interpretation, and much of the limited academic literature on this topic published in the Chinese language tends to focus on presenting historical developments, especially betterment, of the regime rather than providing critical evaluation of its problems. This may or may not be as big a problem as some would suggest, as first China has made some remarkable progresses in the past decades in this field in that many aspects of previously outdated law have crystallized into standards that are comparable with those in Western countries and at the international level; second, it has long been proven throughout the country's modern history that importing any system of international standards without tender consideration and accurate understanding of the particularities of the national context, especially the historical context, is impossible.

However, an overly contextual approach should be avoided. This chapter has two main aims. The first is to provide an overview of the development of the regime, especially the relevant laws, policies and programmes protecting ethnic diversity and religious freedom, focusing not only on legal reforms but also on the changing

H. H. Wei, *Sociocultural Otherness and Minority Justice: A Study on China*,
Ius Gentium: Comparative Perspectives on Law and Justice 88,
https://doi.org/10.1007/978-981-16-9752-4_4

attitudes of both the government and general public. The second is to identify key challenges and obstacles to better recognition and evaluate the plausibility of possible remedies. All is placed within the wider context of Chinese society and politics in exploration of the possibility of a more just, functional and realistic regime for the protection of ethnic and religious diversity in China.

4.1 Part I: Ethnic Diversity and the Chinese State

4.1.1 Protection of Ethnic Minorities: An Overview

China's position on ethnic diversity is complex and constantly changing, and some background contextual facts are necessary to make sense of the developments in the field, their value and impact. The end of the Cultural Revolution in 1976 saw the immediate commence of a period of rapid reforms, replacing radical ideologies with a single-minded quest for economic advancement and overall modernisation of the state. Opening-up exposed the isolated Chinese society to 'the other' reality, which led many to demand not only knowledge and money but also freedom and rights. The period following the student movements of 1989 was much more stable than the West had expected, and China continued to zoom ahead economically, which led to an upgrade in political status at the international stage.

The country's top-down reforms of the ethnic minority rights regime are best understood against not only this recent history but also that of globalization. While critics of globalization accuse it of intensifying inequalities and of giving the misimpression that cultural differences may be eliminated, which is contrary to the ideal and detrimental to many aspects of ethnic minority protection, globalization has also benefited cultural diversity in that it is through processes of globalization that diverse cultures and peoples encounter and interact with each other, which may cause fascination with 'the other', coexistence of cultural differences, and of course also conflicts. In the case of China, it is indeed largely due to globalization that China has become aware of international standards and practices, and its ethnic minorities have become a popular case study of 'when the local meets the global', and it is also only in the era of globalization that China's relations with its own ethnic minorities, who are very small in number and very insignificant in power, may attract global attention.

4.1.2 Ethnic Minorities and Cultural Justice

4.1.2.1 Which Minorities?

The absence of a universally accepted definition of minority rights means that it is not beyond doubt that certain rights exist while others do not, although they are *most commonly* defined or *perceived* as those special rights granted only to members of a recognized minority group, and while most of these rights are individualistic in nature, others, some have forcefully argued, are collective (Kymlicka 2007, Chap. 7). The line between individualistic rights and collective rights begins to blur when the group in question is a cultural or linguistic group, as cultures and languages are necessarily *collective* phenomena, yet many if not all cultural and linguistic rights are held and exercised by the *individual* members of the group, although the group as a collective entity shares the benefits. The International Covenant on Civil and Political Rights (ICCPR) of 1966 was the very first international instrument of a universal nature to contain a provision specifically intended to protect minorities, with Article 27 stating: '[in] those states in which ethnic, religious or linguistic minorities exist, persons belonging to such minorities shall not be denied the right, in community with other members of their group, to enjoy their own culture, to profess and practice their own religion, or use their own language.' To date, this provides the authoritative three essential characteristics of a qualified minority group: *ethnic, religious* and *linguistic* differences, although the actual identification process is often a complex jurisprudential exercise in terms of both criteria and procedure.

The Chinese approach is similar to that of the Council of Europe, which targets the so-called 'national minorities', which commonly refer to 'territorial minorities', 'substate national groups', or 'historically settled homeland groups', which are often used interchangeably in academic literature (Kymlicka 2007, 203). Along similar lines, China has identified fifty-six 'nationalities' based on ethnic, linguistic and religious characteristics, with Han Chinese being by far the majority and the remaining fifty-five as 'national minorities', which makes it the least homogenous country in the region and possibly the world. While some identified minority nationalities are very close in cultural tradition to the Han majority, others, such as the Kazaks and the Uyghurs, have very different cultural practices, languages and religious beliefs and share much greater similarities with Central Asian and Middle Eastern countries. Indeed, these groups having closer cultural ties with foreign lands than with the state in which they situate is the reason why strong minority rights such as *self-governance* and *autonomy* are treated with suspicion by the state.

4.1.2.2 Which Rights?

China has a wide range of laws, resolutions, white papers, decisions of the Standing Committee of the National People's Congress as well as state-sponsored programmes and schemes that target the protection of national minorities. The most (or as some would argue, the least) significant of which is the Constitution. Despite having been criticized as merely aspirational and lacking the kind of legal authority other countries' Constitutions have, three details ought to be observed. The first is that on 14 March 2004, at the 10th National People's Congress, a general provision on human rights was entailed, with article 33 being inserted, which expressly states that 'The State respects and preserves human rights'—a symbolic move at the time. The second is that the Preamble of the Constitution declares that 'it is necessary to combat big-nation chauvinism, mainly Han chauvinism, and also necessary to combat local national chauvinism. The state does its utmost to promote the common prosperity of all nationalities in the country.' It should be noted that officially, Han chauvinism is being treated as a phenomenon of the past, but in reality, especially at times of serious terrorist threats, disparaging attitudes toward certain minority nationalities are strong and unapologetic, tolerated if not backed by official policies. The third is article 4, which grants rights including equality, nondiscrimination, linguistic rights, state assistance in economic and cultural developments, as well as regional autonomy and self-governance to qualified groups.

Similar to international and regional minority rights instruments, Article 4(1) sets the limits of these rights and freedoms, namely, territorial integrity, national unity and public order. The problem is that while we might be able to agree on the general principles, we cannot agree on what actions might damage territorial integrity and political unity and how. The impairment of territorial integrity is more likely to be a complex, gradual and long process rather than a one-off event, or it can be a whole chain of one-off events. A one-off action warranted by the Constitution might have no *immediate* damaging effect on the political unity of the state and might not have been intended to ever have such an effect, and therefore ought to be accommodated and supported by the state; however, such a damaging effect might become apparent in the long run, intended or not, once or if the chain of events is complete. What the Constitution (as well as other relevant instruments that will be examined below) does not tell us is what the determining factor is—*intention* to impair the political unity of the sovereign state, or *actual consequences* (Wei 2016b).

Self-Governance, Autonomy and Political Participation

The rights to self-governance and autonomy, in theory, grant qualified minorities de facto control over an extensive range of internal group affairs in recognition of their ethnic and cultural distinctions as well as historical connections to the land, subject to strict conditions. The Preamble to the Law of the People's Republic of China on Regional National Autonomy 1984 (hereafter Autonomy Law) defines 'regional autonomy' as '[...] minority nationalities, under unified state leadership, practice regional autonomy in areas where they live in concentrated communities and set up organs of self-government for the exercise of the power of autonomy. Regional national autonomy embodies the state's full respect for and guarantee of the right of the minority nationalities to administer their internal affairs and its adherence to the principle of equality, unity and common prosperity for all its nationalities.'

The instrument also provides, in Chaps. 2 and 3, details of the autonomous governments' political and legislative powers and functions, relations with the central government, as well as contains provisions on issues such as facilitation of minority recruitment in this chapter, protection of minority linguistic and religious rights within the region in articles 10 and 11, and relations among the different nationalities living in the same autonomous area in Chap. 5. Among others, it is worth emphasizing that, according to article 17, the chairman of an autonomous region, the prefect of an autonomous prefecture or the head of an autonomous county must be a member of the minority nationality exercising regional autonomy; other posts within the autonomous governments should, whenever possible, be assumed by members of the minority group exercising autonomy or of other minority nationalities living in the region. This policy has been criticized for having enabled minority candidates to gain positions for which they are not qualified, resulting in lack of professionalism and efficiency in the administration. Article 49 requires Han officials working in minority autonomous regions to learn minority languages and minority officials to learn the mainstream Chinese language 'Putonghua'.

The Autonomy Law is evidence that China has, on paper, embraced progressive international minority rights norms, and it is worth noting that this instrument is not new—it has been in force since 1984. However, despite a wide range of impressive powers granted to autonomous governments, opinions regarding China's actual practice of regional autonomy vary greatly. Some argue that the instrument gives qualified minorities real control over their internal affairs; others say that they only have limited power over issues that the state does not consider politically sensitive; some regard the autonomous regimes as merely symbolic and incomparable to autonomous systems in other parts of the world. It also seems to be the case that different autonomous regions enjoy different degrees of autonomy and over different matters, but overall, autonomous rights and powers are much greater in the fields of economy and culture than in those concerning politics and security. In particular, it has been argued that autonomous regions in fact enjoy much less legislative power than ordinary provinces due to political situations, especially secessionist movements in certain minority regions (Zang 2015, 99), despite the fact that article 20 of the Autonomy Law delegates significant legislative powers to autonomous governments, including a qualified right to modify higher legislation.

While the rights to self-government and autonomy are international norms, the author has argued elsewhere in a different context that it should become a recognized fact that many minorities around the globe, including those in China, are not yet in a position to be meaningfully autonomous and urgently need their self-governing capacities upgraded in order to honor autonomy as the ultimate goal (Wei 2016a, 190–207). These capacities should include those to cope with and take advantage of unprecedented change swiftly and effectively; to preserve aspects of collective cultural identity in the face of rapid change; to identify the group's own interests, needs, evaluate opportunities and develop shared purposes and goals; in the absence of a relationship of trust with the state, to establish channels of dialog and communication with the state and independent bodies such as NGOs; to meaningfully participate in state and international decision-making and goal-setting; to develop and maintain continuous and dialogic relationships between the group's internal decision-making bodies and the group's own members, and with the state and the outside world. However, in the current Chinese context, much of these is irrelevant, as how active, capable and skilful national minorities could become entirely depends on whether the state allows them to be, so whether the minorities could make the transition from dependency, through assisted capacity-building and ultimately to meaningful autonomy depends on the state's willingness.

The state's willingness has seemingly manifested positively in one particular context—minority representation in the political system of the state. There are two aspects to this. The better known is guaranteed representation in the National People's Congress, which, despite being a rubber stamp for decisions already made by the ruling party and the central government, has in the past, occasionally, seen articulate delegates pushing for greater reforms. Hence, while each of the fifty-five recognized national minorities is guaranteed at least one seat, their contribution is almost entirely symbolic. In a second, less known aspect of minority participation in state politics, minority contribution is increasingly more visible, namely, that the Han-dominated Chinese government has made concerted efforts to appoint ethnic minorities to top leadership positions *outside* the autonomous regions.

There are two possible explanations. The first is to promote ethnic diversity in the political establishment, which is unlikely. There have always been ethnic minorities occupying important positions at various levels of the government, although it is questionable whether the promotion of diversity has been a consistent purposeful intent. Tying all groups together by showing that they share things in common—in this case positions in the establishment—is more important than emphasizing particularities and celebrating diversities. The second and related is to ease ethnic tensions, which presumes that ethnic minority elites are always representative of the interests of the ethnic group to which they belong.

It is important to note that members within each minority group are differentiated greatly in terms of status attainment, socioeconomic status and otherwise, and different levels of satisfaction in status lead to different political orientations. In the Chinese context, most minority elites are products of state affirmative action programmes (and are therefore thankful and loyal), have studied in Mandarin schools, have taken on Han social and cultural characteristics, and see acculturating into Han society and entering the state system as sociopolitical advancement rather than sociocultural sacrifice (Gladney 2004; Steiner 2010; Zang 2015). In other words, these minorities have benefited a great deal from state polices and integration into mainstream Chinese culture, and as a result, many, either wholeheartedly or pragmatically, have taken on the role of advancing the processes of integration of other minorities into the Han system. Besides, the nature of Chinese politics also means that when interests of the group conflict with those of the party state, ethnic elites are unable to protect the former, however high up they are in the establishment.

Religious Rights

Religion has been claimed to have filled the spiritual vacuum created by the decline in popular faith in socialist ideology in China (Mackerras 2003, 113). While such a statement has perhaps misunderstood the role of religion in the lives of ordinary Chinese, it is true though that religions, be they traditionally Chinese or foreign, have grown in recent years. The ruling Communist Party has adopted an overall tolerant approach to religious activities, although sometimes with conflicting signals. As early as in the *White Paper on Freedom of Religious Belief in China 1997*, the Chinese government acknowledged that widespread religious persecution took place during the Cultural Revolution and brought attention to continuous state efforts at rebuilding respect for religious freedom and diversity. Religious rights for all citizens are identified in article 36 of the Constitution, which aims to guarantee 'freedom of religious belief' and freedom from discrimination on religious grounds, while articles 36(3) and (4) set out limitations of these rights and freedoms by stressing that the state only protects 'normal' religious activities and that religious bodies must not be subject to 'foreign domination'.

The ruling Communist Party is an atheist organization that renders it inherently sceptical toward religion and explains why it keeps religious activities firmly under state control and never hesitates to suppress those that it considers destabling. The overall official tolerance has many reasons. One is the belief that religious influences will fade as socioeconomic circumstances of the people improve. In other words, religion is expected to take its own course toward extinction. Though reality seems to be that as socioeconomic circumstances improve, the distance between ordinary Chinese and the once upon a time far away West has been significantly reduced, the Chinese are now not only in a position to purchase (a great deal of) foreign goods and embrace (some) Western values but also have begun to flirt with Western religions. In reality, all religious groups, places of worship and relevant individuals must openly accept the leadership of the Communist Party and its government, and all religious associations are required by law to register with the state for status evaluation and approval, activities of self-proclaimed preachers are strictly prohibited, and religious activities must not be supportive of or tolerate separatism or disturb public order.

Among those Chinese to whom religion matters the most are perhaps national ethnic minorities, who are overall much more religious in customs, belief and practice than Han Chinese. Unlike Western countries, China has strict restrictions on religious education, and various regulations prohibit school-age children from entering religious places of worship or taking part in religious studies, although in reality, the enforceability of these restrictions is unclear, as religious studies could take place within the private home. In this respect, minorities are not entitled to any greater religious freedom than the Han majority (Castellino and Redondo 2006, 122). What does differentiate them from Han in terms of religious rights and freedoms—and like most international, regional and national minority rights provisions would provide—is that they are entitled to have their own religious holidays, have their dietary restrictions respected and upheld by all, and their religious practices are recognized and accommodated by the state.

It is necessary to point out that, first, China's attitude is similar to that of France, namely, that privately all is free, but in the public domain, religious freedom in the liberal sense is very limited. Second, while the law protects all recognized religions equally, in reality, as is the case in the West, attitudes toward different religions vary greatly, and in the Chinese context, they seem to depend entirely on how closely they are linked to foreign influences and, most importantly, secessionist movements. Third, it should be noted that not all minority traditions are interwoven with religion, and some are much more religious than others. One particularly noteworthy group is the ethnic minorities who are Communist Party members. The Central Committee of the Chinese Communist Party issued in March 1982 that all Party members would be allowed neither to believe in nor practice any religion, as the Party was founded on Marxism-Leninism and thus fundamentally atheist. However, it made an exception for minorities by arguing that since religion was an essential part of their customs, culture and social life, it would exclude the minority Communist Party members from their group if they were forbidden to take part in certain religious activities. Consequently, the policy forbids minority Communist Party members to have religious *beliefs* but allows them to take part in certain religious *practices* such as traditional festivals, rituals and weddings. However, how it is possible really to separate *beliefs* from *practice,* or indeed to forbid beliefs at all, is a complex philosophical question beyond the scope of this chapter.

Minority Education

Ethnic minority education anywhere in the world is a contested concept and challenging project, as it inevitably rests on rigorously debated and sometimes controversial assumptions with long-lasting and often irreversible consequences. The design and function of the Chinese minority education system have been under the influence of four ideological forces to varying extents: Confucianism, Marxism (more specifically Marxism-Leninism), multiculturalism (only to some extent and as a result of attempted indigenisation of Western ideals), and nationalism.

Confucianism is not a uniform body of thought, and there are competing interpretations on many issues. Some argue that 'Confucian culturalism' is highly hierarchical and repressive, under which some groups are inherently entitled to rule, determine how minorities ought to be governed, included or excluded (Leibold and Yangbin 2014, 5), while others claim that, through calling for a hierarchical, paternalistic and duty-bound commitment to peaceful coexistence of diverse cultures and peoples, 'Confucian communitarianism' provides support for state recognition of minorities, though not in terms of protection of 'rights', as it lacks a rights tradition in the Western sense (Leibold and Yangbin 2014).

Marxism adds a layer to the Confucian tradition, and it was under Marxism's heavy influence that minorities first became a question that needed answering, a problem that needed solving. Marxism posits class struggle way above ethnic attachments and cultural differences, and in the case of ethnic minorities, it is believed that different ethnic and cultural groups are at different stages of development and move toward the Communist utopia at their own varying pace, and it is the duty of the Communist Party, the Han Chinese, to educate backward groups into competent communities through state-led education programmes which would guide them along the path toward their ultimate destination (Leibold and Yangbin 2014). As 2.2.4 will show, the same style state/Han-led economic development and social advancement programmes are riddled with controversies and contradictions, although their positive contributions should also be recognized.

Multiculturalism, on the other hand, has a more complex reality. As is the case with many Western ideals, they tend to take on different meanings once imported into the Chinese context. Taking minority linguistic rights as an example, despite an almost universal backlash against multiculturalism as both an ideal and a policy currently taking place throughout the world, a key component of multiculturalism—linguistic rights—has not lost popularity. While both Western and Chinese officials and scholars stress their importance and defend their protection through law, there is in fact little agreement on their value, actual form, practical workability or purpose. In the Chinese context, while multiculturalists would defend linguistic rights simply for being an integral element of minority identity, others would view them merely as a transitional measure while the majority's language 'Putonghua' is being continuously and widely promoted and will continue to dominate.

Nationalism has an inevitable and complicated entanglement with ethnicity in any national context. It helps to identify where individuality stops and community begins and/or vice versa. While nationalism is naturally in tension with the rise of any minority identity, since expressions of minority identity vary greatly from group to group, place to place, the tension between the two also takes many forms, and only a few would create serious problems for the state. It exerts a crucial influence on education, as the latter determines what and how people think about national identity and their own, among many other things. Therefore, if/when nationalism is strong and rising, education tends to present a faithful mirror reflection of that reality.

Under these ideological influences, some working together while others pulling in opposite directions, China's minority education has come to contain the following key components, at least on paper. First, linguistic policy is always a good indicator of state attitudes toward minorities. Other than Articles 4(3) and 121 of the Constitution, which respectively guarantee all nationalities' freedom to use and develop their own spoken and written languages and require autonomous agencies to use local languages in performance of their duties, the Law of the People's Republic of China on the Standard Spoken and Written Chinese Language and a series of State Education Commission Opinions also contain key provisions. Both the Autonomy Law and Education Law guarantee the rights to use minority languages in teaching in minority areas and to have textbooks in minority languages. It should be noted that although law requires that schools with a majority of ethnic students use their own minority language, this does not help either ethnic minorities in majority Han schools or schools with a variety of different ethnic minority students—in which case the language of instruction will almost always be 'Putonghua'.

While language is by all means of crucial importance for the survival of the tradition and culture of any ethnic group, there are significant intergroup and intragroup differences. Minorities with only oral languages are not in a strong position to maintain their language through education, not only because they will not be able to have textbooks printed in the language that they speak. In some groups, the use of their language is widespread, whereas in others, only the elderly can speak it. Hence, uniform application of existing linguistic laws and policies is impossible. The group's attitude is also tied to economic opportunities and status attainment associated with the continuous use or abandonment of the group's language. It is widely argued that realization of minority linguistic rights in the form of provision of education solely or mainly in the minority language is not beneficial in terms of communication and future employment, as mastering the majority language is crucial for anyone in any country to play a meaningful role in society and to get a decent job. These practical difficulties, which always emerge when ideology meets reality, do not have easy solutions, as while some minority groups' linguistic pride and emotional attachment to their language are very powerful, as evident in the reactions to the recent controversial movement to limit the use of Mongolian in the classroom in Inner Mongolia, others have willingly chosen to enter Mandarin-speaking schools and do not seem to consider assimilation a problem.

Another key component of China's minority education policy has been the structural preferential programmes comprising significant preferences for university entry and certain jobs. For instance, ethnic minorities are entitled to lower threshold admission scores, waivered or lowered tuition fees and state-funded remedial programmes if facing financial hardship. Preferential treatment extends to quotas for professional training schools and medical schools, with institutions in economically advanced provinces being paired up with those in minority regions. Independent studies conducted by both Western and Chinese scholars have revealed that preferential education policies have significantly reduced inequalities in employment primarily by granting minority students easier access to secondary and higher education, consequently creating greater opportunities to gain employment (Guo 2013; Mackerras 2003). However, some have sought to criticize such policies from the viewpoint of assimilation, claiming that by the nature of their training, minority professionals, teachers and doctors have become more adapted to the state system rather than to their own culture (Mackerras 2003, 133). While assimilation in this way per se is neither preventable nor entirely undesirable, as it is not forced, there is often a very fine line between *forced* and *voluntary.*

Until recently, unlike in the West especially the United States, where preferential policies are extremely controversial and unpopular, they have been largely uncontroversial in China and widely accepted if not whole-heartedly welcomed by the Han majority. This is surprising considering the tremendously competitive Chinese testing system, especially the annual National Higher Education Entrance Examination ('Gaokao'), which has been described as 'the most pressure-packed examination in the world' (Siegel 2007); thus, preferential admission based on ethnicity can, quite rightly in some respect, be viewed as reverse discrimination, creating minority elites at the expense of Han students. This explains why some Han Chinese have sought in various ways to register themselves as ethnic minorities to avail themselves of these preferential benefits. There has been evidence of resentment, which has never been strong or widespread enough to turn into tension, perhaps partly due to the fact that the grievances and inequalities suffered by ethnic minorities have been frequently and publicly talked about in the state media. It is worth emphasizing that most if not all of China's minority preferential policy programmes are a quota-based form of affirmative action that is currently illegal in the United States.

This renders some recent changes particularly noteworthy. In the past few years a number of provinces have declared that they would stop awarding minority students bonus points for the National Higher Education Entrance Examination—Shandong stopped in 2017, Anhui would stop in 2022, Jiangxi in 2023, Liaoning in 2026, and a number of other provinces such as Hunan, Guangxi, Hainan, Guizhou have either reduced the bonus points or set extra restrictions for qualification. The rationale has been said to be that educational equality between the Han and the minorities has improved so significantly over the years that bonus points now constitute reverse discrimination against Han students.

Economic, Social and Development Rights

China's economic advancement in the past few decades has not benefited all equally. While there has been a general improvement in all regions, the rise of the eastern regions is much more significant than that of the minority-dominated western regions, causing widening inequalities, and minority groups residing in the more developed regions exhibit stronger indicators of socioeconomic development than those residing in the western interior (Zang 2015, 119), although the general living standards of all groups have improved significantly (Guo 2013). China's driven efforts toward advancing the economic development of minority-dominated regions are reflected in laws, preferential policies, and state-sponsored projects. More than ten articles in the Autonomy Law specify the duties of state organs to assist minority-dominated autonomous areas with economic development and social advancement. For instance, articles 28 and 29 require autonomous governments to, under the guidance of state plans, rationally manage, protect and develop the natural resources within the region, and consider and recognize local circumstances when arranging and managing construction projects; article 55 requires the state to implement preferential policies to encourage and attract foreign investment to minority-dominated regions; and according to article 59 the state shall set aside special funds to develop the economy of the autonomous regions, which must not be deducted, withheld or inappropriately used by any state agencies or persons.

While the genuineness of the state's intention to develop these regions for the benefit of their residents should not be doubted, an obvious political and strategic side to it should also be recognized. Since many of the international trade activities in the region are undertaken across state borders, for instance, Inner Mongolia with Mongolia, Xinjiang with Kyrgyzstan and Kazakhstan, Yunnan with Myanmar, and Guangxi with Vietnam, economic developments of these minority-dominated regions are vital for China's economic impact in Central and South Asia. In particular, since China's own oil and gas reserves are relatively modest in comparison to the enormous domestic demand for energy, it has been very keen to build oil and gas pipelines in the region, and indeed, the most important commodities among Xinjiang's various imports from Central Asian countries have been gas and petroleum. Apart from sources of energy, China is most interested in laying railway routes between Chinese cities and Central and Southern Asian countries as well as establishing regional financial organizations. None of these would have been possible without improved economic performance in the ethnic minority areas, which in return will further contribute to the region's socioeconomic advancement.

The most ambitious state-sponsored project in this area has been the Great Western Development Strategy, designed specifically to diminish widespread regionwise inequalities by shifting economic growth away from the eastern regions toward the minority-dominated West, including all five of the autonomous regions plus six other provinces nearby. The project has been widely praised and equally widely criticized. On the one hand, rapid growth in economic activities and opportunities has generated wealth, improved living standards and increased mobility for all within the region. On the other hand, western development has attracted a large number of Han migrants into the region to take up residence and set up businesses. This has gradually fuelled ethnic tension in some areas as the locals feel that economically, the in-coming Han Chinese have benefited disproportionately more from the Strategy that was initially designed to benefit the locals, and politically, Han migration constitutes internal colonization that goes hand in hand with recentralization of state power beneath the surface of regional autonomy (Castellino and Redondo 2006, 136). Most likely, having noticed these concerns, the Ministry of Labor has introduced preferential policies for minority employment in the relevant regions, such as prioritization of employment of minorities, lowered standard of recruitment, and establishment of vocational training schools with lowered threshold of entry for minorities.

One noteworthy phenomenon that shows a different side to the mainstream perception of minorities and minority cultures as being in need of reform and development has been the rapid expansion of ethnic tourism in both Han and minority-dominated regions in recent decades. In Han areas, it tends to take the form of cultural theme parks, 'folk culture villages', in which minority cultures and customs are presented through dance, musical performances and model villages; in minority areas, many minority groups have opened up their own villages to tourism, and purposely built ethnic villages, which resemble the theme parks in Han areas, have also emerged even in isolated and previously inaccessible areas (Mackerras 2003). Understandably, minorities have not benefited equally from tourism, not least because culturally speaking, some have more to offer than others. Many minorities view the acceleration of tourism in a positive light, as it undoubtedly has led to the rapid development of infrastructure, generated a great deal of income and raised the standard of living. By bringing people into contact with each other and with each other's culture, ethnic tourism has also enabled cross-cultural understanding and strengthened awareness of and respect for cultural identity and diversity. However, problems have also emerged and caused criticism.

First, it has been widely argued that the blooming of ethnic tourism has caused destruction of the environment in certain areas, which is a problem that has been openly acknowledged by the state. Second, it is debatable whether ethnic tourism actually does culture any good, as the construction of ethnic villages greatly commercialises minority cultures and traditions and turns authentic cultural practices into staged performances. It has been wondered whether such a commercialised display of culture actually helps culture survive; nevertheless, as Mackerras (2003, 73) points out, it undoubtedly does give it a new reason for existence, namely, to make money. While there is no doubt that tourism has brought money to minority areas, it has also been pointed out that, third, it has benefited some far more than others, and that the state gets the most, minority elites get a decent amount, and ordinary minorities get the least (Mackerras 2003). Fourth and related, it has also been argued that while minorities are mainly involved in the actual work, such as performance in ethnic villages, they have little say in planning or managing the activities which are often operated by Han companies or local governments (Zang 2015, 39).

4.1.3 Perceptions of Threat and Other Systemic Obstacles

This review of China's key ethnic minority rights efforts should reveal that, perhaps surprisingly, both the quality and quantity of most of the instruments are of high standard. The problem is not lack of law, but implementation. While it is impossible to evaluate the success of all laws, policies and programmes on a par, it is achievable to speak of obstacles in general, in so doing which aspects of ethnic minority rights are well protected and which are not will become clear along with the reasons. There are nine interrelated obstacles, some of which the author has examined elsewhere in both English and Chinese publications.

First, criticizing or making suggestions as to how to improve the legal protection of ethnic minorities in China is impossible without a thorough understanding of the Chinese perception and operation of the legal system, which is not only the oldest legal tradition in the world but also a complex mixture of traditional Chinese values and imported Western ideals. It has been argued that there are a great deal of similarities between how Chinese law is perceived and administered today and how it was conceived over 2000 years ago, most notably that law is an administrative tool of the government, representative of the state, both in terms of the sources of law and methods of implementation (Hsu 2003). In other words, law lacks, has always lacked, its independent power. It is not meant to counterbalance or contradict the state but rather to confirm and uphold its preferences. Consequently, just because the law *says* so, it does not mean that it *is* so, and sometimes despite evidence, there is no easy means to prove either way.

This nature of Chinese law means that, second, in regard to ethnic minority rights, the state's attitude toward the ideal of minority recognition *by way of protection of rights* is determinant. While it should be noted that technically speaking, *minority* rights are not strictly *human* rights despite being situated within the international human rights regime (Wei 2016a), a country's attitude toward *human* rights in general is nevertheless always a good indicator of its attitude toward and performance in *minority* rights protection. There remain stubborn obstacles to human rights protection in China, some ideological, some practical, some historical, all intertwined. And while substantial economic advancements in recent decades have removed many practical constraints, as this book shows, for a complex web of reasons, being any sense of an 'other', protecting otherness from the perspective of 'rights', is difficult in China.

In the particular context of ethnic minorities, the reason for this difficulty is a disbelief or distrust in the minority rights rationale and the value of ethnic-cultural diversity. This is the third obstacle. Support for this view may be found in some of the intragroup differences in terms of state treatment, which is related to the perception of threat. For instance, while the Uyghurs and most Hui are Sunni Muslims, the latter group is not viewed as much a threat by the state as the former because of the two groups' different degrees of acculturation. While Hui are descendants of foreign Muslim merchants, militia and officials from Arabian and Central Asian countries in the 7th to fourteenth centuries who intermarried Han Chinese, and that the 2010 census recorded nearly 10.6 million Hui, making them the second largest ethnic minority group in China, they spread all over the country, are very much integrated into Han society, read, speak and write Mandarin Chinese, wear Han costumes and celebrate Han festivals. Whereas the 10.1 million Uyghurs are a Turkic group living in geographic concentration in Xinjiang, which means that the probability of collective action is far greater, wear their own costumes, have their own language, celebrate their own festivals, and have much firmer religious beliefs than the Hui. The more similarities a minority group has with the majority, the more likely it is to invest its future in the mainstream system, to advance its interests through negotiations and reforms within the framework of the status quo, and therefore much less of a threat (Zang 2015, 127–128).

Closely related to this is the fourth, very important factor that determines the way the ethnic minority regime functions, namely, the government's overwhelming emphasis on territorial integrity and national security. What matters most is minorities' loyalty to the state, not cultural diversity. This is very easy to understand if not accept considering the country's turbulent history which saw the country divided up by foreign invaders, past uprisings that the government considers to have threatened its hold on power, as well as the more recent regionwise, urban–rural tension and conflicts due to increased socioeconomic inequality. While it is normal and proper that states fiercely guard their domestic realms, and in light of reliable evidence that threats to national security are real, there have been many instances globally that rights standards are lowered temporarily to deal with the situation, and only the governments themselves are in a position to review and evaluate the evidence in determining the seriousness of the threat. Without dismissing the importance of security and stability, an overwhelming emphasis on them may understandably have an adverse impact on minority rights, especially certain minority rights of certain minority groups, particularly those in the form of self-governance and autonomy of those groups on the state borders.

The fifth, related, obstacle is the threat of terrorism, having created a suspect group worldwide against a backdrop of stereotypes if not racism. Much of the criticism of counterterrorism measures in Western countries applies equally to China, with the Muslim nationalities especially the Uyghurs most affected in the Chinese context, although independent research on the topic is difficult to conduct and data (such as arrest numbers) are not readily available. It is widely felt that anti-terrorism laws and policies have had a disproportionate effect against Muslims, and security is much tighter in the western regions of China than in the rest of the country. This is in a sense understandable, as it would be denying the obvious not to admit that the vast majority, if not all, of terrorist activities successfully carried out in the country have been committed by one particular minority group linked to the East Turkestan Islamic Movement, which is proscribed as a terrorist organization not just by China, the United States but also the UN Security Council. The rapid introduction of a large number of harsh anti-terrorism laws in countries such as the US, UK and Russia in recent decades, which have all controversially expanded state and police powers, has shown that China is not unique in facing this irresolvable problem: when feelings as well as threats of insecurity are very real, it is difficult if not impossible to make sure basic human and minority rights principles are not abandoned.

It should be noted that while China is not new in fighting terrorism, it is new in fighting terrorism with counterterrorism laws, as its very first comprehensive Counter-Terrorism Law was passed only late 2015 and took effect on 1 January 2016. An important and much talked about feature of China's counterterrorism actions is the so-called 'people's strategy', formally recognized by article 5 of the new Counter-Terrorism Law as a key principle. Article 8 requires the authorities to establish coordination mechanisms to mobilize grassroots organizations, which all have the duty to assist state authorities in counterterrorism activities (article 9), set up community volunteer groups (article 74), who, as well as all organizations and individuals who work as informants and provide the state with counterterrorism intelligence (article 44), will be rewarded and honored for providing support in the prevention of terrorism (article 10).

This strategy is not new but newly formally endorsed in a piece of legislation. A widely reported news story in August 2014 described cooperation between the security forces and over 30,000 local residents of Hetian Prefecture in Xinjiang in a successful manhunt for suspected terrorists. The 'people's strategy' does make sense as terrorists come from and live among the people, which makes the people in many ways more informed than the state and its security forces. More importantly, however, the strategy reveals one important aspect of counterterrorism activities of the state that distinguishes them from other state-led actions—that the people tend to be wholeheartedly on the state's side—just as studies reveal that, despite having been harshly criticized by academics and human rights activists, the counterterrorism laws of the US and the UK are very popular among the people, who believe that they fulfil the urgent need in protecting them against terrorist threats, compared to which potential infringements of (mostly terrorists') human rights seem trivial and very hypocritical.

Since counterterrorism activities are much more relevant to certain groups of minorities and their discriminative treatment, the observation that on this matter the people and the state are side by side reveals that in regard to the treatment of minorities, what matters is not just the state's attitude but also the ordinary people's attitude, and under some circumstances, the latter matters more. This is the sixth obstacle to better minority protection in China: the people, more specifically Han Chinese, do not have a sound understanding of the rights and needs of ethnic minorities. China's ethnic relation is in general good, but while the Han are not intentionally racist toward any national minority, they do hold deep-seated prejudices as to which group is the 'civilised core' and which are lazy and backward barbarians in terms of social standing and achievements who need continuous help and guidance. The previously discussed Han fascination with ethnic tourism and 'folk culture villages' says a great deal about Han perception of minorities—while it may be politically incorrect to say so expressly, but for the Han Chinese, some minorities are probably more source of amusement than reason for genuine celebration of cultural diversity or equality. It is highly doubtful that the normative ideal of equality among all nationalities would ever be accepted by the Han, as anyone who qualifies for preferential treatment and special assistance from the state is surely weaker.

These perceptions will not change without the possibility of participation in free, open and rational debate on ethnic and cultural diversity both among the general public and in academia, which is increasingly difficult. This is the seventh obstacle. China is known for its powerful censorship on information on politically sensitive topics, and ethnic relations are among the most sensitive. The author has argued elsewhere that it is meaningless to speak of legal protection of minorities without first engaging in constructive, free, cross-cultural and multifaith dialog, to increase awareness and understanding of multiple groups and diverse perspectives, to enable challenges, criticism and change of direction if necessary in terms both of personal opinion and official position (Wei 2016a, Chap. 7). However, reality is that there is not only very little academic research on minority rights, the general atmosphere also means that ordinary people are neither encouraged nor exactly permitted to think critically on the relevant matters. Hence, for the time being, perceptions of ethnic minorities as well as the corresponding policies will remain unchallenged until the state changes its mind.

What is more alarming than the public's lack of knowledge of minority issues is the administrative cadres' and judicial officials' lack of appropriate training in specialized knowledge and skills in dealing with minority-related matters (Castellino and Redondo 2006, 142). This eighth obstacle is different from the third regarding the state's attitude and is of a more technical nature. It has been said at the beginning of Part 3 that the primary problem with China's ethnic minority protection is not the lack of law but implementation. It is easy to blame it all on the lack of governmental will, but in the Chinese context it could equally be said that, while ideals and standards have been identified and established, ideals will remain ideals and standards will remain standards unless those who are actually doing the job are equipped with sound understanding of their rationale as well as the practical capacities and creativities to make them reality. Problems with both administrative and court systems have become hot topics in recent years, and despite ongoing reforms, they suffer from vital flaws, among which are lack of independent authority and efficiency, inadequate professional training, serious corruption and abuse of power, and local protectionism. Regarding ethnic minorities specifically, despite significant progress in endorsing international norms in Chinese legislation, there is neither enough yearning among judicial officials for detailed knowledge of the rationale behind the relevant laws and policies, nor a genuine eagerness to work out how these norms could actually work in the very peculiar Chinese context. It is one thing to announce protection and quite another to make protection reality.

As already noted, one area of minority protection in which China has done well in making announcements reality is the development of minority-dominated regions. But when viewed from another angle, this constitutes the ninth obstacle. Without questioning the necessity and achievements of many of China's state-sponsored development projects in its western regions, the threat to minority land rights, in particular their right to natural resources, must be highlighted. This is an issue that has troubled many nations (Bell 2014), and the challenge of creating a protection regime that successfully balances minority land rights on the one hand and state-assisted development on the other has yet to be overcome. And it is debatable whether it could ever be overcome, not only because that first, states are seldom genuinely willing to let minorities living on resource-rich lands exercise real control over natural resources, and particularly in China, minority natural resources are first and foremost resources of the state; second, it has been argued whether minorities are actually in a position to meaningfully exercise control over their own land as institutionalised welfare dependency is widespread, which is caused and sustained by state paternalism and top-down interventions, causing many supposedly self-governing minorities to lack the necessary capacities and skills to meaningfully take control, so that they are forever placed at the receiving end—a situation that the state is more than happy to maintain (Wei 2016a); third, the balance between land rights and the right to development is in essence an issue of conflict of rights. Due to the complexity, variety and conflicting nature of human and minority interests, clashes are inevitable and often irresolvable. However, one should be careful with fixating on 'conflict of rights', as it diverts our attention from the fundamental problem at hand—competing cultural values, interests and beliefs (Wei 2016a, 222; McDonald 1998).

4.2 Concluding Part I: Between Ideals and Reality

While it is impossible to label any of China's minority laws and policies as simply right or wrong, because all that are good have side-effects and all that are problematic seem to exist for a good reason, it is nevertheless possible to say that when it comes to ethnic relations and related rights protection, China is clearly a paragon of great contradictions. Despite a large number of laws, policies and programmes, it is arguable that the country is a long way short of meeting international standards. While it is common, and right, to evaluate a country's rights performance against established international standards, it ought to be recognized that the international regime, despite being a phenomenon to be applauded, is far from unproblematic, in that it not only contains unstable concepts and vague standards but also promotes idealistic and unduly abstract ideals. While international law is not supposed to contain detailed instructions as to how rights may be realized in particular national contexts, an inevitable consequence of a one-size-fit-all practice is that it generalizes too much and downplays genuine political variations and particularities of human and cultural experiences, the recognition of which is vital to the spread of human and minority rights ideals (Wei 2016a, 214, 2016b). This is not to excuse any state for not respecting international standards, but rather to acknowledge that international standards are sometimes neither clear nor immediately realizable.

China has long realized this and seems to have developed two approaches in response. The first is the so-called 'rights sequentialism', which is a common claim among developing countries, namely, that the realization of rights has preconditions and takes time. While rights protection does take time and effort, there is the danger that over time, governments may gradually and habitually develop inherent contradictions to full protection of minority rights, especially the stronger rights, e.g., self-governance and autonomy. In particular, rights sequentialism requires and presumes good faith; states are presumed to genuinely and consistently want to bring about full minority protection, which is sadly often not the case. The second, which has gradually replaced the first, is the insistence on a uniquely Chinese approach. It is worth noting that for a very long time, China was not overtly concerned with either being part of the international rights regime or constructing an alternative theory of rights to replace the Western one that it had largely rejected. But recent years have seen China increasingly forcefully stress the importance of a Chinese rights approach. Some say this is a good sign, as the country has seriously started to think systematically how imported rights ideals may take root in Chinese soil, though many attempts have remained theoretical. While others are more pessimistic and interpret this as China returning to hard cultural relativism and in so doing seeking to challenge the universal ideals in a more fundamental way. Whichever is the correct interpretation, until China can really view ethnic minority rights as a mechanism that will assist, not hinder, political stability, social progress and healthy economic growth in the long run, things will not change for the better.

4.3 Part II: Religion in an Atheist State

Just how important or unimportant religion is to China is hard to determine. On the one hand, the country has temples and churches everywhere, demonstrating a strong presence of religious faiths; on the other hand, it is under the continuous rule of the Communist Party, which is by definition atheist, causing one not to expect too much in terms of religious tolerance let alone active promotion. While China has never been a religious country in a Western sense, religion has flourished throughout Chinese history and the country has long been host to a great variety of the most enduring religious traditions in the world, be they homegrown like Confucianism and Taoism, or imported like Buddhism, Christianity and Islam. According to the data published by the State Council's Information Office (2018), China has almost 200 million believers, although one has good reasons to believe this is inaccurate on the low side not least because the exact criteria and procedure of identification are unknown, and it is likely that only people who publicly and explicitly practice their religions and those who are affiliated with an officially recognized religious association are counted.

As will be demonstrated below, China has a wide range of forms of religions or quasi-religions, but only five are officially recognized: Taoism, Buddhism, Protestantism, Catholicism and Islam. While Confucianism has long been the most influential religious-philosophical movement in the country and has enjoyed renewed popularity in recent years, along with traditional folk religions, it is considered only as part of the Chinese cultural heritage rather than religious faith, while other 'spiritual practices' are considered superstitions or cults.

Between 2013 and 2019, the author had an office at the Hongjialou Campus of Shandong University next to the Sacred Heart Cathedral, commonly known as Hongjialou Cathedral, in the city of Jinan, the capital of Shandong Province. The Gothic Revival church, built in the years of 1901 to 1906 and reminiscent of the Notre Dame de Paris, is the largest in the region and cathedral of the Roman Catholic Archdiocese of Jinan. Specializing in human and minority rights means that the author is familiar with stories and reports on religious persecutions at various stages of Chinese history as well as the more recent crackdown on Western holidays and celebrations with religious connotations, which contrast greatly with what the author has witnessed in the past few years at the cathedral. Every Christmas the entire church is lit up and its exceptional golden presence is visible from far away, and the entire church compound is decorated with Christmas lights and decorations, with a giant Christmas tree almost half as tall as the cathedral standing in the middle of the square dripping with ornaments. While traditional Christmas carol services are taking place inside the church, enormous crowds of people with or without religious faith—many of whom are our students at the university—gather outside to share the festive joy and thanksgiving, take photos and share on the social media to spread the fun further.

It is impossible not to be drawn in and touched by the warmth and energy of such gatherings, and it is usually in front of such crowds that the author, an atheist and nonparticipant, wonders: where is the persecution? This part of the chapter attempts to answer this question by exploring three related questions in the Chinese context. First, in the face of conflicting evidence, what exactly is China's official position on religion, and how has it come to be? Second, is it possible to talk about the state's attitude toward religion generally or are different religions treated differently? If so, what are the reasons? Third, all things considered and all factors taken into account, can China be said to be anti-religion, and what are the implications for the protection of religious rights and diversity?

It might be necessary to begin with a mental note on what might go wrong with this analysis. Academic fascination with Chinese religiosity both inside and outside the country is not new, but conducting research on the topic, especially from the perspectives of religious freedom and diversity, is not easy due to the sensitive nature of the subject. The vast majority of the publications to which this chapter has referred have been published in English, although many are written by scholars of Chinese origin, and it seems that the most common path of studying Chinese religiosity is the Western one, along the lines of state-religion relations, which presumes mutual autonomy and noninterference to be the ideal. While this is not necessarily automatically problematic, is has been born out of a particular historical and political context and when applied to China tends to serve the purpose of proving its presumptions, that there is no mutual autonomy and there is a great deal of interference, therefore things are bad. This is not to say that the Western approach is useless, but rather to remind readers that the Chinese reality is complex and cannot be fully understood using only the Western analytical model, Western concepts, and Western ideals.

Having said that, it is equally if not more important to avoid falling into the trap of cultural relativism, so this second half of the chapter aims to demonstrate the complexity of Chinese religiosity by showing, first, the discourse of Chinese religiosity is part of many wider discourses that require careful detangling; second, it would be a mistake to focus only on state-recognized religions and be blind to the fact that the most influential religious or semireligious forces in China are in fact not considered 'religion' at all, yet they are the key to understanding religiosity as otherness in the Chinese context. But before diving into these issues, it is necessary to lay the foundation of analysis with, first, observation of China's secularism and, second, presentation of some basic facts of China's administrative and legal protections and regulations of religious activities.

4.3.1 Key Features in State Regulations of Religious Affairs

Secularism understandably underlines the obstacles to the survival of religion in China: how likely is it for a state run by a single all-powerful political party that is by definition atheist to value religion and religious diversity? Is expecting an atheist party to protect religion comparable to asking a theocratic state to advance atheism? This might be an analogy worth bearing in mind when enquiring about the sort and degree of protection and recognition one could realistically expect in the Chinese context. China is secularist in three senses. First, it is secularist because it has been under continuous Communist rule. Second, it is secularist also due to historical movements of secularization before the Communists took power, as will be shown below. Third, as examination of the legislations and regulations will reveal, it is secularist also in the sense that it seems to have *facially* adopted the Western concept of secularism, which has three key characteristics: strict separation of religious bodies from the institutions and running of the state, freedom of religion for all, meaning that everyone is free to hold, practice and change their religious beliefs within the limits of public order and law, and no discrimination against anyone on grounds of their religious beliefs or nonreligious world views. Yet, as analysis grows, it might become clearer that secularism is not necessarily the underlying principle. Control is. And how to interpret such control is key to understanding not only religious diversity but also how Chinese society functions.

One way of cutting into 'control' of religion is by looking into history where many if not all needs for and functions of 'control' first came into being. While a more comprehensive analysis will be provided in the next section, where the question of whether China is anti-religion is examined, it is necessary to mention here Ching-Kun Yang's ground-breaking book *Religion in Chinese Society* (1961), in which, among many other things, how Chinese state control of religion had a long history of literally thousands of years is examined. He points out that while for the larger part of history religions in China generally supported the regime either by granting supernatural legitimacy or by upholding those traditional values that sustained the political order, throughout Chinese history religions had never stopped periodically challenging the state ideologically and militarily, causing oppression and systemic regulations of religious affairs in return. In fact, many of the contemporary control methods existed long in history, for instance, compulsory registration for religious places of worship. And as will be shown later, while not every single act of state control is reactionary, the memory of having been challenged and threatened once upon a time in history tends to be long-lasting with powerful cumulative effects—this was true in history and is true now.

Yang (1961) presents a picture of the various forms of state regulation of religion in dynastic times, including instituting state-sponsored ritual programmes dedicated to officially recognized deities and cosmic forces, bestowing recognition and support to certain popular cults and religions while prohibiting others, instituting a clerical management system that controlled all aspects of clerical life and activities of places of worship, and so on, which this chapter will not repeat. It is beyond the scope of this chapter to trace the evolution of official regulatory systems from ancient times to modern days in great detail, but it is necessary to say that when the Communist Party came to power in 1949, it considered religions to be the ideological enemy and subversive political forces, but it nevertheless adopted a fairly tactical approach toward the major religions and manifested a certain degree of toleration, as evident in religious freedom being formally incorporated into the 1954 Constitution, although various levels of bodies were set up to control and regulate religious practices, and sectarian religions were banned.

From 1957 to 1966, state policy was centered on increasing economic productivity under central planning. The 'Socialist Transformation' forced religions to disband denominations and to reduce gatherings and venues, and stripped the power, property and influence of the clergy (Yang 2012, 82). During the Cultural Revolution of 1966 to 1976, widespread religious prosecution took place, religions were banned, temples, churches and mosques were shut down, religious statues and artifacts were destroyed, religious personnel were forced to return to lay life while religious leaders and believers were harassed, imprisoned, and even killed. This period of severe religious persecution has been officially acknowledged by the Chinese government. Interestingly though, even during the Cultural Revolution, the 1975 Constitution kept the clause on religious freedom but also added the 'freedom of atheist propaganda' (Yang 2012, 74).

The end and negation of the Cultural Revolution soon brought religions back to life, although it has been argued that during the Cultural Revolution, religions only disappeared from the public scene but never died. However, there are conflicting views as to whether the reform era under the pragmatic leadership of Deng Xiaoping was in fact a period of toleration and enlightenment for religion. On the one hand, it is argued that it was, as although atheism remained the guiding principle, beginning in 1979, a limited number of churches, temples and mosques were allowed to reopen for services, so it was in this year that the total ban on religion could be said to have been lifted, leading to rapid expansion and revival of religious activities in later years (Mackerras 2003, 115). On the other hand, it is argued that if one counts the large number of circulars, ordinances and administrative orders issued in this period with the purpose of controlling and regulating religion, one would reach the conclusion that it was in fact an era of strengthened, not lightened, regulation (Yang 2012, 75–76).

This is not to deny the fact governments then and now have officially acknowledged that widespread religious prosecution took place during the Cultural Revolution, or that religious upsurge outpaced regulatory expansion during the Deng's reform era in spite of accelerated state efforts at control, but this has been attributed to the fact that economic development was the central task of the leadership at that time, causing many to want to justify a tolerant approach to religion and to put religion to good use for economic gains, for instance building temples and turning them into tourist attractions (Yang 2012, 77). In other words, it was pragmatism that prevailed, not necessarily respect for religion or religious diversity.

A number of administrative and legal instruments that both protect and restrict religious beliefs and practices need to be noted. The first is 'Document 19' of 1982, officially known as 'The Basic Viewpoint and Policy on the Religious Affairs during the Socialist Period of Our Country', which provides a succinct account of the Communist Party's understanding of religion and sets the tone for religious policy in China ever since. It declares religion to be a historical phenomenon pertaining to a definite period in the development of human society, with its own cycle of emergence, development, and demise. It considers the emergence of the earliest religious mentality to be reflecting primitive peoples' sense of awe toward natural phenomena at a time when the production level was low, and with greater social, economic and educational developments such as those advocated and instituted by Socialism and Communism, the document asserts that religion will eventually disappear from human history.

Such an understanding of religion has provided the atheist government with a justification to accommodate the existence of religion and tolerate a certain degree of religious diversity—let nature take its course—hence the illuminating statements in Part Four of the Document that warn against dealing with matters of religion simplistically, setting believers and nonbelievers against each other by exaggerating their differences and forgetting their common ground, discriminating against and prosecuting believers. It even expressly states that matters of religious belief are matters of citizens' free personal choice. But 'let it be' has never been the official attitude—the Document directs that atheist propaganda must be carried out unremittingly across the country, declares that while the political power of a socialist state can in no way be used to promote any one religion or to forbid any one religion, it only recognizes 'normal' religious beliefs and practices, and that such religions must fulfil the state-mandated obligation of being 'patriotic' in the sense that they must not oppose the

Communist Party's leadership or the Socialist system, or damage national or ethnic unity (Yu 2005, 2). Notably, it grants legal existence only to Buddhism, Daoism, Islam, Protestantism and Catholicism under state-sanctioned 'patriotic associations' and not to any other religions or associations.

In line with the spirits of Document 19 is the Chinese Constitution, which is often considered both the most prominent and the least useful. It reaffirms in article 36 freedom of religious belief, nondiscrimination against any religion or believers, while stipulating also that only 'normal' religious activities will be accommodated, in that such activities must not disrupt public order, impair the health of citizens or interfere with the educational system. Significantly, religious bodies and affairs must not be subject to any foreign domination. A number of key words are noteworthy. First, while it forbids on paper discrimination against anyone on the basis of religion, it does not in reality apply to positions in the government or in the military. While there are senior members of the government who are not Communist Party members, the majority are and thus sworn-in nonbelievers in any religion; Communist party membership or at least Communist Youth League membership are normally prerequisites for joining the military, in which religious beliefs and practices are strictly forbidden.

Second, 'normal religious activities' are those carried out by religious bodies that have been registered and are therefore officially recognized by the state. Those groups that are not recognized, for instance, underground churches and gatherings, are not protected by the Constitution, even if they belong to a recognized religion. If religious activities carried out by recognized groups fail to conform to the many laws and regulations governing religious activities, for instance, by disrupting the order of society, they are not protected by the Constitution. Falun Gong and Jehovah's Witnesses are considered cults, not religions, and therefore are not protected by the Constitution. The vagueness and the consequent elasticity of many of such provisions mean that in practice, what counts as 'normal' is entirely determined by the state, especially the United Front Department and the Public Security Bureau, and even a well-intentioned official may end up drastically restricting religious or quasi-religious activities in some situations, especially during political and ideological campaigns.

Third, religious interference of the state's education system is banned, to the extent that while religion may be mentioned in an educational context, it must not be taught with the intention of converting a person to that religious faith. And while all of the official religious associations run schools to train their own personnel, these schools must gain approval from the Religious Affairs Bureau, conform to and synchronize with the national educational system and curricular requirements, and be overseen by the Ministry of Education. This means that students in these schools will only spend some of their time learning the contents of their religions and the rest studying the subjects that their counterparts in regular schools study (Chau 2011, 18). The rationale is simple—one must become a good citizen first before qualifying as a competent clerical member of their religion.

In addition to the Constitution, in 2004, the same year in which the Constitution was amended, the 57th Standing Committee of the State Council issued its Regulations on Religious Affairs, which was amended in June 2017 and came into force in

February 2018. The following articles are noteworthy which demonstrate the inherited spirit of Document 19: Article 4 stipulates that the state shall protect normal religious activities according to law, actively direct religions to adapt to the socialist society; Article 6 states that departments of religious affairs of the people's governments at or above the county level shall lawfully regulate religious affairs that concern national interests and public interests; Article 7 stipulates that the establishment, changes and dissolution of religious groups must be registered in accordance with the relevant provisions of the state's administration of social groups; Article 8 lists the functions to which religious groups are entitled: assisting governments at all levels in the implementation of laws, regulations, rules and policies, protecting the legitimate rights of citizens with religious beliefs, guiding religious affairs, developing rules and regulations and urging the implementation thereof, researching religious culture, interpreting religious doctrines, developing religious ideology, conducting religious education and training, managing the clergy, performing other functions as prescribed by laws, regulations, rules and bylaws of the religious group.

Article 11 stipulates that religious institutions of education may be established only by religious organizations at the national level, provincial level, and those of autonomous regions and municipalities directly under the Central Government, and that no other organization or individual may establish any religious institution of education; Articles 40 and 41 stipulate that religious gatherings shall take place only within established premises of religious activities, nonreligious organizations, nonreligious institutions of education, nonreligious venues, nondesignated temporary event locations may not organize or host religious activities, or accept religious donations, and nonreligious organizations, nonreligious institutions of education and nonreligious venues may not conduct religious education or organize Chinese citizens to go abroad for religion-related meetings, trainings or other activities; and Article 47 requires that online engagement in religious information services be examined and approved by religious affairs departments of above provincial level governments and be conducted in accordance with the state's internet information services management regulations.

It is important to note that the government today has deployed not only regulatory strategies from various periods of the past but has also implemented modern ones befitting secularist ideologies and specific requirements of the current regime (Chau 2019, 168). Until March 2018, all religious affairs in China were overseen by the State Administration of Religions Affairs (SARA), a department under the State Council and closely connected to the Communist Party's United Front Work Department, which manages relations with organizations and individuals inside and outside China that are not part of the Communist Party to ensure they are supportive of its rule.[1] In March 2018, in accordance with the 'Deepening Party and State Institutional Reform Plan' issued by the 19th Communist Party Central Committee, SARA was dissolved as an independent bureau and became part of the United Front Work Department, which took over all of SARA's functions and made SARA's director the deputy director of the United Front Work Department—a telling move that could help clarify

[1] Its official website: http://www.zytzb.gov.cn/html/index.html.

the context in which analysis is to be carried out in this chapter. SARA is now called the National Religious Affairs Administration.

Previously under the supervision of SARA and now the United Front Work Department are China's five state-endorsed religious organizations representing the five recognized religions: Chinese Taoist Association, Buddhist Association of China, the Three-Self Patriotic Movement of the Protestant Churches in China, Chinese Patriotic Catholic Association, and the Islamic Association of China. On the surface, they are nongovernmental organizations, but in fact, they function as an extension and delegation of SARA and local religious affairs bureaus for the internal management of their respective faiths, under whose supervision they select religious leaders, register religious venues, and ensure followers' beliefs and activities are in line with government policies. For instance, while the provincial-level Three-Self Patriotic Movement Committee in principle has the power of approval to ordain ministers, they must gain prior approval of the candidate from the provincial religious affairs bureau, and while the prefecture-level Committee may appoint senior pastors of local churches, such appointments must first be approved by the same-level religious affairs bureau (Yang 2012, 81–82).

A fairly recent instrument explains well the relationship between religious groups and government bodies as well as the attitude of the government toward religion and religious diversity. In February 2020, the Administrative Measures for Religious Groups came into effect, which requires religious groups to gain prior government approval for nearly all aspects of their operations. Among others, Article 3 stipulates that all religious activities of unregistered groups are banned in China without prior approval of the government; Article 5 requires religious groups to follow the directions of the leadership of the Communist Party and uphold the 'sinicization' of religion, which means promoting doctrines that comply with the government's version of traditional Chinese values and socialist principles; Article 17 stipulates that religious groups should spread the ideology of the Communist Party among religious personnel and believers and educate them to follow the leadership of the Party and support the socialist system; and Article 22 stipulates that religious groups should search in their religious teachings for those principles that promote social harmony and development, and that religious doctrines ought to be interpreted in compliance with traditional Chinese cultural values and the developmental needs of the country.

There are other administrative and legal instruments that are listed on the official website of the National Religious Affairs Administration that this chapter will not go through. It is worth noting though that in addition to these legislations and rules targeting Chinese citizens, there are also rules governing the religious activities of foreigners living in China, considering that foreign religious influence is feared the most. The government in 2000 issued the Detailed Instructions on the Implementation of the Administrative Rules for the Religious Activities of Foreigners within the Borders of the People's Republic of China, and reiterated, clarified and expanded the rules contained in the 1994 Administrative Rules for the Religious Activities of Foreigners within the Borders of the People's Republic of China. Noteworthy provisions include, among others: Article 7 states that foreigners should carry out their religious activities only in legally-registered and state approved temples, mosques or churches; Article 11 stipulates that with the state's approval foreigners may bring religious articles into the country for academic or cultural exchange purposes; Article 12 prohibits the following from entering the country: items in numbers that exceed the reasonable amount that a single individual would use, or those that do not conform to the scope set by Article 11, or those with content that is threatening to national security and public interest; Article 16 stipulates that foreigners should not interfere with the internal affairs of religious groups or with the selection of religious personnel, must not, in any name or form, set up religious organizations, bodies, activity centers or run religious schools or training classes; Article 17 forbids foreigners from appointing Chinese citizens as religious ministers, converting Chinese citizens, engaging in unauthorized preaching or teaching, preaching, teaching or conducting religious activities at an unregistered place, conducting religious activities with participation of Chinese citizens at a temporary religious site without the presence of Chinese religious personnel, creating or selling religious materials, publishing electronic religious materials and other religious items, disseminating religious promotional materials.

These key features of Chinese law and policy on religion reveal that while there have been changes and adjustments in different periods since the Communist Party came to power in 1949, there have been no substantive deviations from the principles established in Document 19. Overall, the state emphasizes freedom to *have* religious belief and downplays freedom to *practice* and engage in religious activities, as evident in consistent policies of control and regulation. Drawing boundaries and setting limits for freedoms are not per se problematic, as there are no limitless freedoms in theory or practice and all religious freedoms in all countries are subject to some limitations determined by the state. But some have thoroughly measured the specifics of Chinese provisions against the United Nations treaties and find that while the Chinese government's restrictive measures are not entirely unjustified, many have gone further than international norms and are excessive (Kolodner 1994; Zhu 2010; Zhang and Zhu 2011; Yang 2013), rendering it doubtful that Chinese law protects the same range of belief and outward manifestation that is recognized by international law, despite that Chinese provisions appear to have joined the International Covenant on Civil and Political Rights in prohibiting discrimination on grounds of religion. But does this necessarily mean China is anti-religion?

4.3.2 (Why) is China Anti-Religion?

To answer this question, it is necessary to first consider what are the signs that indicate that China *is* anti-religion, what are the signs that indicate that China is *not* anti-religion, if the former, what are the reasons that China *is* anti-religion, and if the latter, what are the reasons that China is *not* anti-religion—although the presumption should always be that things are never as simple as anti- or not anti-. A convincing sign that China might not be anti-religion is that the country has been home to a large number of religions for thousands of years—some have even claimed that before the modernist transformations of the twentieth century under both the Republican and Communist regimes, China had one of the richest and most diverse religious cultures in the world (Chau 2011, 1). And having been continuously ruled by the Communists for over seventy years, anyone who has visited China could bear witness that the country has functioning temples, churches and mosques everywhere, and that many traditional festivals, which the Chinese take very seriously and are national holidays, have strong religious elements in their celebrations and rituals, although they are often not considered to be religion but rather part of culture and tradition.

A sign that China might be anti-religion is that there has never been a period in China's long history in which the state has pursued a neutral policy or acquired a relaxed attitude toward religion, and criticism over modern China's hard stance on religion has been one of the most serious and consistent allegations since the country began to attract attention from the international human rights community. The analysis of the administrative and legal regulations of religion above in Sect. 4.3.1 is evidence that, as an atheist political party, despite having always advocated a certain degree and form of toleration, the Communist Party has always been suspicious if not resentful toward religion, and such sentiments have grown in recent years in that the state's firm belief in (being in) control is increasingly obvious. To understand its implications on the reality and future of religion in China, one needs to thoughtfully consider how this has come to be. There are several interrelated reasons. It is worth repeating that it was not the Communists who started the long history of official antipathy toward religion in China. Rather, it could be traced all the way back to as early as the fourth century B.C., when learned men began to equate religion with superstitions—a belief rooted in Confucianism.

4.3.2.1 Confucian Roots and State-Religion Relations

Despite the long presence of religion in Chinese history both past and contemporary, unlike in the West, institutional religions, or religious institutions, have never played an important role let alone a dominant one in China's culture, society or politics. What has played a vital role though, over the past two thousand and five hundred years no less, is Confucianism. It has long been debated whether Confucianism is a religion. On the one hand, it does address topics such as heaven, spirits and reverence of ancestors, believes in rituals as a means of maintaining order and restoring tradition, and thus has some of the characteristics, power and social functions as a theistic religion. On the other hand, it functions more as a code of conduct and a way of life by stressing societal structure, family values, filial piety, and harmony of relationships that are hierarchical but beneficial to both individuals and society—in other words, it emphasizes earthly existence rather than an otherworldly source of spiritual values and thus is more of a social, ethical and political philosophy than a religion. Confucian ideals of living and ways of governing have continuously impacted the functioning of the Chinese state and how society sees religion; traditionally, when Confucianism ruled supreme, any ideology or belief system that did not conform to Confucian teachings and ideals would be considered heresy or superstition.

While Confucianists' powerful attacks on any faith or activity that they considered heresy had never stopped over the past thousands of years, Yang (1961) argues that historically it was not the actual teachings, the ideology itself, that directly caused the othering and prosecution of other faiths, in that it was not the theological or philosophical differences that generated religious prosecution but rather pragmatic political considerations of the regime. He maintains that there were no pure ideological clashes between Confucianism and other faiths, as the former always refused to discuss supernatural issues, and although it later labeled Buddhism and Taoism heretic, it in fact officially or unofficially incorporated the essence of the teachings of both without any objection from the state. Clearly, mere theoretical differences alone were insufficient to be the foundation of political hostility. What was sufficient was of a more practical cast, namely, the (rather rational) fear (backed by numerous events throughout history) that religious faiths or movements could threaten the rule of the regime built on Confucian orthodoxy—a well-known example was the war fought between the Qing Dynasty and the Christian movement of the Taiping Heavenly Kingdom from 1850 to 1864.

In addition to and closely related to remaining in power, maintaining existing socioeconomic order was a key motivation that constituted an important driving force behind historical religious persecutions, once again hiding behind Confucian ideals. This can best be explained through Yang (1961)'s distinction between 'institutional religion' and 'diffused religion', which, despite criticism, is straight to the point in helping us understand why the Chinese state is so powerful, historically and now, in relation to religion, and why religions in general, be they homegrown or imported, historically or now, are so weak in relation to the state. According to Yang, an institutional religion is a system of religious life having an independent theology or cosmic interpretation of the universe and human events, an independent form of worship consisting of symbols (gods, spirits and their images) and rituals, and an independent organization of personnel to facilitate the interpretation of theological views and to pursue cultic worship (Yang 1961, 294–295)—for instance Buddhism, Daoism, Christianity and Islam.

A 'diffused religion' is one having its theology, cults and personnel so intimately diffused into one or more secular social institutions that they become a part of the concept, rituals, and structure of the latter, thus having no significant independent existence of its own—for instance folk religions, and Confucianism, whose rituals and ideals were historically very much part of the Chinese social fabric, styles of life and ways of governing, rendering them religions in the arena of the everyday life of both the people and the state. Their rituals or ideals were so diffused into secular social institutions that they became indistinguishable. It also means that these rituals and ideals and the secular systems were highly compatible, they complemented and supported each other, and by so merging the diffused religions became dependent on the secular institutions for their survival, and secular institutions, having incorporated elements of diffused religions into their socioeconomic order, needed to uphold the status quo in order to maintain the existing order and structure—hence the special relationship between Confucianism and the state and the former's supreme status.

This explains why institutional religions, which were latecomers compared to the many diffused religions, had no chance of growing powerful in Chinese history, as when they came into being or entered China, they were immediately confronted with a mature and powerful system with a well-developed particular type of relationship with its existing (diffused) religions—that of incorporation—and with a clear preference—that of the existing rituals and beliefs that were already part of everyday functioning, compatible and supportive of the regime, providing the ordinary people with philosophical as well as practical guidance as to how to live lives. This is also why Yu (2005, 3) notes that there has never been a period in China's long stretch of history in which the regime has adopted a neutral policy toward organized religious movements—as such movements always tend to challenge something that is already taken for granted, foundational and central to society and the regime—for instance, Buddhism challenges the traditional kinship system and calls on people to abandon secular socioeconomic life and relations, thereby also challenging the sociopolitical regime that builds on the kinship system and those secular relations.

The relevance of all this today is that the ideals of Confucianism remain firmly incorporated into the modern Chinese state, which in the past few years has been deliberately engineering its revival. If in dynastic times state and society had a particular attitude toward and relationship with institutional religions because of the influence of Confucianism, today with the revival of Confucianism, the same attitude and relationship would likely also be dominant. The difference is that today, there are new ideologies that complement and reinforce those attitudes and relationships.

4.3.2.2 Marxism, Atheism and Communist Rule

While not having started the anti-religious attitude, the Communist rulers have inherited their predecessors' position on religion, which fits comfortably with another ideology that has militated against Western-style religious freedom: Marxism, which presents doctrinal opposition to all religious teachings. It should be noted that it was during the earlier days of the Communist period that Marxism, which saw the essence of religion as the spiritual opium of the people, presented an especially formidable obstacle to religious freedom. Nowadays, despite the theoretical conflict between Marxism and religion, contemporary leaders have not advocated the abolition of religious practices. Rather, while the Party strictly forbids its members to hold and practice religion, it has tolerated though not encouraged nonparty members to hold and practice religions to the extent that such beliefs and practices do not obstruct the nation's progress along the socialist road and that all religions are required to officially declare obedience to the Party. Clearly, how religion has managed to survive if not thrive under atheist Communist rule raises interesting theoretical and practical questions regarding the interactions of atheist states and theist ideologies.

It is wrong though to speak of 'Marxist atheism' as a whole, as it takes multiple forms, each has been influential at different stages and among different people and with different policy implications. To understand contemporary China's religious position is to figure out how these various forms have come to be, coexist and impact each other and the regime's thought and behavior as a whole. Marxist atheism in the Chinese context has been said to take three main forms—militant atheism, enlightenment atheism and mild atheism—in order of their degree of anti-religiousness (Yang 2012, 45). While militant atheism sees an urgent need to use harsh social and political measures to control and eradicate religion as a dangerous political ideology serving the interests of the exploiting classes, enlightenment atheism regards religion as an illusory or false consciousness that is backward and nonscientific, thus allowing a limited degree of religious freedom but hopes to bring about its decline through scientific development, mass education and political propaganda, and mild atheism wants even greater tolerance of religion (Yang 2012, 46).

These different versions of atheism are important for understanding the historical evolution of religious freedom and hence the varying degrees of religious otherness at different stages in China. Influenced by the New Culture movement, many leading members of the Chinese Communist Party adopted Marxism-Leninism during its early days and engaged in aggressive attacks on both traditional Chinese culture and religion. The new regime founded in 1949 also adhered firmly to the Soviet position, and during the Cultural Revolution (1966–1976), militant atheism continued to be dominant. When the Cultural Revolution ended and Deng Xiaoping became the paramount leader, launching comprehensive economic reforms, a period of apparently greater religious tolerance based on enlightenment atheism began as pragmatism prevailed in all aspects of social life. Enlightenment atheism was visibly embodied in Document 19 of 1982, as examined previously, and it was during this period that theoreticians began to engage in genuine debate about religion, with the liberal-leaning ones reigning in the end, causing many to soften their position toward mild atheism or even further.

There is more than one way to have a softened position on religion, one of which is to see religion as culture, the advantages of which are obvious. First, when religion is viewed as part of culture, as a cultural phenomenon, what are normally considered to be its flaws immediately become tolerable. People are less determined to demand its scientific provability or question its ideological incorrectness, thereby eliminating two major sources of suspicion and discomfort. As 'culture' has a much softer appearance than 'religion', both the state and society are more likely to let it be; hence, religion as part of culture has more of a chance of survival than on its own. Second, 'religion' is precise, while 'culture' is a much broader domain with no fixed boundaries; hence, a cultural approach to religion is more interdisciplinary and further-reaching. People from a large number of disciplines may all contribute to the study of religion from their respective angles, at the same time bringing these subjects to the attention of those who did not previously consider them related or relevant. Once interdisciplinary and multidisciplinary dialog becomes possible, third, religion becomes more relatable and therefore more understandable to a larger number of people, thereby increasing its chance of survival and recognition.

How soft can one's position be on religion depends on various factors, one of which appears to be profession and the associated level of education. For instance, seeing religion as a cultural component was most popular in the 1990s, producing, among Chinese intellectuals who used to be very critical of religion, a group of 'cultural Christians' who were either very sympathetic toward Christianity or had taken up the Christian faith themselves. They spread Christianity like fashion in the cities, in which people were drawn to the religion through reading their publications rather than through contact with ordinary believers or churches (Yang 2012, 57). Apart from cultural Christians, many intellectuals were/are sympathetic toward other faiths and believers too, such as Buddhism, Daoism, but perhaps less so Islam. In contrast, the continuous presence of militant atheism is most noticeable among military and retired officers whose perception of religion tends to be hostile (Yang 2013, 8). Clearly, the level of education and the everyday atmosphere in which one lives and works determine the level of tolerance if not acceptance.

4.3.2.3 'Asian Values'

A third factor is the so-called 'Asian Values', or 'Chinese Values'. A full examination of minorities and sociocultural otherness cannot bypass the debate of 'Asian Values', though a consensus on the precise meaning and content of which is difficult to reach. While it is wrong to say that China completely denies the universality of human rights ideals, it has increasingly referred to the uniqueness of Chinese culture, national context and values in recent years in its critique of mainstream Western ideals and conceptions of rights. The harmonizing 'Chinese values' in both the Chinese and other Asian contexts typically manifest three key characteristics, among others. First, largely due to its colonial pasts, China firmly adheres to the principle of state sovereignty both when dealing with internal ethnic-religious tensions and especially when responding to criticisms from the outside world. This emphasis on sovereignty is one of the reasons why neither China nor any other Asian country has taken steps to suggest developing regional systems of human and minority rights protection, and also the emphasis that religious belief and practice in China must be free from foreign domination.

Second and related, due to the continuous influence of Confucianism, the country prefers to deal with rights issues through internal and external cooperation instead of confrontation, which is seen as a style excessively favored by the West. It also expects ethnic-religious minorities within its borders to voice and advance their claims on the same principles. This preference based on collective cultural and behavioral habits also renders the country easily offended and likely to consider itself confronted whenever criticized or whenever a strong claim of diversity and otherness is voiced.

Third, China emphasizes the collective over the individual in that individual rights must not compromise the greater good of a well-ordered society (Wei 2016a; Frick 2019, 67). To the extent that religious freedom as a concept is viewed not only as an idea imported from *foreign* land but also as an *individual* liberty, such freedom and associated rights must be completed with duties to the nation and be subordinate to the collective interests of the state and society as a whole, which is the case for any human and minority right in China but especially so in the realm of religion given its theistic nature. While all religious freedoms and activities are subject to legitimate constraints under national and international laws, so the fact that religious freedoms take second place after state interests per se is not automatically a problem. What might be a problem is how many constraints there are, for what purposes, and whether they are necessary and proportional to these purposes.

4.3.2.4 Nationalism and Patriotism

Modern nationalism was first introduced into China in the late nineteenth century and early twentieth century, when Chinese intellectuals and politicians began to promote modernity programmes to reform the country and to eliminate all religions in order to build up a powerful modern Chinese state. This connection between nationalism and modernity was imported from the West and had its roots in the teachings of John Locke, who began to promote the separation of state and religion four hundred years ago on the grounds that the state and society could only mobilize their resources and talents effectively if they could be free from the interference of religion in secular matters; and Immanuel Kant, who considered religion to be irrational and harmful to modernity and should be confined to the private spheres of families and religious institutions; and also Emile Durkheim, who similarly viewed religion as superstitious and harmful to modernity, which ought to be replaced by science (Kuo 2017, 17).

This modernity approach, despite having been criticized for being only partially correct in terms of empirical evidence and normative implications, continues to heavily influence society's conception of religion as well as the state's religious policies in China today. And arguably, it was during the most recent decade that 'Chinese nationalism' gradually accelerated into 'Chinese patriotism', which in many respects manifests the characteristics and functions of a state religion, which would require other religions to be submissive and to integrate it into their own theologies, teachings and organizational structures. This being the bottom-line, it remains to be seen how Chinese patriotism is to interact with religions in the years to come, which will very much depend on how and in what direction itself may evolve. But the prospects will not look the same for all religions.

4.3.3 Internal Diversity and Broader Issues

This section does not present a comprehensive picture of all religions but focuses on analyzing the reasons why different religions have experienced their respective difficulties. In recent years, instead of equally repressing or promoting all religions, China has taken firm steps to promote Confucianism, in part perhaps to counter the rapid increase of Christianity (Yang 2012, 77). This reminds us that it is not right to treat all religions on a par and talk about treatment of religion in general, attempting to reach a conclusion as to whether the state is anti-religion or not. There is always internal diversity in terms of intensity and methods of state regulation as well as societal attitudes toward different religions for a variety of sociocultural and political reasons. Additionally, local factors are seldom the only determinants, and global events or incidents taking place in a faraway region may have a long-lasting impact very close to home, as most visibly demonstrated in the case of Islam, with a few incidents that have taken place in China in the past few years indicating that Islam and Muslims' difficulties in this country are largely due to their global image and the emotions that certain events have generated, rational or irrational.

4.3.3.1 Islam: Global Challenges and Local Emotions

Islam is by far the most prevalent of all institutional religions in China, and the three most populous nationalities among its adherents are the Hui, the Uygurs and the Kazaks. The strength of Islamic culture and religion among Muslims in China varies greatly, at one extreme with many Hui who do not actually believe in Islam or follow Islamic dietary proscriptions, and at the other extreme many Uygurs adhere fiercely to their tradition and religious teachings (Mackerras 2003, 119). Three incidents concerning Muslims in 2017 unveiled telling and seriously underexamined collective emotions of Chinese society and their enormous impact on the construction of 'the other' and differential treatment between different religious groups.

The first began in July 2017 when a 'halal' button appeared on the leading Chinese food delivery app Meituan, promising to deliver halal food in separate boxes that would not be used for nonhalal food. Very soon a social media war erupted with netizens taking no time to label the company's move a sign of pan-Islamification of secular China and discrimination against non-Muslims, causing many users to delete the app en masse in protest. The company later issued a statement explaining that the halal option was the idea of local representatives in a Muslim-majority city, Linxia in Gansu Province, without prior approval of the company and that it would be available only in selected Muslim-majority cities. This explanation had almost no effect on those fiery netizens who continued to attack the company on the internet with comments that turned increasingly and explicitly Islamophobic, racist and nationalistic.

The second incident came to public attention in September 2017, when a university in eastern China introduced Muslim-only shower cabins, offering much greater privacy than regular communal shower rooms, where dozens of students would usually shower together. Anhui University of Science and Technology explained this decision in an announcement that according to the Koran, showering was a private act for Muslims and should not be seen by others, so out of full respect for the customs of Muslim students and in consideration of their growing number, the university decided to open shower areas exclusively dedicated to them. The announcement urged students to understand this decision, respect each other and promote integrity among ethnic groups. This decision provoked heated debates on social media, leading to widespread display of anti-Muslim sentiments and even hate speech against 'unfair Muslim privilege'.

The third controversy took place in November 2017, when it was brought to public attention that Huawei, the prominent Chinese smartphone brand, had added to its latest model, 'Mate 10 Pro', a built-in Muslim prayer reminder alongside a function to locate nearby mosques. These features were displayed on one of the company's advertisements in China, which triggered a flood of angry responses on social media attacking the features as, along very similar lines to those of the earlier two incidents, giving preferential treatment to Muslims, discriminating against non-Muslims, signs of Islamification of China, even supporting terrorism. Many even called for a boycott of the company and its products. In response, on 16 November 2017, Huawei issued a harsh statement threatening to take legal actions against those netizens who carried out what it believed to be vicious attacks on the company's reputation by opportunistically distorting the facts. It also stated expressly that the model with the Muslim alarm function had been a customer-centric strategy and specifically designed for 'a foreign region' and would not be available on the Chinese market. After this statement, although the anti-Muslim sentiment that the incident sparked did not disappear, some of the earliest online posts attacking the company were deleted along with some anti-Muslim comments and heated discussions. Huawei also removed the advertisement that displayed those features from its website and other platforms.

The negative emotions that these three cases have revealed are easy to identify, namely, and to varying degrees, fear, anger, and even hatred, resulting from complex interactions between historical events and new provocations, between faraway fears and local uncertainties, between insecurities of the state and everyday concerns of ordinary citizens, between the fact of cultural diversity and the ideal of national unity and cultural purity, between competing interpretations of the relationship between the nation state and personal sense of belonging. In essence, they all concern the positioning of cultural and religious minorities in relation to the state and the majority, which involves complex issues of citizenship and belonging, and calls especially for attention to be paid to the collective emotions that form the basis of popular support for some forms of discrimination.

In particular, the stigma associated with Islam and the Muslim community in the West has been embraced in China in this age of globalization and the internet, in which information, speculations, insecurities and tensions travel fast and far despite significantly different national contexts and social constructs of Muslim identity. Having a large Muslim population, the widely reported mass-mediated terrorist attacks mainly in the West but occasionally also in China have kept the sense of uncertainty and anxiety alive within Chinese borders, about who the enemies are, what might happen next, how most effectively to proceed with the project of cultural unification. Fears are normal and even healthy, and as long as critical thinking is encouraged, negative emotions may well lead to rational and practical solutions. But Chinese society is not one in which citizens may easily develop critical capacities through the exercise of free thinking or expression. People seldom have the opportunity, or indeed will, to engage in critical discussions about cultural diversity, ethnic belonging and minority rights, or any reflective critical debate about any official stance or policy of the state.

What the state decides goes, oversimplifications and mistakes tend to remain uncorrected unless the state corrects them first. It is in such an atmosphere that negative emotions remain unchecked and volatile, sustaining unstable and problematic though understandable conceptions of inequality and belonging.

It is against this background that the underlying reasons for these societal emotions and their impact on the collective sense of justice may be highlighted. First, despite always having multiple cultures and ethnic groups, China has never been multicultural. While speaking of 'the Chinese culture' as such is oversimplifying the matter, on the whole, throughout history, the country has always valued convergence over divergence, sameness over difference, unity over diversity, harmony over conflict (which tends to be caused by diversity, so it is believed), and community over the individual. This is an important reason why China is uncomfortable with the Western rights language, which in many ways serves private interests rather than those of the community. This has necessarily led to a lack of multicultural thinking, which has meant that the state and its people have a particular way of thinking of ethnic diversity and differences as a result of authoritarian deliberation, and that it manifests cultural insensitivity if not borderline racism.

Second and related, government stance on human and minority rights has left its mark on society. China's position on human and minority rights appears to be constantly changing and therefore difficult to analyze and easy to misunderstand (Wei 2016b, 215). Until the most recent decades, China had serious reservations about the international human rights regime and its ideals, which it labeled political weapons employed by the West to undermine the Socialist state. Until recent years, the past three decades witnessed a gradual but sure change in China's style if not attitude in dealing with human and minority rights issues and especially in the handling of attacks from the West, in that instead of taking a defensive position and hiding in denial, the country acquired a newfound confidence as evident in significant resources and personnel dedicated to facilitating contacts with the West and bettering mutual understanding, participating in and hosting bilateral and multilateral human rights talks on selective categories of rights such as women's rights, children's rights and disability rights which the state consider to be uncontroversial (Wei 2016b).

While attitude of the state inevitably led to awakening of the people's rights senses, it should be noted that this confidence has been that of the state rather than of the people, in that while the state more frequently than before discusses human rights (albeit almost entirely in a defensive tone), the ordinary people's opportunities to talk about rights issues at all let alone critically remain limited—they are used to looking to the state for official guidance, which means problems and confusions will arise when/if official position is unclear or constantly changing.

Third, a few decades back when China entered its reform era and finally opened up to the West, it was thirsty, passionate, open-minded and in anticipation of great things to come. It gained a habit of almost unquestionably embracing everything Western, from ideology to commercial goods, from language to lifestyle, good and bad. An important fact is that China opened up to the West at a time of rising terrorism outside China and secessionist movements in the minority-dominated regions inside China. In other words, internationally and nationally, there were a great deal of political uncertainties that were related to ethnic diversity, cultural clashes, and Islam, often with the consequence of intensifying feelings of identity and rising nationalism. While secessionist movements and terrorism are not reported in the same way as they are in the West—in fact with just a few exceptions, ethnicity-related secessionist movements or terrorist acts were/are seldom mentioned in China let alone discussed openly in detail like in the West—but news coverage of those events taking place in other parts of the world is enough for the Chinese society to be acquainted with fragments of the issues and infected with the emotions, and Islamophobia. This is not to say that Islamophobia is entirely imported, but that as is the case with all national contexts in which Muslims have had issues, there is always a wider, international atmosphere from which national collective emotions gain inspiration, a sense of association, and a sense of justification.

This relates to a fourth factor. Unlike in the West, where free speech rules supreme, in China, there is a limited range of safe topics for open discussion, and such safe topics generally fall within the economic, social and cultural arena. There exists limited free space for open discussion and information exchange on topics such as religion and ethnic identity, although both are very much part of culture which sometimes gives the impression that they might be 'safe', but it is not their cultural element that renders them 'unsafe' but their association with geo-politics, internal diversity and ethnic relations. Lack of free space for discussion of ethnic issues, coupled with lack of free flow of information, has several consequences.

The first is society's lack of knowledge on ethnicity issues, cultural diversity, Islam and Muslims, which means misunderstandings and misimpressions will always remain uncorrected while genuine differences and conflicts are dealt with simplistically. Second, in such an atmosphere, emotions can easily overrule the necessity of rational debate and enquiries, leading to a collective sense of overconfidence and a false sense of being powerful. Third, overdriven nationalistic emotions often rule out the possibility of real cross-cultural dialog, making people not want to get to know each other or engage in conversations, leaving no real chance for the minorities to (re)present themselves, especially in ways that are contrary to mainstream conceptions of them. Fourth, consequently and over time, the masses will not only lose the curiosity to take an interest in ethnic-cultural issues but will also fail to see the necessity, and miss the opportunity, to build up the capacity to develop critical skills to debate matters that are crucial in a modern society in which different cultures and peoples ought to meaningfully coexist. Fifth, when and where people have limited freedom to express individuality or critically engage in public discussions, when they do get the chance to experience that freedom, they tend to let loose, pick easy targets and attack scapegoats. The psychology is easy to understand—if the majority of people are unfree to diverge, why should the minorities be free to be different?

4.3.3.2 Catholicism, the Century of Humiliation, Sinicization

Catholicism, in contrast, is facing very different challenges due to interactions with the state and society, both historical and present, of a very different nature. Apart from the four examined above, another important factor has determined the Chinese state's attitude toward religion—its 'century of humiliation'—the modern impact of which takes the form of conflict between state sovereignty and religious autonomy, and which affects mainly the Chinese Catholic community but is intertwined also with religious policies for and attitudes toward Tibetan Buddhism and Islam. The 'century of humiliation' refers specifically to the period of 110 years between the beginning of the First Opium War in 1839 and the end of the Chinese civil war in 1949, which saw the loss of Chinese territories as well as humiliating treaties and concessions made to foreign invaders, highlighting the harsh pain and intense shock dealt to China's self-confidence and worldview by the intrusion of an outside world that had until that time remained a distant unknown. It was during this period that China was forced to rethink its position in the world and begun to form a conscious awareness of the concept of an international arena, the power relations within which would determine its fate and left the country deeply wounded.

Modern studies on China, especially those in the field of human and minority rights, have grossly underestimated the strength, length and depth of the impact of these 110 years on China's self-image and projection of the world. Although the past 73 years since the end of that century have seen China gradually becoming adept at working within the international system, and that its participation in global political, military and economic arenas has showcased a country that is able to—when it wants to—function within existing international arrangements, the country has a noticeable habit of periodically referring back to the century of humiliation, especially when attacked on the international stage. While some may explain this as the ruling party's conscious strategy of highlighting its success in leading the country out of the shadow and enhancing support for party leadership, the more personal, psychological reason perhaps reflects more accurately the collective emotions that are driving much of China's diplomatic and political actions domestically and internationally—that the country has never put that century behind and continues to harbor a high degree of hurt and anger which is easily lit, rendering some of the country's policies and actions more emotional than rational. Accurately appreciating the impact of the intense lingering emotions generated by long-gone history is the key to understanding many of China's attitudes and actions dealing with foreigners. This association with foreigners has presented Christianity in China with unique challenges.

Despite its long presence in China and significant intertwinement with Chinese society and culture, Christianity is still viewed by many as a 'foreign' religion and for that reason continues to generate suspicion among both political elites and ordinary nonbelievers, mainly for three reasons. The first is that, compared to others, Christian believers appear to be more resistant to government regulation. Lim (2013, 2) talks about a 'politics of Christianity' in China and notes, on the one hand, the state's determination to exert control over all religious matters, and on the other, Chinese Christians' intense ambivalence toward such control. This might seem particularly worrying to the authorities considering that, second, unlike the Muslims who in history came to China without any intention to seek concerts but primarily to trade, the main purpose of the Christian missionaries was the proselytization of the Chinese people, which was why Christianity was and is considered by many as a heterodox religion and hence an ideological-political threat (Israeli 1980; Lim 2013). Third and related, as already examined in Sect. 4.3.1, a key concern of the state is foreign interference of China's religious and in turn political affairs. It is important to note that all religions, including Daoism, Buddhism and popular religions, cultivate relations with foreign countries and groups, but none has generated as much suspicion as Christians, since the former are considered authentically Chinese (even though Buddhism is in fact an import) and the latter is viewed as foreign.

A good example is Chinese Catholics' complex relations with the Vatican. While the Vatican insists on religious autonomy and has the right to appoint bishops in all Catholic communities around the globe, China does not recognize this power and has been appointing its own bishops, and the Chinese Catholic Church is independent of that of Rome. There are possibly five interrelated reasons. The first is the lingering effects of the painful memories of the century of humiliation noted above. The second is likely to be the fact that during the Chinese civil war between 1945 and 1949, the Vatican sided with the Kuomintang (KMT) government and moved its embassy to Taiwan after the KMT was defeated (Kuo 2017, 38). Third and related to this, the Vatican remains one of the few countries that recognize Taiwan as an independent state. The fourth reason might be that the Vatican is not only the headquarters of the entire Catholic community on earth but also itself a sovereign state. Allowing a foreign sovereign state to appoint religious clergy in China brings back memories and causes concerns not only to the nationalists. Fifth, the Vatican's role in the collapse of the USSR is unlikely to have been forgotten.

Having said that, the relationship between the Chinese government and the Vatican has appeared to be warming up slightly since Pope Francis came to power, as evident in two notable events. First, the Pope's plane was allowed, in August 2014, to fly over Chinese airspace en route to South Korea, making him the first ever Pope to fly over China, for which he sent a friendly message from onboard to President Xi to wish him and the nation well. China's friendly gesture was in great contrast to its treatment of Pope John Paul II, whose requests to fly over Chinese airspace en route to South Korea were rejected twice. Second, in September 2018 and after decades of discussion, the Chinese Foreign Ministry signed an Interim Agreement with the Vatican on the delicate matter of appointment of bishops, which was renewed in October 2020, extending the experimental phase of implementation for two further years until October 2022. This provisional agreement apparently allows the Chinese government to propose bishop candidates to the Vatican, and the Pope will pick from the list, rendering that while the Pope does not have full autonomy, his authority is partially recognized. Whether this means that all Chinese bishops are now in communion with Rome is unclear. It is worth noting that according to a Vatican newspaper, two Chinese bishops were appointed in October 2020 according to the regulatory framework stipulated in the agreement. There is no openly available information on this matter in China.

Either way such an agreement is of historic significance, but neither the agreement nor its extension has attracted much public attention in China, possibly due to, first, lack of general interest in religion, second, that the Foreign Ministry reported the news extremely briefly, almost in passing—in two sentences. However, a recently passed instrument casts serious doubt over the precise wording (which was never disclosed to the public) and actual effectiveness of the Interim Agreement, and has been called a violation of the 2018 agreement by the Catholic News Agency. The Administrative Measures for Religious Clergy (2021), not mentioning the Vatican or the agreement, provides that China's own state-run Catholic Church, the Chinese Catholic Patriotic Association, will be selecting, approving and ordaining candidates for the episcopate—and these new rules came into effect on 1st May. Article 16 requires the Chinese Catholic Bishops Conference to submit information about the new bishop to the State Administration for Religious Affairs, and the new bishop, after being registered in official database, along with all members of religious clergy, 'should love the motherland, support the leadership of the Chinese Communist Party, support the socialist system, abide by the Constitution, laws, regulations, and rules, practice the core values of socialism, adhere to the principle of independent and self-administered religion in China, adhere to the direction of the Sinicization of religion in China"—the new rules' Article 3 states.

It is clear that Catholicism, more than any other religion, reminds China of the importance of national sovereignty; hence, it more than any other religion feels the impact of what has come to be known as the process of sinicization—the aim of which is to turn 'Catholicism in China', which may well be viewed as an unfinished Western project with all its foreign connections, historical baggage and future implications, into 'Catholicism made in China', or 'Chinese Catholicism', which will be a new form of the old religion with Chinese characteristics, demonstrating that it has not just taken root in China, it has in fact grown out of the Chinese soil. The impact of sinicization on ordinary people's religious practices has yet to unfold completely. An interesting finding, which is consistent with the author's own observations, may be worth highlighting. Yao and Badham (2007) note that among Chinese Christian believers, there are more females than males and more elderly people than younger ones, and the educational level is lower than the national average. The fact that the more disadvantaged people in society—the minorities within minorities—tend to turn to this faith should not only help us appreciate the functions of this religion in the everyday life of different members of society but may also provide an angle of examining more precisely how the practice of religion relates to social involvement in this new age of sinicization.

4.3.3.3 (Non-Tibetan) Buddhism as Culture and Buddhism as Religion

Foreign roots, however, do not necessarily guarantee suspicion and suppression. Although also subject to extensive regulation and control, Buddhism is rarely targeted with direct suppressive interventions despite also being imported—from India no less which is not exactly friendly toward China. Buddhism has a long history in China, and since its recovery from the Cultural Revolution, it has progressively regained favor among the Chinese people, with a large number of citizens engaging in Buddhist activities, although such engagement alone does not necessarily render them Buddhists, and the precise number of Buddhists is hard to estimate accurately as the Buddhist conversion process is much less formal than say the Christian one

(Chau 2011, 32). But the overall 'advantages' of Buddhism over other religions are easy to identify.

First, as noted above, one way of taking up a soft position on religion, hence rendering religion less threatening to the state, is to view religion as a part of culture. Two cultural elements have made this easier to accomplish for Buddhism even though it is subjected to all the same formal regulations and controls that the other religions are. The first is martial arts, and the second is the revival of classical literature. In 1981, the well-known movie *Shaolin Temple* was released. Filmed on the ruined site of the actual Shaolin Temple in Henan Province, the legend of the fight of the martial monks against a military rebellion in the seventh century attracted millions of viewers when it was first shown in mainland China in 1982, among them were many young people who were not representative of lay Buddhists at that time who consisted mostly of the middle-aged and the elderly. The popularity of this film quickly led to the production of a series of similarly themed films, television programmes and literature, further intensifying popular interest in everything to do the temple (Chau 2011, 33–34).

The martial arts literature, in which Buddhist temples, symbols and monks always play an indispensable role, has also contributed a great deal to the rehabilitation of popular interest in Buddhism. After the end of the Cultural Revolution, when this form of traditional literature was reintroduced back to the mainland from Hong Kong in the 1980s when the reforms commenced, stories about learning combat skills combined with legends of love and revenge took the country by storm. Around the same time, classical literary works and folk tales such as *Journey to the West,* a fictional account of the legends about the pilgrimage of the famous Buddhist monk Xuanzang from China to India in search of sutras, also made a come-back, and TV adaptations of these literary works went absolutely viral. It is important to note that what fascinated the country at first were martial arts and folk-tales, not Buddhism the religion. But it was due to the influence of these works and tales that society saw/see Buddhist temples, symbols and monks in a very positive light, which was and remains rare and significant (Chau 2011, 34).

The second and related advantage of Buddhism over other religions in China is the fact that the official Buddhist institutions have taken advantage of the success of the popular culture and use it to spread Buddhism in China effectively and legally—by promoting the 'Buddhist culture' rather than the 'Buddhist religion', a sound strategy which was first articulated in two articles in 1986 by Zhao Puchu (1907–2000), then President of the Buddhist Association of China, with the effect of deflecting political hostility and justifying the existence of Buddhism in this country. He argued in 'We Should Study the Influence of Buddhism on Chinese Culture' and 'The Relationship between Buddhism and Chinese Culture' that, throughout the long history of China, Buddhism had contributed to and benefited all aspects of Chinese culture, and that its existence in contemporary China should also be seen as constructive rather than harmful, since traditional culture, with Buddhist contributions and elements, cannot be dissociated from modern culture, and that the Chinese should draw all the valuable essence of traditional culture to enrich and develop a new, modern, socialist national culture (Chau 2011, 35).

It is important to note the striking similarities between Zhao's expression and that of the current government's position on religion—that religious teachings and values should be interpreted in accordance with those not just of Chinese culture, but of *traditional* Chinese culture. Hereafter, both Zhao himself and official Buddhist institutions have published a large number of articles affirming the positive role of Buddhism in the formation and development of Chinese culture, traditional Chinese culture. Besides, the success of this 'Buddhism as culture rather than religion' strategy is also in the fact that it has not only been expressed in abstract theory, on paper, but has also been carried out in practice, as evident in institutional Buddhism's participation in a wide range of cultural productions in order to spread its social influence further and continuously (Chau 2011, 35–36).

The third advantage of Buddhism over other religions is the associated economic benefits, especially those that can be extracted from tourism to Buddhist sites. At approximately the same time that the *Shaolin Temple* was shown in the mainland in 1982, domestic tourism began to develop rapidly. The success of the movie and the similarly themed movies that followed lit up enthusiasm of pilgrim-tourists. For instance, according to Wang and Zheng (2006), there were 200,000 visits to Shaolin Temple in the period between September 1974, when it first opened as a tourist site, and the end of 1978. In contrast, in 1982 alone, when the movie was first shown in the mainland, the number of visits jumped to 700,000, and by 1984, this number had more than trebled (Chau 2011, 34). Buddhist temples and monasteries, with traditional architecture and magnificent surrounding sceneries, have been popular tourist destinations ever since, and Buddhism-themed handicrafts, ornaments and art have never been out of fashion, generating a great deal of revenue. It is worth noting that Shaolin Temple, which has invested significant funds in the promotion of the Shaolin Culture, has registered 'Shaolin' and 'Shaolin Temple' as trademarks both inside China and abroad. Daoist temples and churches are of course also tourist attractions, but being homegrown, the former do not face the same kind of pressure, neither have they had the opportunity to benefit from free advertising in popular culture; the latter, being imported from the West and associated with the above-examined controversial part of Chinese history, economic benefits alone can do little.

Furthermore, it is not just the 'hard' and martial arts-related side of Buddhism that casts religion in a positive light and attracts popular attention. The fourth advantage of Buddhism over other religions in China is its 'softness'. Whenever one thinks of Buddhism and its teachings, one thinks of gentleness and compassion as not only essential elements of wisdom but also a good, sensible way of life. Many people consider being a Buddhist means that person is kind, tolerant and vegetarian—qualities that fit well within a harmonious society and are in great contrast to what have been perceived to be the essential elements of other imported religions.

4.4 Concluding Part II: Reasonable Expectations in the Age of Sinicization

In the past few years, China appears to have witnessed a hard-line turn on religion. On the policy level, several key guiding principles have been firmly established. First, religious affairs must be actively guided to adapt to the socialist system and society, support Party leadership and the political regime, and serve the overall interests of the nation and the Chinese people (State Council Information Office 2018). Second and related, religions and religious dialog should be promoted as an instrument for implementing official state policy objectives, for instance, facilitating connections with those countries that are hosting Belt and Road Initiative projects. Third and most importantly, and as already noted in this chapter, the word 'sinicization' has been making increasing appearances on the media and in print, meaning that the Party and the government are increasingly forceful in developing and promoting policies that shape religious practices in China into what they consider to be the Chinese identity, assimilating religious beliefs with China's traditional culture, promoting patriotic education and activities within religious communities in order for them to exhibit Chinese characteristics and ways of thinking.

Part II has not aimed to present a comprehensive situational analysis of religion in China, but has rather stressed the centrality of relationality in Chinese religious life, in order to demonstrate the connections and interactions between religions and other sociocultural and political elements in the wider society, and to identify sources of distrust, fear and disconnections. In many ways, if not every way, in order to understand state-religion relations in China, one must first understand state-society relations, present-past relations, local-foreign relations, which have never been mutually independent of each other, and to recognize that the Chinese mentality toward religion has pretty much remained unchanged throughout the country's long history, hence periodically repeating the same conflicts and revealing the same emotions—which means that it might well be pointless to keep discussing the theories and repeating 'prosecution is wrong' if the history is not sufficiently addressed and the emotions not tentatively dealt with. However, overemphasizing the long-lasting impact of history or reopening questions that now firmly belong in the past may in fact be detrimental to dealing with the present and looking into the future. In the search for practical solutions, the Chinese do not seem to be very good at letting go heavy baggage and starting afresh. Nor do present circumstances require or permit.

References

Bell A (2014) Relating indigenous and settler identities: beyond domination. Palgrave Macmillan

Castellino J, Redondo ED (2006) Minority rights in Asia. Oxford University Press

Chau AY (ed) (2011) Religion in contemporary China: revitalisation and innovation. Routledge, Abingdon

Chau AY (2019) Religion in China: tie that bind. Polity Press, Cambridge

Frick M-L (2019) Human rights and relative universalism. Palgrave Macmillan
Gladney DC (2004) Responses to Chinese rule: patterns of cooperation and opposition. In: Frederick Starr S (ed) Xinjiang: China's muslim borderland. M.E. Sharpe, Armonk, NY, pp 375–396
Guo R (2013) China's ethnic minorities: social and economic indicators. Routledge
Hsu S (ed) (2003) Understanding China's legal system. New York University Press
Israeli R (1980) Muslims in China. Curzon Press, London
Kolodner E (1994) Religious rights in China: a comparison of international human rights law and Chinese domestic legislation. Pacific Basin Law J 12:407
Kuo C (2017) Religion and nationalism in Chinese societies. Amsterdam University Press
Kuo L (2018) Chinese cities crack down on Christmas celebrations. at https://www.theguardian.com/world/2018/dec/24/china-cracks-down-on-christmas-celebrations. The Guardian, 24 Dec 2018
Kymlicka W (2007) Multicultural Odysseys: navigating the new international politics of diversity. Oxford University Press
Leibold J, Yangbin C (2014) Minority education in China. Hong Kong University Press, Hong Kong
Lim FKG (ed) (2013) Christianity in contemporary China: socio-cultural perspectives. Routledge, Abingdon
Mackerras C (2003) China's ethnic minorities and globalization. RoutledgeCurzon
McDonald L (1998) Can collective and individual rights coexist? Melbourne University Law Review 22(1998):310–336
Siegel B (2007) Stressful times for Chinese students. TIME magazine, 12 June 2007
Steiner N (2010) Negotiating policy and identity in Uyghur China: realizing a Uyghur community policy. Wittenberg Univ East Asian Stud J 35:43–56
The State Council Information Office of the People's Republic of China (2018) China's policies and practices on protecting freedom of religious belief. http://www.gov.cn/xinwen/2018-04/03/content_5279419.htm. April 2018
Wang G, Zheng C (2006) Shaolinsi: shangyechao zhong de chushi zitai (Shaolin Temple: An Other-worldly Attitude in the Tide of Business). Zhongguo xinwen zhoukan (Chinese News Weekly), pp 40–47
Wei HH (2016a) A dialogical concept of minority rights. Brill, Leiden
Wei HH (2016b) Asking the minority question in China. J Compar Law 11(2):214–234
Yang CK (1961) Religion in Chinese society: a study of contemporary social functions of religion and some of their historical factors. University of California Press, Berkeley and Los Angeles
Yang F (2012) Religion in China: survival & revival under communist rule. Oxford University Press, New York
Yang F (2013) A research agenda on religious freedom in China. Rev Faith Int Affairs 2(2)
Yao X, Badham P (2007) Religious experience in contemporary China. University of Wales Press, Cardiff
Yu AC (2005) State and religion in China: historical and textual perspectives. Open Court
Zang X (2015) Ethnicity in China. Polity Press, Cambridge
Zhang Q, Zhu Y (2011) Religious freedom and its legal restrictions in China. Brigham Young Univ Law Rev 3:783–818
Zhu G (2010) Prosecuting "Evil Cults": a critical examination of law regarding freedom of religious belief in Mainland China. Hum Rights Quart 32(3):471–501

Chapter 5
Intimacy and the Policing of Virtue

5.1 Introduction: Intimacy as Otherness

Many if not all aspects of otherness covered in this book have something to do with social change, which in China tends to be automatically associated with 'revolution'—cultural revolution, information revolution, revolutionary reform—all emphasizing the speed, scale, scope, and impact of change. Chapter 1 has noted that in the past few decades, China is said to have experienced a 'sexual revolution', leading some academics and the media to talk about the phenomenon and its manifestations as the result of cultural clashes, 'when East meets West', when conventional Chinese society and especially its younger generation finally embrace modern expressions of sex and sexuality, implying the belatedness and justifiability of this revolution. This chapter looks closely at two controversial topics related to this so-called sexual revolution. While neither is taboo exactly, neither is talked much about openly, or they only tend to be talked about in a particular light due to their association with illegality, immorality, and shame.

A popular view holds that there is a link between political liberalization and sexual liberalization, in that just as the former implies greater political participation and personal autonomy on the part of the individual, sexual liberalization also presupposes some form of modernization and an atmosphere of greater personal freedom, in which individuals gain greater liberty to conduct their sexual affairs according to their own wishes and desires (Jeffreys 2006, 44). Indeed, freedom in the realm of sex and sexuality is often considered a reliable marker of progress and modernization. This appears to be an accurate description of China's reform era a few decades ago when this so-called sexual revolution first appeared, when there was not only a dramatic increase in public displays of affections and sexual intimacy which were previously unthinkable in conventional China; it also caused the emergence of a gay culture which was already examined in Chap. 1; it was also accompanied by a vibrant albeit illegal sex industry.

H. H. Wei, *Sociocultural Otherness and Minority Justice: A Study on China*,
Ius Gentium: Comparative Perspectives on Law and Justice 88,
https://doi.org/10.1007/978-981-16-9752-4_5

Part I of this chapter examines commercial sex at a time when the party-state has once again turned conservative and has expressed a great deal of anxiety about what it considers to be sexual promiscuity and immoral conducts. Social, moral and cultural discourses in relation to sex and so much more are increasingly conducted according to considerations that are historical, traditionally Chinese, and conservative. The author does not focus on examining prostitution as a feminist issue by debating whether it is a person's right to sell one's body for financial gain; neither does she emphasize it as a crime, which it is in China, or debate the necessity and effectiveness of the relevant laws and police crackdowns over the years—although both feminist debates and existing laws and policies will be considered to set the scene. Neither does the chapter seek to choose a side between the abolitionists and those who want to legalize prostitution. Instead, attention focuses on the social, cultural and economic factors that determine China's perception of prostitution, as well as the reasons behind those who buy and sell sex in various ways.

Much of the analysis conducted here is enabled by and dependent on invaluable fieldwork conducted by Chinese sociologists, which gives this chapter an additional aim of introducing their names to readers who are not yet familiar with them. It is important for readers to know that despite social stigma and increased policing of virtue, which renders studying such topics increasingly difficult and easy to misunderstand, Chinese sociologists have conducted dedicated studies on this subject over the years, in whose works those who are normally considered 'the other' are treated as simply real people who, for their own reasons, have to make a living in an illegal way. It is rather surprising that in a society such as China, these academics have managed to adopt a softer approach and present those involved in prostitution in a rather neutral, even sympathetic light. It is only with such a mentality that it is possible to understand the meaning of the re-emergence of prostitution during the reform era after decades of apparent absence and what it reveals about China's changing conceptions and particularities of modernity.

Part II moves on to another topic concerning intimacy and sexuality. When analyzing the sociocultural aspects of Chinese society, scholarship, especially Western scholarship, tends to emphasize change and transformation, and in doing so has at times neglected the powerful forces of cultural continuity (Jankowiak and Moore 2017, 6). The three topics examined in Part II—cohabitation, extramarital relations, and singlehood—are termed 'alternative family life' by the author, indicating that the otherness of these alternative lifestyle choices is due to the persistent presence of one predominant and conventional way of family life—that of a legal marriage based upon a stated promise of loyalty protected by the state. While the Chinese family and marriage have undergone significant changes not only in the past decades, the basic ideals, expectations, structure and functions all remain the same. By examining the social origins, determinants and functions of cohabitation, extramarital relations and singlehood in a conservative national context, how cultural tradition and morality interfere with and shape people's private life becomes apparent, in so doing the commonly presumed power relations in such relationships as well as social expectations to the extent of social pressure, are re-examined. In particular, this chapter makes a connection between identity politics and the search for intimacy, emphasizing not the immorality or pragmatism of certain lifestyle choices but the interplay between unsatisfied basic human needs on the one hand, and social, economic, cultural and technological factors on the other in the generation of the driving forces behind personal choices.

5.2 Part I: Prostitution, Intimacy and Power Relations

5.2.1 Setting the Scene: Prostitution in a Changing China

The subject of prostitution offers a surprisingly useful vehicle for examining not only sociocultural changes in China but also the interaction between the development of politics and that of sexual culture, particularly through observing how the official discourse on the subject has changed over time and with reference to the anxiety and fear that China's sexual revolution in general and prostitution in particular have generated for both the authorities and ordinary people. In much the same way as the other issues covered in this book, it is a controversial phenomenon that both attracts attention and causes people to want to look away due to the shame and stigma attached to it, and that societal conception of it has changed and continues to change with the sociocultural and political atmosphere of the country.

In keeping with Marxist theoretical guidance, the early Chinese Communist Party viewed prostitution as an expression of moral decadence and a sign of the degraded position of women under feudal-capitalist patriarchy and therefore incompatible with socialist ideals. Hence, after taking power in 1949, the CCP embarked upon a series of campaigns that had supposedly eradicated prostitution from the mainland by the late 1950s, which was viewed as one of the major achievements of the Maoist regime (Jeffreys 2012, 2), although others said that it never disappeared completely; rather, the rates were extremely low due to the population's lack of mobility, opportunities and funds as a result of central planning of everything. Stories such as those of former prostitutes who were liberated and fully transformed into exemplary factory workers were also widely told during this period.

The re-emergence of prostitution historically coincided with the commence of China's economic reforms and opening-up to the West in late 1978 under the leadership of Deng Xiaoping. Although it remains debatable whether there was a causal link as such, the cause of prostitution becoming a problem could be attributed to the dramatic changes taking place in the country at that time that caused some commentators to call it a second industrial revolution, resulting not only in the wholesale transformation of China's economy but also the largest internal migration in human history, and it was this huge flood of rural people rushing into the cities seeking opportunities and wealth that provided the sex industry with a large portion of its workforce. Although the assertion that prostitution was completely absent during the Maoist era has always been challenged—thereby challenging the claim that it had 'come back'—it remains true that the subject of prostitution did not become a serious governmental and intellectual concern until the reforms were well on the way, and it became a serious concern only because it was sufficiently widespread and continued to grow, giving rise also to the widely held opinion that, just like so many other things that were/are wrong with the Chinese society, the growing problem of prostitution particularly during the reform era was the result of Western moral corruption.

The prevalence of prostitution in China is difficult to say for certain as figures relating to the number of sexual service providers vary according to different sources and estimates. What is certain is that the abolitionist policy that was enforced during the Maoist era—with the ultimate aim of eliminating prostitution eventually—has been inherited and enjoys continuous support today. Over the past few decades since the reform era, China has put in place a wide range of legislations and regulations that outlaws sex work and third-party involvement in sex work, including but not limited to the first Criminal Law in 1979, the 1987 Regulations, the 1984 Criminal Law, the 1991 Decision on Strictly Forbidding the Selling and Buying of Sex, 1991 Decision on Severe Punishment of Criminals Who Abduct and Traffic in or Kidnap Women and Children, the 1992 Law on Protecting the Rights and Interests of Women, the 1997 Revised Criminal Law, the 1999 Entertainment Regulations, and so on. The public Security Bureau would enforce these laws through police raids as a part of periodic crackdowns, which were campaigns that would tend to last varying periods of time. Dewey, Zheng and Orchard (2016, 10) note that such raids would also come in different forms: regular and shock raids, timed and random raids, systematic and block raids, daytime and night raids.

However, despite illegality, prostitution has proven to be a resilient industry, with massage parlours, karaoke bars, hair salons, and high-end clubs all being common sites for commercial sexual services. This chapter invites readers to consider why it is necessary to pay attention to prostitution in China and how best to cut into the subject, which may be answered together. First, the subject of prostitution has always been presented over simplistically, binarily, in opposition to moral and legitimate sex, as simply immoral sex and illegitimate sex. It is important to note the internal diversity of personal motivations and individual circumstances so as to truly understand the subject and those involved. Second and related, as a sociocultural phenomenon, it is necessary to place it within the larger societal context and examine its relationship and interaction with other social forces that play a key role in generating, sustaining but also condemning the phenomenon, for instance moral and cultural traditions, feminist influences, changes in the wider sexual culture, as well as challenges presented by the job market. Third, considering the complex sociocultural and economic reality, this chapter also explores what it means to take a middle path between abolition and legitimization, and examines prostitution as a subject of sociocultural otherness rather than crime.

5.2.2 *Beyond Crime: Prostitution as Sociocultural Otherness*

Rather than speaking of this subject in the only way it is supposed to be spoken of, that it is a serious legal and moral crime that ought to be condemned and eliminated, it is important to compare and contrast the variety of ways of looking at prostitution within the Chinese context, taking particular note that it concerns a wide range of questions, not only those of sexuality, sexual culture, the institution of marriage, but also the trafficking of women, internal migration, the labor market, economic and social inequality, even the construction and perception of modernity. While this chapter does not fully cover all of these aspects, it hopes to serve at least as a reminder of the danger and injustice of oversimplification.

5.2.2.1 Moral Decadence

Prostitution is a topic that sparks many ethical debates and is among one of those actions that are considered immoral *ipso facto*. Claims to morality and virtue in the realm of sexuality are no news in any culture, and there appear to be three most commonly defended ethical views that uphold the immorality of prostitution. The first is the naturalistic theories of sexual ethics upheld by the Catholic Church, according to which all actions that a human performs are supposed to be aimed at their good, and whether or not an act constitutes a fulfilment of the human good ought to be determined according to natural law. Saint Thomas Aquinas ([1264] 1975) concludes that sexual acts must be guided by reason and performed only when proper human functions are fulfilled—for the propagation of the species—and that sexual intercourse for any other purpose, including but not limited to prostitution, is unnatural and immoral.

These naturalistic theories have secular formulations as well as very similar cultural expressions in Chinese culture, in which consensual sexual relations without marriage, let alone selling and purchasing sex, have always been considered to be morally inferior, although in different periods of Chinese history, they attract different degrees and forms of condemnation or penalties if any. In much of contemporary China, particularly during the previous reform era, societal moral perception and treatment of prostitution has been full of contradictions. On the one hand, the country has pushed for a market society in which the so-called evils of the market have had space and time to grow—sexual liberation and sexual freedom, or as some would prefer, sexual promiscuity and moral corruption—which have presented serious challenges to traditional ethics and moral values that have long been considered to be the bedrock of Chinese society.

But on the other hand, discussions and debates about sex and sexuality have also grown, allowing space, albeit limited, for influential sociologists such as Pan Suiming, Li Yinhe, Huang Ying Ying to examine and present to the public the complex relations between sex, power and morality, and announce that a society does not have to be puritan in order to be decent and civilized (Li 2008; Pan 2017; Pan and Huang 2013; Jeffreys 2006, 46). Pan Suiming, Huang Ying Ying, and Ding Yu have also produced several works on Chinese prostitutes over the past many years, telling their stories, calling for greater understanding and gentler treatment. The consequence of reading such nonmainstream works in a characteristically socially conservative society appears to be that, while one may not consider prostitution to be absolutely morally corrupt, few can entirely accept it, which corresponds to the fact that despite the enormous and continuous sociocultural changes that have taken place in the past decades, mainstream perception of prostitution has changed very little.

The second commonly expressed point of view that could be employed to condemn prostitution on moral grounds is the so-called 'no sex without love' view. This more modern expression of conventional sexual morality appears to have been attributed to the late Roger Scruton (1944–2020). In *Sexual Desire: A Moral Philosophy of the Erotic,* Scruton argues that unlike the claims of the Catholic Church, the natural function of sex is not procreation but to express love and to recognize the personal existence of another individual, and that it is not animal instincts that motivate sexual desires but a complex system of human intentions and reciprocal response mediated by the concept of the person—in other words, purely human (Scruton 1986). Sexual perversions are therefore immoral. Prostitution clearly does not meet his criteria of moral sex.

This is also a widely held belief in China, in that sex should be at least affection-based if not love-based, which could of course happen with or without the formal institution of marriage, as modern patterns of dating and courtship in many ways oppose tradition in its purest form. Without getting into a detailed philosophical analysis of the differences between affection, love, lust, passion and so on, it is sufficient to point out that since prostitution is by nature commercial, whether or not there is affection or other related emotions involved as the act happens does not seem to alter its sociocultural positioning in the Chinese context. Exactly how widely held this 'no sex without love/affection' view is remains unknown, but it is important to know and as will explained in more detail below that sex for other purposes including casual sex has received growing tolerance, even recognition, among the younger generations, which no doubt will affect their perception of prostitution as a sexual act, legal or not.

The third view that may be employed to condemn prostitution is the radical feminist position, which claims that inherent in all sexual acts are the subjugation and objectification of women and that prostitution is the ultimate way to achieve this. Feminist philosophy in general emphasizes the inequalities and oppression that women suffer as a group in society. Such inequalities and oppression are usually attributed to the male-dominated patriarchy that has had a long history and is very much alive today—a representative example being the Chinese society. While different branches of feminism tend to agree with this general description of women's position in society, their precise views on sex and sexuality vary. And it is not possible to understand prostitution in any cultural context without first appreciating the substantial extent to which different branches of feminists disagree over prostitution's nature, social meaning, impact, moral and legal status, and indeed their projection of women.

5.2.2.2 Feminism, Feminisms

At one extreme is the anti-prostitution group, which, following Catharine Mackinnon, relies almost exclusively on radical feminist theorizations of sex and sexuality as a social construct of male power, defined by men and forced upon women (Jeffreys 2004, 76). They believe that in any society, it is gender and sexuality rather than economic class that are the primacy contradiction in women's lives, and thus oppose the institution of prostitution, which they consider to be the ultimate in the reduction of women to objects that can be purchased and sold, on the grounds that it is a key part of a patriarchal system of oppression that denies women their full status as human beings (Jeffreys 2004, 76). This rendition of men as oppressors and women as helpless victims has led this group to construct monolithic representations of women and of their needs, which have proven to be self-defeating in some respects and limited in applicability in others, resulting in criticisms such as that they have been blinded by gender differences and gender differences alone and have ignored other equally if not more important factors such as race, sexual orientation, tolerability of the culture in question, and so on.

The vast majority who oppose this radical feminist depiction of prostitution share not exactly a pro-prostitution perspective as such but rather an anti-anti-prostitution perspective (Jeffreys 2004, 79). They also see prostitution as an unconventional form of work for women, but nevertheless maintain that women have the right to choose to engage in such work should their personal circumstances deem it necessary. In other words, they see it as a kind of work, demeaning, but work nonetheless. This is not to deny that there are also those at the other extreme who see prostitution as an exercise of women's autonomy and freedom to do as one sees fit with one's body—a view that has been criticized for endorsing promiscuous sex in the name of liberty. As this chapter will show, while this radically liberal approach is highly problematic and does not reflect the complex lived reality of those engaged in prostitution in most if not the vast majority of circumstances, prostitution is nevertheless internally diverse in terms of forms as well as personal circumstances of those involved in it, and that it does appear to be true that in some forms of prostitution those who sell their bodies do seem to have done so out of autonomy, even enjoyment and pursuit of sexual pleasure, and getting paid for it.

The utility of these feminist responses to prostitution is arguably limited in the Chinese context, in that in many ways the Chinese responses, or the Chinese response, is a departure from any meaningful theoretical debate at all, in that while attacking prostitution from theoretical points of view is normal, employing theories to defend prostitution has been extremely rare, partly due to the lack of a necessary space within which such socioculturally controversial views may be freely exchanged, and partly due to a general lack of societal as well as academic interest in the subject.

5.2.2.3 Sexual Liberation

A perhaps more useful (though also questionable) angle of looking at prostitution in China is to see it as part of a 'sexual revolution' as a result of the East meeting the West, through which the ordinary Chinese, especially the younger generations, get the chance to embrace the 'liberal' and 'progressive' sexual ideals and practices of the Western world, causing the Chinese culture in many respects to increasingly resemble that of the free West—such convergence nowadays is increasingly seen in a negative light. It is a useful angle in that it places the subject more firmly within the context of social change, particularly the dramatic shifts that took place during the reform era; it is questionable as it may be argued that it was the economic side of things—dramatic increase in purchase power, internal migration, opportunities to engage in prostitution activities at a wide range of venues—rather than a change in attitude, that has caused the phenomenon.

Although the two are of course inseparable. As already mentioned in earlier chapters, whether what took place could be called a revolution as such may be debatable, what is beyond doubt is that during the reform era when prostitution began to re-emerge, there was a widely felt sense of comprehensive liberation, or liberalization, in many aspects of the people's personal and social lives, including sexual life. However, of course, being sexually liberal does not necessarily mean supportive of prostitution, and the reality was and has always been much less straightforward, in that the dramatic changes in the sexual culture during the reform era in fact revived many traditional cultural practices, such as that of concubinage but now in the modern disguise of mistress-keeping, having multiple sexual partners, or frequent visits to prostitutes.

But it is easy to blame it all on the exposure to foreign, sexually liberal, culture, as while at that time as well as now, exposure to foreign culture is considered necessary, the state has always been concerned with the detrimental impact that some foreign cultural elements may have on the socialist values and traditional Chinese culture. In the sexual field, the state and society are particularly worried about Western notions and practices of sexual freedom and sexual liberation corrupting Chinese youth (Jeffreys 2006, 45)—in much the same way that Western notions and practices of political freedom and political liberalism would corrupt the Chinese people.

5.2.2.4 Prostitution and Labor

A fairly obvious fact that has received no official recognition is that prostitution in contemporary China has been shaped by changing labor market conditions. There are several aspects to this observation. First, the growing literature on China's internal rural-to-urban migrant workers shows that a significant part of the female migrant population has entered the sex industry to work as lower-class prostitutes (Sun 2020; Jeffreys and Yu 2015, 103) and that the reason that they left their hometowns in the first place was not necessarily the lack of work but the search for better-paying work (Jeffreys 2004, 12). This points to the second aspect of the reality of prostitution in

China, namely, that it has economic lure, which explains its continued growth and rapid spread during the reform era when restrictions placed upon people's movements from the less developed rural regions to the cities were lifted. In the presence of unemployment and huge socioeconomic inequality today, prostitution is likely to appear particularly lucrative as an income-generating activity for less advantaged women, despite the government's implementation of tougher controls and punishment.

However, it would be wrong to assume that only poor women enter prostitution. This leads to the third aspect which will be explored in greater detail in Sect. 5.2.4 below, that there are diverse forms of selling and buying sex, reflecting different individual circumstances, motivations and needs of those engaged in it, to which tentative attention ought to be paid if an accurate and realistic understanding of prostitution in China is to be gained. While this chapter does not attempt to examine all forms of prostitution, it wants to draw attention to the less typical types of selling sex as well as the less noticeable reasons for selling and buying. But before getting into the details, it is necessary to examine why some types of prostitution have received less attention than others, and why some previously unnoticed categories of sex buyers deserve urgent, friendly, attention—against the background of how prostitution is currently presented and studied in China compared to how the author believes it ought to be presented and studied.

5.2.3 Simplifications of Reality

Prostitution is not one of those subjects that could easily generate interest let alone dedication from those outside the fields of human and minority rights, gender and sexuality, and when and where it does attract attention, it is usually for the wrong reasons. In the absence of sufficient academic research and a complete lack of public discourse, prostitution and prostitutes have been presented in the way that they are normally presented in most cultures—as problems and scandals. While the legality of prostitution in China is not open to debate and will probably never be, which necessarily limits what is achievable in terms of society's treatment of sex workers; what is more relevant and important than cold questions of legality and morality, is whether we have really understood the phenomenon, whether we have accurately identified the driving forces behind sex-selling and sex-buying, whether we have acquired enough information and knowledge about those individuals involved in such work, and whether we care to do so.

How a controversial subject or group is presented is of great significance in an environment in which public discourses on such topics are often not possible, rendering that members of society tend to readily take on what is handed to them, especially in the absence of sufficient opportunities, and willingness, to gain first-hand knowledge. Hence, it is of crucial importance that the problems with how the subject of prostitution is currently being presented are clearly identified and frankly confronted, particularly the fact that the mainstream presentation today is static, binary and a grossly simplified version of reality. There are several aspects to this.

First, the fact that selling sex and soliciting prostitutes are illegal in China has prevented people from feeling the need to ask profound questions about important concepts in relation to the subject of prostitution on the one hand, for instance stigma, discrimination, sexual desires, poverty, and on the other from making tentative enquiries into the personal lives of those involved in the trade. Prostitution is portrayed as an ugly social, legal and moral problem, and prostitutes are lazy women who make easy money by lying on their back and profit without much effort. Once this image becomes fixated, it becomes unnecessary to ever ask 'how do women in prostitution really make money and at what cost?' or 'is prostitution really that simple and effortless?'. The general public tends to stop at cold hard data but considers themselves as having acquired all the necessary information on the subject, for instance, the number of prostitution-related cases in a given year, the estimated number of prostitutes at a given time in a given place, the number of police crackdowns in the area, or existing laws, regulations and policies. Such highly abstract and fragmented information does not reveal anything meaningful about the 'person' that the data are supposed to represent.

On this point, three aspects are worth highlighting here. First, on stigma and discrimination, state regulation of transactional sexual exchange always reflects prevailing sociocultural beliefs about a wide range of issues, such as the appropriate forms of sexual expressions, the role of the state in the regulation of adult consensual sexual relations, freedom from sexual exploitation, social and moral decency and so on. Out of the three main approaches to prostitution—criminalization, decriminalization, legalization—China has firmly adhered to the first, which has had a number of consequences: the illegality and stigma associated with their work reduces their bargaining power with clients and significantly increases their risks of abuse and exploitation; their mistrust of the authorities hinders their possibilities to get health treatment when and where necessary, contact social services, or report crimes committed against them; and if caught, criminal records of prostitution-related offences will further limit their already very limited abilities to obtain employment, housing and other benefits and opportunities that may be life-changing (Dewey et al. 2016); and their bad image created by criminalization significantly impacts on societal conception of them, hindering their possibility of having a normal life.

Criminalization has also hindered their possibility of having a decent working environment, which is the second, better known aspect nevertheless worth highlighting. Studies have found that instead of eliminating prostitution, criminalization has resulted in a violent and exploitative working environment that threatens the health and safety of many sex workers, whose sociolegal status renders them extremely vulnerable in their dealings with the police, clients, madams, bar bouncers, gangsters, other sex workers who may bully or otherwise take advantage of them in respective ways (Sun 2020; Huang and Pan 2014; Dewey et al. 2016; Jeffreys 2012). Under criminalization, sex workers are also much less able to negotiate the terms of sexual transaction, including condom use, which is made worse by the fact that condoms are often considered evidence of sex work during police raids. This is not saying that legalization is the way out, which is completely out of the question in China. However, rather than emphasizing the health and safety consequences of illegality, which are of course serious issues, the underlying reasons why society does not consider violence and discrimination against this group a problem deserves attention.

The third aspect worth highlighting is that, thankfully, in the face of a general lack of interest in sex workers' everyday lives, Chinese sociologists such as Pan Suiming, Huang Yingying and Ding Yu have continuously been engaged in field studies on prostitution and prostitutes over the past two decades, aiming to get to know the real person, tell their full stories and present their lived experiences, difficulties, relationships and emotions, so that the public may become willing to consider better treatment for these people if not afford them social recognition. In addition to conducting research on controversial topics such as the strategies that prostitutes and their managers employ to resist police crackdowns (Huang and Pan 2014), the most invaluable contributions that they and their team have made are the collection of personal stories of prostitutes revealing previously untold facts of their everyday life, social interactions, their families, and how they do business.

Challenging the oversimplistic presentations of the lived realities of people of the sex trade, such field studies are based on first-hand interactions with prostitutes, which often require making friends with them, living with and observing them over a lengthy period of time, which all involve a certain degree of danger due to the illegal nature of prostitution as well as possibilities of misunderstanding. Unlike the cold hard data, these studies tend to build around questions concerning very personal details of the prostitutes' lives as real persons, such as how they balance their normal family life with selling sex, whether their family members know of their job, if so what they think of it, what the personal circumstances are that have motivated them to get into the sex trade in the first place, whether they are able to form romantic relationships outside business hours, whether they have meaningful interactions and relations with the clients or is it just sex, how they befriend other prostitutes and support each other in their hours of need, what their expectations are in life, what they think of the state's official stance on prostitution, how they themselves see trading sex for money, how they wish to be viewed by society, and so on.

Ding (2016) depicts the width and complexity of sex workers' duties as extending far beyond sexual services and involving a wide range of social and interpersonal skills. Considering themselves 'emotional laborers', the female sex workers in Ding's research are self-trained experts in switching between different roles in different circumstances and according to the needs of the clients, for instance, a skilful icebreaker, a tentative listener, a drinking buddy, a good dance partner, and a gentle companion. Apart from good relations with the clients, they must also ensure they are always on good terms with the madams, managers and other sex workers so that they do not create trouble. Such observations have led Ding (2016, 236) to criticize the move to rename 'prostitution' 'sex work' and to argue that while this move's intention of neutralizing commercial sex work makes sense, it nevertheless emphasizes 'sex', which is only a partial element in the services provided by many in this industry.

Furthermore, and very importantly, Ding (2016) highlights the choice element in many sex workers' decisions to enter the sex industry and emphasizes their urge to become a meaningful part of urban life through cashing in on their youth and sexual appeal. Instead of condemning them and claiming the moral high ground, China's rural–urban divide and widespread socioeconomic inequality are presented as the key driving forces behind such decisions. Many of the female sex workers she studied come from less developed rural regions and have previously worked in poorly paid factories. While they are physically present in cities, the country's household registration system, as examined in Chap. 3, denies them a full urban status, and their low socioeconomic position renders it even less likely for them to fully experience urban life and take advantage of the opportunities that it has to offer.

While becoming a genuinely meaningful part of urban life is beyond their reach, what they can do is to work on the surface—by taking good care of their appearances, looking modern and sexually attractive, making good money by providing sexual services to urban men, spending a large proportion of their income on fashionable clothing and makeup, joining the gym, establishing social networks and connections—all of which enable them to acquire the experience of *looking and living like* an urban woman, without actually *being* one. In other words, entering the sex industry provides them with a chance to experience—the key word being 'experience'—a lifestyle that would otherwise remain out of their reach due to the largely unshakable social hierarchy.

It would be ideal if the works of Ding Yu, Pan Suiming and Huang Yingying may be more widely disseminated and discussed. Instead of focusing on either law or morality, they shine the spotlight on the people themselves, provide answers to those questions that make up a more complete picture of the lived realities of those involved, present different angles that may or may not generate public interest, and most importantly establish a connection between the controversial subject and identity politics. Such works are likely to promote understanding, even sympathy, and greater willingness to engage in the subject, which may help challenge a related second aspect of the mainstream simplistic presentation of prostitution in China—that not enough effort has been spent on studying prostitution relationally. This has two meanings. The first is that more attention should be directed toward examining the personal relationships of those involved in the sex industry, be they family relations, friendships formed at work, romantic relations past and present, or how they interact with the neighbors. Just like any member of a given society, those who engage in sex work are social beings, whose personal choices always have social and contextual determinants as well as social and contextual consequences.

The second meaning of this proposed relational approach is that it is of vital importance to examine the interaction between the phenomenon of prostitution and other structural factors, emphasizing the structural and more fundamental causes of people's choices. The opening of this chapter has already placed the re-emergence of prostitution in China within the larger historical context of the reform era, linking the phenomenon to socioeconomic changes and structural factors, particularly rising and widespread inequality, rural–urban divide, internal migration, and interactions with Western ideals and lifestyles. The aim should be to present the whole set of facts and analysis of the wide range of interactions, thereby diluting individual responsibilities without completely denying their existence.

The third aspect of the existing overly simplistic presentation of prostitution is that attention has predominantly, if not entirely, been on the sellers of sex, ignoring the necessary other half of the sexual encounter—the buyers. This selective focus is a global phenomenon that is hard to understand, especially considering that sex buyers in diverse cultural settings have been found to have an increased burden of sexually transmitted infections and HIV/AIDS, and surveys conducted in the UK and China, for instance, show that sex buyers are significantly more likely than non-sex buyers to report a history of sexually transmitted diseases (Ward et al. 2005; Huang et al. 2011). Despite being global, in a sense, this lack of focus on sex buyers also reveals the patriarchal nature of Chinese society (in which most sellers are women and most buyers are men) and also explains why when condemning prostitution, female sex sellers tend to attract more severe criticism than male buyers.

The correction of this requires not only more honest and comprehensive studies of prostitution and more real-life observations, but also theoretical examinations and investigations into key concepts and social relations. As already mentioned earlier, the lack of public discourse and theoretical engagements has produced a static understanding of the phenomenon. This points to the fourth aspect of the oversimplistic presentation and societal perception of the subject, namely, that the importance of theory and theoretical debate must not be overlooked if we are to fully understand the reality of this group.

5.2.4 The Multifaceted Reality of Human Needs

One important but willingly neglected aspect of prostitution concerns the human and emotional needs that are likely to have been involved. This section does not seek to present a comprehensive evaluation of all the needs elements of this phenomenon or of all the people involved. Rather, attention is directed toward some of the less noticeable aspects of selling and buying sex, with an emphasis on the satisfaction of different needs in different circumstances and less on moral and sociocultural evils. Chinese society is not one that is good at talking about satisfaction of basic human and emotional needs, least of all in such a controversial context, through such a stigmatized means, even though and perhaps especially because it is obvious.

As already pointed out above, buyer-focused Chinese studies on the motives, attitudes and behavior of clients appear to be lacking in the mainland, but Western studies, albeit also very limited, may shed important light on who buys sex and why, as while sociocultural contexts vary, basic human needs and how people choose to satisfy those needs may not. Farley et al. (2015) find that men who pay for sex tend to score higher than those who do not on measures of impersonal sexual interactions and hostile masculinity; they are less empathetic toward prostituted women and see them as intrinsically different from others, indicating that these men share many characteristics with those who are at risk of committing sexual aggression.

Apart from a higher degree of acceptance of sexual violence, male clients of prostitution have been found to express more permissive attitudes toward extramarital sex; they also think about sex more frequently than noncliments, report a higher frequency of masturbation and accessing pornography (Davis et al 2020; Monto and Milrod 2014; Farley et al. 2012). In their explorations of why men pay for sex, Ward et al. (2005) mention rising divorce rates as well as an increase in the proportion of men who have never been married, indicating that male sex buyers often lack relational and committed sex (Farley et al 2015) or are otherwise dissatisfied with their sex lives, lonely, as well as have a certain degree of freedom in their private lives due to lack of attachment and therefore lack of constraints.

Furthermore, empirical studies conducted cross-culturally have confirmed that men would buy sex for the following broad reasons: desire for certain sexual acts that are not generally accessible in their conventional relationships; desire for variety and change; the element of excitement and thrill in the risky nature of various forms of commercial sex; fear of commitment and avoidance of intimacy; inability to have a conventional, noncommercial, relationship; fulfilment of sexual urge; less or no pressure on sexual performance (Campbell 1998; Monto 2000; Atchison et al. 1998; Chu 2018).

On the other hand are the sex sellers' needs, which tend to rise out of unfortunate personal circumstances—the need to escape poverty in the countryside, to support oneself after leaving an abusive marriage, to make a living in a competitive society without decent education and necessary qualifications, to provide for the family, to satisfy one's materialistic needs in the face of growing wealth and income inequalities, to feel wanted for one's physical attractiveness and sexual appeal, and as Ding (2016) above claims, also the need to feel less like an outsider in an alien environment. But as the subsection below will show, it would be wrong to assume that everyone enters prostitution out of some form of desperation or feelings of unworthiness, or that life as a sex seller is always utterly miserable and open to exploitation. The reality is more diverse than anticipated, and everyone's motivations vary according to personal circumstances, which give rise to very diverse needs—as demonstrated by the phenomenon of 'compensated dating'.

5.2.4.1 Compensated Dating

'Compensated dating', or 'yuanjiao' in Chinese, is nothing new in China, with dating websites, social media, apps and modeling agencies helping in the past many years to facilitate relationships in which one side (usually a young girl or woman) offers friendly companionships or sexual favors to the other side (usually an older man) who in return provides monetary or social benefits, which may include a wide range of things such as an expensive night out, tuition fees, luxury goods, overseas holidays, shelter, cash, and sometimes drugs. The author initially hesitated to include 'compensated dating' as a modern form of prostitution, as when it first originated in Japan in the early 1990s, it did not in fact incorporate a sexual aspect but referred only to young girls providing companionships to older male clients. But today, sex has become a primary element in compensated dating, and even though the term does not automatically equal sexual exchanges, in the majority of cases, it does involve a variety of sexual interactions (Chu 2018, 5). It is worth noting that the Japanese government has officially required the term 'prostitution' to denote any situation that has previously been regarded as 'compensated dating' (Udagawa 2007; Chu 2018).

Prostitution or not, an examination of its key features is necessary for two reasons. First, it is a modern and much less straightforward form of sex-selling, lacking many of the traditional key features of prostitution, therefore providing a worthy contrast and further proving the complexity and diversity of the trade. Second and related, it calls the conventional interpretations of client-prostitute power balance into question and sheds important light on the emotional needs of those who buy compensated dating—if it is only sex that they are after, why don't they just purchase traditional forms of prostitution, which is often much cheaper and much less time-consuming? The answer is that they have more than just sex in mind, but for a variety of reasons are only able or prefer to get it this way.

First, Chu (2018) shows that for men who purchase compensated dating, emotional comfort and intimacy are more important than physical pleasure. These men, for whatever reason, are unable to form a conventional romantic relationship or simply have the need for variety or for the occasional girlfriend experience, but nevertheless consider traditional sex workers too commercial and the lack of emotional connection a turn-off. Compensated dating, being much less mechanical and more sensual, is able to offer them a personalized experience that caters to their specific needs and desires, which could consist of a wide range of elements.

One of such needs and desires is in fact to look after and protect the girls or women from whom they have purchased compensated dating, to the extent that some would create a list of all the men who have behaved badly in the past and circulate throughout the community of compensated dating so that the women involved could be warned. Working guidelines have also been drawn up for the women containing detailed information on psychological preparation as well as practical knowledge that they ought to acquire before entering the compensated dating world (Chu 2018, 119). Some men would even offer financial assistance to a woman just to prevent her from going on dates with other clients. All of these manifest not only men's superior financial and social status but also feelings and emotions that strongly resemble those in a conventional intimate relationship.

Second and interestingly, men who purchase compensated dating seem to consider the women offering such services to be intrinsically different from those engaged in traditional sex work. They see the former as normal, clean, innocent and pure, with whom men are able and willing to form a genuine connection, even to develop a proper relationship (Chu 2018; Milrod and Monto 2017). In fact, Chu (2018) notes that it is not uncommon for genuine friendships or noncommercial relationships to form in the field of compensated dating, which is why this form of meeting people is so important for both men and women. Besides, the fact that compared to traditional sex workers, women involved in compensated dating tend to be more selective with regard to whom they have sex with also makes men feel like 'the chosen one' (Chu 2018).

Furthermore, the fact that men who purchase sex consider women who sell sex in the traditional way unclean and too mechanical is worth emphasizing and brings out a different side to sex-buying—that many clients are in fact after comfort, support, connection, security about their masculinity, rather than mere sexual intercourse, indicating that should they have the chance to engage in a normal, noncommercial, committed and connected relationship, they would, but for the time being compensated dating is the closest thing.

One of the reasons is that, third, many of these men do not have the courage to visit traditional brothels either because of the stigma attached to such establishments or lack of confidence in their own attractiveness. The fact that compensated dating is usually initiated and arranged online or on social media provides sufficient space for their self-confidence to grow, can therefore greatly reduce their fear and embarrassment and enhance their powerfulness. This indicates a shift of power balance between the client and the seller in compensated dating, blurs the line between the dominant and the dominated, the powerful and the weak, the provider and the receiver, the protector and the protected, thereby calling into question who really is in charge, who needs whom more, whether selling sex necessarily implies objectification and exploitation of women as it is commonly presumed, and ultimately whether it really is that immoral.

To defend particular aspects of compensated dating does not equal defending compensated dating as a whole, let alone defending prostitution. Afterall its status as a form of prostitution is still open to debate. If its functions of emotional support and intimate connection may be viewed in a positive, nonmaterialistic, light, once the girls' or women's reasons for engaging in compensated dating are taken into account, one's perception may alter. Research suggests that many young girls voluntarily participate in compensated dating because it offers a quick and easy way to make money and to meet rich men with influence, as well as to gain a sense of self-worth and security that the power of luxury and consumption may bring (Jeffreys and Yu 2015; Chu 2018). Unlike those who engage in traditional prostitution, many of these girls and young women are from comfortable backgrounds, get into the field for the sex as well as for the money, and often do not draw a clear line between work sex and private sex, which many of them believe are similar if not the same (Chu 2018, 113; Jeffreys 2012, 55).

For them, monogamy is neither necessary nor required for intimate relationships in a modern society, and this is perhaps the key difference between compensated dating and normal dating with the men taking care of the bills—the former is not committed and provided as a service, whereas the latter is committed and noncommercial even though there is money involved. This is the main reason why society considers compensated dating a clear sign of moral decay and is very disturbed when news reports reveal that young school girls or college students are found to have been engaging in compensated dating. The explosive growth of the internet and social media makes setting up such a date or relationship extremely easy, and rising socioeconomic inequalities will push an increasing number of girls into the field in search of an easy way out. This has become a serious concern in Chinese society.

5.2.4.2 Elderly Sex Buyers

In recent years, articles have begun to appear talking about a previously unnoticed group of Chinese sex buyers—the elderly. Cultural conditioning has determined that when we consider the lives of older people, we do not tend to discuss sexuality and often assume that aging brings dramatic changes to one's sexual appetite and will eventually render sexual fulfilment an irrelevant topic to this group. However, sometimes, an unexpected event may bring about a dramatic change in awareness and understanding, and an elderly man buying sex and getting caught is such an event that constitutes a grim window into the loneliness and desperation that have motivated old men to grasp at the opportunities of commercial sexual interactions.

Elderly men buying sex first came to public attention when a sharp rise in HIV infections among Chinese men above the age of 60 was revealed as having risen from 8,391 cases in 2012 to 19,815 cases in 2017 and to 24,465 cases in 2018, accounting for 16.46% of that year's total infections (Huang et al. 2020; Koetse 2018). Extramarital heterosexual sex was found to be the main means of transmission for elderly men, and marital sex was the main means of transmission for elderly women. This was a piece of shocking news, as it had been popular belief that older adults did not constitute a risk population for HIV infection, as they were socially more conservative with less sexual urges. Hence, clearly contrary to common belief, older people are active in pursuing sex in their later lives, and when their urges are not met, an increasing number will go out and look for sex partners at public places such as ballrooms, public bathrooms, dancing groups, and many will seek prostitution most commonly at low-cost commercial sex venues (Tang et al. 2014; Zhou et al 2014). Their general lack of safe sex awareness is the key reason behind the rising infections of sexually transmitted diseases and HIV/AIDS among this group.

As already examined in Chap. 3, China is a rapidly aging society. Ignoring the sexual needs of this massive and growing group is potentially a major problem for the country. Although media discussions remain rare, the topic is no longer taboo, and a growing number of commentators are urging society to start facing and talking about this uncomfortable subject. Specifically, it is important to first realize that the belief that older people have no sexual interest or should not have sexual interest is erroneous and stereotypical, and that it is such misconceptions that play a vital role in preventing older people from enjoying healthy and safe sex and in causing them to feel shame when experiencing sexual urges or wanting to pursue an active sex life. This should be understood within the Chinese familial and marital context, in which when emotional fulfilment is no longer attained and loving sentiments no longer live on, many if not the majority of Chinese marriages do not break up but rather tend to survive on 'inertia', in that while the couple continue to live together, they are emotionally and sexually withdrawn and indifferent toward each other, the sense of deeply shared affection is absent (Jankowiak and Moore 2017, 123), causing those who can to search for affection and sex elsewhere.

In particular, research shows that compared to older men, older women seem to have less sexual desires and interest (Lindau et al. 2007), which is a major reason for sexual incompatibility within marriage and for men to engage in extramarital and commercial sex. Whether and how much of this gender variation is culturally determined is unknown and impossible to know for sure, but clearly sexuality among older adults should receive greater attention from society as well as from within the group itself. Efforts to reshape societal and individual perceptions are needed in all forms of media and education. Better training for health care providers, particularly those working with older people, is essential in increasing understanding and awareness of elderly sexual needs. The basic message that should be spread out soon and which should be easy to achieve, is that the sexual desires and needs of the elderly are normal, natural, and healthy.

This does not automatically mean that all forms of elderly sexual fulfilment are normal, natural, healthy and should be advocated. The fact that elderly sexuality first came to public attention due to rising HIV infections reminds us of how homosexuality first entered public discourse in China—also with the rise of HIV/AIDS. As examined in Chap. 1, growing public attention to HIV/AIDS underscored the intrinsic tie between homosexual activities and the spread of the disease, which further strengthened fear and stigma related both to HIV/AIDS and the homosexual community. Similarly, elderly sexuality's linkage to HIV infections and prostitution, while reflecting actual facts, is also going to strengthen stereotypes and further demonise elderly sexuality, sexually transmitted diseases and HIV/AIDS, and prostitution, which ought to be taken into consideration when designing and implementing policies of education and intervention.

5.2.4.3 Rural-To-Urban Migrants Revisited

Chapter 3 has already looked at the impact of structural reforms on migrant workers. While female sexual service providers come from all walks of life and multiple sectors of society, a common stereotype is that they are mostly young and poorly educated rural-to-urban migrants. As mentioned previously in this chapter, while some migrant women have been forced into prostitution by severe social and financial hardship, many enter prostitution voluntarily as a means to escape dead-end jobs and in search of upward mobility, because prostitution is able to provide them with more disposable income and flexible working hours (Jeffreys and Yu 2015, 100). While few migrants regard sex work as a permanent, full-time profession, many work intermittently in factories as well as sell sex. It is worth noting that migrant women who work as sex workers are often mothers and daughters, wives and girlfriends, who in most cases opt to sell their bodies to provide for their children and family. Astonishingly, their husbands or boyfriends sometimes work as their pimps and protectors (Sun 2020). Many of these women strongly believe that there is nothing wrong with sex-selling, as they are working to earn honest money just like anyone else, whereas others are ashamed of what they do and are scared of being caught for their transgressive activities (Sun 2020).

A connection is made between transgression and socioeconomic inequality, or more specifically, how the former interacts with, contributes to and shapes the latter.

On 9 September 2013, the *Economic Weekly,* a widely read and influential publication in China, featured a leading story entitled ‘Foxconn’s night life’, claiming to present a trueful account of what life was like for Foxconn workers in the commercial and recreational spaces outside the industrial complexes in the cities of Shenzhen and Zhengzhou. According to the controversial piece based on interviews with the workers, a considerable number of female Foxconn workers sold sex to their male coworkers in their spare time for additional income. Some even ended up leaving their factory work to become full-time sex workers.

Four days after the publication of this piece, the Foxconn Workers’ Union issued a public protest describing the article as being in poor taste and insulting to the 400,000 female workers at Foxconn who were hard-working and dedicated, demanding withdrawal of the article and a public apology, highlighting also the piece’s failure to include the perspective of the management. It is worth pointing out here that the Foxconn Workers’ Union consistently sided with the management and was silent on a wide range of critical issues concerning the workers’ welfare, including but not limited to the previously mentioned suicides (Ngai et al 2014; Sun 2020).

On 25 September, *China Women’s News,* the official newspaper of the All-China Women’s Federation, weighed in on the debate by publishing a commentary that pointed out that, while a small number of Foxconn female workers did engage in some illegal activities, the vast majority were good. It criticized the *Economic Weekly* piece for catering to poor taste by claiming in the article that the women workers were making a rationalist economic decision by engaging in sex work, and urged the Workers’ Union to do more than issuing protesting words and to take concrete steps to protect the workers’ rights and dignity (Sun 2020).

This story is a good example of the functioning of the moralistic framework within which the subject of prostitution is talked about, in that it insists on the binary division between the good woman and the bad woman, the morally acceptable and the morally unacceptable, irrespective of their personal circumstances. By failing to dig deeper or acknowledge the fact that migrant women’s decision to engage in whatever profession is determined not by free will but by rural–urban divides, class division, socioeconomic inequality and capital exploitation, the message is simplified—that selling sex to gain additional income is demeaning, shameful and immoral, thereby ruling out alternative considerations and pathways. One such possible pathway is to have a socioeconomic framework of analysis instead of a moral framework, the applicability of which is not limited to rural-to-urban migrant workers engaged in prostitution but to all sex sellers generally.

Such an approach is necessary because, first, a normative framework, which often evokes tradition, law and order, stigmatizes rural migrant women who sell sex to support their children and family. Without denying the unlawfulness of sex-selling, it should nevertheless be possible to recognize its respectful and dignified aspects. A socioeconomic framework can more realistically reflect what is going on in this complex sociocultural field, within which the state, the market and various social forces all shape societal perception of what is acceptable and what is not, which often oversimplifies social, cultural and personal circumstances. Second, as the example of rural migrant workers shows, rather than moral competence or decency, it is the structural factors, rural–urban divides and socioeconomic inequality that shape individuals' choices and consequently determine their position and respectability in society. Therefore, third and related, the connection between sexual intimacy and sex-selling on the one hand, and rational financial and social considerations on the other, ought to be made more explicit so as to enable more tentative analysis.

Fourth, an important but hardly discussed aspect of prostitution that this chapter has not explored is the fact that people of all sexes—women, men, transgendered—engage in prostitution. Research shows that not only middle-aged women on holidays from Taiwan and Hong Kong sometimes purchase male companionship and sexual services but also young mainland women in search of uncomplicated sex (Miller 2006). Ding (2008) notes that female sex workers in the Pearl River Delta region sometimes purchase sex from male migrants to affirm their higher-class status and to have fun. It was also mentioned in Chap. 1 that some young men from poor rural areas work as male sex workers in cities and offer sexual services to women as well as men. It was also noted previously that many of the young men who provide sexual services to other men self-identify as heterosexual but would do it for the money, while those who are bisexual or gay express concerns over their triply stigmatized identity as homosexual, rural-to-urban migrants and prostitutes (Jeffreys and Yu 2015, 104). A socioeconomic framework can help better examine these 'minorities within minorities' in this female-dominated industry, and will generate additional information on changes in sexual culture as well as gender relations.

5.3 Concluding Part I

Both inside the country and overseas, academic research on prostitution in China has been very limited, and the limited work has most often focused on either law or morality. Part I has sought to emphasize the importance of studying this group not just in terms of business but also in terms of identity and human needs, especially how structural factors have influenced or even determined how individuals make life choices, through which their sense of self-identity is either revealed or concealed, and their needs are either satisfied or remain unfulfilled. Once the structural causes of personal choices are identified, particularly through exploring the subjective experiences of those involved in prostitution, it becomes possible to appreciate the call for society to adopt a more lenient attitude toward these people without having to officially change the laws, polices or state position, although the effects and consequences of recognizing that the root cause of many issues is unrelated to morals are far from predetermined.

Furthermore, without calling for legalization of prostitution, it is nevertheless worthwhile to consider the possibility of developing intervention strategies and services that are unique for the people who are involved in prostitution. For instance, they may be in need of services for assistance in coping with histories of victimization, such as substance abuse treatments, suicide prevention, and counseling services that address sexual and other forms of violence. Whether such violence is perpetrated by family members, partners, strangers, clients or pimps could have different impacts on the individual's psychosocial development and physical well-being. Services must be able to address these multiple possible sources of violence and their respective consequences.

Additionally, the nature and social perception of prostitution could render it difficult for those involved to develop and maintain healthy support networks, such as close family members, supportive friends, and sympathetic professional service providers. Intervention and outreach efforts ought to have this in mind and need to include realistic coping strategies that these people can employ in specific circumstances. They may also be interested in being linked with services that would provide them with more options in life, for instance, safe housing, food and shelter, clothing, skills training, education opportunities, and job placements—which could all potentially lead them away from prostitution.

But how it is possible to provide these services in an environment that criminalizes and discriminates against prostitution requires careful thinking and could perhaps gain inspiration from the rationale behind the 100% Condom Use Programme—that without altering the ultimate goal of eliminating prostitution eventually, it is nevertheless necessary to employ pragmatic transitional methods to deal with the more urgent problems at hand. Whether legalization or some form of partial recognition is likely to take place in the near future does not appear to be something we need to be overly preoccupied with.

5.4 Part II: Social Expectations and Alternative Family Life

5.4.1 Enduring Philosophies and Changing Practices

There are a number of features characterizing China's family life today, reflecting the paradoxes in both the familial sphere and society in general. Traditionally, the ideal family type respects Confucian values, is multigenerational and organized around both parental willingness to sacrifice for their dependents and the dependents' total obedience toward the parents, although this is no longer the primary bases of familial organization or emotional bonds for a large proportion of modern Chinese families. The impact of the era of economic reforms has been felt not only on the redistributive system, class formation and the economy but also on traditional family life, which took a directional shift during the reform era in terms of property, care of kin, decisions about fertility, and very importantly conceptions of intimacy (Jankowiak and Moore 2017). It was during this period that individual interests and emotional and intimate needs began to come into play and gain recognition, and despite continuous emphasis on collective consciousness, collective institutions and collective emotions, state policies during this period gave sufficient space for the growth of individualism.

A direct consequence of this in the private and familial sphere has been the weakening, not disappearance, of the consensus over what the ideal family life is, as well as the weakening, not disappearance, of an utter agreement on the ideal division of labor or performance of roles within the family. While society remains characteristically conservative and promotes a particular type of familial pattern, the reality is that instead of the single promoted family type, there are multiple forms of union that are allowed to exist, with or without varying degrees of societal recognition and appreciation, and individuals, unlike in the past, tend to care less about what others and society think of their life choices and ways of living, although wanting societal acceptance is only natural.

It is impossible to understand the emergence and functions of alternative ways of union without first appreciating the mainstream form of union—legal marriage. Traditional Chinese marriage was patriarchal and tended to be arranged by parents who would prejudge the overall suitability of the potential son/daughter-in-law on behalf of their children, often with the aim of strengthening the family as a viable socioeconomic unit. Since traditional Chinese families would go to great lengths to keep unmarried men and women from socializing together, romantic, intimate and sexual inclinations of unmarried people were suppressed by tradition and ideology, parents were often in a position to make marriage arrangements without any distractions of romance let alone sexual encounters (Jankowiak and Moore 2017, 74), having only family interests in mind.

While Maoist and liberal ideologies in the twentieth century very much undermined the traditional family system in its purest form, it was never eliminated entirely and its influence lingered on into the modern days, when many parents would still exercise some form of control over their children's private life and 'arrange' their marriages though perhaps not quite forcefully—it is not only a sociocultural habit but also an entitlement. A difference is that while in the old days, family interests were paramount when marriages were arranged, now the children's interests tend to be determinant—as judged by the parents' standards and criteria. An important reason for this lingered-on 'habit' of the parents is the economic control that most parents still exercise over their children and their future prospects, which is why young people who live in an urban environment where economic opportunities are more available and varied (and the culture is also cosmopolitan) tend to have greater freedom over their own ways of living and marriages. However, even in such environments, the pervasive Confucian ideology that empowered males and elders, backed up by a society that stands ready to enforce its precepts, means that young people generally would let their parents have a say in matters concerning marriage and family life (Jankowiak and Moore 2017, 75).

It is commonly assumed that the idea of affection-based marriage/relationship was introduced into China as a consequence of contact with the West, and that while family has always been one of life's central experiences in China, the ideal of a love-based marriage never existed until the East met the West (Pan 2015, 280). This is not to simplistically assume that arranged marriages were/are always loveless, but as Pan (2015) puts it, in regard to marriage, traditionally the Chinese were nowhere near as familiar or preoccupied with the idea of love as those in the West and that 'romantic love' in China has a history of only approximately eighty years (Pan 2015,

281). Some would rebut this by referring the modern readers to ancient Chinese literature and folkloristic sources with lines and words expressing passion and yearning, indicating that 'romantic love' in China has a history not of eighty years, but of thousands of years, in fact it is pre-Confucian (Jankowiak and Moore 2017, 84). It was only necessary for the traditional patriarchal structures to weaken to a point where young people were granted the opportunity to do what they had always inclined to do—marry someone they were strongly attracted to, which was a genetically-based universal human need (Jankowiak and Fischer 1992).

The reform era is said to have enabled another phenomenon—the dating culture—due to the coming into play of various driving forces that effectively changed the Chinese courtship culture: risen availability of personal wealth, maturing of the single-child generation, expansion of urban leisure venues, rapid growth of the middle class, availability of the internet, and a sharp awareness of Western dating habits (Jankowiak and Moore 2017, 101–102). While the pre-reform era generations believed that, whatever the nature of the marriage bond, love or not love, it ought to be nurtured and expressed within the family, within the officially recognized relationship called marriage; during the reform era, perhaps for the first time in Chinese history, the unmarried population had a great deal of resources at their disposal and an equally great deal of opportunities to explore the previous unexperienced. While Chinese society has always believed that fulfilment of familial and social obligations is an essential part of marriage and family—pre-, during- and post-reform era—it was during the reform era that fulfilment of obligations ceased to be the singularly central feature, partly due to the maturation of a generation that understood the importance of pragmatism and the advancement of personal well-being and interests.

This generates two oppositional possibilities in regard to private life due to individual variations in pragmatism and personal interests: first, entering relationships for pragmatic purposes in the economic and opportunistic sense; second, prioritizing personal needs for intense feelings, romance, and intimacy as advancement of personal interests. Perhaps much more so than Westerners, many Chinese still view dating and getting married as a pragmatic affair, in that attention should not be fixated on finding love as such, but should rather be on generating a sense of safety and stability by entering into a formal relation with 'the right person', for instance someone with similar background, similar education and similar ideals, and most importantly perhaps, a stable income and career—which is normally expected of the man—so that he can sustain the family in the long-term. As one contestant on a popular dating show puts it, 'I would rather cry in a BMW than laugh on a bicycle', which is an extreme but telling example of this type of pragmatism.

In contrast, the second possibility generated by pragmatism and advancement of personal interests mentioned above gives rise to four possible choices of relationship and forms of union to fulfil their personal needs: marriage based on love, love without marriage (or 'relationship or cohabitation based on love'), love outside marriage (extramarital relations), and singlehood if no such bond has been formed with anyone and the person involved does not wish to comprise. While this is by far not the only reason why an increasing number of people choose singlehood over relationships and marriage, it is the reason on which this chapter focuses. The remainder of the chapter examines each of these choices in turn, contextually and from multiple disciplinary perspectives, evaluates the functions and meanings of their existence in a society that not only greatly values family as a vital unit that provides its members with mutual support and personal care, but also believes that the extent to which a family is able to meet such an expectation normally depends on a healthy and stable *martial* relationship.

New conceptions and practices of love, marriage and union point toward individual self-fulfilment and satisfaction, away from sacrificing oneself for the family, unconditionally serving the parents, in-laws and children, and by extension away from obeying those old rules that teach people to so behave. While individual citizens are no longer subjects of the old constraining familial regime and may to varying extents behave according to one's own wishes, the state, which continues to embody notions of sexuality and family with deep historical roots in its official policies, has a lot more to worry about and appears increasingly concerned as divorce rates continue to rise in the past fifteen years or so—in 2018, approximately 4.5 million couples filed for divorce, in 2019 this figure rose to 4.7 million.

In May 2020, a new law was passed and came into effect on the first day of 2021, imposing a mandatory 'cooling off period' of 30 days upon anyone who would file for divorce. If either side of the couple decides to call off the divorce during that period, the aggrieved party must apply for divorce again, and the 30-day clock starts anew. The intention of the state is clear—to discourage frustrated couples from splitting up by making divorce a harder and lengthier process and curbing impulsive divorces especially. Interestingly and despite quarantine during the COVID-19 pandemic, the second half of 2020 saw a sharp rise in the number of couples rushing to file for divorce before the controversial new law came into effect. This is telling in a country that proudly places familial harmony at the center of its culture, where divorce was previously—and even now still in some places—unthinkable, irresponsible and even shameful.

Related to a high divorce rate are two other phenomena that have equally caused the government a great deal of concern—a low fertility rate and a low marriage registration rate. In 2020, China's number of births saw a 15% decline compared with 2019, and annual population growth rate dropped to a new low of less than 0.3%, which no doubt was the reason why the government rushed to introduce a new three-child policy in May 2021, vividly demonstrating how concerned it was about falling fertility and rapid population decline. Low levels of fertility can indeed have profound implications, particularly for a country like China: a shrinking working-age population could severely affect the country's socioeconomic development, which had brought the country so much international influence in the past few decades; changing the age structure, particularly a rapidly aging national population, will also bring unprecedented challenges and heavily burden the health system.

China also recorded its lowest marriage registration rate in nearly two decades in 2020, with some 8.1 million couples registering for marriage, which only accounted for 60% of those in 2013 when such registrations saw a peak. The declining marriage rate not only indicates changing attitudes toward matrimony and family life among the younger generations but also predicts a continuation of low fertility in the country, as while neither the Marriage Law nor the Population and Family Planning Law expressly forbids or allows single parenthood, and that the former in fact expressly guarantees equal rights for children born out of wedlock, the reality is that the laws presume that anyone having children is married, and the treatment of single parents and children born to single parents is often left up to the discretion of local governments, which have adopted varying stances, with some having denied children born out of wedlock household registration ('*hukou*') which determines access to state education and healthcare.

It is in such a societal atmosphere that enduring traditional philosophies and emerging new practices encounter, interact, and conflict, revealing a distinct and powerful process of individualization in the private lives of Chinese individuals, deep contradictions between tradition and modernity, between collective norms and personal preferences, between social stratification and individual pursuit of fulfilment take place and ought to be captured. In the same spirit as Part I, Part II does not employ an overly moralistic perspective but rather focuses on the structural, socioeconomic and emotional determinants of individual decisions and experiences.

5.4.2 Extramarital Relations: Morality, Power Relations, and Identity

While many factors can jeopardise a spousal relationship, the most effective is perhaps infidelity, and the discovery of a spouse's involvement in an extramarital affair is possibly one of the most hurtful events in a socially conservative society, which tends to result in rapid deterioration in the quality of the marriage though not necessarily divorce. Almost all societies and cultures have explicit or implicit standards regarding fidelity, and historically, when and where religion had a strong influence on social norms, all major religions of the world had very specific expectations of fidelity in marriage. In many countries, infidelity is not only grounds for divorce but also has legal consequences with both public and personal consequences, while in others, for instance where Islamic law functions, infidelity is severely punished.

Extramarital relations are seldom if ever openly and systematically studied, not least because people tend to be secretive about them, rendering cases hard to find and reliable data absent, hence little is known about the prevalence and correlates of such affairs; but also that just like everywhere else, there are widely accepted sociocultural standards of behavior against such relations, the breach of which will attract moral condemnation, and in some situations, for instance if a government official is involved, disciplinary and legal punishments. But it would be wrong not to look closer at extramarital affairs in contemporary China, as, first, it partially explains the high and rising divorce rate despite all that the government has done in preventing people from getting divorced; second, it is central to understanding gender differences and gender equality in sexuality in China; and third, looking beyond (though without ignoring) morality and examining extramarital relations as demonstrations of complex yet natural human needs and desires, may help us better understand the characteristically sexually repressed society in which such needs and desires are not always easily satisfied. It is a particular way of obtaining intimacy that could help us understand the larger social impacts on human sexuality, and vice versa.

Attitudes toward extramarital affairs are a good angle to examine gender differences and inequality in society in general and in sexuality in particular. It is a widely held belief that men and women have different attitudes toward extramarital affairs, and that men are more likely than women to have affairs, partly because in all societies men are more likely than women to have high income and to use that income to facilitate extramarital relations. Traditional biosocial theories also hold that men's promiscuous behaviors are largely due to biology, and that maximizing the number of partners is a way of men showing their masculinity, contrasting with women maximizing their births to hold on to relationships and stability. Feminist theories, on the other hand, believe that such discrepancies between males and females are socially constructed; hence, if opportunities and social conditions permit, women, just like men, will also maximize their number of partners.

Related to this is the perspective that sexuality has always been a power struggle, in that throughout Chinese history, men (and culture) have managed to carefully confine women's sexuality within the family, particularly in the old days when polygamy was legal and rich and power men had concubines, women were men's private property and were bearers of inhumane cultural practices of foot-binding which had the unspoken purpose of ensuring women's fidelity, which was tightly connected to the honor of the entire family, by making it difficult for them to move around and socialize.

Although concubines and polygamy have long been replaced by modern monogamous marriage arrangements, this long sociocultural legacy has kept Chinese women's tolerance of their men's infidelity relatively high, and the more traditional Chinese women generally have more tolerance of their husbands' being involved in extramarital affairs than their more modern counterparts. This legacy has also given rise to men's double standards regarding gender and sexuality, in that while on the one hand they expect their wives to be faithful, on the other hand and especially at the peak of the reform era in the late 1990s and early 2000s when social controls were significantly loosened, under the combined influences of deep-rooted feudalist male dominance, imported Western ideologies, a sense of personal freedom, and newly (re)emerged opportunities of commercialized sexuality, men—not just rich and powerful men—could explore a freer sexual lifestyle, have extramarital relations or keep mistresses, adding some modern Western flavors to a long Chinese tradition.

While unlike in the feudalist period, extramarital affairs in contemporary China are expected to be relatively invisible, in recent decades, articles and stories of extramarital affairs have made frequent appearances on the media and social media, generating a great deal of interest not least because of people's natural crave for all that is private and hidden. First, as already noted, the divorce rate in China has been rising consistently and rapidly despite various measures put in place to make getting divorced that much more difficult. This has generated a great deal of debate on the popular press and social media, which tend to link this trend to a corresponding growth in extramarital adventures. It should be noted that, to the best of the author's knowledge, no research has been conducted on whether there has indeed been a corresponding or even a significant increase in infidelity. The point is that the frequent reporting on divorce, particularly divorce of famous people, has generated interest in extramarital affairs, which is one of the leading causes of divorce.

Second, the frequent news stories that some corrupt officials have been brought down and jailed for, among others, keeping mistresses, tend to further provoke interest and extended reporting in the current climate, partly because, third and related, the Chinese society has in recent years taken a conservative turn in some social aspects often at the expense of privacy, as evident in, for instance, the high frequency of public exposure of corrupt officials' extramarital activities, and the return of some long-disappeared harsh terms used by the mainstream media, such as '*tongjian*', which usually translates as 'adultery' but in fact has a much more morally condemning and humiliating effect. For quite some time, this term has largely disappeared and has been replaced with mild and more neutral terms such as '*hunwaiqing*' or '*hunwailian*' ('extramarital love').

Extramarital affairs are a good angle to look into gender inequality. Chang (1999) offers a typology of classifying extramarital affairs into four types: the traditional saviour type, which is the closest to the traditional legacy of concubinage, in which one party (usually the man) has the power, money and opportunity to provide material and other support to a much weaker, often much younger and dependent partner (usually the woman), thereby playing the role of a dominant paternal figure; the unhappy housewives type, in which the unhappy and lonely wife, who is taken for granted and unsatisfied by the husband, begins an affair with someone who is not necessarily rich or powerful but is willing and able to provide spiritual support and cares for the often traditional woman who is either not able or not willing to get a divorce; the soul-mate type, in which, for instance, a modern and independent woman, who does not care for money or marriage, has an affair with a married man for true love and genuine connection, often promising not to break up his marriage; and finally the instrumental type, in which one party has an affair with another for pragmatic purposes and personal gain, for instance a modern woman having a secret affair with a powerful man in order to advance her career.

While Chang's typology automatically assumes that the weaker party, or the beneficiary, is the woman, the reality is that men may well be the weaker dependent party in such a relationship, although it should be admitted that in the vast majority of such cases the woman is the weaker one, so Chang's depiction is not exactly gender stereotype. Furthermore, if we look only at the women involved in these four types of relationships, while those in the first two types tend to be women with conservative values—either that men should look after and 'save' women, or that even if the marriage is an unhappy one the decision to get divorced should not be taken lightly, the women in the last two types tend to be modern and independent—in that they are in a position to not expect the man to provide for them, not to care about money or marriage, but only about love and connection. This is another reason, besides and oppositional to the lingering influence of tradition and old cultural practices, why extramarital affairs are achievable for men in this contemporary, supposedly universally monogamous, new world—not because women remain weak and dependent, but exactly the opposite—it is precisely women's increased independence and autonomy that have rendered extramarital affairs not only accessible but also enjoyable due to the lack of excessive baggage compared to the past.

The implication of this observation for the feminist theories is not optimistic, as it seems that modernization and enhanced opportunities for women in society proposed by feminists have not necessarily generated progression toward equality when it comes to intimacy and sexuality—in a way it makes women more willing (and able) to become 'the other woman' for love, in effect allowing the old cultural legacy to take advantage of new changes, returning men (and women) to the old feudalist lifestyle in this particular respect—and many women do not consider this inequality, but falling in love. But on the other hand, it is arguable that there is a big difference between women in the old days and modern women now—the former often did not have a choice, whereas in the last two types of extramarital relations, it is often the autonomous choice of modern women to enter such a relationship. Indeed, the more modern and independent the mistress is, the more threatening she is likely to be perceived by the wife, as the husband has less of a reason to break up such a relationship.

This leads to an important point that Western feminist theories, which focus on gender equality and gender politics between men and women, tend not to address—that the conflicting interests between the women involved, the awkward tension between the wife and the mistress, deserve greater attention, particularly in those scenarios where there is neither direct confrontation between the parties nor immediate threat to the marriage. The soulmate type of extramarital relationship is illuminating on this particular point, in that the modern mistress seeks neither money nor marriage from the man, but the affair itself is still damaging to the wife's interest in terms of someone else sharing her husband's affection, time and resources. There is always the possibility though that as the affair progresses, the modern woman's position and attitude may change, and she becomes more of a confrontational threat and demands more.

Directing attention toward the conflicts of interest and tensions between the women serves at least three purposes. First, it may help explain why Chinese societal attitudes toward extramarital affairs remain highly disapproving. Zhang et al. (2012) show that the Chinese popular disapproval of extramarital sex has not softened and is of a much higher disapproval level than in formerly socialist European countries. Focusing on the women in a patriarchal society, in which they are usually presumed to have the most to lose as a result of extramarital relations, can better reveal what exactly is at stake. It is important to note the difference between 'extramarital sex' and 'extramarital relations' though, as the former includes commercial sex, whereas the latter refers to extramarital sexual liaisons that usually have some emotional involvement and last a certain period of time, and it is the latter that this chapter examines.

Second, paying more attention to the roles and concerns of women may also provide insights into related fields and subjects such as spousal violence, sexually transmitted diseases, and even class division. Xiao (2018) has examined the wide range of motivations that have pushed people into forming extramarital relations, focusing particularly on men and women belonging in the subordinate classes, revealing how the interactions between intimate social relations and monetary exchange have helped the people involved to gain support, dignity and self-respect which mean different things to different people, and experiencing intimacy in extramarital relations also has different impact on people in different classes, although satisfaction of some sorts of needs is that one thing they all have in common.

Third, paying more attention to the women involved does not have to mean diverting attention from the men, but rather may help us challenge presumptions. For instance, Jeffreys (2010) provides a unique angle to examine extramarital affairs in China—the involvement of private investigators in collecting legally admissible evidence on behalf of women who either want to know if their husbands are having an affair or seek to initiate or expedite contested divorce proceedings. While the exact number of private investigators involved in such businesses is unknown due to the indeterminate legal status of such work, it is widely understood that such work is primarily concerned with the investigation of male infidelity, which explains why private investigators doing such work are usually nicknamed 'second wife assassins' or 'mistress killers'. This gender-specific depiction obscures the fact that women also engage in extramarital affairs and men also hire private investigators.

These agencies are believed to use surveillance techniques that properly belong to law-enforcement authorities, such as tailing, using recording devices and hidden cameras, but without respecting the procedural rules that govern the use of such techniques. Although it has been insisted that professional spying equipment or illegal technology such as bugging devices or pinhole cameras are never used, such statements are hard to believe due to not only the lack of regulation of the trade but also and especially the high demand for such services, which reflects two issues.

First, private detective work provides a necessary supplement to public services by undertaking tasks that the relevant authorities such as the police, lawyers, legal-aid centers or the All-China Women's Federation are unable or unwilling to perform adequately—either because the issue is considered too trivial, or the means is illegal and/or immoral, or that the private nature of the matter renders intervention difficult. It is understandable that in the face of very limited options, a frustrated spouse, especially a woman, is willing to pay for services that can guarantee results—legally or illegally is probably one of the last things on their mind.

Second, many of the tasks that these agencies perform not only intrude on normal police work but also constitute invasion of privacy, though supporters would argue that such work aims to protect women's rights by speedily gathering evidence that cannot be gathered in any other way, and which will lead to punishment of the wrongdoer and just compensation for the injured party, in so doing it performs an important and necessary social service by upholding the Marriage Law, traditional family values and the institution of marriage, as well as contributing to the establishment of a more transparent government as extramarital affairs are often linked to corruption. In other words, employing controversial means is a small price to pay in the absence of more proper and more effective methods to tackle the problem, and if anything needs to change, it is that the state should introduce clear rules governing this field of work on the basis of an acknowledgment that it performs a valuable service, and that its capacity to investigate needs to be regulated and restricted, not banned. But the bottom-line is that their existence is necessary.

Furthermore, these agencies are not the only ones that need regulation and guidance. For instance, it is doubtful that law enforcement authorities and members of the general public can adequately distinguish between bigamy, cohabitation, casual sex, love affair and extramarital relations. Article 1042 of the Civil Code of the People's Republic of China, adopted on 28 May 2020 and came into effect on 1 January 2021, replacing the Marriage Law, stipulates that bigamy is prohibited and that no one who has a spouse may cohabit with another person. In practice, however, it is difficult to establish legally and exactly when and if such a second, illegal relationship has commenced. The conventional presumption that the cheating spouse and the third party are both 'guilty' also further blurs the line between extramarital relations that break the law and those that do not (which are the vast majority).

Another factor that further complicates the matter is that, while the private life and even extramarital affairs of ordinary citizens are increasingly viewed as a private matter for the individuals themselves to solve, and if such matters ought to be judged, they should be judged morally and privately; in contrast, it has become a trend since the commence of the anti-corruption campaign that extramarital affairs of Communist Party members and government officials attract not only Party disciplinary penalties but often also legal punishments, irrespective of whether they entail corruption or not though they very often do. In other words, Communist Party members and government officials are subject to a higher behavioral standard than ordinary citizens.

In light of these problems and details, it is foreseeable that devolving investigatory powers to private investigators in cases involving suspected adultery, particularly those that involve allegations of corruption of government officials, would encourage further unnecessary intrusion into citizens' private affairs, and the extent to which individual rights and privacy should be abrogated in the pursuit of so-called justice in a case of spousal infidelity does not get to be critically debated. Among others, three points of debate are worth considering in the Chinese context: the first concerns motivations or justifications for extramarital relations; the second concerns different types of extramarital relations; and the third concerns gender differences.

Without denying that extramarital relations are immoral, it should nevertheless be possible to recognize that an overly simplistic condemnation diverts attention from other and deeper issues, particularly those related to human needs. The literature reveals that sexual needs, emotional intimacy and romantic love are among the major motivations for extramarital involvement (Glass and Wright 1992; Thompson 1984): sexual needs include those for sexual excitement, variety and enjoyment; emotional intimacy includes reasons and needs that strongly resemble and reflect aspects of a close nonsexual friendship, such as self-esteem, mutual understanding and respect, companionship, and intellectual sharing; romantic love refers to experiencing romance and falling in love. While different cultures tend to emphasize different justifications, these findings explain why a simple promotion of traditional family values and exemplary models with regard to marital relationships will not prevent people from entering extramarital relationships.

Specifically, in the Chinese context, while the strength of the link between marital status and personal well-being is often emphasized and marriage is promoted as an ideal unit that can best provide an environment in which sexual intimacy, emotional security and romantic love are available, the extent to which marriage can actually meet these expectations, which depends on so many factors in addition to the marriage being stable, healthy and fulfilling, is seldom discussed honestly or critically. While few will disagree that people need close relationships to satisfy their need for belonging, which is vital for personal well-being, some might doubt whether it is the best means, as it seems that nonmarital relationships can serve that purpose just as well.

It should also be remembered that extramarital relations can take different forms—sexual, or emotional—or a combination of both sexual satisfaction and deep emotional attachment. In-depth studies are needed to discover the likely differentiated associations between different motivations and actual behavior in such a relationship, and whether, for instance, sexual motivations are associated more with men and emotional motivations more with women as commonly presumed, and whether society is more tolerant when romantic love and not just intimacy is present in an extramarital relationship—presuming the difference between the two is possible to tell.

5.4.3 Cohabitation: Morality, Intimacy, and Broader Issues

It is against this historical and contemporary background of changing familial patterns and difficulties associated with marriage that cohabitation has become more prevalent in China in recent decades, although its role, meaning and social functions have seldom been carefully looked at—partly due to its lack of official recognition as a desirable form of union—hence the lack of suitable data, which stands in great contrast to the many other well-documented aspects of changes in family life that China has experienced over the past decades. It is important to carefully analyze the phenomenon of rising cohabitation in China as an alternative form of familial union for three reasons.

First, in contrast to many other phenomena analyzed in this book, which have very strong Chinese characteristics if not uniquely Chinese, the rise of cohabitation in China is very much part of a global trend, but while many explanations have been proposed for the emergence and rise of cohabitation in Western countries where cohabitation very much resembles marriage—for instance the rise of secularism, individualism, decreased attraction of legal marriage, economic factors, improved social status of women, reduced stigma attached to premarital sex and unmarried sexual relations, and so on—little is known or said about why an increasing number of Chinese are choosing to form cohabiting unions rather than entering into a legal marriage in a socially conservative country. The exact reasons need to be brought to the surface, as cohabitation is a form of otherness that says something about the sociocultural atmosphere of the country.

Second and related, thus far, most research on cohabitation has been conducted in developed societies such as European countries and the US, producing results that are indicative and reflective of particular stages and manifestations of economic, social and cultural development—for instance, cohabitation is more common among people who hold liberal values and who have low economic prospects (Manning and Smock 1995; Yu and Xie 2015, 609). Chinese society has undergone tremendous social and institutional changes in recent decades, and it would be worthwhile to purposefully study how, if, these changes have caused the rise and diffusion of cohabitation and how, if, entering cohabiting unions has helped people cope with changes. Of particular interest would be to examine the relationship between cohabitation and broader issues such as gender, class, education, migration, and power relations—both within the cohabiting unions and the larger society.

Third and importantly, until very recently, cohabitation was widely considered in China to be a socially deviant and immoral behavior, and even now cohabiting individuals, especially men, are expected to treat cohabitation as preparation for serious commitment to eventual marriage. This partial and conditional social acceptance is perhaps a main reason why cohabiting Chinese couples have a high chance of marrying eventually, and according to studies, it remains rare for a person to have multiple cohabitation experiences, especially among those born before 1980. It has also been pointed out that the very limited studies on cohabitation rates in China do not even collect information from respondents who did not ultimately marry their cohabiting partners (Yu and Xie 2015, 613–614), rendering the prevalence likely to be seriously underestimated. What then does the recent spread of cohabitation tell us of the status of traditional morality in Chinese society today? Is traditional morality ever the driving factor? What is the relationship between morality and intimacy? How big a role does morality play in the face of economic disadvantage which might be corrected by cohabitation rather than marriage? Ultimately, considering the quiet tolerance if not complete acceptance of cohabitation, can this form of union still be considered 'otherness'?

Against China's long tradition of social (and once upon a time, legal) intolerance of premarital cohabitation and premarital sex, a number of contextual causes have enabled the quiet yet significant emergence and diffusion of cohabitation. The first is legal change. The 2001 amendment to the Chinese Marriage Law of 1980 decriminalized cohabitation by changing the wording from 'illegal cohabitation' to 'nonmarital cohabitation', which sent out a clear signal changing the public's reception. This is comparable to the social impact of the decriminalization of homosexual activities in 1997 and the removal of homosexuality from the nation's official list of mental illnesses. Though the latter is likely to have received much more publication than the former due to the nature and style of queer rights activism; whereas private lifestyle, as the name suggests, is private.

The second is ideational change. Modification, if not utter renewal, of traditional social norms generated by the development and modernization of society has caused changes in familial behavior. It has been argued that there is a reciprocal link between the development of modern societies and the development of modern families. According to this system of ideas called 'developmental idealism', the more developed a society is the more advanced its family system will be, and the signs that a family system is advanced are the presence of gender equality, respect of freedom and consent, marriage at later age, planned and low fertility, and it is under such a system that people will be allowed to encounter alternative forms of union and willing to accept that which form of union to enter is the free choice of the individual (Thornton 2001, 2005; Yu and Xie 2015, 610).

Examination of the Chinese public's attitudes toward marriage, fertility and other related familial behaviors seems to affirm the influence of developmental idealism. Attitudes toward fertility is particularly telling of its relationship with the nation's socioeconomic development, as while the long-term impact of the now abolished One Child Policy is undeniable, the government's fear that the country will soon enter a phase of negative population growth is real—young people seem to have simply ignored official encouragements to have more children, often citing rising costs of childbearing and wanting to invest more time, space and resources on themselves.

A third cause is the encounter and acceptance of Western lifestyles, especially Western ideals of private life. A direct benefit enjoyed by ordinary Chinese of the open-door policy during the reform era has been that people are granted the chance to become familiar with Western culture and lifestyles through television programmes, magazines, newspapers, the internet, and most directly through travel, causing many to become aware of and acceptant of Western ideals, ways of life and familial practices including cohabitation. The atmosphere then is different from now. At the time many studies on China observed rising individualism alongside comprehensive westernization, which significantly weakened the constraining restrictions of traditional social norms on individual choice and behavior, especially in relation to private lifestyle, causing increased tolerance toward premarital sex, casual sex, unmarried childbearing, and cohabitation (Yu and Xie 2015, 612).

When society returns to a former stage and degree of conservativeness as it now has, acceptance and practice of cohabitation may not necessarily decrease, as when the public sphere becomes increasingly restrictive in terms of choice and expression, private life is a sphere in which freedom may be retained and people may 'let it out' and make up for what is lacking in public. The element of privacy in private life, another concept learned as a result of greater openness to Western cultures and which has gained increasing awareness among the people especially the educated in recent years, is another reason that choices in private life such as cohabitation may be less vulnerable to judgments of society and others.

The fourth related factor is economic development, which, by creating a greater range of economic and career opportunities through the expansion of education, industrialization and migration of the workforce, has enabled the pursuit of greater freedom and a wider range of personal choices in at least three aspects. First, as mentioned previously in the first section, people simply have more money, more opportunities and a wider range of places to meet people with whom they may enter into relationships. Second, while in traditional Chinese societies and families, children live with their parents until they get married (and many continue to live with their parents under the same roof even after they get married), modern societies have enabled early departure of children from the parental home and parental control, granting them more if not complete freedom to choose their lifestyle including cohabitation. But living independently, especially in urban environments, often means high and rising living expenses, which is even more reason for people to cohabit, especially as a transitional stage in order to accumulate economic resources for marriage—this is the third aspect.

The fifth and related contextual factor is the improvement of education, especially women's education, not least because education broadens perspectives by providing alternative options (which is why cohabitation tends to be more common in China among those with higher education levels), but also that education has enabled women's economic independence from men, causing their needs and gains from marriage to decline, rendering cohabitation a realistically possible alternative form of intimate relationship, and whether or not it leads eventually to marriage matters less than before. Furthermore, an increasing number of women are delaying marriage to obtain a higher degree or have a career, which is another reason for them to seek sex or enter into cohabiting relations rather than straight into marriage.

The sixth contextual cause is migration. Chapter 3 has examined the powerful impact of internal migration on both society and the individual. In relation to cohabitation specifically, there are several possible explanations for how large-scale migration is likely to have played an important role in the emergence of cohabitation in China. First, while traditional family values predominate in rural areas, urban residents in cosmopolitan cities have experienced much earlier and greater exposure to Western influence, cosmopolitan life and ideals of diversity and pluralism; consequently, they are more tolerant of cohabitation than their rural counterparts. Second, privacy enjoys greater respect and protection in cities, while in rural areas, people often need to worry about other people's opinions regarding their own choices of life. In the cities, this is much less of a concern, not least because much of private life is able to be concealed from others.

Third, being far away from home and family, migrant workers experience a great deal of loneliness and emotional need for comfort, leading some to seek out and enter into cohabiting relations when that someone comes along and if housing arrangements permit. Fourth, considering that migrant workers tend to be low-paid and urban housing costs tend to be high, migrant couples who are in a sexual relation are likely to consider living together in order to reduce housing and other living expenses. And fifth, in the absence of parental guidance and supervision, migrant youth can easily try out premarital sex or cohabitation, which also fills the void of loneliness caused by being far away from home.

As noted at the beginning of Part II, despite significant changes and shifts in attitudes, sociocultural continuity needs to be emphasized, and rising from which the constraining factors that render people unaccepting or hesitant toward cohabitation, despite the increasingly tolerant environment regarding these issues, may be derived. First, in general, lower social status is associated with less tolerance of nontraditional behaviors such as cohabitation; second, cohabitation is less common among people with a lower level of education, which is measured normally by years of schooling; third, Communist Party members have a much lower likelihood of premarital cohabitation than nonmembers; and fourth, less economically developed regions are less tolerant of such nontraditional family behaviors (Yu and Xie 2015).

5.4.4 Changing (?) Perceptions of Singlehood

The growing rate of cohabitation should inspire us to rethink not only our expectations of marriage but also our conception of singlehood. For the purposes of this part, 'singlehood' is defined in relation to those people who are not engaged in a committed long-term relationship and do not have children. This definition does not include the social categories of single parents, widows, divorcees, or unmarried people who share their lives with a partner, which are all forms of nonmarriage regularly conceptualized under the general umbrella of singlehood (Lahad 2017, 2). While such a broad conception is not adopted in this chapter, it does remind us that singlehood is diverse in nature and manifestation; it varies, for example, by gender, age, class, religion and ethnicity, rendering it a sociocultural and relational construct rather than a mere individual experience, reflecting widespread understandings of social relations, identities and expectations.

As already noted above, China is unquestionably a pro-marriage country, not due to religious influences but cultural beliefs. Chinese social expectation appears to be that everyone will marry at the appropriate age and then have a child, or at least should enter a relationship with the specific purpose of marrying that person eventually, and few observers would question that cultural expectations, community standards, public policies and personal attitudes elevate the status and value of heterosexual marriage relative to single life. But the largely unconditional support for marriage and family has not stopped the emergence of rising singlehood. While the comparison between 'married' and 'single' appears to be straightforward, the common grounds and similarities between the two groups as well as their shared challenges are never mentioned, whereas the differences, particularly those differences where the single fare worse than the married, are much talked about and often attributed to the less desirable aspects of singlehood and even to the personal deficiencies of single persons themselves—in addition to loneliness and sadness, singles are often perceived as unable to commit, unfulfilled, immature, selfish and too picky (McKeown 2015).

Before diving into deeper issues, it is easy to provide the question 'why is singlehood rising in China?' with a fairly straightforward answer. First, as already examined above, society is changing, as are the functions and expectations of marriage and family, rendering singlehood properly a choice for some, especially those in large cities or are influenced by urbanization. Second, rising levels of education also mean that more and more people are delaying marriage, as the length of time it takes to complete one's education has prolonged. Of particular relevance is the improvement of women's education, rendering the cultural ideals of early marriage, traditional lifestyle and dependence on the husband less attractive. It is also worth mentioning in passing that when a Chinese woman is too educated, it in fact limits her choices in male partners, as being too educated, just like being too rich, places men under pressure and in discomfort in a traditional patriarchal society.

Third, despite a clear preference for marriage, Chinese society is much more tolerant than before and is more acceptant of singlehood, so that people who are single, especially those who remain single by choice in pursuit of a modern lifestyle, can stay single without unbearable social pressure. Society, which remains characteristically conservative socially, often needs to be reminded though that being single does not necessarily mean being without intimate relations, which is one of the reasons why many find it hard to believe some people would actually choose to be single, as in their minds they are choosing loneliness over togetherness and intimacy, which is just not necessarily the case. Fourth, modern life places young people under increasing economic pressure, rendering marriage a huge responsibility relationally as well as financially. Hence, if one is able to resist the pressure and stigmatization that do exist albeit only subtly in many contexts and situations, singlehood offers a great deal of attraction in a modern, expensive, busy society.

This leads us to look more closely at whether singlehood is indeed a stigmatized status. A key component of the stigma process is that the affected person experiences discrimination and status loss, which may have harmful consequences for their life opportunities and affect their physical, mental or financial well-being. According to this criterion, it seems to be an overstatement to say that singles are stigmatized in the Chinese context, as even if singles have encountered stereotypical attitudes, such attitudes will have to translate into actual discriminatory behaviors and policies that have turned them into a disadvantaged group in an important life domain in order to constitute 'stigma'—which does not seem to have happened. Similar to what Byrne and Carr (2005) have described, the discriminatory treatments that singles may experience in Chinese society occur largely in informal and interpersonal exchanges rather than institutionally.

There are several reasons for such informal and interpersonal discrimination. First, demographic patterns and other social conditions have changed faster than cultural values. While social changes have created a sociocultural context in which singles may live fulfilling and respectable lives, cultural values continue to endorse the traditional ideology of marriage, leaving singles in a cultural lag. Second, as is the case in any society, marriage is not only simply taken for granted as the natural norm but also associated with the provision of resources and rights, rendering it an institution of social privilege compared to singlehood, and any institution or system of privilege is likely to be resistant to change, as their ideologies tend to have been universalized and internalized by the vast majority of members of society if not all.

Universality and internalization tend to mean that, third, any information that might reveal the problematic aspects of the marital institution tends not to be critically reviewed but ignored, and anyone whose behavior appears not to have conformed to such universal ideals—by remaining single for instance—is likely to invite scrutiny, mockery, and criticism, which are in fact often perfectly well-meaning. The lack of institutional discrimination may be interpreted as highlighting that the single status is perhaps less important to personal identity and social experience than other characteristics—many of which have been examined in this book—which tend to have more dominant implications, for instance gender, class, rural–urban divides, according to which the effects of singlehood as a contingent notion vary (Lahad 2012).

The powerful influence of gender, for instance, seems to have cross-cultural validity. While critical Chinese studies are lacking, a good number of works about single women has been published in the past two decades in the West, revealing the gendered complexity of singlehood that is also true in China—single women of a certain age tend to face significantly more judgment than single men of the same age, as evident in the derogatory names such as 'spinster' and 'husband hunter', which imply that they are desperate to be in a relationship but have failed. Other cultural expressions that mock them, such as 'old maid' and 'leftover women', characterise them as overly selective, unable to make timely choices and uptight about getting married until time runs out (Lahad 2017, 9). By explaining their situation through the sociology of time, single women are often portrayed as unwisely being on hold, empty, unwanted, having wasted too much time for nothing, and the older the single woman is the more scrutiny (as well as sympathy) she seems to attract, revealing the societal assumption that singlehood should only be temporal, or it will inevitably degrade into a miserable, vulnerable and lonely later life (Lahad 2017, 6).

The situation becomes even more difficult for women once we factor in class. Ip and Peeren (2019) note how rural-to-urban migrant women in Shanghai legitimate their relationship status and live with the stigmatization of their singlehood. They find that the stigma attached to women with rural backgrounds is strongly sensed by these women, which hinders their opportunities to find a desirable person to marry. Unlike those urban 'leftover women' who are considered by some to be undesirable for being too well educated or having too successful a career, thus putting men under huge pressure, rural migrant women are considered undesirable simply because of their rural origins. As a result, they are excluded from the Shanghai marriage market and tend to end up marrying migrant men from their home provinces (Zhang 2013). They also face potential stigmatization in their hometowns. As noted previously, many migrant women work in urban hair and beauty salons, which could potentially generate gossip back home about their supposed impropriety and immorality in cities for supposedly having behaved in a way that a single or married woman living away from her husband should not (Ip and Peeren 2019, 672).

It is important to note that background also affects men in this respect. Li et al. (2010) note that a rising proportion of men in China's rural areas are experiencing prolonged and even permanent singlehood for two related reasons. The first is the change in the sex ratio in the country and the growing shortage of women on the marriage market; the second is poverty, which many have reported to be the main reason not only for their singlehood but also a key obstacle to their access to active sexuality. This double penalty imposed by poverty places these men in a situation of social discrimination, especially in rural areas where high value is placed upon marriage and strong social pressure is exerted on single men. A wide range of frustrations—emotional, familial, sexual—has been expressed by many (Li et al. 2010).

5.5 Chapter Conclusion: When Norms Conflict with Needs

Different historical stages and a wide range of sociocultural determinants have delivered a very complex and multilayered impact on how the Chinese view and practice intimacy. In the wake of so much social change in such a short period of time, a wide range of messages has been embedded in public discourses on and cultural representations of intimacy, and relatedly gender roles, the family and sexuality in contemporary Chinese settings. These messages are both a mix of, as well as a move beyond, Chinese tradition/familism and Western influence/individualism. While this chapter has probably not done justice to such a complex issue in such limited space, it hopes to have shown that intimacy has a place in understanding social change and modern citizenship in contemporary China, however problematic or insignificant that place may be. It is also important not to stop at preliminary conclusions but think harder on their implications and future directions.

First, it is very important for social sciences scholars studying these groups or phenomena to move away from simplistic binary thinking and simple contrasts of moral versus immoral, legal versus illegal, married versus unmarried. More fine-grained categories of situations, personal choices and pathways are required to characterize the diverse experiences of the people covered in this chapter, and it is only when scholars can abandon taken-for-granted demarcations can they truly work out the interplay of multiple factors and uncover the distinctive challenges and experiences of these highly heterogeneous categories of people.

Second, this chapter hopes to have reinforced the importance of sharing personal narratives and presenting diversified pictures. Personal stories of marginalized groups, when shared with honesty and commitment, have the capacity to reveal how abstract ideologies and expectations play out in everyday lives, thereby deepening the understanding of these people's experiences and our own perceptions. Hence, in order to prevent misunderstandings and prejudices, more in-depth qualitative studies are urgently needed. It is also through tentative examination of real-life individual stories that one is able to examine how personal agency interacts with structural restraints. In addition, it is equally important for more attention to be paid to those who do the 'othering', their reasons and motivations, as well as their personal life stories.

Third, improving the quality of life for the people covered in this chapter requires tackling the fundamental causes of challenges, discrimination and stigma. This chapter has hoped to show the variety of social forces and structures that have had an impact on the groups in concern, and the paradigms and strict categorizations that constantly define and constrain people's behavior and ways of life. They constitute the reasons why it can be so difficult to resist and challenge many of the existing convictions about the practices covered in this chapter. In identifying new research questions and paving the way for further studies or data collection initiatives, it is important to locate the relevant issues and groups within a broader critical context and theory, so that how patterns of behavior alter or not alter in response to changing political circumstances, sociocultural and economic situations as well as emotional needs may be more vividly revealed.

Fourth and related, it is worth repeating the importance of paying more attention to the role of individual needs for intimacy in such controversial subjects—which is particularly difficult to achieve in a socially and emotionally repressed society like China—and to the fact that there is not a single ideal way of satisfying these needs which every family, union or individual can aspire to conform. It might be necessary to admit or at least consider that there is possibly a range of ideal types based partly on enduring traditions in a given context, partly on the demands of local collective and personal conditions, partly on the emotional and other needs of the individual. At the end of the day, as traditional and social values and practices in these domains become unsettled, people venturing into uncharted waters in their familial, spousal and sexual relationships is understandable if not automatically respectable, and it invites tentative observation and analysis, not simplistic praise or condemnation.

References

Aquinas T ([1264], (1975)) Summa contra gentiles, book three: providence. University of Notre Dame Press, Part II

Atchison C, Fraser L, Lowman J (1998) Men who buy sex: preliminary findings of an exploratory study. In: Elias B, Elias and Brewer (eds) Prostitution: on whores, Hustlers and Johns. Prometheus Books, New York, pp 172–203

Byrne A, Carr D (2005) Caught in the cultural lag: the stigma of singlehood. Psychol Inquiry 16(2, 3):84–91

Campbell R (1998) Invisible men: making visible male clients of female prostitutes in Merseyside. In: Elias B, Elias and Brewer (eds) Prostitution: on whores, Hustlers and Johns. Prometheus Books, New York, pp 155–171

Chang J-S (1999) Extramarital affairs: marital mores, gender politics, and infidelity in Taiwan. Modern China 25(1):69–99

Chu CS, Kwan, (2018) Compensating dating: buying and selling sex in cyberspace. Palgrave Macmillan, Singapore

Davis A, Vaillancourt T, Arnocky S (2020) The dark tetrad and male clients of female sex work. Front Psychol 11:577171

Dewey S, Zheng T, Orchard T (2016) Sex workers and criminalization in North America and China: ethical and legal issues in exclusionary regimes. Springer

De Y, Patricia A (2015) Understanding and treating chronic shame: a relational/neurobiological approach. Routledge, New York

Ding Y (2008) Transitions and new possibilities of sex work: Xiaojies' perception of work and way of life in the Pearl River Delta thesis submitted for the degree of Doctor of Philosophy at the University of Hong Kong. https://core.ac.uk/display/37891894

Ding Y (2016) Desires: transitions and new possibilities of sex work in the pearl river delta area. Social Sciences Academic Press, Beijing (China) (in Chinese)

Erikson EH (1968) Identity: youth and crisis. W. W. Norton, New York

Farley M et al (2012) A thorn in the heart: Cambodian men who buy sex'. In: Paper presented at the 'focus on men who buy sex: discourage men's demand of prostitution, stop sex trafficking' conference. Phnom Penh, Cambodia

Farley M et al (2015) Comparing sex buyers with men who do not buy sex: new data on prostitution and trafficking. J Interpers Violence 32(23):2015
Glass S, Wright T (1992) Justifications for extramarital relationships: the association between attitudes, behaviors and gender. J Sex Res 29(3):361–387
Heatherton TF, Kleck RE, Hebl MR, Hull JG (eds) The social psychology of stigma. The Guilford Press, New York
Hershatter G (1999) Dangerous pleasures: prostitution and modernity and twentieth-century Shanghai. University of California Press, Berkeley and Los Angeles
Huang Y, Suiming P (2014) Government crackdown of sex work in China: responses from female sex workers and implications for their health. Glob Public Health 9(9):1067–1079
Huang ZJ et al (2011) Bridge population: sex workers or their clients? STI prevalence and risk behaviors of clients of female sex workers in China. AIDS Care 23(Suppl):45–53
Huang L, Qiao L, Yutong Z (2020) Ignored, unmentionable desire: elderly Chinese struggle to satisfy sexual urges. Global Times
Ip PTT, Peeren E (2019) Exploiting the distance between conflicting norms: female rural-to-urban migrant workers in Shanghai negotiating stigma around singlehood and marriage. Eur J Cult Stud 22(5–6):665–683
Jankowiak WR, Fischer E (1992) A cross-cultural perspective on romantic love. Ethnology 31(2):149–155
Jankowiak WR, Moore RL (2017) Family life in China. Polity, Cambridge
Jeffreys E (2004) China, sex and prostitution. Routledge Curzon, Abingdon
Jeffreys E (ed) (2006) Sex and sexuality in China. Routledge, Abingdon
Jeffreys E (2010) Regulating private affairs in contemporary China: Private investigators and the policing of spousal infidelity. China Information 24(2):149–167
Jeffreys E (2012) Prostitution scandals in China: policing. Media Soc, Routledge, Abingdon
Jeffreys E, Yu H (2015) Sex in China. Polity, Cambridge
Koetse M (2018) 'Let's talk about sex, grandpa: HIV on the rise among China's elderly men. Whatsonweibo.com
Lahad K (2012) Singlehood, waiting, and the sociology of time. Sociol Forum 27(1)
Lahad K (2017) A table for one: a critical reading of singlehood. Manchester University Press, Gender and Time, Manchester
Li S, Qunlin Z, Xueyan Y (2010) Male singlehood, poverty and sexuality in rural China: an exploratory survey' population (English Edition) 65(4):679–694
Li YH (2008) Learning from sexuality. Epoch Literature and Art Press, Changchun (in Chinese)
Lindau ST et al (2007) A study of sexuality and health among older adults in the United States. N Engl J Med 357:762–774
Manning WD, Smock PJ (1995) Why marry? race and the transition to marriage among cohabitors. Demography 32(4):509–520
Mann SL (2011) Gender and sexuality in modern Chinese history. Cambridge University Press, New York
McKeown JKL (2015) I will not be wearing heels tonight! a feminist exploration of singlehood, dating, and leisure'. J Leisure Res 47(4)485–500
Miller T (2006) Boys flocking to be "ducks" for China's bored housewives. Observer
Milrod C, Monto M (2017) Older male clients of female sex workers in the United States. Arch Sex Behav 46(6):1867–1876
Monto M (2000) Why Men Seek Out Prostitutes. In: Weitzer R (ed) Sex for sale: prostitution, pornography, and the sex industry. Routledge, New York, pp 67–83
Monto M, Milrod C (2014) Ordinary or peculiar men? Comparing the customers of prostitutes with a nationally representative sample of men. Int J Offender Ther Comp Criminol 58(7):802–820
Ngai P et al (2014) Worker-intellectual unity: suicide, trans-border sociological intervention, and the Foxconn-Apple connection. Curr Sociol 62(2):209–222
Pan L (2015) When true love came to China. Hong Kong University Press, Hong Kong

Pan S (2017) The "Sexuality " of Chinese from 2000 to 2015: the main data analysis of the four national total population sample surveys. Hong Kong: 1908 Ltd (in Chinese)

Pan S, Huang Y (2013) Change of sex: the sexual life of Chinese in the 21st century. China Renmin University Press, Beijing (in Chinese)

Rowbotham J, Muravyeva M, Nash D (eds) Shame, blame and culpability: crime and violence in the modern state, Routledge, Abingdon

Scruton R (1986) Sexual desire: a moral philosophy of the erotic. The Free Press, New York

Sun W, Lei W (2017) In search of intimacy in China: the emergence of advice media for the privatized self. Commun Cult Critique 10(2017):20–38

Sun W (2020) Dark intimacy and the moral economy of sex: rural migrants and the cultural politics of transgression. China Inf 00:1–22

Tang Z et al (2014) Aphrodisiac use associated with HIV infection in elderly male clients of low-cost commercial sex venues in Guangxi, China: a matched case-control study. PLOS ONE 9(10):e109452

Thompson AP (1984) Emotional and sexual components of extramarital relations. J Marriage Fam 46(1):35–43

Thornton A (2001) The developmental paradigm, reading history sideways, and family change. Demography 38(4):449–465

Thornton A (2005) Reading history sideways: the fallacy and enduring impact of the developmental paradigm on family life. University of Chicago Press, Chicago

Udagawa Y (2007) Compensated dating in Japan: an exploration of anomie and social change in Japan. University of Central Missouri, Missouri

Ward H et al (2005) Who pays for sex? anal increasing prevalence of female commercial sex contacts among men in Britain. Sex Trans Infect 81:467–471

Xiao S (2018) Desire and dignity: class, gender and intimacy in transitional Social Sciences Academic Press (China), China, Beijing (in Chinese)

Yu J, Xie Yu (2015) Cohabitation in China: trends and determinants. Popul Dev Rev 41(4):607–628

Zhang N, Parish W, Huang Y, Pan S (2012) Sexual infidelity in China: prevalence and gender-specific correlates. Arch Sex Behav 41:861–873

Zhang NN (2013) Rural women migrant returnees in contemporary China. J Peasant Stud 40(1):171–188

Zhou Y et al (2014) Motivations for sexual risk behaviors among older men in Shanghai, China: a qualitative study. BMC Public Health 2014(14):802

Chapter 6
Expression and the Nation State

This chapter does not seek to provide a full picture of freedom of expression in the Chinese mainland. Rather, it examines two means of expression that have not received widespread attention. The first is the seldom studied artistic freedom, which has both brought new challenges to the already limited freedom as well as created new freedom due to art's unique nature and means of expression. Part I of the chapter aims to provide an interdisciplinary analysis of the necessity and possibility of accommodating controversial forms of artistic expression in China. Against the country's cultural, political and social background and situated within the larger atmosphere, the author draws on political, legal and artistic theories in combination with analysis of historical as well as recent incidents in the Chinese art field to explore the complexity and value of the 'otherness' of controversial art in general and in the Chinese context in particular. Employing a comparative method in highlighting the controversy surrounding the word 'controversial' itself, the author emphasizes that the value of free artistic expression goes way beyond art and presents arguments as to why China can and should accommodate artistic forms and expressions that are considered to be contrary to the core values of the nation and society, despite difficulties.

The second form of expression covered in this chapter is controversial, behavioral as well as emotional in nature—the so-called Human Flesh Search Engine (HFSE hereafter), which is an extreme but highly effective online collective behavior in China with a diversity of possible purposes, from tracing down people, fact-checking, bullying, to exposing immoral behaviors of individuals or corruption. It calls for collaborative search among internet users to provide information on a person or an event in order to reveal the hidden truth of an incident or the identity of an individual. It typically begins with a widespread online post depicting an immoral event or a questionable behavior, which will be followed up with the provision of details of the event or person involved by a wide range of possible parties. Ordinary netizens play a key role through their voluntary participation in denouncing the guilty party by commenting on existing information or providing further information. The effects of

H. H. Wei, *Sociocultural Otherness and Minority Justice: A Study on China*,
Ius Gentium: Comparative Perspectives on Law and Justice 88,
https://doi.org/10.1007/978-981-16-9752-4_6

HFSE incidents vary; sometimes they could be violent and severely disrupt a person's everyday life. The commonly talked about negative effects of HFSE include invasion of privacy, slander and bully; but its positive functions are also obvious, for instance and as will be shown in this chapter, it has become a highly effective means to expose and bring down corrupt officials, as under the pressure of public opinion and hard evidence, the authorities will often step in and conduct investigations, no doubt with one of the purposes of ending the online collective expression has quickly as possible.

These two forms of expression constitute 'sociocultural otherness' in different but related ways. First, they are 'otherness' in the sense that they are seldom studied. Second, they are 'otherness' because they are considered unacceptable in their respective ways. In the case of controversial artistic expressions, they are unacceptable in that they are radical, challenge traditional standards of beauty, disobey widely accepted societal and behavioral norms; in the case of HFSE actions, they are illegal and often constitute invasion of privacy, even violence. They are 'otherness' also in a third and most important sense, in that they each reveal important truths about China from an unexpected angle, thereby challenging something rather fundamental.

6.1 Part I: Freedom of Expression and Controversial Art

6.1.1 Introduction: Controversial Art as Cultural Otherness

The notion of 'art' employed in this chapter is constructed broadly to include the widest range of human activities in creating visual, auditory or performing works, both demonstrating the artists' technical skills as well as expressing their conceptual and imaginative ideas, either intended to be appreciated for their emotional power, or to express social, political, cultural points of view, or simply to create a piece of work for the sake of creating a piece of work without having any underlying purposes or deeper meaning, or the purposes or meanings are open to varying interpretations (Freeland 2001). The examples used in this chapter are 'controversial' art forms either because they are radical, extreme presentations that challenge tradition and morality, standards of beauty, comprehensive especially behavioral conformity, societal harmony and unity, collective habit and appreciation of the value of obedience—cultural, social, political.

Controversial art is not new to China but rather has been present since the 1980s, although what was considered controversial then may not be controversial now, what was not controversial then may be controversial now, and some have remained unchanged. There is much controversy surrounding the word 'controversial', not only that it is highly subjective, heavily context-dependent, and constantly changing. By nature, and however one wants to define it, 'controversial artistic expressions' tend to be neither conservative on the means of communication nor physically pleasing to the eye (Julius 2002; Attwood et al. 2013). In the morally paternalistic Chinese society, they have been, in their diverse ways, viewed, condemned or punished for being physically and/or morally ugly, harmful, and/or dangerous. The question is to whom, in what ways, and are they really?

Exploring and hoping to provide answers to 'to whom, in what ways, and are they really harmful and dangerous' constitute the purpose of this chapter, which issues a philosophical invitation to engage in critical examinations on the proper place of controversial art in mainland China by presenting two related questions for thought—does China need controversial art, and relatedly how and why should the Chinese learn to coexist with art forms and expressions that they habitually want to supress? Bear in mind that throughout human history and in all cultures, the works of artists have been subject to restrictions and censorship, all countries have some forms of limitations on freedom of expression, and in relation to artistic expressions, legal constraints and censorship tend to take the form of obscenity law, nuisance law, public security law, prior restraints such as customs interception and film board censorship, and in those countries in which powerful religious influences exist—blasphemy law (Kearns 2013; Bezanson 2009).

This chapter does not consider artistic freedom in a vacuum but places the phenomenon of controversial art firmly within the contemporary Chinese context, constructs a tentative exploration into the social, cultural and political constraints of being controversial in any way artistically in China, in the hope of truly understanding the relevant issues first before providing the answers. This is not a project aiming to advance cultural relativism—quite the contrary—it hopes to find realistic ways forward toward meaningful protection of universal freedom of (artistic) expression based on appreciation of genuine cultural differences and accurate understanding of the interactions between various forces and factors. It is a kind of culturally sensitive universalism.

Controversial art is a complex cultural phenomenon that should be distinguished from mere contemporary art, although it ought to be analyzed against the background of the development of the latter. Following the end of the Cultural Revolution and the death of Mao, a period of comprehensive and radical rethinking of progressive modernity commenced, involving not only the opening up of China to outside economic and cultural influences but also the reconstruction of the country's internal space for greater autonomous forms and expressions of economic and cultural activities. As a result, divergence from official modes of expression began to appear and led to what some called a tripartite division of art production alongside socialist realist art which was mainstream at the time: a return to the traditional forms of Chinese art-making; an officially supported modern art that tended toward anodyne formalist mixing of traditional Chinese and modern Western techniques; and a largely unofficial though in recent years increasingly recognized and powerful modern art that draws strongly on Western modernism and postmodernism (Gladston 2016, 7), although even this last form is not a mere extension or copy of Western influences but with strong local Chinese cultural elements.

It is important to note that, for a long time, contemporary art was outside the sociocultural, economic and political interests of the ruling party, until the late 1990s and early 2000s, an example being that the development of extreme forms of body art in the late 1990s led to the handing down in 2001 of the Ministry of Culture

Notice outlawing pornography and extreme forms of bodily violence in the name of art. Though it was perhaps the 2000 Shanghai Biennale, at which a programme of globalization was facilitated and experimental exhibitions were organized to test the public roles of contemporary art, that the Chinese government began to take a serious interest in contemporary art as a progressive manifestation of Chinese modernity. This growing awareness has had two long-lasting consequences.

The first is a shift in outlook away from the prior concentration on economic and social reforms toward a more fundamental, structural, coordination of socioeconomic and cultural interests in support of the country's continuing modernization, involving the development of official policies on the cultural industries as well as the use of cultural diplomacy abroad on the international stage. The second and related is a total transformation in attitude toward the political management of culture in general, art and especially contemporary art, in that not only has mainstream politics begun to pay close attention but also that art, including contemporary art, is expected to be compatible with the political interests of the ruling party and the state.

While sociocultural and political conditions differ from those during the Cultural Revolution, the persistent desire of the state to manage culture is continuously felt and must not be underestimated. Hence, while contemporary art, including some controversial forms of art, saw progressive institutionalisation during the 2000s and now enjoys a continuous presence in major cosmopolitan cities, it should not be interpreted unequivocally as a sign of increased cultural liberalization or of greater tolerance of cultural divergence let alone social critique—especially not now. When society changes, art changes, the limitations placed upon art change, and since modern controversial art tends to represent dramatic change or radical expression, it causes discomfort and makes people worry, especially in a society that has in recent years made a conservative U-turn culturally and comprehensively (O'Dea 2017).

'Why is China uncomfortable with or even afraid of controversial art?' is an important question to ask. First, in many people's opinion, controversial art is, as its name suggests, controversial, weird, and abnormal, thereby testing and challenging society's levels of tolerance and standards of decency, inviting and even craving strong reactions and harsh criticism (Julius 2002; Mey 2007). While in free societies this is not usually a problem (though it sometimes can be), in others it potentially is. Second, it tends to express negative rather than positive emotions and thoughts in ways that are not mainstream, in order to imagine, explore and express discomfort, fear and uncertainties in life—such discomfort, fear and uncertainties tend to spread when they are on public display.

Third, controversial art, particularly performance art, went through a period of 'radicalization' in China in the late 1990s and early 2000s, during which period a number of very radical exhibitions, such as 'Post-Sense Sensibility' in 1999, 'Infatuated with Injury' and 'Fuck Off' in 2000, effectively turned questions of aesthetics into something much more serious and violent—as the use of dead animals and human body parts, the pictorial documentation of an artist eating a dead baby, or injecting the artists' blood through a tube into the mouths of two dead babies, practically declared war on law, morality and humanity. Such performances and displays were increasingly widely seen as attention-seeking shows with absolutely no regard for common social decency and were for the sole purpose of self-expression irrespective of costs or consequences. This radical period has left a permanent mark and has been the key reason why while experimental art in general is allowed to be on public display at exhibitions in China, performance art is banned.

Considering these three points above in conjunction with the fact that all works of art can perform a social function—in that it is created for an audience, it can effectively express and communicate certain points of view to its audience, it can therefore influence and potentially alter the thinking and collective behavior of the audience—its potential political implications are likely to be another reason why they are treated with caution, especially considering that the Chinese state has long been familiar with the power of art, as evident in the propaganda artworks during the Sino-Japanese War and the Civil War in the 1930s and 1940s as well as during the Cultural Revolution. One of the earlier speeches of the current top leader at a literary gathering in Beijing pronounced that art should serve the people, which was another piece of evidence of the state's awareness of the powerful influence and functions of art, including nonmainstream, controversial, art.

6.1.2 External and Internal Restraints of Artistic Freedom

It is important to remember that all forms of expression, including artistic expression, are subject to legitimate limitations, be they external or internal (Kearns 2013). External limits result from conflict between freedom of expression on the one hand and rights and considerations that represent the opposite positions or interests; internal limits are agreed principles or restrictions placed upon the means, content and/or context of expression.

On external limits, hence rights conflict, it is difficult to talk about 'controversial art' as a whole, as it consists of a wide range of manifestations, so using artistic expressions that communicate some form of disrespect or even hatred as an example, it presents a difficult issue for liberals, as it reveals a conflict between their two most cherished values. On the one hand, a liberal society prides itself on its acceptance and celebration of cultural diversity and pluralism, on its fostering of equal respect for all members of all cultural groups, on rejecting all forms of discrimination on grounds of culture, ethnicity, national origin, religious affiliation, gender, age, disability, sexual orientation and so on. But at the same time, a firm commitment to freedom of expression requires liberals to tolerate the expression of opinions that they considered abhorrent (Sumner 2004). A good example in the field of controversial art is *Piss Christ*, a 1987 photograph by American artist Andres Serrano, which depicts a small plastic crucifix submerged in a glass tank of the artist's own urine. Works such as this expose a contradiction between liberal equality and liberal freedom, a dilemma that presents itself as a conflict of rights—between a liberty-right to express and a claim-right to equal protection and equal consideration.

Speaking of such rights conflicts in a nonliberal society like China also makes sense, as conflicts of rights and interests are a matter of fact anywhere rather than confined to liberal societies. But it makes less sense, as, first, in a place where liberal freedoms are not upheld to the extent or in the way as they are in the West, conflicts tend to be much less intense as the natural tendency is to affirm values of the mainstream, rendering any balancing exercise less meaningful; second and related, speaking of rights conflicts in the Chinese context could also be dangerous and misleading, as such an approach could easily be hijacked to become excuses for substandard protection.

The internal limits, in comparison, are those principles, freestanding or not, that legitimately constrain freedom of artistic expression. Three are particularly noteworthy: the Harm Principle, the Moralism Principle, and the Paternalism Principle, which all overlap and share key elements. While they are applicable in different contexts, since harm, morality, and decency tend to have different meanings and scopes in different cultures, the applicability of these principles and the balancing exercises employed tend to vary. Each shall be examined within the Chinese context, illustrated using real examples from the art field.

6.1.3 Harm and Controversial Art

In the famous *On Liberty,* John Stuart Mill seeks a general principle that will define the limits of social interference with the activities of individuals. The kinds of interference that he has in mind include not only formal mechanisms of the state such as laws and regulations, but also the more informal forms of interference of the dominant social groups that may oppress or silence the minorities for being different—what he calls 'the tyranny of the majority'. His statement of the principle of liberty is well known: 'the only purpose for which power can be rightfully exercised over any member of a civilized community, against his will, is to prevent harm to others. His own good, either physical or moral, is not a sufficient warrant' (Mill [1859] 2006). In other words, where harm to others is involved, individuals may rightfully be subject to coercion or control, while in their purely personal conduct that affects no other and no such harm is involved, their liberty ought to be protected. According to Mill, personal conduct may involve three things: the inward domain of consciousness, comprising conscience, thought, feeling, opinion and the like; living out one's own plan of life (that does not cause harm to others); and voluntary association with others (that does not harm third parties).

It is important to note that Mill does not include the activity of expressing and publishing opinions on this list, which does not mean that he excludes freedom of expression from the protection region of personal liberty—quite the contrary. Rather, he considers such activities to belong to that part of the conduct of an individual that concerns other people rather than purely personal, and is capable of causing harm to others. But he nevertheless urges nearly absolute protection against social interference of freedom of expression, thereby attaching a very special importance to it and granting it anomalous treatment within his overall scheme. His reason for giving expression this privileged status is that liberty of expression and discussion is almost as important as the liberty of thought itself, and that freedom to hold any opinion is worth little without the companion freedom to freely express, discuss and circulate. Most importantly, censorship will cause valuable truths to be suppressed, discourage inquiry, lead dominant or orthodox opinions to be held as dead letters, and in general disserve the mental well-being of mankind (Sumner 2004, 25–26). Hence, by recognizing on the one hand that expression is a social act capable of causing harm and on the other advocating for its near-absolute protection, Mill leaves open the question when interference with expression may be justified, which should be settled on a case-by-case basis.

Furthermore, it is crucial to note that when speaking of expression, Mill seems to have in mind strictly the expression of opinions, with his primary focus seemingly on political expression, particularly concerning safeguarding discussions of opinions about morals, religion, politics, social relations and the business of life. This is perhaps comparable to determining the level of scrutiny according to the social value of the speech in question, a principle laid down in the landmark decision *Chaplinsky v. New Hampshire* (1942), namely, that not all speech is of equal value, therefore rendering different protection. Examples of 'low value speech' include commercial speech, obscenity, libel, incitement, fighting words and child pornography, the 'low value' of which is due to the fact that they do not constitute an essential part of any exposition of ideas and are of such slight value as a step to truth that any benefit that may be derived from their protection is clearly outweighed by the social interest of order and morality' (Sadurski 1999, 41).[1] This does not mean that such speech should be totally unprotected. Rather, their protection is subject to a balancing of costs and benefits, which would be improper in the case of 'high value' speech.

Opponents of such a view reject the gradation of speech into higher and lower values, emphasizing the serious risks of entrusting an authoritative body with the power to assign different values to different categories of speech even before considering their actual harm and impact, which would be contrary to the libertarian approach to freedom of speech (Sadurski 1999, 41–42), which is particularly relevant in the Chinese context. However, it ought to be recognized that uniformity in the level of protection for all forms of speech could in fact be damaging to the general protection of free speech by an across-the-board lowering of the standard of scrutiny of restrictions placed upon expression. But if, as Cass Sunstein puts it, a well-functioning system of free expression must inevitably distinguish between different kinds of speech, it ultimately could mean that some forms of expression could be considered so remote from the rationale for free expression that there is simply no need to afford it any protection—which in effect is a moral judgment (Sadurski 1999, 43).

Furthermore, if one is to claim that a particular speech is of low value, in theory, the reasons should be harm-independent; otherwise, the principle would simply collapse into the Harm Principle, which renders it wholly unnecessary to differentiate between the types or values of different forms of expression. But in reality, especially considering that a predetermined focus on categorization may in fact divert attention away

[1] 315 U.S. 568 (1942), at 571–572.

from the actual consequences of the expression if any, the expression-harm connection appears to be more reliable and makes more sense, particularly considering that the term 'expression' has a very broad connotation for ordinary people and as it is employed in this chapter, extending well beyond the articulation of opinions in the narrow sense to include a wide range of means of communication and expression, such as art. But this creates additional problems—for many of the art pieces covered in this chapter, it is debatable whether they should be categorized as 'speech/expression' (which enjoys a higher degree of protection under the principle of freedom of expression) or 'act/conduct' (which is subject to the normal operation of the Harm Principle). Attempting to make such a distinction is indeed problematic and particularly crude to those communicative artistic acts that deserve special attention, not least because any speech/expression is communicated through some act/conduct, and many forms of conduct/act are expressive with the specific aim to communicate ideas or emotions, to the extent that it does not just *carry* speech, it *is* speech, or it is equivalent to speech in terms of purpose and impact (Maitra and McGowan 2012; Sadurski 1999, 43–47).

This is why an examination of the controversial art pieces covered in this chapter is worthy—as is very often the case in the modern world, art is a powerful sociocultural and political tool for expressing opinions about all the important issues that Mill considers to deserve near-absolute protection, although they do not fit exactly with Mill's definition of expression. It would hence be interesting to compare and contrast Mill's view with what might be considered harmful artistic expression in real life and in the Chinese context, with four questions in mind: first, what type of harm to others is relevant for the purposes of the principle in its application to artistic expressions—physical, psychological, moral? Second, how is harm to be determined and differentiated from, say, offence (Feinberg 1984; Feinberg 1985; Winston 2012)? Third, must the harm in question be caused to humans, or can it be caused to animals or the environment? And fourth, must there be actual harm or just the potential of harm? This chapter is not able to provide definite answers to these questions—if definite answers ever exist—but examining various forms of Chinese artistic expression with these questions in mind helps understand the complexity of the situation.

On the morning of 5 February 1989, artists and critics nervously marked the opening of the *China/Avant-Garde* exhibition, which was an unprecedented and monumental display of modern art at the National Art Gallery in central Beijing, with the aim of showing, categorizing and canonizing the conceptual and experimental artworks that had flowered throughout China during the reform era, which brought greater freedom to the country (Munroe et al. 2017, 81). The exhibition was very important symbolically, as it was taking place in an institution that epitomised political orthodoxy. It also turned out to be encyclopaedic and chaotic, not least because the 300 something works were selected by a team of academics and critics whose tastes and aims were not aligned, but also that despite that performance artists had been officially banned from the space (and those who were allowed to exhibit were forbidden from discussing pornography or politics), somehow they managed to get in and tried their best to provoke. One of them was Xiao Lu, whose gunshot performance brought the exhibition to an abrupt close by officials and riot police.

Xiao Lu's artwork at the exhibition, *Dialog* (1989), showed a man and a woman calling each other in two separate phone booths, between which there was a red phone on a table with its receiver dangling off the hook. At approximately 11:10, Xiao Lu fired two gunshots into this piece, leading to her arrest along with the man who provided her with the gun. There was great confusion about Xiao Lu's actual intention. Many seriously politicized her action given the political climate at the time, while she herself issued a statement after her arrest, announcing that she was not at all interested in politics and her action was purely artistic—it was her way of showing the intense emotions that she was experiencing in life at that time; there were also those who praised the artistic significance of the work and considered it the curtain call of the revolutionary New Wave and an opening volley for China's entry into modern art. However this piece should be interpreted, the potential physical harm that it could have caused to those at the exhibition as well as the emotional and psychological impact of firing a gun in public were obvious.

Returning to the third question asked above—must the harm in question be caused to humans or can it be caused primarily to, say, animals or the environment, which of course inevitably also harms the humans? The examples used here to help examine this question seem to also bring out the interactions between harm and morality. In October 2017, three controversial art pieces on display at the *Art and China after 1989: Theatre of the World* exhibition at the Guggenheim in New York were quickly removed after public complaints about them all featuring animal abuse. The exhibition was intended to present the creative and critical expressions of a very bold contemporary art movement spanning the years 1989 to 2008, arguably the most transformative period of modern Chinese history, offering a fresh interpretive survey of Chinese experimental art framed by the end of the Cold War, the spread of globalization and the rise of modern China. Focusing primarily on conceptual art, the exhibition examined how two generations of artists had interpreted the sweeping transformations that had brought China to the center of the world's attention as well as its art into a global artistic context (Munroe et al. 2017, 9).

The three pieces that were removed were Sun Yuan and Peng Yu's *Dogs That Cannot Touch Each Other* (2003), Xu Bing's *A Case Study of Transference* (1994) and Huang Yong Ping's *Theatre of the World* (1993). In *Dogs That Cannot Touch Each Other* (2003), eight nonmotorized exercise treadmills were arranged in two rows facing each other, and then eight American pit bulls were ceremonially walked to the treadmills so that they also faced each other in two rows. The bound dogs instinctively began to run, creating a frenetic scene in which they were barking loudly and trying to attack the dogs in front. The piece was meant to be a simulacrum of social violence, one that used the anxiety and aggravation of the bound American pit bulls as an allegory to interrogate the extent to which human thoughts and behavior were constricted by the often unavoidable manipulations of others and our everyday environment, exposing particularly the relational conditions vividly in detail (Munroe et al. 2017, 204).

A Case Study of Transference (1994), an exploration of the relationship between man, nature and culture, featured two live breeding pigs—a male boar stamped in ink with gibberish composed of the Roman alphabet and a sow stamped with illegible, invented Chinese characters—that became the unwitting protagonists of a performance piece. Xu Bing, the artist, initially intended the piece to be a humorous cultural allegory, in which the pigs—hybrids of American Yorkshire and Chinese Changbai Breeds—enacted a violent but productive meeting of the West and the East. The onlookers' self-conscious reactions when watching the two creatures that were devoid of human consciousness yet carrying on their bodies the marks of human civilization and engaging in the most primal form of 'social intercourse' without any shame were also the focus of the artist's attention. The civilized humans were expected to ask themselves, while watching natural instincts and desires on display, how much had culture changed us? (Munroe et al. 2017, 164).

Huang Yong Ping's *Theatre of the World* (1993) was a quiet spectacle staged in a faceted table/cage shaped like a tortoise, in which there was a living arena of the natural world with swarms of spiders, scorpions, crickets, cockroaches, black beetles, centipedes, lizards, geckos, toads and snakes, and they would dart, attack and devour each other in front of onlookers' eyes. The artist's design for the piece referred to the panopticon, with a central arena-like space that opened onto a series of compartments or cells radiating along the periphery. An institutional building, a system of control as well as the title of a book written by the English philosopher Jeremy Bentham in 1791, the panopticon was conceived by him as a prison structure that would allow the inspector to view criminals without them knowing when or whether they were being watched. Foucault, who clearly inspired Huang, reappraised Bentham's invention in his *Discipline and Punish: The Birth of the Prison* (1975), reading in it a disciplinary power that extended to other institutions in the modern world (Munroe et al. 2017, 82).

As noted previously, the removal of these three Chinese pieces from the exhibition was due to public complaints of animal cruelty, although arguably these complaints and protests brought these pieces a great deal more attention than they ever intended to. While protests and complaints were severe enough to render it necessary for the museum to remove the pieces, many also criticized the Guggenheim for having failed to protect freedom of artistic expression in the face of the conservative and normalizing forces of social decency and morality. What might be a more suitable reason though to ban the pieces was that such performances could cause psychological and emotional harms to some onlookers, especially children—by causing physical harm to the animals. Such harms could arguably be minimized though through restrictions of time, manner and circumstances—for instance if the American pit bulls would only be allowed to run on the treadmills for say five minutes before the imposition of a break; or if children below the ages of 16 would not be allowed to view the pieces—all of which would compromise the intended impact of the performances. But it remains a moot point whether they should have been completely prohibited solely on grounds of their content and means of expression. It is also arguable that these examples of controversial art relate more to 'distress', 'offence', than 'harm', which requires in-depth analysis that is beyond the scope of this chapter.

6.1.4 Morality and Controversial Art

The relationship between art and morality is manifold and complex, although it is generally agreed that the realm of the aesthetic cannot, and should not, be divorced from the realm of the moral (Bermúdez and Gardner 2003), but what this would entail in reality, in specific contexts, is open to debate and many interpretations (Ben-Dor 2011; Cashell 2009). Although Mill's Harm Principle is generally understood to exclude moral harm and distress, it does remind us of the close connection between harm and morality, specifically of the fact that moral corruption is very much a type of harm. However, 'morality' is a broad conception and tends to be more encompassing in some cultures than others, giving rise to the difficulty that regulating, restraining or prohibiting artistic expression on moral grounds must first define morality, a task that may be completed according to a number of criteria or standards.

The first possible test as to whether an artistic expression is moral is judgment according to 'community standards'. In theory, community standards are not set by those of the lowest taste or the highest taste, or by the most conservative or the least conservative; rather, they should represent standards of average thinking and feeling of society. Such collective standards should normally have three key features: they tend to be contemporary and change to varying degrees as social norms change; the community in question, as it has been argued, is the country as a whole—in other words, the standards are national, acts and expressions are judged according to 'Chinese' standards; and most importantly, they should be standards of tolerance rather than standards of taste (Sumner 2004, 93–94).

In reality, and especially in authoritarian states, determining community standards is both difficult and easy, and certainly controversial. First, it is unclear how such reliable standards may be determined—from representatives, opinion surveys or some experts? Despite such difficulties, second, community standards often mean opinions of the state, or of the majority, and for that reason tend to be presumed to be unquestionably objective, although in reality they are often subjective and biased, representing the views of certain groups and excluding those of others. Third and related, community standards tend to be considered a matter of fact beyond criticism or challenge and therefore are standards of taste rather than tolerance as they should be, often concealing the real reason for expectations of conformity.

The second possible test is that of 'internal necessities', according to which the publication of some questionable content would not count as undue if it had literary or artistic merit and if the treatment did not exceed what was necessary to the development of its themes (Sumner 2004, 96). Arguments from the literary and artistic perspective are appropriate when the items for consideration are serious works of art—serious but controversial—for instance Lady Chatterley's Lover in its historical context, or a controversial painting from a reputable gallery, although this does open up the philosophical question as to what makes a piece of work a piece of art, which is beyond the scope of this chapter. However, very often, no credible case of literary or artistic merit could be made for the art piece in question; neither does every artist bother to try hard; and indeed not everyone who makes art is an 'artist' in the strictest sense.

This renders a possible third test—also a variation of the Harm Principle—worthy of consideration: using sexually explicit publications as an example, a piece of artwork may be considered problematic if the work portrays persons in a degrading manner, for instance as objects of violence, cruelty or other forms of dehumanizing treatment. In other words, the underlying principle is that controversial content should not be automatically prohibited, but subjecting anyone to degradation and humiliation in such publications should be. A good example is pornography. While depicting pornographic materials in the name of art-making is banned in China, there are always the questions of what constitutes degradation and how degrading is degrading, which concern all forms of controversial artistic expressions. And once in a while it seems there is also the question—degrading whom or what?

In April 2019, a Chinese performance artist, known as Siyuan Zhuji, sparked controversy for posting photos on an art website and on social media of himself laying naked next to his late father's remains after exhuming the bones and arranging them into a skeleton, a day after the Tomb-Sweeping Day which was China's annual festival to pay respect to the departed. According to the artist, he was only three years old when his father died of liver cancer, and it had been his dream to take a photo with his father's remains, which he considered to be a very personal expression of his feelings. These photos went viral on the internet and attracted widespread and severe condemnation calling the act a disrespectful, immoral and shameless shot for fame, which eventually led to suspension of his social media account.

Some commentators considered digging up the bones alone morally unacceptable, and the fact that the artist used his father as a tool for a so-called piece of art was against all rules and traditions of filial piety. Others argued that it was the phototaking and then posting online that were problematic—if it was not for the purpose of fame and attention seeking, why not just hang your 'art' up at home rather than posting online and sharing with the world? There were also supporters who considered it a brave act that dared to go beyond the boundaries of moral principles so that a direct conversation between the departed and the living could be enabled—art is subjective, what others think does not make the piece more or less of a piece of art.

While not exactly the same, this case is comparable with art-making that involves the use of dead animals, which was very common during the previously discussed radical period of the late 1990s and early 2000s. On 28th May 2000, artist Wu Gaozhong performed '*Birthday*' in a park in Nanjing: he rented a butchered buffalo from the local market, took away its viscera, spread rose pedals inside and around its stomach, entered the stomach naked to stay in it. His assistant sewed up the stomach with a string. Wu stayed inside the buffalo's body for ten minutes, during which he caressed the inside of the stomach, then pulled the stiches and string apart to get out. He then stood next to the buffalo's body and threw rose pedals in the air. Hugely controversial, Wu claimed that he had a special feeling of closeness and a sense of security and protection while inside the body of the buffalo, as if he was being comforted by his mother (Fok 2013).

These two performances share similarities, rendering it possible to defend or criticize them together. First, there is degradation involved in both the case of the father's remains and that of the dead buffalo. Second, both artists have clearly employed the shock factor as a tool to attract attention either to themselves or to the point they wish to make. Third, it seems that the only thing that matters is the artist's personal experience gained from the performance. This is perhaps the crucial difference between these two performances and the previously mentioned *Theatre of the World* (1993) of Huang Yong Ping—what is on public display in these two performances appears to be self-satisfaction and self-satisfaction only, at the expense of exploitation of human and animal remains as well as the viewers' comfort.

6.1.5 Paternalism and Controversial Art

The Paternalism Principle in this context is a liberty-limiting principle that recognizes the need to prevent self-inflicted harm as a legitimate reason for some form of intervention, coercion or prohibition. The key distinction between what might be called 'hard paternalism' and 'soft paternalism' has to do with the weight attached to the degree of voluntariness of a person's action in a one-party case and the voluntariness of his consent in a two-party case. Hard paternalism will accept that it is necessary to protect competent adults against their own will from harmful consequences even of their fully voluntary choices and undertakings, whereas the spirit of soft paternalism is closer to John Stuart Mill's liberalism than to the protectiveness of hard paternalism, which holds that the state has the right to prevent self-regarding harmful action when but only when that action is substantially nonvoluntary or when temporary intervention is necessary in order to establish whether it is voluntary—giving rise to the question of whether soft paternalism is an independent liberty-limiting principle at all (Feinberg 1986, 12).

A good arena within which paternalism may be examined is that of performance art, highly controversial and banned in China's mainstream art circles, often associated with savage and weird acts, obscenity and public display of violence and blood in the name of art, which are all prohibited by official directives from the Ministry of Culture. Its controversy not only comes from presumed association with weirdness, violence and obscenity, but also that many contain deeper meanings and may be interpreted as voicing criticisms of the establishment in a powerful and confrontational way. While being a cast of experimental art means that performance art is meant to voice critical reflections on matters concerning the social reality through the creation of striking imagery or performance of certain acts that push the boundaries, the Chinese reality is one in which all forms of art are increasingly shaped into productions that can cause pleasurable aesthetic feelings or make constructive contributions toward social progress and well-being. In other words, while since the mid-1990s artists have been largely left alone to make pretty much any kind of art as long as they do not directly challenge the government, in recent years art has increasingly been required to conform to mainstream and traditional standards of normality and pleasantness, in that not only it needs to be pleasing to the eye but also must be easily understood by the majority. This is not to say that experimental and conceptual art is prohibited, but rather the free space is smaller than before, and being weird and controversial is no longer as acceptable as it was once upon a time.

A telling example is He Yunchang, a performance artist in Beijing known for highly controversial performance artworks involving acts of physical endurance, self-mutilation and violence, often demonstrating an obsession with the infliction of harm and injury. In *One Meter of Democracy* (2010), He asked 25 people (who were artists, critics and curators all of similar age to He) to vote in a secret ballot to decide whether he should have a 1 meter long and 0.5 to 1 cm deep cut down the right-hand side of his body starting from below the collarbone all the way down to the knee. With 3 abstentions, 12 against 10 people voted for the cut, which would be made and then stitched up by a female surgent. The artist then underwent such a surgical operation, naked, fully conscious and screaming in pain all the way, with all 25 voters watching, the entire process of which was recorded. The painful and troublesome recovery process took approximately 60 days according to the artist himself, leaving a large scar down the right-hand side of his body.

This performance art piece constitutes a major departure from standard pleasurable aesthetics and is a faithful and consistent representation of the artist's usual style, that is, to use the body as a tool, even a weapon, through pushing the boundaries of social decency and morality, breaking institutional and systematic restrictions placed upon such performances and everyday behavior, to convey certain messages. The messages or deeper meaning of this piece, if there is any, may be interpreted in various ways. First, people who are critical of performance art would say that such performances are nothing more than attention-seeking shows of self-absorbed people. Second, the name of the piece suggests that the artist intends to convey his perceptions of democracy and appears to have exposed the problems in the design and process of democratic voting. By focusing the viewers' attention on the lack of consideration and ill consequences of the tyranny of the majority realized through democracy, it issues a warning that further democratization in China is likely to cause infliction of serious injury to the country. But at the same time, it could equally be argued that despite appearances, this piece was pro-democracy by demonstrating what could happen to those in power should the people be given a free vote.

Third, pro-democracy or not, it is also arguable that the chief intention of the artist has been to simply express his rebellion toward the constraints of the state and society and his desire and determination to break free irrespective of the consequences—both in terms of the physical and mental harm that he had to endure during and after the performance, and the social condemnation that this piece would undoubtedly attract upon coming into public attention—and it is only as a side-effect that this process of rebellion and breaking free reminds people of what the society lacks: democracy and empathy. If this was indeed the artist's primary intention, the danger of such a piece being performed in a society in which critical thinking and expression are constrained becomes apparent, that it causes fear and thereby enhances an overly simplistic view of democracy in a society that has never experienced or understood real democracy, which will only hinder further discussion of its pros and cons.

There are several elements of such performances that could lead the artist into trouble. The first is the association with democracy, which needs no detailed explanation. The second is the nudity. It is beyond doubt that the police would stop him if he were performing naked in public in China, although it is ironic that the only two times that he encountered police interventions in his artistic career thus far for performing naked in public were in the United States, not in China (Wang 2014, 23), indicating that the restrictive nature of society in this regard is irrespective of political systems. The third and related is the hard paternalistic concern that hurting oneself or inviting others to hurt oneself in the name of making art should attract intervention. What makes things a little difficult, at least from an artistically interpretative point of view, is that if the brutality of the artist's methodology is essential to the conveyance of the meaning of the piece, for instance if the brutality is a reflection of the brutality of the social reality as he sees it, which has prompted him to use his body to make a primitive sacrifice in order to demonstrate the position, the will and the struggle of the weak in an overpowering system, as well as the artist's refusal of the normalizing pressure that comes from widely upheld rationalities and conventions (Wang 2014, 14, 24).

This was of course not the first time that the artist had created such astonishing yet conceptually thought-provoking performance art that challenged the paternalism principle. On 8 August 2008, the opening day of the much-anticipated 2008 Beijing Olympics, He Yunchang had a twenty-five-centimeter section of bone excised from the eighth rib of his left side. He originally had planned to have a longer rib extracted but decided to accept the surgeon's cautioning suggestion in selecting the eighth in order to minimize potential harm. Removing a rib in the name of making art was so shocking that it took him a few years to negotiate and eventually find a hospital in his home province Yunnan, which was the only hospital that he could convince to carry out such a medically unnecessary operation. He then fashioned the rib into a necklace that was used as a prop in a series of photographs. Two questions arise. First, does the fact that such performances are often photographed or recorded render them more controversial and in need of intervention, or the performances per se are reason enough to attract intervention? Second, does the type of self-inflicted harm matter?

It is easy to understand why photography and video documentation are often employed by performance artists as a primary methodology in China—performance work is formally prohibited in Chinese art institutions, so photographic and video documentation has been an important strategy for both exhibiting artworks as well as building catalogs and spreading ideas and influences, enabling the artists and their work to become more influential than a one-off event performed in a confined space and to catch the attention of faraway viewers, curators and collectors—which also makes the work more 'dangerous'. This is particularly important for artists who are not mainstream or are poorly connected, not that it guarantees attention but it helps.

Regarding whether the type of self-inflicted harm matters and indeed what types of self-inflicted harm should count, the controversial case of the late Datong Dazhang is thought-provoking. Datong Dazhang, an ex-soldier and then audit clerk at a bank, was an outlier living a Bohemian lifestyle who sought to establish himself outside official structures and frameworks through paintings, conceptual artworks and performances, which were all completely disregarded, rendering him a decided failure as an artist during his lifetime by usual standards. He was so relegated to the very margins of the Chinese contemporary art world that few had known of him until his suicide by hanging in his apartment at 00:00 on 1 January 2000, which was interpreted as the final piece of his performance art, though not in the strictest sense as there was no audience present to witness his suicide, it was considered to be an act that was true to self and a devout self-expression in which he sacrificed his body and released his soul for his artistic passion (Chun 2016). He left a note announcing that his suicide was a predestined personal decision and asked others, among other things, to dump his body outside the crematorium.

Whether or not suicide constitutes 'self-inflicted harm' is a philosophical question beyond the scope of this chapter. But for obvious reasons, while it would be wrong to encourage others to follow suit in the name of art, it would also be wrong, and impossible, to forbid such acts. Indeed, Dazhang was not the first and only artist to have committed suicide in the name of art—Qi Li, for instance, died at the age of 23 during a public display in which he slowly froze his body performing the *Ice Burial* (Fok 2013). This example again causes one to wonder whether Dazhang's suicide could in fact be considered to be for the purpose of art at all, as it was not a performance in the literal sense due to the lack of an audience.

Paternalism, or perhaps more accurately strict moralism, also manifests in another way, testament to the continuing challenges that conservative normalizing expectations present to those who are outsiders. In 2017, Ge Yulu, then a recent graduate with a Master's Degree in Experimental Art from China Central Academy of Fine Arts rose to fame in China because of one of his artworks: the authorities and the media recently discovered that he had secretly named a road after himself by sticking up a fake street sign on an unnamed street and successfully fooled Google and Baidu maps. Ge, whose name coincidentally ends with 'Lu', which means road or street in Chinese, carried out this project as part of his thesis. Although his project came to public attention in 2017 after media exposure, it in fact started four years ago when he first moved to the capital, in which he would search for unnamed streets and put up fake signs that would normally be torn down immediately by urban management officers. But somehow this one had managed to escape the attention of the authorities until now.

His behavior sparked controversy and debate. Insisting that it was never his intention to actually own a road, Ge claimed that he merely wanted to create a space of imagination and fun in the boring real world, without having given much thought to public order and governance. Supporters of him would praise his creativity and argue that while it was not exactly good behavior, it was nevertheless a kind of harmless wrong-doing that brought smiles onto many people's faces. Besides, in its uniquely naughty way, it inspired people to think about their relationship with the city and how public space should be governed. Hoping the authorities would allow the fake street sign to remain where it was or even turn it into a tourist site, some would even compare Ge's project with graffiti in the West and argued that, while graffiti was illegal in much of the Western world, as long as it was not violent, offensive or in violation of rights, the authorities would usually be very tolerant and let it be—a good example being the fascination with the world-renowned British graffiti artist Banksy.

However, the fake street sign was nevertheless taken down soon after media exposure—a decision that was not hard to defend considering the Chinese context. First, according to the authorities, the street had already had an official name since 2005; it just did not have an official sign before Ge put up his fake one. Second, Ge had not only put up fake road signs but had also tempered with surveillance cameras in the past in the name of experimental art—he once stared into a surveillance camera on the street for hours until the policeman behind the camera showed up and had a serious talk with him. He explained his act as questioning the power of surveillance and that the 'eye contact' with the person behind the camera was romantic and warm. The fact that surveillance cameras were involved means that it is possible to interpret his act as a form of civic protest rather than just being naughty, and Chinese society is not one that welcomes civic protests. A similar act of Ge's led to him being punished for a disciplinary violation in July 2017—he placed a fake penis on top of the university's flag post in one of his video installations.

Third and related, in any society, how humorous one is allowed to be in public is never just a matter of right and wrong in a vacuum but concerns the role of humor in society and the relationship between humor and regulation, particularly the boundaries placed upon humor (Bucaria and Barra 2016, 210)—and in this particular case, when and under what conditions it is OK to play around in the name of art. This is a very broad area, and all societies and cultures debate what constitutes 'appropriate' humor, which is more than a question of political correctness which is itself historically and culturally specific. Idealistically speaking, there is no point in having regulations or being concerned about the content or means of delivery of humorous acts or expressions unless it is obvious or foreseeable that such humor can affect society in undesirable ways. But in the Chinese context, in which there is often an unexamined assumption that a certain kind of humor or irony can have negative and widespread effects on society, it is often difficult to defend certain humorous but controversial expressions in concrete terms.

However, it ought to be remembered that in none of the above cases the artist in question encountered any disproportional intervention. This leads to two preliminary conclusions. First, the social role and cultural power of such artistic expressions ought to be acknowledged, in that they are able to say or do things that would be absolutely unacceptable should they be said or done in other ways. A telling illustration is Ge Yulu's eye-to-eye confrontation with the surveillance camera. Should he have questioned or confronted the power of surveillance, say, in an academic essay, he would likely to get in trouble. In contrast, by being silly and irresponsible, he managed to get away with just a lecture. However, second, such artistic expressions are open to diverse interpretations, rendering the real intent of the artist not always immediately apparent. Hence, it is possible that had there not been sufficient opportunity for the artist to explain or for the viewers to explore, staring at the surveillance camera could well just be staring at the surveillance camera and nothing more. Third, it seems that for this type of artistic expression that constitutes harmless wrong-doing, Chinese society is tolerant enough though not quite up to the standards of the free West.

6.2 Concluding Part I: Is it a Matter of Cultural Sensitivity?

Theoretically speaking, justifications of freedom of artistic expression are usually fourfold: search for the truth, exercise of individual autonomy, legitimacy of a democratic state, and the value of tolerance. In reality, however, and particularly in a unique national context such as China, it all seems to somehow land on cultural sensitivity. Whether or not art should be culturally sensitive probably depends on what being culturally sensitive means and entails, both generally and in specific national contexts. Generally speaking, cultural sensitivity is the knowledge, awareness, and acceptance of other cultures, other cultural identities, and cultural differences. In the Chinese context and in relation to controversial art, cultural sensitivity seems to translate into the knowledge, awareness and acceptance of the limitations placed upon freedom to practice controversial art generated not simply by the Chinese culture as such but more so perhaps by the state's ideology and style of governing. This gives rise to the question of whether what is, or what should be, in concern is a matter of cultural sensitivity at all.

The value of controversial art lies precisely in what renders it controversial, that it challenges underlying conservatism of mainstream attitudes to art and beyond. By doing so, it generates sparks and inspires conversation. To protect controversial art does not need to mean protect all artistic expressions that are controversial, as who is putting up a show for the sake of seeking attention and who is exploring something deep through artistic albeit controversial means is more than often fairly obvious. However, the problem is often that the former will not necessarily be punished while the latter could be prohibited. In other words, the meaningful tends to be considered more threatening than the meaningless, and only a selected few will be willing and able to dig deep into why the artists choose to do art this way, which tends to tell a great deal of story as art is never just art. Furthermore, the snowballing effect is also a cause for concern in China—that if controversial art is allowed to challenge art, controversial something else can also challenge other things, and habits are infectious, learnt and passed on, which is likely to generate fear, anger, and action—which is why Part I has asked more questions than it can answer, reflecting the reality of controversial art as otherness in China and beyond.

6.3 Part II: Human Flesh Search Engine as Collective Action

The internet has revolutionized almost every aspect of Chinese daily life in recent decades. In February 2021, the China Internet Network Information Center published its 47th statistical report on China's internet usage and development, according to which, by the end of 2020, the total number of Chinese internet users had reached 0.989 billion, 99.7% of whom had accessed the internet on their mobile phones, which means 70% of the Chinese population can now get online anywhere, at any time, instantly, rendering not only that the information flow is faster but also that expression and exchange of opinion in public is more active. Such a sense of freedom can bring many benefits, especially in a censored society, but at the same time could also cause controversies and problems in certain circumstances—one of which is the so-called 'Human Flesh Search Engine' (HFSE), which refers to human interactions and collaborative sharing of information for the purpose of tracking down people online or offline for various reasons, including but not limited to locating missing persons, exposure of misbehavior or transgressions, fact-checking, bullying, or simply slandering. Hence, it is a type of human-assisted search engine mechanism as well as a form of collective action.

While different HFSE incidents could differ in terms of trigger, target, motivation, purpose, and patterns of the development of the storyline, they share many common features. First, the key actors in HFSE incidents are always internet users working together, using their contacts and conventional search engines to achieve a common goal; second, these incidents usually take place in cyberplace, although as the cases in this chapter illustrate, often there are offline consequences too, such as threatening phone calls or other harassing behavior; third, the trigger for HFSE is usually the online exposure of someone's misbehavior, real or fabricated, or transgression of generally accepted norms, real or fabricated; and fourth, the process of HFSE usually consists of exposure, searching and sharing of information, naming and shaming, and eventual consequences. While HFSE is often labeled a form of online vigilantism that victimizes people on the internet, it is important to remember the diversity of purposes that it has achieved, go beneath the surface and examine the underlying aspects that could not be observed at first glance, and especially examine why the phenomenon emerged in the first place and what purpose it has achieved that cannot be achieved through other means. In other words, there must be something that should be done but has not been done that renders HFSE necessary for some people, for some purposes, rendering a more systematic and multidimensional, if not neutral, examination of the phenomenon necessary.

Furthermore, a sound understanding of the Chinese reality should give rise to the observation that a contextual analytical approach ought to be adopted to fully understand HFSE. This has several implications. First, HFSEs should be studied in the context of *offline* social, cultural and political conditions that have not only shaped individuals' *online* behavior but also determined how people communicate generally in real life. Particularly, HFSE should be seen as a telling phenomenon that depicts in its own unique way how participation nonetheless takes place in a censored social space in which whether or not meaningful engagement can take place depends very much on the topic. Second, an examination of this phenomenon should not focus solely on its irrational, and in some situations, violent, nature; rather, the individual and collective emotions behind, the realities that have generated such emotions, and why people choose to express emotions in this particular way, should also be tentatively analyzed. Third, studying HFSE should have an even higher purpose than to use the internet as a vehicle for understanding expression in the Chinese context, it is a unique gateway also to understanding how the state and its people interact, at what expense, with what consequences.

6.3.1 Context, Key Features and Controversies

6.3.1.1 Key Features of HFSE

It is necessary to begin the analysis with a presentation of the essential features of HFSE, although any internet user should be familiar with them. The first is that the number of possible participants in an HFSE action could potentially be very large due to the size of the Chinese internet population and the number of people using mobile phones to access the internet. The fact that information travels far, fast, freely and interactively is also encouraging for people who seek or want to share information for whatever purpose. The second is online anonymity, which is the most significant difference between the real world and cyberspace. Anonymity has dual effects. On the one hand, it protects democratic discourse and enables people to communicate more openly and honestly knowing that their identity is concealed. This is particularly important in China, as censorship injects a certain degree of fear, or at least carefulness, into everyone's mind when they speak in public, especially when face to face. The social norm of always maintaining harmony with others will also cause people to hesitate, especially when they have something negative to say. This becomes less of a problem online despite cyberspace also being censored, as people feel only partly exposed, unlike in real life, and tend to feel freer to express and condemn.

On the other hand, while the feeling that they have escaped the ever-present gaze of the state (though this is not true) may turn some into heroes (for instance, in exposing corrupt officials, defending the weak, or searching and sharing information to help find a missing person), it can also turn others into unaccountable bullies who view online anonymity as the 'umbrella' keeping them safe from blame and responsibility. The fact that HFSE is always a group event may also give the impression that individual responsibility is diminished, wrongfully entitling some people to say or do whatever they like, generating irresponsible behavior and giving rise to dubious information that lacks credibility. In Le Bon's ([1895] 2003) words, it is the crowds that allow people to feel anonymous and thus less responsible for their own actions, which may bring out the violent, the criminal, the very worst, in people.

The third feature is efficiency and openness. As the examples below will demonstrate, it could take just one slight piece of personal information to trigger the chain of information gathering and sharing, which could take a matter of days or even hours for the individual to be totally exposed in cyberspace. The reason for such efficiency is of course the large number of participants and hence a diverse range of sources of information, which are unrivalled by any other type of formal search mechanism. Besides, all the information gathered is made public online and shared with everyone for an indeterminant period of time, enabling further searches and hence further expansion of the influence unless deleted. The fourth feature is dual character, in that some aspects of HFSE is legal, others illegal, some aspects moral, others immoral, controversial, even violent and criminal, which need not be explained in detail here, and much of course depends on the motivation and purpose of the HFSE incident in question, which can be explored through examining two real examples of HFSE incidents so that at least a partial insight into the mechanism's diverse targets, motivations, purposes and functions may be gained.

6.3.1.2 Diverse Targets and Purposes

In December 2008, a Beijing court delivered a landmark verdict in December 2008, which ruled that a man named Wang Fei's privacy had been invaded and reputation had been damaged by his late wife Jiang's university classmate, Zhang Leyi, who posted online diary excerpts of Jiang (who committed suicide upon discovering her husband's extramarital affair) containing details of Wang's infidelity, his real name, family address and the name of his employer. The internet company that hosted the comments was also held reliable. Zhang and the internet company were ordered to pay Wang 5,000 RMB and 3,000 RMB, respectively. This was the very first case against the 'human flesh search engine' that had reached court in China, in which internet users, who, upon reading Zhang's posts, were angered by the story and mounted a cyber manhunt for Wang, causing Wang to be forced to resign and have trouble finding another job after strangers tracked him down and contacted the companies where he and his lover worked. Threatening words were painted on his family's door, and his photos, address and phone numbers were made public on the internet.

Two interrelated emotional elements are present in this case that directly caused internet users to collaborate and take part in this HFSE incident: sympathy and moral shock. Sympathy is an emotion that is often the precondition of the type of HFSE actions aiming to bring about some form of redress by exposing moral misbehavior. While the emotion itself does not directly cause any action or movement, it plays the vital role of bringing people together by creating a shared sentiment as well as a common goal, the rightful pursuit of which becomes the reason for participation in a movement. Emotion also determines the scale of the action, in that the greater the number of people experiencing sympathetic emotion is, the larger the population of potential participants could be. But in this type of cases, sympathy for the weaker party is never the only emotion felt by the HFSE participants—on the other side of the coin is always disapproval, resentment, or shock caused by some violations of certain social or moral standards of behavior—in other words emotions felt toward the stronger party, which itself is a mobilizing force.

The mobilizing power of moral shocks is well studied. A moral shock effect can expand consciousness and turn bystanders into comrades who are not only reconnected with their own feelings and moral convictions but are also connected with others who share those feelings and convictions (Jasper and Poulsen 1995; Jasper 1997; Wettergren 2005). In the absence of pre-existing social networks, moral shocks are often the first step toward recruitment of strangers into taking part in an action or movement, and such moral shocks are often triggered by an unexpected event or release of a piece of information that causes a public sense of moral outrage that may intensify over time as the information spreads further—such as in the above case that the wife committed suicide upon discovering her husband's extramarital affair. The values and norms that the moral shocks reveal are firmly situated in the wider sociocultural context (Solove 2007); in other words, they are social, collective, attitudes and positions rather than just some individual's personal opinion, and when these values and norms are shaken or threatened—for instance in the above case by the husband's extramarital affair—the moral indignation and outrage toward particular targets will soon emerge and spread, causing more to join in the action in defense of the weak and the moral. There are comparable examples of Chinese internet users exposing those who abuse animals, elderly or disabled people.

Another well-known HFSE case but of a different nature than the one examined above was that of Zhou Jiugeng, then chief of the Real Estate Management Bureau in the Jiangning District of Nanjing, the capital of Jiangsu Province. On 10 December 2008, Zhou stated in an interview that his bureau would closely monitor the real estate market and punish developers who would sell properties at a price that was lower than the cost. At the time due to high prices in some Chinese cities, many new properties went unsold, forcing developers to dramatically lower their prices in order to relieve the problem of overstock. Zhou's statement was widely reported and soon caused a wave of anger among internet users who considered his comments highly insensitive about the fact that property prices had significantly exceeded ordinary people's affordability, which was a source of great concern and grievance among the general population, who were of the view that the government should take measures to lower property prices to a generally affordable level rather than encourage developers to keep the prices high.

The anger soon spread in cyberspace, and in the following days more and more information about Zhou was revealed online, for instance he smoked luxury brand cigarettes and wore an expensive watch which he should not have been able to afford with his public servant's salary, and that his brother was a real estate developer, hinting that his interview comments were meant to protect family interests. On 20 December, the district government first responded by announcing that an inquiry into Zhou's conducts had been started; on 28 December, Zhou was dismissed due to his inappropriate comments and for misusing public funds to purchase luxury goods. Soon more and more details about Zhou's corruption began to surface; for instance, between 2003 and 2008, he accepted over 1 million RMB as bribery. On 10 October 2009, Zhou was sentenced to 11 years in jail for corruption.

The controversy as well as the power of HFSE are plain for all to see in this case, which unlike the previous case, is clearly politically focused, namely, that Zhou's corruption would not have been exposed and he would not have been punished had public attention focused solely on his interview remarks. Rather, the public was so angry that they began to search for evidence that might raise suspicions of corruption, clearly with the aim of making him pay for what he said. In this way, they were not just a group of internet users any more but a group with multiple shared sentiments, in this case discontent with high property prices, anger at the insensitivity of those in charge, and general grievances caused by cases of official corruption that they had heard or read about. Once again, the wider reality of the country is of vital importance. The fact that in offline real life, an ordinary citizen removing corrupt officials is a near impossible task, let alone so efficiently, renders HFSE particularly appealing in the eye of those who want to expose suspected corruption or simply want to let the anger out. To understand this fully requires one to place HFSE in two particular wider contexts that overlap: the offline social, cultural and political context of Chinese society, and the unique atmosphere of cyberspace.

6.3.1.3 Sociocultural and Political Context

It is important to point out that HFSE is not uniquely Chinese but rather has been employed in various forms all over the world to achieve similar purposes, although it is widely believed that the phenomenon has originated from Chinese cyberspace. Neither is HFSE the only form of human- and technology-assisted online action—for instance, it shares many common features with crowdsourcing, which is a business practice that takes advantage of collective intelligence of the general public and obtains information and services from a large number of people, paid or unpaid, typically through an open call on the internet, to gain insights into what customers really need and want. Hence, certain types of HFSE actions, for instance, those looking for a missing person by posting their information on an online forum and requesting internet users to provide information, are crowdsourcing. There are, however, uniquely Chinese contextual reasons—social, cultural, political—for the occurrence and equivocal public reception of HFSE actions.

First of all, in many respects, HFSE is a reconstruction of traditional Chinese social relations and moral order. Chinese culture had always provided fertile soil for actions such as HFSE even before the internet age. The traditional Chinese community is predominantly rural and based on kinship and close family relations, in which community members interact at high frequency, share and know a great deal about each other, causing a lack of clear boundaries between the group and the individual. Unlike modern communities with closed doors and an emphasis on privacy, in a traditional community that has retained many primitive characteristics of social relations, the search, collection and sharing of information are all human-assisted; everything from news to gossips passes from person to person and then spreads, which is clearly HFSE in primitive form.

As will be shown below, the traditional moral order built on the basis of such a community and Confucian ethics is the deeper cultural reason why HFSEs can easily develop into violence despite being firmly wrapped under the cloak of morality. The essence of Confucian ethics may be summarized into three principles: everyone has the heart of goodness, morality transcends interests, and morality is self-disciplinary. Distinguishable from Western rationalism based on human nature, Confucianism emphasizes the unification of individual value and societal value, and upholds that the morality of society as a whole is the sum of the morality of each and every member of society. By emphasizing the inevitable relationship between the individual and society—that is, only when every member of society upholds a high moral standard, pursues the collectively recognized good and condemns the collectively recognized evil, can harmony and security be created in society—individuals who grow up in such an atmosphere easily feel entitled to attack those individuals or behaviors that contravene the singular moral order, and it is for this reason that China has had a long history of moral condemnation, from adulterous men and women being paraded in the streets, even killed by lynching, to public humiliation, imprisonment, torture and harassment into suicide of the so-called class enemies during the Cultural Revolution, which are all typical manifestations of 'moral trial' in ethics-based Chinese society. In many ways, HFSE is merely this old practice adapting to the new age.

An important difference between this new age and the old is the possibility of becoming aware of and adopting values other than those of the mainstream. The series of political and sociocultural movements in the most recent centuries, the comprehensive economic reforms and urbanization that have taken place in the past decades, especially the influence of Western sociocultural and political thought, have enormously impacted and weakened the traditional social relations and moral order in China. While it may not be right to say that the country has become immoral as a result of the reforms and transformations, it is true that some behaviors that were traditionally unacceptable are now often tolerated and unpunished, causing some to claim that the increase in immoral behaviors has led to a dubious reality in which mainstream traditional Chinese values are weakened, not entirely eliminated, which has further caused a strange situation in which people tend to be very tolerant toward one's own immoral behaviors and very critical toward and ready to condemn other people's similarly immoral behaviors, creating motivations for HFSE actions. The psychology is complex and perhaps also straightforward—while immoral behaviors increase due to self-indulgence, moral order may be reconstructed in the heart by condemning others, and the wide coverage of the internet in China has provided an efficient and secure way to achieve the latter.

Second, the influence of 'wuxia', a genre of traditional Chinese fiction concerning the adventures of martial artists in ancient China, plays an important part. The word 'wuxia' is a compound composed of the elements 'wu' (literally 'martial', 'military', or 'armed') and 'xia' (literally 'chivalrous', 'vigilante' or 'hero'). Although 'wuxia' as a name of a genre is a recent coinage, stories about 'xia' date back over 2000 years, the eight common attributes of which are often listed as benevolence, justice, individualism, loyalty, courage, truthfulness, disregard for wealth, and desire for glory. Above all, it emphasizes seeking vengeance and bringing villains to justice.

In such stories, a martial artist who follows the code of 'xia' is often referred to as a 'xiake' (literally 'follower of xia'), which is sometimes translated as 'swordsman' or 'swordswoman', and anyone who deserves such a name is often a hero who typically originates from the lower social classes and does not serve any lord, rights and redresses wrongs, fights for righteousness, removes evil oppressors and brings retribution for past misdeeds.

Thousands of years of influence of 'xia' have had a great impact on the Chinese national temperament, and HFSE has created a modern opportunity for ordinary people to personally experience what being a chivalrous hero feels like. In this respect, it is important to know that while xiakes were respected by the masses, they were feared by those in power and were outsiders in the feudal system, whose stringent political hierarchy and social structure placed the ordinary people firmly at the bottom of society. The concentration of unlimited power led to widespread corruption and suffering of powerless ordinary people. But due to distrust of the centralized public power and the feudal justice system and consequently concerns over the cost and outcome of litigation under such a system, when the vulnerable encountered disputes and violations, they would rather place their trust in private relief and the help of xiakes, who were righteous, just, efficient and understood grassroots pains, rather than seeking formal legal resolution from the ruling classes.

Hence, if reconstruction of traditional moral order is the reason for those who take part in HFSE incidents that concern immoral behaviors in private life, the influence of 'xiake' and the belief in private relief can better explain those politically focused HFSE actions (such as anti-corruption). The contemporary Chinese system has retained many feudal elements in that power is highly centralized and lacks independently accountable mechanisms for supervision and correction, giving rise to widespread corruption. Despite the severe crackdowns on corruption in recent years, the silence of the state media over certain events and limited space for public discourse have generated the necessary atmosphere in which the spirit of xiake may be revived in the form of HFSE. On the one hand, through bravely exposing corruption and the unknown truths of politics, HFSE plays the role of watchdog which constitutes a warning to other corrupt officials; on the other hand, it also becomes the modern extension of private relief under the old feudal system, to which those who have failed to gain justice through administrative or legal means may now turn.

While the presence of such an alternative means of seeking justice is proof that the public relief system does not always function as it should, and that in the absence of immediate solutions private relief methods such as HFSE necessarily fill the gap; the fact that HFSE actions often fail to observe procedural norms and boundaries should not be concealed by the fact that they can effectively produce results. Additionally, the more effective HFSE actions may be, the less likely that people will place their trust in administrative and legal means, causing further damage to the system.

Third, for a very long time, 'privacy' had been an alien concept in the Chinese tradition. In the Chinese language, 'privacy' means seclusion and implies secrecy rather than respect for personal space and liberty. Under the influence of traditional Chinese legal culture engraved with Confucian ethics, the social consciousness of Chinese society emphasizes collectivity over the individual, the family as a whole over its individual members, and upholds a traditional sense of justice that places the interests of the state and society way above individual welfare and rights. One of the ultimate aims of Confucian ethics is to maintain the structure, stability and prosperity of the family and, by extension, those of society and the state. It requires individuals with different identities and class positions to act accordingly and obey the respective social norms specific to the group to which they belong—based on the belief that an individual is a member of a collectivity, not in the sense according to individualism. The pursuit of order and harmony is collectivist in nature, which has not only greatly impacted how the Chinese think and act but has also determined how human and minority rights issues are approached: rights exist within the ethical relationships of the pre-existing social framework, should only be realized provided obligations to the community have been fulfilled, and should the interests of the state, community and family require one to surrender their individual rights and freedoms, one should do so. In such an atmosphere, awareness of privacy was absent in the old days, and weak now.

Fourth and perhaps most importantly, as already touched upon in the discussions on private relief, the lack of offline solutions is a driving force behind participation in HFSE incidents, the details of which will be explored below. Much depends on the nature of the HFSE event in question, but this point may be better explored from the perspective that HFSE is a form of online collective action, an analysis of which may be conducted using the market metaphor of 'demand, supply, mobilization' process as proposed by Klandermans and Van Stekelenburg (2013), according to whom 'demand' refers to the mobilizing potential and participants' motivations for taking part in a collective action, 'supply' refers to the opportunities and resources used to entice people to participate in such events, and 'mobilization' is the process or mechanism that links 'demand' and 'supply' and makes things actually happen.

6.3.2 The Role of the Internet and HFSE as Collective Action

6.3.2.1 Demand: Grievances and Motivations

The root cause for any HFSE incident is usually some sort of discontent stemming from the real world (though the internet could also produce new grievances that could cause engagement or protest). The reform era has witnessed not only rapid economic development but also the import of many Western ideals and practices, arousing in many Chinese a consciousness and willingness to participate in the public domain. But meaningful participation is not always easy, especially for issues that concern politics and ideology. Limited official channels for expression let alone resistance in the real world have led some to feel the need to seek out and propagate information on incidents or other people's stories that exemplify their own discontent (Pei 2000). In other words, grievances or discontent do not need to be one's own for someone to partake in an HFSE incident. But in order for people to participate in HFSE events, the presence of widespread grievances alone is not sufficient—they must be transformed into motivations, which, according to Klandermans (1997), could include instrumental, identity and ideological motivations.

However, just as most events do not involve only one single grievance, most HFSE incidents could have more than one motivation behind. For example, the case of Zhou Jiugeng mentioned previously is associated with a number of possible grievances, such as official corruption, abuse of power, social injustice and unjust distribution of power and resources, which directly and adversely affect ordinary people's economic situation. The motivations for those who have taken part in bringing down Zhou could thus be multiple. For instance, some could have decided to take part in order to *instrumentally* take advantage of the new media to demand their interests in being able to purchase properties at a fair price and their rights to social and economic justice. Others may have joined on the basis of a common *identity* that is based on common beliefs and background in order to express care for the fate of those who are in similar situations—for instance, in the case of Zhou Jiugeng, such a shared identity is that of all those people who are not able to afford properties or consider the price too high—and those who take part either identify with the group at stake or with the movement as the chosen means to bring about justice.

Unlike these two types of motivations, *ideological* motivation expressed through this means is rare in the Chinese context, as HFSE incidents that have the purpose of opposing the existing political system and mainstream ideology will not be allowed to take place, not least because of the political reality but also that Confucianism cultivates obedience to authority, while market economic values place material interests and pragmatism above political and ideological faiths. It seems that only when the issue of concern is international, against foreign targets, has something to do with China's national interest that ideological motivation gets to play a role in initiating Chinese people's participation in online collective actions. A telling example is what followed after the NATO bombing of the Chinese embassy in Belgrade in May 1999, causing anti-American sentiments to soar among the Chinese all over the world. Despite a huge wave of angry protests and demonstrations with government backings that spread across China, a number of online collective actions were also noteworthy. For instance, members of the Honker Union of China, a patriotic group of highly skilled hackers, launched a series of attacks on US websites; and the *People's Daily* set up a 'protest forum' for Chinese internet users to post nationalistic and angry messages online.

Over the years, there has been a limited number of collective actions of such nature—against foreign targets (be they individuals, organizations or governments) and concerning Chinese national interests—for instance, an online petition took place in 2005 to oppose Japan's bid for a permanent seat on the UN Security Council, which collected 30 million signatures. It is these rare occasions of government-backed or at least government-tolerated collective actions that have helped, perhaps unintentionally, popularize online protests and activities such as HFSE. It is important to note that once an online collective action receives government backing, it becomes a low-cost and low-risk activity—something that it normally is *not* in the Chinese context—through transforming the collective action into collective expressions of nationalism in digital modes, which in turn creates an atmosphere that precludes many choices except the one that supports the national cause—out loud and in unison.

6.3.2.2 Supply: The Significance of the Internet

The key factors influencing participation in collective action are resources and opportunities available to the aggrieved, which explains why grievances are ubiquitous but collective actions are rare in any context (McCarthy and Zald 1987). The fact that HFSE is able to thrive online in China is a clear indication that the internet has obvious advantages over traditional communication means for HFSE purposes, or that in order to achieve the same purposes, they often have to do things differently should other means of communication need to be employed. The advantages of the internet are reflected in the key features of HFSE, as mentioned at the beginning of Sect. 6.3.1, which explains its role in stimulating collective action online.

First, online interactions allow individuals to mobilize far more quickly, efficiently, and often at no or very low costs, and unlike direct calls for gathering in real life, the powers of online mass communication do not depend on existing social networks, which allows internet users who are complete strangers to each other to gather upon discovering common interests or concerns. This renders people much more willing and confident to engage in online actions, either dedicatedly or as free riders, thereby lowering the threshold for voluntary contributions and in turn altering the fundamental mechanisms of participation, which is the second advantage.

Third and as already mentioned previously, anonymity of the internet has profound behavioral impact on individuals, as while in face-to-face interactions everyone must worry about more than just the information they convey—for instance their appearances and class may render them less confident than they should be, in the virtual world it is much easier to present oneself favorably (without necessarily having to lie) and therefore be accepted. This flexibility in identity construction and image formation might also be a factor that encourages people to get online and participate. In other words, fourth and related, in cyberspace, everyone is visibly equal without differences in wealth and background, thereby eliminating some obstacles to communication that are present in offline real life.

Fifth, in Chinese society, organized gathering for a common purpose is often a cause for concern for the state. But the unique features of the internet mean that HFSE is spontaneous and often leaderless and does not depend on establishing or maintaining pre-existing social networks of players; rather, just by simply linking, searching, sharing and interacting, a group is formed, and a great deal can be achieved online rather than offline and at a much faster speed.

It is important to note, however, that cyberspace reveals the real world rather than replaces it, which has two main implications. First, when studying this online phenomenon, the feet should firmly remain on the offline ground, and attention should focus on the phenomenon's offline enablers. Instead of the general sociocultural and political reality that has already been examined in Sect. 6.3.1, attention here should focus specifically on how the application and function of the internet is related to what particular aspect of the wider offline circumstances to which people are exposed—specifically, considering that despite the diverse motivations and purposes of HFSE actions, HFSE is by nature a form of collective action, attention should be on not how the internet facilitates the occurrence of HFSE per se, but on its precise role in arousing and strengthening motivation to participate.

Second and related, the virtual world reflects the real world also in the sense that the internet is not free but censored. The Chinese government is highly vigilant over possible negative political influence arising from rapid internet development, and enormous efforts have been made to politically and administratively regulate the internet by legal and administrative measures (Zheng and Wu 2005, 516). Behavioral norms and duties for internet users and service providers have been formulated, requesting, for instance, that information that harms the interest of the state should not be posted online, and that it is the responsibility of the service providers to monitor and censor the information posted on the websites. However, exactly what harms the interests of the state is open to interpretation.

Apart from formal rules and policies, there are also broader and indirect censorship strategies, for instance, through the automatic filtering of keywords or by employing human labor (including but not limited to the internet police) to physically monitor and delete sensitive words and topics. A direct result of constantly emphasizing national and public interests in everyday life as well as in the context of internet usage and punishing serious violators publicly to set an example has been that the internet community has gradually learned to self-censor, discipline and control themselves (Svensson 2014). If their online discussions are considered by the government to have crossed the line, for instance if sensitive topics are discussed or collective actions are called for, websites may be blocked or shut down, accounts may be closed and individuals may be held accountable or even imprisoned.

The fact that the country's online policies reflect and imitate paternalistic offline policies, with the similar aim of promoting the development of a harmonious society and consolidating the government's authority, leads to three interrelated questions. First, technically speaking, how does an online collective action such as HFSE actually take place in China? Second, if online and offline environments are not entirely dissimilar and collective action is normally closely watched and hard to carry out, what does the fact that HFSE exits, despite being illegal no less, tell us? And third, has HFSE actually succeeded in challenging the state or anything mainstream? The first two questions will be considered in Sect. 6.3.2.3 below, and the third will be examined in Sect. 6.3.3.

6.3.2.3 Mobilization: Implications and Complexities

HFSE incidents seem to have the following key features or steps. The first is the creation of as large a pool as possible of sympathizers by bringing to their attention a grievance, explaining the details of the events or actions to evoke their emotions and willingness to partake. Different issues attract different attention and evoke different emotions in different people. In the Chinese context, issues concerning corruption, extreme wealth or extreme poverty and those with a nationalistic connotation seem to attract more attention than other topics from internet users. As long as there is a basic pool of sympathizers to begin with, it is possible to spread the call for action further.

The second feature is that, unlike in Western democratic countries in which collective actions are organized and typically part of a long-term campaign or social movement with a clear and shared objective, HFSE incidents in China are transient, spontaneous, self-organized or unorganized and tend to finish as soon as the triggering event has ended. In other words, instead of being ideology-based, organization-based, identity-based, HFSE appears to be issue-based and temporary, and for that reason appears more self-empowering than empowering others, more emotion-driven and could be generated by something very trivial.

The third, which is particularly necessary in the Chinese context, is to somehow avoid censorship or at least lower the risk of being censored or suffering consequences. Much of course depends on whether the incident is politically focused, but it is worth remembering that HFSE as a general action is illegal. There are many possible strategies though. For instance, talking about particular topics on a website that is entirely unrelated to the topic in question, rendering it unexpected and therefore harder or at least slower to be detected; employing the strategy of the use of abstract or coded language to protect and conceal the true message, rendering it understandable only to those relevant.

Furthermore, should it be necessary or desirable for the information posted to be widely received and have maximum impact, as is the case in most HFSE actions, a useful strategy is to gain the attention and alliance of state-controlled traditional media, in turn and in effect gaining state approval. Should this be the strategy the involvement of the central media is particularly important if internet users want to expose the misconduct of government officials especially those at lower levels, which is why officials in China are particularly afraid of media exposure rather than mere collective actions taking place at a fixed place and at a particular time. The psychology underneath is the memory and therefore fear of the long tradition of public naming and shaming. While participation in traditional offline collective action may also gain attention and support from state-controlled media, the internet makes everything faster and easier.

This provides a partial answer to the second question above: if online and offline environments are not entirely dissimilar and collective action is normally closely watched and hard to carry out, what does the fact that HFSE exits online, despite being illegal no less, tell us? The answers are fourfold. First, as explained in the paragraph above, there are strategies one can employ to carry out collective actions on the internet. Second, while the nature, motivation and purpose of HFSE incidents differ, the majority of them seem to concern private morality, which does not constitute a cause for state concern. The fact that HFSE itself is illegal hence in theory ought to be intervened is of course important, but the fact that it is hardly ever just a one-off event but often a chain of events renders timely and effective intervention difficult. Those HFSE incidents that are politically focused thus far all aim at exposing corrupt officials, which is in alignment with the ongoing anti-corruption campaign in the country and therefore carries little political risk, and the fact that previous HFSE incidents of this nature have often incurred formal investigations of the exposed official will no doubt inspire others to do the same.

Third, while Chinese cyberspace is not free, total control is neither possible nor desirable (or sought after by the state); thus, collective actions such as HFSE are not an impossible enterprise. Although rules, regulations and technology enable the authorities to block or filter the flow of information, they also provide opportunities for internet users to counteract such efforts, for instance, through the use of 'proxy' technologies to overcome the firewall set up by the regime. An essential portion of internet users, especially young people, have learned how to circumvent official blockages to access foreign websites—not necessarily as an act of protest but merely out of necessity of acquiring information—which are skills that people in a free society will not need to possess. Perhaps contrary to common belief, it is certain that the Chinese government knows that it is not in its best interest to have total control over the internet, as the operation of the socioeconomic system and so much more depends on a relatively free flow of information, which is also essential for keeping the people reasonably satisfied.

There is clear evidence that should the government want to completely block proxy technology software to render foreign websites entirely inaccessible, it can, as proven in the fact that whenever there are important state events such as when the National People's Congress opens its annual session, it becomes that much harder and often impossible to overcome the firewall, but as soon as such events end, the proxy technologies start working again and foreign websites become once again accessible. It is thus arguable that the government has decided that in order to achieve its twin goals of maintaining a relatively free flow of information on the one hand and a tight control of politically sensitive information on the other (Zheng and Wu 2005, 519), it is better to filter than to block, to periodically block than to block permanently. Besides, as Hardin (1990) points out, a state does not need to go to the extremes and become truly a 'gunman' state to solicit social obedience from its citizens—it can simply develop 'conventions' by setting clear examples of 'reasonable behavior' to draw boundaries and punish those who cross those boundaries.

Fourth and related, it is also possible that the state, while having taken a clear stance against HFSE in general, considering its many necessary aspects and important functions, has intentionally kept a reasonable relaxed cyberspace for it to nevertheless function so as to learn of public concerns, and also to grant people an opportunity to simply let it out for whatever reason, rationally or not. All these complexities and contextual realities make it difficult to decisively defend or condemn HFSE. What makes it even harder to take a stance is if one attempts an answer to the third question posted at the end of Sect. 6.3.2.2—that have HFSE actions actually succeeded in challenging the state or anything mainstream?

6.3.3 Goodness, Badness, Otherness

In the West, the influence of the internet and internet-based collective action on civil participation and democracy is widely studied. Many argue that the internet has substantially promoted the formation, development and growth of civil society and has made genuine democratic participation possible to a much wider range of people than before the internet came into being, by providing ordinary people with both resources and opportunities to expand their participation (Hill and Hughes 1998), including through online collective action. Some have noted both the key role that the internet has played in the collapse of authoritarian regimes as well as being a continuous threat to other similar states (Zheng and Wu 2005, 510). In contrast, others are more pessimistic about the internet and internet-based activities on democracy, arguing that while the internet makes it easy for ordinary people to express and participate, it also makes it easy for governments to regulate, both by controlling its underlying code and by shaping the legal and social environment in which it operates (Lessig 1999). Others argue that intensive use of the internet may diminish social capital, counter any gains in participatory equality, damage the public sphere and cause fragmentation and polarization, which will ultimately undermine democratic participation (Sunstein 2001; Barber 1998).

It is perhaps important to go beyond the arguments for or against a positive or negative impact of the internet and internet-based activities on democratic development in China, as there is evidence supporting both arguments. Here, it is important to clarify that the third question asked above was whether HFSE has challenged the state, not whether internet-based collective action in general has challenged the state, although it is necessary to attempt an answer to the latter question first as HFSE is a form of internet-based collective action. The quick answer is that the internet and internet-based collective action have not been able to pose a serious threat to the Chinese state, although they have caused some, albeit often limited, changes, in some circumstances. While this is not the place to provide a detailed analysis of all of the representative cases, a simple summary of two is sufficient to highlight the role of the internet in the unfolding of these collective actions in the information age.

On 20 March 2003, Sun Zhigang, a 27-year-old young man, was beaten to death by eight inmates at the infirmary of a custody and repatriation center in Guangzhou, the capital of Guangdong Province, after failing to provide proof of identification and was thus detained under the 'Measures for the Custody and Repatriation of Vagrant Beggars in Cities', which was passed in 1982 with the original aim of providing shelter for homeless people in the cities but in reality had become a means for local governments to protect their own residents against outsiders and what they considered to be trouble makers, including the poor, migrant workers, kidnapped women who were then sold in the underground market, and petitioners.

After details of Sun's case came to public attention through the media and the internet, it caused a widespread sense of outrage against the custody and repatriation system, and people from all over the country began to rally against it in their own ways and called for change. People with experiences similar to those of Sun posted their stories online to share with the country; academics wrote articles questioning the constitutionality of the system; three students submitted a petition both in person (to the Standing Committee of the National People's Congress) and posted an online call for the government to re-examine the custody and repatriation system (Zheng and Wu 2005, 530). Debate about the case soon evolved into more general concerns about inequality and human rights abuses. On 20 June 2003, then Premier Wen Jiabao declared that the custody and repatriation system would be abolished from 1 August, making Sun's case possibly the very first incident of a civilian death causing the repeal of a state regulation in the People's Republic.

A second example is much more recent. Li Wenliang was a Chinese ophthalmologist known for raising public awareness of early COVID-19 infections in Wuhan upon receiving an internal diagnostic report of a suspected severe acute respiratory syndrome (SARS) patient from other doctors, which he in turn shared with his friends and from whom he demanded confidentiality. But the report nevertheless started to circulate, subsequently causing rumors of another deadly SARS outbreak to spread on Chinese social media platforms, for which Dr Li was summoned and admonished by Wuhan police. The outbreak was later confirmed not to be SARS but a new coronavirus. Dr Li returned to work, contracted the virus while treating an infected patient, and died at the age of only 33 on 7 February 2020.

His death generated deeply painful and complex emotions in China, in which a large number of people, in utter confusion at this earliest stage of the disease, had been following his status on social media platforms. Wuhan residents placed flowers outside his hospital, lit candles, and blew whistles as a tribute to the whistle blower. On the same day as Dr Li's death, China's highest anti-corruption body, the National Supervisory Commission, initiated a comprehensive investigation into the issues concerning Dr Li in response to high public demand on the internet and social media platforms. He was subsequently exonerated, his admonishment was revoked, and an official apology was made to his family.

While he has now officially been honored by the state as a 'martyr'—the highest honor the government can bestow on a citizen who dies from serving the country—his death has left a great deal behind. People began to discuss the importance of whistle blowing and free speech both in the specific context of the COVID-19 pandemic and generally in China. Even to this day, people continue to leave messages in the response section below his very last Sina Weibo social media message, paying tributes, expressing sorrow, or simply saying hello. How have these actions influenced the state is evident in the important role the internet has played in these processes—without the internet, few would have heard of the details of Dr Li's story, there would have been no collective expression or demand, and very possibly no reaction from the state.

Considering the general intolerant atmosphere in China of collective actions, a question naturally comes to mind: why have some online collective actions failed while others have succeeded? Zheng and Wu (2005) point out that interaction strategies are determinant: if a given collective action is perceived as undermining the legitimacy of the state, for instance, if it presents direct challenges to the state or the ruling party, it is likely to invite crackdown and doomed to fail. But not just any challenge—it needs to be to the extent of being able to *undermine*. In the above two cases, while criticisms are direct, widespread, and directed against the state, they are within reasonable bounds—the first one was rational constructive debate about state laws and policies, the second was deeply emotional and humane and took place at a difficult time, which, despite having generated calls for free speech, still rendered it hard for any government to take any coordinated action against it. This might well be the reason that the government responded to the collective emotions unusually well by quickly launching a high-level investigation into Dr Li's admonishment and honoring him with the highest level of state recognition.

Furthermore, the two cases also have something else in common: the collective actions involved constitute 'voice', which is similar to what Hardin (1990, 360) calls 'cooperation interaction'. When members of the public express their dissatisfaction directly to the authorities or anyone indeed, the listening party has to be engaged in a search for the causes and possible solutions to their dissatisfaction. By voicing their opinions, members of the public try to change in a constructive manner certain practices or policies of society, not to escape from its objectionable state of affairs, whether through direct petitions to those in charge or through various types of collective actions to mobilize public opinion (Hirschman 1970).

It is generally the case that such collective 'voice' activities do not usually pose a direct *threat* to the state, despite often involving various degrees and types of criticism and challenges—these are criticisms and challenges to which the state is willing to listen and make an attempt at a possible solution. In other words, these collective voice activities are acceptable to the state, as they do not aim to overthrow or undermine the state, but rather constitute a mechanism that provides the state with feedback so that the authority's legitimacy may be strengthened. Many of the HFSE activities belong in this category—particularly those that aim to expose corrupt officials—while they directly and efficiently expose malpractices and mismanagement in China's political system, they nevertheless provide the leadership with opportunities to strengthen itself, thereby rendering the collective action in question a challenge that aims to benefit, not a threat that aims to undermine.

This leads one to consider more carefully how useful HFSE, particularly those HFSE actions that are politically focused, could be in the Chinese context and what changes it may bring. The answer is fourfold. First, when considering the usefulness of HFSE in China, it is important to do so in comparison to real-life collective actions such as protests, which the Chinese state tends to prevent at all costs. Having said that, small-scale and isolated protests have a long history in China, and are expected, if not welcomed, let alone invited, by the government as a means of identifying and dealing with discontented members of society. But protests remain difficult to realize in China.

However, as already noted, protests or similar actions on the internet are much harder to control, and since the leadership has allowed social media to flourish, it has also allowed a fuller rang of negative expressions about the state and its officials to flourish. As a result, online actions such as those anti-corruption HFSE incidents have been very effective at embarrassing and indeed bringing down the officials involved, as it seems that the state has realized that looking bad and being embarrassed do not in fact threaten their hold on power as long as these actions are occasional, isolated, and quiet down quickly—as already noted also, politically focused HFSE incidents in China are almost always issue-based rather than part of a long-term organized programme, as soon as the issue in question has been dealt with, the incident ends.

Second, when considering the usefulness of HFSE in China, expectations need to be reasonable, in that it would be entirely unrealistic to expect either this particular type of online collective action or internet activities in general to lead to anything close to a democratic system in the foreseeable future. O'Donnell and Schmitter (1986, 9) make a distinction between 'liberalization' and 'democratization' and argue that liberalization can take place within the existing authoritarian political framework, as the rulers may tolerate or even promote liberalization *in certain spaces* for individual and group actions in order to relieve pressures and obtain information and support without having to alter the structure of authority, that is, without becoming truly accountable to the citizenry for their actions or subjecting their claim to rule to genuine competitive elections.

In other words, liberalization can exist without democratization, that is, liberalization in certain areas and on certain subjects, leading to what they call 'liberalized authoritarianism'. This accurately explains the function of many HFSE actions or what is expected of them—they serve important purposes that are useful to the leadership without threatening their rule, while at the same time giving the masses a certain degree of freedom of expression and powerfulness especially in those politically focused incidents (King et al. 2013). It is important to note that all those corrupt officials who have been exposed by HFSE are local rather than high-ranking. Such exposure of higher up officials will normally only be able to appear after they have already been condemned by the state, rather than initiated by the people.

Third and related, it is important to remember that while HFSE does not generally threaten the state, it very much threatens the individual being exposed in various ways, which attracts a different degree of condemnation if any at all. This relates to reasonable expectations in another sense, a good way to demonstrate which would be from the angle of rights conflict. There is a great deal of potential for rights conflict in HFSE incidents, rendering it difficult to judge the goodness or badness of such actions. It seems that much would depend on whether the person or issue in question concerns public interest.

HFSE in the public domain refers to incidents that involve the search and sharing of information on officials or events in which the public has vested interest, and the rights conflict takes the form of that between citizens' freedom of expression and the right to know on the one hand and the privacy of public servants on the other. It is widely accepted across cultures that, unlike ordinary citizens, public servants must significantly waive the right to privacy in favor of transparency, but this does not mean a complete surrender of the right. It seems that a distinction must be made between information that is inherent to the public servant's official position and information that is not and therefore affects only their private life. While this balancing task is easy in theory, it is not in practice, especially in the absence of clear guidelines and rules. While it could justifiably be said that the protection of a public servant's right to private and personal information is necessary provided that such protection does not prevent due accountability, online anonymity offers a certain degree of protection to irrational, offensive and insulting behaviors which tend to lead to overexposure and damage not just to the reputation of the official but also that of people related to them, such as relatives, colleagues and friends.

Rights conflicts are most acute in HFSE incidents that concern private life, in which ordinary people are the most common victims of actions that very much constitute group violence regardless of the initial motivation of the participants. People who are so targeted may be divided into two categories: ordinary people being exposed for something they have done in everyday life, and parties in some kind of news event. In such situations, conflicts take place between citizens' rights to comment and to participate in open discussions on the one hand, and the affected person's rights to privacy, reputation and protection of personal information on the other. As mentioned previously, in such incidents and unlike HFSE actions that are politically focused, privately related HFSE actions usually center on some person's private conduct's infringement upon widely held moral norms, which usually has nothing to do with public interest and tends to draw on highly subjective criteria. It would seem that in such situations, in theory and simplistically speaking, the affected person's interests of privacy and reputation should receive absolute protection against HFSE, although what would this entail in practice could only be determined on a case-by-case basis.

The fourth usefulness of HFSE in the Chinese context may be revealed if HFSE actions are seen as individual or collective expressions of emotion, which would extend the context of HFSE beyond sociocultural and historical realms into contemporary politics. Emotion as a complex reaction pattern is multifaceted with psychological, behavioral and experiential elements, truthfully revealing what an individual, or a group of individuals, finds significant in their personal life and society, how they have become conscious of these significant issues and events as well as how they choose to deal with them. Instead of one-sidedly condemning HFSE, it might be more fruitful to make this connection between online behavior and expression of emotion more explicit, which would constitute a trustworthy angle from which to observe and analyze changes in societal temperament, which would in turn contribute to what the Chinese state cares the most – harmony and stability.

References

Attwood F, Campbell V, Hunter IQ, Lockyer S (2013) Controversial images: media representations on the edge. Palgrave Macmillan, Basingstoke

Barber B (1998) The new telecommunications technology: endless frontier or end of democracy. In: Noll RG, Price ME (eds) A communications cornucopia. Brookings Institution, Washington, DC, pp 72–98

Ben-Dor O (ed) (2011) Law and art: justice, ethics and aesthetics. Routledge, Abingdon

Bermúdez JL, Gardner S (eds) (2003) Art and morality. Routledge, Abingdon

Bezanson RP (2009) Art and freedom of speech. University of Illinois Press, Urbana

Bucaria C, Barra L (eds) (2016) Taboo comedy: television and controversial humor. Palgrave Macmillan, London
Cashell K (2009) Aftershock: the ethics of contemporary transgressive art. I.B. Tauris, London
Chun J (2016) Attempting to find closure. J R Asiatic Soc China 76(No. 1):75–91
Feinberg J (1984) Harm to others: the moral limits of the criminal law. Oxford University Press, New York
Feinberg J (1985) Offense to others: the moral limits of the criminal law. Oxford University Press, New York
Feinberg J (1986) Harm to self: the moral limits of the criminal law. Oxford University Press, New York
Fok S (2013) Life and death: art and the body in contemporary china. University of Chicago Press, Chicago
Freeland C (2001) But is it art? Oxford University Press, New York
Gladston P (2016) Deconstructing contemporary chinese art: selected critical writings and conversations, 2007–2014. Springer
Hardin R (1990) The social evolution of cooperation. In: Cook KS, Levi M (eds) The limits of rationality. University of Chicago Press, Chicago, pp 358–376
Hill KA, Hughes JE (1998) Cyberpolitics: citizen activism in the age of the Internet. Rowman & Littlefield, Lanham, MD
Hirschman AO (1970) Exit, voice and loyalty: responses to decline in firms, organizations, and states. Harvard University Press, Cambridge, MA
Jasper JM (1997) The art of moral protest: culture, biography, and creativity in social movements. University of Chicago Press, Chicago
Jasper JM, Poulsen JD (1995) Recruiting strangers and friends: moral shocks and social networks in animal rights and anti-nuclear protests. Soc Probl 42(No. 4)
Julius A (2002) Transgressions: the offences of art. The University of Chicago Press, Chicago
Kearns P (2013) Freedom of artistic expression: essays on culture and legal censure. Hart Publishing, Oxford
King G, Pan J, Roberts ME (2013) How censorship in China allows government criticism but silences collective expression. Am Polit Sci Rev 107(Issue 2):326–343
Klandermans B (1997) The social psychology of protest. Basil Blackwell, Oxford
Klandermans B, Van Stekelenburg J (2013) Social movements and the dynamics of collective action. In: Huddy DOSL, Levy JL (eds) The Oxford handbook of political psychology, 2nd edn. Oxford University Press, Oxford
Le Bon G ([1895] 2003) The crowd: a study of the popular mind. Dover Publications Inc.
Lessig L (1999) Code and other laws of cyberspace. Basic Books, New York
Maitra I, McGowan MK (eds) (2012) Speech & harm: controversies over free speech. Oxford University Press, Oxford
McCarthy JD, Zald MN (1987) Social movements in an organizational society. Transaction Publishers, New Brunswick, New Jersey
Mey K (2007) Art & obscenity. I.B. Tauris, New York
Mill JS ([1859] 2006) On liberty and the subjection of women. Penguin Classics, London
Munroe A, Philip T, Hou H (2017) Art and China after 1989: theatre of the world. Guggenheim Museum Publications, New York
O'Dea M (2017) The Phoenix years: art, resistance, and the making of modern China. Pegasus Books Ltd., New York
O'Donnell G, Schmitter PC (1986) Transitions from authoritarian rule: tentative conclusions about uncertain future. Johns Hopkins University Press, Baltimore
Pei M (2000) Rights and resistance: the changing context of the dissident movement in China. In: Elizabeth JP, Mark S (eds) Chinese society: change, conflict and resistance. RoutledgeCurzon, London and New York
Sadurski W (1999) Freedom of speech and its limits. Kluwer Academic Publishers, Dordrecht
Solove DJ (2007) The future of reputation. Vail-Ballou Press

Sumner LW (2004) The hateful and the obscene: studies in the limits of free expression. University of Toronto Press, Toronto
Sunstein Cass (2001) Republic.com. Princeton University Press, Princeton
Svensson M (2014) Voice, power and connectivity in China's microblogosphere: digital divides on Sina Weibo. China Inf 28(2):168–188
Wang M (2014) The primitive and unproductive body: He Yunchang and his performance art. Yishu J Contemp Chin Art 13(Issue 4):6–25
Wettergren ÅSA (2005) Mobilization and the Moral Shock: Adbusters Media Foundation. In: Flam H, King D (eds) Emotions and Social Movements. Routledge, London, Chap 6
Winston B (2012) A right to offend. Bloomsbury, London
Zheng Y, Wu G (2005) Information technology, public space, and collective action in China. Comp Polit Stud 38(No.5):507–536

Conclusion: Beyond Otherness

This book has a particular approach and a particular intellectual agenda—the former places great emphasis on context, and the latter aims to demonstrate the extreme complexity of the context, rendering that any attempt to oversimplify things will not only hinder mutual understanding but will also and more damagingly make rational self-perception unlikely and self-correction impossible. It is only on the basis of such a recognition that good questions may arise, and good questions should lead to further explorations and new discoveries rather than merely confirming one's inherited wisdom and pre-existing beliefs.

For various reasons, the difficulty of studying sociocultural otherness in China is not beyond the realm of imagination, and the author has not been able to cover all the topics that she originally intended to cover for those various reasons. Consequently, this book has perhaps not been a comprehensive presentation of the reality of sociocultural otherness in China and therefore carries the slight risk of selective representation under certain light, which gives rise to the need to state so expressly. However, it is neither possible nor necessary to cover everything in order to achieve the purposes of this project, namely, to demonstrate the degree of complexity of sociocultural otherness in the Chinese context, explore the underlying causes and interplay of factors, through the examination of representative subjects of theoretical and empirical reflection.

Furthermore, it is hoped that what has been covered in this book constitutes a step in the right direction, and that it is sufficient to show that China's sociocultural otherness is not only fascinating but also has profound implications not only for the fate of this country but also for that of the entire world. While any conclusion of such a complex and important subject can only be to a large extent inconclusive, this concluding chapter nevertheless draws this project to its end with some thoughts on future prospects.

H. H. Wei, *Sociocultural Otherness and Minority Justice: A Study on China*,
Ius Gentium: Comparative Perspectives on Law and Justice 88,
https://doi.org/10.1007/978-981-16-9752-4

Diversity and Cultural Continuity

The particular stance regarding sociocultural otherness adopted by a researcher or their institution can prevent the exploration of certain kinds of perspectives and issues while emphasizing heavily, if not solely, on their chosen ones of personal and institutional preference. This could potentially have serious ethical and political implications, to which tentative attention must be drawn should this worthy subject be taken on by anyone. It is also essential that the researcher is extra careful when considering the implications of their work with respect to whom and what it represents, the terms on which it engages in such representations and discussions, and once published or otherwise disseminated, the political ends to which their findings may be put, if at all.

This is a challenge confronting social sciences researchers in many cultures but may be more so in some contexts than in others, which requires cultural sensitivity and skills but, above all, honesty and commitment to one's chosen area of study. To understand sociocultural otherness is to understand and appreciate diversity—diversity of peoples, diversity of cultures, diversity of situations, diversity of ideas—without serious engagement with which it would be impossible to construct a better, more just, society. This has at least two implications.

While it is unnecessary to presume before the commence of any minority rights project that anything to do with otherness would necessarily cause trouble, it is nevertheless important to think hard on how to conduct and present such a project in a culturally sensitive way without compromising truth or professionalism. Paine (2004) said that a long habit of not thinking a thing wrong would give it a superficial appearance of being right, which would tend to cause a formidable outcry in defense of custom and tradition, but time would make more converts than reason. This accurately describes the challenges and difficulties that the Chinese context has generated for those who do not belong in the mainstream. It seems that an important task for any researcher in this field ought to be to ensure that certain topics can appear in the public discourse and that conversations and debates are kept alive.

This relates to a point made in one of the chapters earlier that the power of existence could be far greater than the power of resistance—both for ideas and peoples—which is both a matter of pragmatic academic skills as well as accurate understanding of historical, political and sociocultural realities of China. Simply by merely existing rather than presenting the ideas in an overly prepolitical way and being seen as putting up a fight, which would further enhance the image of 'the other' and causing more fear and suspicion, one would be pleasantly surprised to find that some subjects, despite being nonmainstream and normally a source of controversy, nevertheless have a space to grow (Wei 2016). In other words, it is important to learn how to gently push forward, but just remember to push forward.

The second implication is that diversity ought to be examined not in an idealistic vacuum but firmly within the context of the Chinese reality. As already pointed out in the reasoning before, many like to carry out analyses of contemporary Chinese issues against the background of the country's rapid change and constant transformation in the past few decades. Once the readers have read this book in its entirety, it should become apparent that more urgent attention should instead be focused on the forces of cultural continuity rather than change—it is not what *has* changed but rather what *has not* changed that most affects recognition of sociocultural otherness and treatment of 'the other' in China. The author would go one step forward in saying that any examination of China's minority situations should be based on the presumption that the country's political climate will not change in the foreseeable future.

Memory and Security

This book has sought to draw the explicit connection between China's past experiences and historical pains with the state's general attitude toward any kind of otherness. The Durkheimian tradition in social thought sees collective memory as central to the reproduction of society and unification of the group—collective memory as defined as the recollections of a shared past that are passed on through ongoing processes of commemoration, either written down, painted, or otherwise represented and communicated. The collective story unites individuals culturally and gives rise to a collective identity (Eyerman 2019, 25) that has a great deal of implications for sociocultural minorities.

From this perspective, not only is the past collectively shaped, so is and perhaps especially the present. In the specific context of China and as this book has demonstrated, the long-lasting impact of the country's painful colonial past, particularly how it affects state-minority relations, majority-minority relations, and the general attitude toward divergence from the mainstream, is seriously understudied and underestimated. Such recognition calls for a historical approach to studying sociocultural otherness as well as relevant important concepts such as 'risk' and 'security'. It is, however, worth repeating once again that emphasizing historical and cultural particularities does not equal a call for an overly contextual approach—which ought to be avoided in fact. What it does call for is a tentative search for those underlying causes that have previously been ignored or undervalued. Neither does it intend to make excuses for intolerance, but rather to get to the roots of intolerance.

A related note is that, an unintended but welcomed consequence of writing this book has been that the author has now started another, temporarily entitled *Emotions and Minoritisation*, on how collective memories and historical pains determine who may be 'othered', in what ways and for what reasons. Attention will focus on the continuous unfolding and reworking of historical traumas and how they generate collective emotions that determine minorities' fate.

Discourses and Exclusion

To better understand sociocultural otherness in China, it is important to pay more attention to critical discourse studies, which have long focused on issues of power, domination, social inequality, and on the relevance of gender and sexuality, class, race, culture and so on in the study of text and talk. Through its focus on language use in situations of inequality and injustice, this discipline aims to uncover and demystify certain social processes to make mechanisms of discrimination, manipulation and propaganda more explicit (Wodak 1989; Riggins (ed.) 1997). Much attention has also been focused on the role of the mass media in the construction and reproduction of dominant ideologies, the study of which will no doubt inspire understanding of the dominated 'other' in the present context.

Furthermore, instead of speaking for subjects that can only be spoken for or spoken of via a particular narrative that privileges the mainstream mentality, it would be worthwhile to really explore the possibility of developing a different order of criticality from within the system, which would require calling into question the existing, in many ways simplistic, discourses that have shaped our understanding of contemporary China's sociocultural otherness—for instance human rights versus Chinese values, universal validity of human rights versus a Chinese theory of human rights. Though how this may be achieved requires much thought and skill. This is not at all to deny the so-called Chinese characteristics or that many truth statements are contextually constituted, but to emphasize that tactically challenging the ways in which both China and the groups in question are conventionally read is a necessary precursor to providing other ways of seeing, doing, understanding—which will no doubt create uncertainty.

Uncertainty and Certainty

Apart from other qualities, an important mark of an advanced and psychologically healthy society is the ability to accept and live with uncertainty and ambiguity, but only as much as there really is uncertainty or ambiguity. Uncertainty is no virtue when the facts are beyond doubt, and ambiguity is obfuscation when absolute terms and expressions are applicable. Accepting that the world is full of uncertainty and ambiguity should not stop people from being certain about many things, but it does sometimes kill the wisdom and ability to tell the difference. In many ways, uncertainty is an invaluable thing in the Chinese context, as it potentially marks the beginning of a never-ending investigation. But the real problem appears to be that few actually care about what might work and what might not work and therefore see the necessity and urgency to face reality and search for solutions. In the face of conceptual, methodological and institutional uncertainties, while recognizing that we all deploy protocols and stipulations when identifying, organizing and framing issues of debate, and it follows that all discussions of minorities and sociocultural otherness, including but not limited to those covered in this book, imply a like simplification and framing of inquiry, the author calls for a more tentative, more critical, more comprehensive and continuous scholarly engagement with Chinese minority issues.

References

Eyerman R (2019) Memory. Palgrave Macmillan, Trauma and Identity

Paine T [1776] (2004) Common sense. Penguin Books, London

Riggins SH (ed) (1997) The language and politics of exclusion: others in discourse. Sage Publications, Thousand Oaks, California

Wei HH (2016) Asking the minority question in China. J Comp Law 11(2):214–234
Wodak R (ed) (1989) Language, power and ideology. John Benjamins, Philadelphia

The manufacturer's authorised representative in the EU is Springer Nature Customer Service Centre GmbH, Europaplatz 3, 69115 Heidelberg, Germany. If you have any concerns regarding our products, please contact ProductSafety@springernature.com

Printed and bound by CPI Group (UK) Ltd, Croydon, CR0 4YY
30/09/2026
02225234-0008